Tim

Tim Mackintosh-Smith's f... ...
Land, won the 1998 Thomas Cook/*Daily Telegraph* Travel Book
Award and is now regarded as a classic of Arabian description. His
books on Ibn Battutah's adventures in the old Islamic world and in
India, *Travels with a Tangerine* and *The Hall of a Thousand Columns*,
were received to huge critical acclaim. His journeys in search of
Ibn Battutah have also been turned into a major BBC television
series. For the past twenty-five years his home has been the Yemeni
capital San'a, where he lives in a tower-house on top of the ancient
Sabaean city and next door to the modern donkey market.

Martin Yeoman

Martin Yeoman, illustrator of the book, is a painter, draughts-
man, sculptor and etcher whose work can be found in a number
of notable British collections, including those of HM The Queen,
HRH The Prince of Wales and the British Museum.

Praise for Landfalls

'*Landfalls* is a beautifully written account of Islamic life and culture
in the twenty-first century . . . Whether he is looking for proof
of demons [in] the Maldives or indulging in a delirious dance [in]
Guinea . . . Tim Mackintosh-Smith's book is a joyous celebration
of cultural diversity' *Sunday Times*

'Mackintosh-Smith has brought to life not just the man but also the
time in which he lived . . . *Landfalls* is well paced, erudite, amusing
. . . and almost always fascinating . . . It proves that reports of the
death of the travel book are premature. Far from it. With its mix of
literary adventure, biography and autobiography, this book suggests
that, in the right hands, the genre can be as flexible, energetic and
rewarding as ever' *Literary Review*

'Dazzling . . . Half Sherlock Holmes, half Paddy Leigh Fermor,
Mr Mackintosh-Smith possesses an enthusiasm, stamina and intelligence that have all been tested on the trail' *Country Life*

Praise for The Hall of a Thousand Columns

'With his hallmark combination of irreverence and empathy, Mackintosh-Smith . . . has confected a curiously addictive blend of history, travel and jokes. But above all, he engages with ideas, and his aim is that of the novelist – to send a bucket down into the sub-conscious . . . The author's passion and intelligence give the book remarkable authenticity . . . intriguing and joyous' *Guardian*

'Few writers have the talent to pull off a notable trilogy in any genre . . . [Mackintosh-Smith's] talent is not in doubt . . . The author appears as an enthusiastic researcher, a thirsty drinker and a traveller who allows little to deter him from his path' *Sunday Times*

'This is engrossing writing to transport even the most languid arm-chair traveller' *Daily Express*

'The wellspring of his writing is his profound immersion in a Muslim culture . . . the strength of his work derives from his posi-tion as both insider and outsider in the Arab world . . . Mackintosh-Smith is in that same learned yet good-humoured tradition [as Leigh Fermor]' *Daily Telegraph*

'Mixing Ibn Battutah's account with his own encounters and jour-neys, Mackintosh-Smith creates an enchanting text . . . This is an engrossing book' *Independent*

'Another triumph, travel writing of the very highest order and the perfect riposte to any publisher or agent who has been predicting the demise of the genre' *The Spectator*

'Mackintosh-Smith's zest and enthusiasm carry all before them and are combined with such a stream of irreverent observations and tan-gential snippets that there is hardly a page where you are not both creasing your brow in disagreement and then chuckling in delight' *Literary Review*

'Part travel book, part biography, part detective story, this is a gripping read and a fitting testament to the Prince of Travellers' *Wanderlust*

Praise for Travels With a Tangerine

'Mackintosh-Smith is an intrepid and determined traveller, with an uncanny instinct for right turnings and the necessary conviction to pursue them . . . Mixing archaic language . . . with a twenty-first-century sensibility, fogeyism with an appetite for fun, food and a good smoke, he slips effortlessly between our world and that of the fourteenth century. In so doing, he has created a gripping and accomplished travel book' *Sunday Times*

'With the *Travels* of IB (as he affectionately thinks of him) in hand, Mackintosh-Smith here follows his predecessor's trail as far as the Crimea, seeking what remains of the sights Battutah saw, skilfully evoking those that have vanished, all the while remaining alert to the deep connections between modern Muslim society and the past. The result is an immensely engaging book' *Daily Telegraph*

'Battutah couldn't enjoy a better champion than Mackintosh-Smith . . . This is a considerable book, mind-broadening not only in the way that it revives the history of a remarkable traveller, but also for its representation of modern Islam as tolerant, hospitable, humorous and cultured' *The Times*

'Sometimes, as [Mackintosh-Smith] travels from Cairo to the Crimea, across deserts, into assassins' strongholds, it seems that Ibn Battutah is just a swish of a robe ahead' *Independent*

'A brilliant, erudite and entertaining literary coup' *Time*

'A fluent Arabist who has lived in Yemen for the best part of two decades, Mackintosh-Smith is an accomplished etymologist who delights in his field of research and shares Ibn Battutah's roving intellectual curiosity, if not his boundless sexual appetite . . . *Travels with a Tangerine* has all the makings of a classic' *The Spectator*

By the same author

Yemen: Travels in Dictionary Land
Travels with a Tangerine: A Journey in the Footnotes of
Ibn Battutah
The Hall of a Thousand Columns: Hindustan to Malabar
with Ibn Battutah
The Travels of Ibn Battutah *(editor)*

LANDFALLS

On the Edge of Islam
from Zanzibar to the Alhambra

Tim Mackintosh-Smith

with illustrations by Martin Yeoman

JOHN MURRAY

First published in Great Britain in 2010 by John Murray (Publishers)
An Hachette UK Company

First published in paperback in 2011

1

© Tim Mackintosh-Smith 2010

The right of Tim Mackintosh-Smith to be identified as the Author of the Work has
been asserted by him in accordance with the Copyright, Designs and Patents Act 1988.

Illustrations © Martin Yeoman

Maps by Rosie Collins

All rights reserved. Apart from any use permitted under UK copyright law no part of this
publication may be reproduced, stored in a retrieval system, or transmitted, in any form
or by any means without the prior written permission of the publisher, nor be otherwise
circulated in any form of binding or cover other than that in which it is published and
without a similar condition being imposed on the subsequent purchaser.

A CIP catalogue record for this title is available from the British Library

ISBN 978-0-7195-6778-0

Typeset in Monotype Bembo by Servis Filmsetting Ltd, Stockport, Cheshire

Printed and bound by Clays Ltd, St Ives plc

John Murray policy is to use papers that are natural, renewable and recyclable
products and made from wood grown in sustainable forests. The logging and
manufacturing processes are expected to conform to the environmental
regulations of the country of origin.

John Murray (Publishers)
338 Euston Road
London NW1 3BH

www.johnmurray.co.uk

خاض البحار وجازها ثم ارتمى   يفلي الفلا بنجيّة صيهود

Across the seas he rode, and then was cast ashore
To ride a sleek swift camel through the arid sands.

Abu 'l-Qasim ibn Abu 'l-Afiyah

مسحتُ الأرض شرقاً ثم غرباً   أسائل عن عواقب كل حي

I've taken measure of the earth, both east and west,
And asked its peoples what their past has left behind.

Muhammad ibn Muhammad al-Abdari

لا تبك إلفاً نأى ولا داراً   ودُر مع الدهـر كيفما دارا

واتخذ الناس كلهم مسكناً   ومثّل الأرض كلها داراً

For far-off home and friends shed not a tear –
Turn with the twists of time, nor fear to roam;
Make mankind everywhere your dwelling-place,
And look upon the whole world as your home.

Attributed to Musa ibn Abd al-Malik Ibn Sa'id

For Ianthe, Tim, Ben, Laila and Fergus

Contents

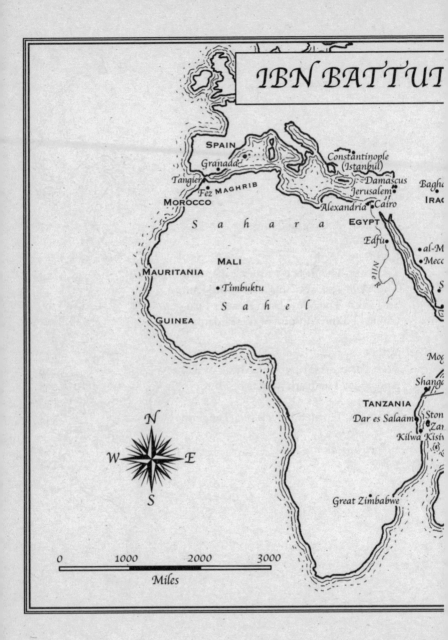

IBN BATTUT

SPAIN

Granada

Constantinople
(Istanbul)

Tangier

Damascus

Fez MAGHRIB

Jerusalem

Baght

MOROCCO

Alexandria Cairo

IRAC

S a h a r a

EGYPT

Edfu

al-M

Mecc

MALI

MAURITANIA

Timbuktu

Nile R.

S

S a h e l

GUINEA

Mog

Shang

TANZANIA

Dar es Salaam

Ston

Zai

Kilwa Kisi

Great Zimbabwe

N

W   E

S

Miles

0   1000   2000   3000

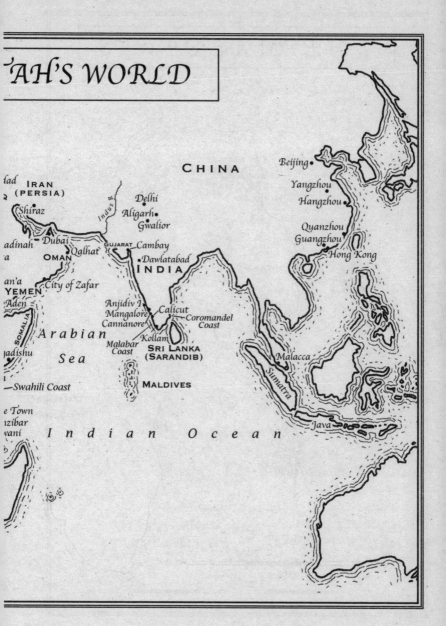

THE MALDIVES

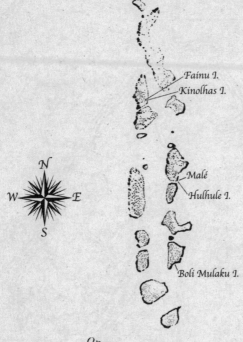

Fainu I.

Kinolhas I.

N
W E
S

Malé

Hulhule I.

Boli Mulaku I.

One-and-a-Half-Degree Channel

Huvadhoo Atoll

Viligili I.

Faares I.

Vaadhoo I.

Equatorial Channel

Fua Mulaku I.

| 0 | 75 | 150 | 225 | 300 |

Miles

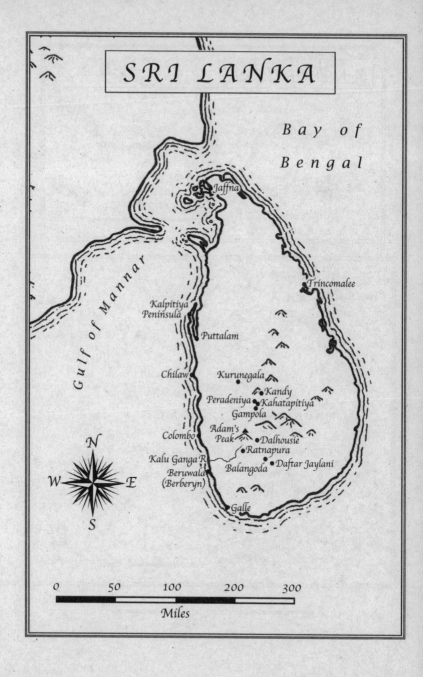

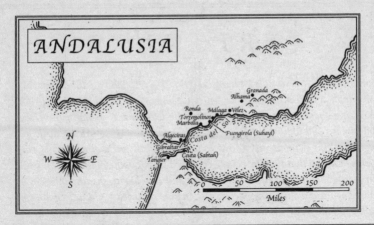

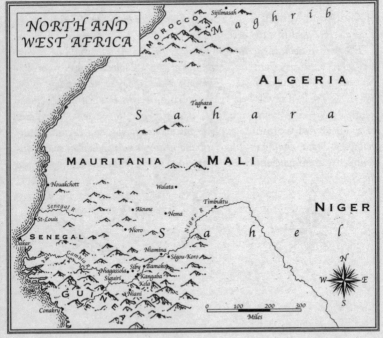

Ibn Battutah (more fully, Shams al-Din Abu Abdallah Muhammad ibn Abdallah Ibn Battutah al-Lawati al-Tanji) was born in 1304 in the Moroccan port city of Tangier. In 1325 he left home to perform the Mecca pilgrimage and to further his studies in Islamic law. As it turned out, he was not to return permanently to the land of his birth for another twenty-nine years. During that time he wandered over a huge swathe of the known world in search of employment, enlightenment and enjoyment, visiting lands as far apart as the Swahili coast, southern Russia, south-east China, Spain and sub-Saharan West Africa. Back in Morocco he recorded his travelling memories in a book entitled The Precious Gift for Lookers into the Marvels of Cities and Wonders of Travel, known for short as the Rihlah or Travels. He died in 1368 or 1369.

The present book is the third in a trilogy that in Arabic would be termed a dhayl, a literary 'tail' or 'train (of a robe)', following on from Ibn Battutah's own book of travels. Each part of the trilogy is independent of the others. The first, Travels with a Tangerine, revisits Ibn Battutah's earlier journeys between Morocco and the Eurasian steppe; the second, The Hall of a Thousand Columns, explores his long residence and eventful wanderings in India, ending in shipwreck and penury on the Malabar coast; this volume traces his adventures on the far-flung shores of the Indian Ocean and the Sahara.

Preamble

A Hole in Time

Picture a miniature from an Arabic manuscript, its colours still jewel-bright after two-thirds of a millennium. In the centre is a small middle-aged man, shown full-face, in full flow, in the act of raising a finger to add a point to an exclamation. His animated figure is flanked by those of two other men, their faces seen in profile. The one on his right is young; he is listening eagerly. The other is an elderly man with his chin in his hand, frowning and plainly sceptical. All three wear turbans and robes and are sitting on a rich carpet by a fountain in front of a pavilion in a garden. In the background – or rather, in the lapis-blue sky above the pavilion, for there is no perspective – is a malachite hill with a cresting of jasper battlements. Opposite this hovers a mountain with an icing of snow. (If you have visited Granada you may recognize these two features, stylized though they are, as the hill of the Alhambra and the Sierra Nevada.) Beyond the frame of the picture the armies of Christian Spain are encamped, out of sight but never out of mind: it is 1350, and the sultanate of Granada is an Islamic island in a Christian peninsula. But the little man in the middle is telling his listeners – the one fascinated, the other dubious – of further horizons, of a wider world where the civilization of Islam had travelled, like him, to the limits. (Also like him, it had fathered offspring out on the edge; their hybrid complexions would become apparent with time.) Below the miniature is a caption in Arabic: *Shaykh Abu Abdallah, known as Ibn Battutah, recounts the wonders and marvels of his travels.*

Throughout my own travels in search of that mobile central figure, Ibn Battutah of Tangier, this image of him in the garden has recurred in my mind. It arises from an encounter towards the end

I

of his wanderings, when he had already spent a quarter of a century roaming the known world in search of enlightenment, employment and relief for his chronically itchy feet. To look at, I suppose the scene is a composite made up from real miniatures of the period. But to me it has its own reality, that of a moment seen through a hole in time.

Everything in the moment, the miniature, is unnaturally clear. The absence of depth flattens each element of the scene into a pressed specimen of itself, floating on the surface of the instant. The flowers are immediately identifiable – iris, lupin, lavender – and a historian of textiles would be able to guess the provenance of the men's robes. Only one thing refuses to reveal itself definitively: the face of Ibn Battutah. Each time I examine it, the features are different.

I've always wanted to know what the man I spend so much time with actually looked like. Of course it doesn't really matter; *figura animi magis quam corporis*. Still, it is an intriguing question, if only to this individualistical age in which the ultimate expression of self-hood is the look, the face, and the pinnacle of celebrity is to become an 'icon'. Ibn Battutah himself only lets on that he had a beard; all I've found out beyond that, so far, is that he was probably small and thin.

It didn't help that on the way to the starting point of this journey I dropped into the Ibn Battuta Mall.* This is a vast shopping centre in Dubai, nearly a mile long and situated (I think by what is commonly called coincidence) at the precise mid-point of the eastern and western extremities of IB's travels. Its interior décor is a rather successful pastiche of some of the great buildings in the lands IB visited – oriental orientalism. In addition to its commercial function, it seeks to 'edutain' visitors about the traveller and his world. To this end, IB kept manifesting before my eyes, and as in my miniature he was different every time. He was an Arab cousin of Pinocchio in the cartoon adventure showing on a child-height screen in Tunisia Court. He was a Hollywood male lead, handsome and pensive – vaguely Brad Pitt, with an unscary beard – in the

---

* I prefer 'Ibn Battutah', but it's not unacceptable to drop the *h*. To avoid arguments and do my bit to save trees, I call him 'IB'.

promotional hand-outs ('Live the Adventure!'). He was a wrinkle-free greybeard in the illustrated children's book, *Ibn Battuta and the Sufi* – read it: you too can benefit from the mystical alternative to cosmetic surgery. He appeared in the live host-body of auburn-bearded Greg from South Africa, pacing the Mall from Andalusia to China and back again in fourteenth-century rig and imparting miniaturized versions of his adventures to interested punters – Greg-IB can collapse the real IB's ten Indian years into twenty seconds flat. And I even bumped, softly, into IB's Pinocchio avatar, brought to life by a roaming person in a padded suit, straight from Disneyworld; or Dislamworld.

In his Mall, IB was an icon in search of an image. I suppose the image will never be found, that I'll never look IB in the face. It's not so much because he's dead; rather, because he always seems to be ahead. (Those familiar expressions of time and motion and space – the past is behind us, the future is in front of us, dead and gone, here and now – don't always work.) All I can do is follow and observe, like those physicists who try to form a picture of their inscrutable particles from the traces they have left behind. Of just how strange some of IB's traces would prove to be, and in what unexpected places I would come across them, I as yet had no idea. Some things cannot be looked for, but only found.

The way around the edge of IB's world is a long one. With this in mind, I went and bought the thing I'd come to the Ibn Battuta Mall to get, a pair of walking boots. As the Filipina saleswoman handed me my receipt, she asked if I was going far for my holidays.

From an island south of Zanzibar, I thought, *by way of ocean, desert, mountains, atolls, Sarandib, China, Timbuktu, palaces, temples, wonders, marvels, holes in time, to a garden in Granada.* 'Oh, here, there and everywhere,' I said.

East

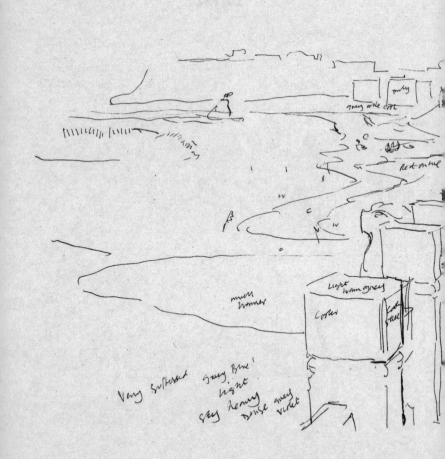

grey ochre diff

puly

Red ochre

Light warm greens

much warmer

Cooler

Very suffused grey Blue
light
grey heavy
Dense grey violet

Tanzania

The Palace by the Sea

Think, in this battered caravanserai
Whose portals are alternate night and day,
How sultan after sultan with his pomp
Abode his hour or two, and went his way.

Edward Fitzgerald, *The Rubáiyát of Omar Khayyám*

Kilwa Kisiwani

I thought it would be easy to find: just keep left along the cliff. Perhaps I've missed a turn. And now the path is forking once again. I stop for a moment, breathing in the smell of the island, a scent released by the early-morning rain. It rises rich, dark, smoky, as if all these centuries of sun have kippered the red earth of Kilwa Kisiwani.

Left, towards the unseen ocean, along the less trodden fork. The track dies in a patch of abandoned garden lapped by a scrub of doum palm. I retrace my steps. The only landmarks are the wintering baobabs, leafless in August, shining silver in this light that flooded out the rain. Further on there is a cottage. A thin white dog ambles up to sniff me; a green bicycle is leaning against the mud wall. (Dog and bike are the only members of either species I've seen on Kilwa.) There is a man, repairing fish-traps. He stops his work and looks at me, surprised for a moment.

'Husuni Kubwa?' I ask. He nods, rises, beckons to me to follow. Soon we're making our way down a slope to a mangrove-tangled shore. Behind the mangroves, still hidden, is the ocean. We reach a staircase cut into the cliff. My guide goes back to his fish–traps. I climb the steps, up towards blackened coral walls.

'Husuni . . . Kubwa,' I say, catching my breath. 'The Big Palace. Big . . . steps . . . too. And not a word about it . . . from you. How could you forget it?' It's become a habit, talking to the other man who has led me here, Muhammad son of Abdallah of Tangier, known as Ibn Battutah, known to me as IB. He doesn't answer. Our long-distance relationship is one-sided, mostly. But his silent ghost and his garrulous book have haunted me for a dozen years. I've haunted him back, shadowed him from the Pillars of Hercules to the end of India; left gaps, admittedly, and this was one of them. But now here we are, on another shore – there it is at last, the sea – and this time I will follow him to the ends of his earth, to both of them; to his antipodes. 'People on the surface of the earth', the geographer al-Dimashqi wrote not long before IB set off from home in 1325, 'are like barleycorns stuck all round an apple. Wherever they live, their feet are on the ground and their heads are in the air . . . Thus the soles of the feet of people at the two extremities of the inhabited world, China and Spain, face each other.'

We have a long way to go, a lot of footsteps. So why have I made IB backtrack more than a decade from where I left him last, in India – round half an ocean, down into the wrong hemisphere, to a small island off the southern coast of Tanzania? Mainly because it's as good a place as any from which to look east, and to watch his wider world unfold. Also, to be honest, because of the name. *Kilwa Kisiwani*: from names like that journeys are spun.

*

To watch the development of maps of the Old World, IB's world, is like following the progress of a huge and very slow-growing foetus. Over the centuries, formless coasts swell with new-found knowledge, subcontinents inflate, peninsulas sprout. Potential Americas and Australias, imagined but undelineated, have yet to surface from the amniotic dark of the Circumambient Sea. As its limbs take shape, the great lone hunched Afro-Eurasian landmass uncurls.

It is a long and uneven gestation. Ptolemy's Mediterranean,

seen from second-century Alexandria, is almost fully formed; but the far eastern end of his world is an embryonic blob in which Africa and China are conjoined, making the Indian Ocean an enclosed pond. It was Ptolemy's Arab heirs who opened it up. Al-Mas'udi reported in the tenth century that some timbers of a teak ship had been found floating off Crete. Not only was the wood from the east, but the planks were 'sewn' together with coir cordage – a shipbuilding technique known in the Indian Ocean but not in the Mediterranean. The two seas, he concluded, must connect. Two hundred years on, the world map of al-Idrisi shows an island-crowded Indian Ocean the same length as the Mediterranean but narrower north to south. It is only just open-ended: the tip of his Malayan Peninsula almost touches Mozambique, and a detached Korea swims in the slender gulf that separates China from Africa.

Africa would eventually stretch out from its foetal position. Not many years after the Portuguese rounded the Cape in 1488, the Arab navigator Sulayman al-Mahri reported their claim that the continent reached further south than anyone had thought, and then turned sharp north-west at what they called the cape of 'Bunasfarans' – Bõa Esperança. That European doubling of the Cape of Good Hope was a turning point for the Indian Ocean, a final opening up – but also a closing down of the old trade routes. Within a few decades, the Portuguese had forged a chain of forts around the shores and islands from Kilwa Kisiwani to Malacca, and imposed gunboats and passports on waters innocent of fire-power and frontiers. The modern map and the modern world were born together. For those who lived on its shores, the Indian Ocean had just got much bigger and much harder to cross.

In the fourteenth century, however, that ocean still felt as small as it looked in the atlas of the age. IB had probably never seen a map of it when he sailed into it in 1330 on his first big venture beyond the Arab world, into the Islamic periphery; but he writes as if he had, compressing the miles. He covers the 1,800-mile crossing of the open sea from Kilwa Kisiwani to Zafar in Oman, for example, in seven words of Arabic, nine of English – 'We sailed from Kilwa to the city of Zafar.' Admittedly, he rarely writes about land- or seascape unless it gets in the way. But that is the point: the

Indian Ocean was an easy sea to sail. It was the common property of a rich, eclectic, cosmopolitan culture held together by trade, the monsoon and Islam. There were fellow-Muslims, often fellow-Arabs, in every major port, and the chance, if you hitched a ride on a well-found vessel powered by the right wind, of covering a steady seventy or eighty nautical miles a day – perhaps five times faster than land travel at the sort of speed a lumbering caravan could make. For IB the Indian Ocean dhow was, *mutatis mutandis*, the equivalent of air travel for us; in the Mediterranean with its fickle winds, you were as likely to end up where you started as to get where you wanted. So when maps of IB's age show, say, the actual 3,000 miles from Kilwa to Sarandib – Serendip, today's Sri Lanka – as being closer than the actual 200 miles from Libya to Greece, they reflect a relative reality. Like that of the London Tube map, it is a reality in which ease of connection is as valid a measure as miles. Seen from IB's Kilwa, that wider eastern periphery where I mean to follow him – the Maldives, India, Sarandib, China – might as well be just over the horizon.

*

I reach the top of the steps. There's a roofless antechamber flanked by more small rooms and then I'm confronted by a long sunken courtyard backed by a pile of jagged walls – and by the realization that here, on this now secluded island of Kilwa Kisiwani, where wattle and daub are the architectural order of the day and a bicycle looks futuristic, there was a time of richness, of greatness. These buildings were once the most splendid in all sub-Saharan Africa.

And IB, who – unless the archaeologists are way out in their dating – was here when they were gleaming new, didn't even mention them. It beats me how, twenty-five years on, he could remember the exact ingredients of the pickles he had with his lunch in Mogadishu on the way here and the fact that its ruler wore silk underwear on Fridays, and yet forget this whopping palace by the sea. You simply can't miss it, up on its cliff overlooking the bay; unless you're IB. He was the man who, as we'll see, went to Granada *and missed the Alhambra*.

He does however make up for his blind spot regarding large royal residences by noticing trivia that other people forget – like pickles and underpants; and, above all, by noticing people. His Kilwa is populated by citizens 'of a solid black colour, with scarified faces', ruled over by the humble and generous Sultan Hasan, and visited by a crowd of droppers-in including merchants, dervishes and scrounging Meccan notables – the latter were *sharifs*, descendants of the Prophet Muhammad whose pedigrees IB, a walking Islamic *Debrett*, remembered to the third generation.

Now they all seem so far away, those people; dots seen across the gulf of time. I only have lizards for company in Husuni Kubwa. There's one, nodding on a fragment of collapsed frieze. Another lizard lounges on a massive chunk of masonry, oddly shaped – a section of ribbed dome, I realize. It resembles the jaw of a gigantic clam, as if coral stone has suffered not a sea-change, but a sea-reversion.

I make for the shade of a wall in one of the rooms by the stair-head, to jot down thoughts I know will get drowned out by all this richness and strangeness. Between jottings my gaze wanders over the mottled surface of the lime-plaster, darkened but still smooth and hard ten lifetimes after it was put on. Something, a shape, appears out of the swirls of grey and black. A graffito, a doodle: a dhow with a single mast and a triangle of bare rigging, emerging from the wall like a ship out of a mist. Someone must have scratched it into the rock-hard plaster while it was still wet, someone squatting where I am now – I feel for an instant that I'm looking over his shoulder, at some point in the few hours it took for the lime to set. A point in time becalmed by this act of inscription. I continue my own inscription, aware that the gulf has narrowed a little.

A last look at that hieroglyph of travel scratched into the wall. I want to share the discovery, but there's no one here. The only humans visible are themselves dots, on board the sailing dhows down below in Kilwa Bay, becalmed on the narrow arm of ocean between island and mainland. *Dud ala ud*, the old sea-fearing inland Arabs called sailors before they too went seafaring – ticks on sticks. I half close my eyes and see them sailing the centuries, bringing celadon bowls and Hangzhou brocade transshipped from junks in distant Malabar.

Nowadays they're coasting in kerosene and mangrove poles.

I pass through the sunken court and emerge again above that sweeping view of Kilwa Bay – and, immediately below and perfectly placed to take in the vista, is a scalloped octagonal swimming pool, in such good shape it looks as if it could be filled again today. A rich man's pool, one for Tiberius on Capri or Getty at Malibu. Further on, another sunken court, its terraced landward end rising in nine steep steps like the seating in an ancient theatre, to the remains of a pavilion – a sort of sultanic opera-box, perched above the drama of arrival and embarkation down in the bay. The side walls of this court are pierced with pigeonholes, dozens of them. Or rather, lamp-holes: the insides are still lined with a layer of soot that flakes off in my fingers. Bigger holes – niches, alcoves – line a rank of rooms beyond the court. My mind's eye fills them with treasures from those imagined argosies in the bay. 'Their lighted houses were aglow', a poet wrote of the wealthy rulers of another Swahili island-state, Pate,

> With lamps of crystal and brass.
> Their nights were as day.
> They lived amid beauty and honour,
> Surrounded by the finest porcelain.

I pick up a tiny fragment of sea-green tile, Persian perhaps, more eloquent than poems.

Another sunken court, more labyrinths of rooms – and then I step into a huge empty quadrangle, fifty yards square and nearly as big in area as all the rest of the palace put together, surrounded by the collapsing remains of windowless chambers. It was Neville Chittick, the British archaeologist who dug here in the 1950s and 1960s, who realized that this big hollow square with its elephant-grey walls was the commercial heart of Kilwa. At first sight it seems strange for a palace and a warehouse to share a party wall. But then I remember I've seen something like it before, across the ocean in the Indian port of Cannanore. There the Ali Rajas – Muslim merchant-princes of the monsoon, like IB's Sultan Hasan – lived in a semi-detached relationship with their godowns. This was Husuni Kubwa's business end, and if the rest of the palace looks oceanward to India and China, this battered caravanserai is Janus-faced, with half its gaze inland, on Africa.

*

Most of IB's brief account of Kilwa is about the builder of Husuni Kubwa, Sultan Hasan, fourth ruler of a dynasty whose origins were in the southern Arabian region of Hadramawt. 'He is called Abu 'l-Mawahib [the Father of Gifts],' IB wrote, 'because of the many presents that he gives.' IB doesn't mention what Hasan gave him – he usually does, and he never fails to name and shame a stingy potentate – but it must have been a fair amount to earn the sultan immortalization as 'generous . . . humble . . . respectful of men of religion . . . worthy . . . open-handed'. Sultan Hasan could afford to be generous. He was awash in two African commodities, stored in the chambers of his warehouse court – slaves, and ivory. A visiting dervish from Yemen, IB says, ended up with a gift of two loads of ivory and twenty slaves. (The slaves solved the problem of how to carry the ivory, but they must have cramped the style of a solitary wandering ascetic.) And then there was a third commodity, one that IB says the sultan seldom gave away. He had good reason not to: Husuni Kubwa was built on it. To monopolize it was, and is, a ticket to power for aspiring African sultans and dictators. It has outlasted the fashion for slaves and ivory, and will probably be lusted after when the current tastes for oil, uranium and even diamonds have passed. The third commodity was gold.

By the time IB reached Kilwa in 1330, it had become the main channel through which southern African gold flowed to the outside world. In the first part of the fourteenth century, that flow had increased from a trickle to an outpour. The economies of Europe and the Near East were turning more and more to gold as currency, and the world price of the metal took off. This was the time when the inland metropolis of Great Zimbabwe, in whose territory the mines lay, became truly great. In Kilwa, Husuni Kubwa was the built expression of that buoyant graph line.

But how could a small offshore island a thousand miles north-east of the Zimbabwean mines have cornered the gold export market? The answer lies in that great biannual rhythm of the ocean, the *mawsim* – the Arabic 'season' for sailing, the English 'monsoon'.

Riding the north-east monsoon from Arabia or Persia, the furthest south you could sail in Africa, while still giving yourself time to trade and to catch the south-west monsoon home, was Kilwa. Go any further and you were likely to get stuck for a year waiting for the wind to turn. Ports further south gathered fables; Kilwa gathered merchants, and money.

So too did the land that lies at the end of IB's travels round the edge of the Old World, the West African empire of Mali. Viewed from Kilwa, that other African Eldorado seems as far off as China (it nearly is, in linear terms), or further – to ride the monsoon to Canton was one thing, to cross the thick of Africa a near impossibility. But the *sawahil* of East Africa (the 'coasts' of the ocean, the origin of 'Swahili') and their singular, the *sahil* of the west (the 'coast' of the desert, the origin of 'Sahel'), were both part of the same world-system. Both were lapped by vast empty spaces, one of water, one of sand, whose emptiness helped rather than hindered the movement across them of goods and people and ideas. Trade powered the revolution of these two great spheres of interaction, Islam lubricated it; and in Europe, the Near East and Central Asia other spheres revolved, all of them turning in concert through a rare half-century of harmony that began with the end of the Crusades and the taming of the Mongols and died with the Black Death. IB began his travels in the middle of that age, and in a life of landfalls saw more of that harmonious world than any other human being; probably, in fact, saw more of the globe than anyone since apes walked upright. Just as important, he made it home alive and got down on paper what he saw. History can be thankful: he is the eye-witness of that concordant age, even if he did forget the odd palace.

But we have wandered from Kilwa. Here, in the fold of the map, in the lap of that uncurling foetal Africa, I root around the sultan's amphibious caravanserai where the treasures of the interior were stored with those of the shore – tortoiseshell, and ambergris ('dragonspit', as the Chinese customs ledgers call it) – and with the brocades and porcelain that came from across the ocean, from the great industrial power-house of Yuan-dynasty China. The Sino-African trading relationship is the same today, manufactured goods in return for raw materials; even if tusks and silks are now copper ore and DVD players.

Husuni Kubwa shows how some things don't change. At the same time, like all the best ruins, it is a reminder that the muta-bility of power and wealth is itself a constant. The fourteenth-century world that IB travelled in may have been only hemiglobalized, its communications slow and indirect; but its markets, like today's, were linked in a precarious web. When, in the middle of the century, the Black Death struck, the world economy slumped and the price of gold plunged; it dragged Kilwa down with it, and that other golden kingdom, Mali. Husuni Kubwa, this sprawling palace of the monsoon winds, was abandoned and – except for a brief tenancy by M. Morice, a French slaver who camped out here in the eighteenth century –. has been empty ever since.

The scales tip, the graph-line dips,' and Thebes and Babylon, Kilwa and Mali and Great Zimbabwe, London and New York begin their inevitable decline.

★

Still clutching my bit of green tile, I retrace my steps. I want to look once more at the doodle of the dhow, to catch again that fleeting feeling of looking over someone's shoulder, of someone being here in this emptiness.

There *is* someone here. Someone's voice: an Arabic voice, telling of . . .

He looks up from his book mid-word, wide-eyed, as if I'm a ghost. I greet him gently in Arabic, wondering if *he's* the ghost. Shock turns to smile; he returns the greeting, looks me up and down, takes in my battered shoulder-bag, my boots from the Ibn Battuta Mall, now red with the earth of Kilwa. 'You are a . . . stranger, a traveller,' he says, still in Arabic, proud of the words. 'Please say *du'a* for me.'

Du'a. Prayer. I hesitate, looking at the young face under the crumpled embroidered cap; but Arabic is a language of prayers, and I'm already improvizing one – '. . . success . . . wisdom . . . guidance . . .' – even as I wonder why he asked.

'Amen,' he says. Then I remember. 'Blessed are the strangers,' the Prophet Muhammad said. Strangers, people on the road, pick up *barakah*, blessing, with the dust on their boots. (Or their hands,

17

I recall – IB's host in his next stop, Zafar, actually drank the blessing-infused water the traveller had washed his hands in.)

Yahya shows me his textbooks, piled on a piece of fallen wall in his study in the ruins: a primer, a grammar, a Qur'an reciters' manual. I apologize for distracting him, but he says, in his careful, halting Arabic, 'It is not a problem. Today is Thursday. It is the day for gathering firewood. I must help my friends.'

As Yahya leads me back through the ruins in the direction of the village, I ask him what he knows about Sultan Hasan.

'Who is he?'

'The sultan who built Husuni Kubwa.'

'I don't know him.'

I get the same answer from Yahya's friend, a fellow-student whom we meet in the brush just beyond the caravanserai. He shakes his head, when Yahya has relieved it of the bundle of twigs he's been carrying. 'They say the king who built this place kept his gold down there,' he says, pointing to a deep square well. 'That is what I have heard.'

That was all. 'And Ibn Battutah?' I ask. 'The traveller from Morocco?'

Again, I draw a blank. So too with the rest of their fellow-students, who are converging on the village with the fuel for next week's cooking fires. They put down their loads, and we sit on a *baraza*, a cool lime-plastered bench running along the front of the house where they board. Ridwan, their leader, tells me about the *madrasahs* on Kilwa. 'It is the centre for Islamic studies for the whole of this coast,' he says with pride. 'There are a hundred boarders from the mainland, and a few students from Kilwa, like me.'

All this is news to me; I'd hardly given a thought to the island's present. Ridwan seems incurious about its past. 'Husuni Kubwa? It is very old,' he says with a shrug.

Other than that one gleam of gold in the well, I hear nothing of the glittering past of Kilwa Kisiwani. I've come to excavate memories and have found a void. The sultans have gone their way, leaving their battered caravanserai and crumbling palace to the lizards, and the students.

★

Back at the house where I'd spent the night, I hoped that my host, Muhammad Mwanga, Kilwa's chief of Ofisi ya Mambo ya Kale – the Office of Old Things, or Antiquities – would be able to fill in the silence between IB's voice and the voices of the present. But he had gone off to a wife on the mainland, leaving me in the hands of his island spouse. Her only appearances were to bring food. I now sat eating my lone lunch – rice, fish, squid and dik-dik stewed with okra; Mrs Mwanga must have thought I needed feeding up after my antiquarian rambles.

As I ate, something kept catching my eye: a briar pipe, sitting on Mrs Mwanga's sideboard next to a tin of Davidoff tobacco. It was a puzzling object. Mr Mwanga, in his white-framed shades and Hawaiian shirt, hadn't looked like a pipe-smoker. Neither did his wife. I began to wonder if they had a mystery lodger . . . an ex-Assistant District Commissioner from Tanganyika days, perhaps, who had stayed on and would soon stride in wearing enormous shorts and call me 'old chap'. The puzzle of the pipe was soon solved, however, by the arrival of the Mwangas' other guest, a youthful French ethnologist called Pascal Bacuez. He had fallen under the spell of Kilwa, he explained, and had been staying there on and off for the last ten years. Yes, he said, the pipe was his. It suited a Sorbonne ethnologist, I thought: it went with the *tristes tropiques*.

As we were finishing off the last of the dik-dik another arrival appeared in the Mwangas' front parlour, a tall man, fortyish, in shapeless trousers, a baggy T-shirt, a string of old glass beads and a billy-goat beard. 'Meet Ahmad,' said Pascal, 'my friend and principal informant.' There was something strange about Ahmad – a feral energy that seemed to possess his stringy body. I saw it in his eyes, felt it in his handshake. You wouldn't want to meet him in the woods . . .

Without warning, still holding my hand, holding me with his eyes, he flew off into Kiswahili – a rollicking rhythmic monologue, a rat-tat-tat of syllables; interspersed, I realized, with the pops and twangs of Arabic. I picked up a repeated name – ' . . . Shaykh Abd al-Qadir . . .' – then snatches of sufi litanies and odds and ends of Qur'anic verses and Islamic prayers, the names of angels, of devils, of jinn, jagged Arabic and pitter-patter Swahili careering in a headlong fugue of sounds in which he never released me from the grip of his gaze.

The mad monologue ended as abruptly as it had begun. For a moment more, Ahmad studied me, the rabbit in the headlamps; then freed me with a burst of laughter. 'You history man,' Ahmad stated in English, serious again. I nodded. 'Know then', he continued in Arabic, 'that Kilwa was founded by Solomon the son of David, on both of whom be peace. Know also that many *sharifs* have come to Kilwa.' I thought of the scrounging *sharifs* IB met here, and wondered if Ahmad would fill in some of the blanks of the past. But his brief history of Kilwa had ended. He smiled, shook my hand again and left.

Still headlamp-eyed, I turned to Pascal. 'Ahmad is Kilwa's ex-witch-doctor,' he said.

The idea of a Muslim witch-doctor, even an ex- one, threw me. The terms seemed mutually exclusive: Islam as I knew it was about as tolerant of witchcraft as the judges of Salem, Massachusetts. But Pascal's revelation gave sense of a sort to that strange bilingual performance, in which all those fragments of Arabic, sampled from sources that ranged from impeccably orthodox through mystical to downright occult, were laid on to an indigenous Kiswahili backing track. The mesmeric Ahmad intrigued me even more. And, I learned later, he wasn't exactly an 'ex-' witch-doctor.

'Since he came back from Dar es Salaam he's been planning to set up in the business again,' Pascal said that evening as we sat on the *baraza* by the door of Mr Mwanga's house. I'd just had an open-air ladle-shower in the back yard, under a night sky so bright it seemed not just lit by stars but paved with them: you could have walked the Milky Way. Now, I could see Pascal's pipe-smoke silhouetted against the constellations and, to our left, the billowing black form of a big mango tree that they called Mwembe Ladu, the Mango Struck by Lightning. A few passers-by, their footfalls damped by the dust of the track, had stopped to chat with Pascal; they spoke in slow soft island speech, filled with long pauses and aaahs. Now the village was silent. Apart from a glimmer of lamplight from a neighbouring cottage, we might have been the only signs of waking human life on Kilwa Kisiwani.

'Ahmad summons the jinn,' Pascal went on. 'They come and enter him and help him to perform exorcisms.'

I took this in. 'It doesn't sound very Islamic.'

'Well, he gives it all an Islamic basis. Part of the summoning process involves reciting phrases from the Qadiri *dhikr* and so on.' I recalled those snatches of sufi litany I'd heard. 'And most of his jinn are good Muslim ones from Arabia. He's got a favourite, an Arabian female jinni called Karimah. And there are others. They come and possess him in a set order.'

'So there's a sort of *placement*, an etiquette.'

'Yes, but the infidel foreign jinn aren't so well behaved. There are American jinn, who are very malevolent. And British jinn.'

'How do they rate?' I asked, feeling defensive about my fellow country-... well, not country*men*, but one has to keep the side up.

'Not as bad as the American ones.'

'Phew,' I said. 'But how does Ahmad get hold of these infidel jinn? I mean, he'd hardly be able to lure them with Islamic recitations.'

'He uses all sorts of things. Including beer and whisky.'

'What, as libations?'

'No,' Pascal said, laughing. 'He drinks them!'

The idea was fascinating. I could picture rowdy redneck jinn pouring into Ahmad's body with the Kentucky sourmash, and more genial British genies possessing him with appreciative sniffs as the ice-cubes squeaked and cracked: jinn and tonic. (In my mind's eye, one of the latter took on the form of an old schoolmaster of mine. 'Never forget the school motto, chaps,' he would say with a bibulous wink. '*Spiritus intus alit* − "The spirit nourishes within . . . "') Fascinating, but most definitely unislamic, this use of spirits to summon spirits. 'Try telling all this to a judge in Saudi Arabia,' I said.

'Ahmad doesn't only use alcohol. I've introduced him to pipe-smoking, and he now uses that in his jinn-summoning.'

Weren't ethnologists supposed to make sure they didn't import any elements from their own society into that of the people they were studying? Whatever, I didn't doubt that pipe-smoke, like alcohol fumes, would be an irresistible attractant for certain types of jinn. My former house in Yemen had been haunted by a hubble-bubble-smoking jinni; I could imagine Pascal's briar conjuring a whole host of infidel spirits, some in enormous shorts, others in deerstalkers, one – inspired by my late cousin Douglas, a pipe-smoking dean – in a dog-collar, all wafting in along curling whiffs of smoke like the children in the old advertisement for Bisto gravy powder: 'Aaah, Davidoff!'

As Pascal refilled his own pipe, I thought more about the implications of Ahmad's witch-doctoring. Alcohol may be forbidden in Islam, and tobacco frowned on by the puritanical; but belief in jinn is incumbent on Muslims. All the same, the idea of deliberately getting possessed by them in order to perform exorcisms was, to say the least, heterodox. 'Doesn't this all go against the flow?' I asked Pascal. 'I mean, the more recent trend in Islam seems to have been towards a rigid sort of orthodoxy.'

'Well, yes,' Pascal said. 'But they're not like that on Kilwa. Not long ago, for example, some Tablighis came here from Pakistan, and they didn't like them at all.' The Tablighis, I recalled, are a missionary group with puritan tendencies. 'And, do you know, in all the years I've been coming to Kilwa not a single person has ever tried to convert me.'

'I noticed they're pretty laid back on that score,' I said. Neither Yahya nor Ridwan had asked me the question that would have been popped in minutes, if not seconds, by many of their Arab peers: Are you a Muslim? No one had even asked me where I was from. Feeling multiply at home as I do, and disliking being pinned down, I found the incuriosity refreshing.

We talked on into the night, about Ahmad and his jinn, about the strange meeting of beliefs – *métissage*, Pascal termed it – in which waves of Islam had overlaid, but not obliterated, indigenous religious ideas. The result was a many-layered sedimentary pile, a sort of supernatural compost-heap in which, although we might at first only see the latest additions, the deeper strata were no less live, fermenting in the dark. It would all have horrified the orthodox IB. And some of the strata, I learned, were very deep and dark indeed.

'You remember Ahmad talked about the *sharifs* coming to Kilwa?' Pascal asked me. I did. They had come and been honoured for their noble blood, inherited from the prophet of Islam, since at least the time of IB: he met those Meccan *sharifs* here, enjoying the sultan's largesse. 'They've got a special position here. You see, Ahmad uses his powers for exorcism and healing. But the *sharifs* have another sort of power – *karamah*. And it doesn't matter if they're dead.'

Karamah was a word I knew well. IB used it often, and meant by it a grace bestowed by God on saintly people. The term covered a wide range of gifts, from the ability to foresee future events to a knack for guessing a visitor's favourite pudding; the sort of things which, in a latter-day world thought devoid of miracles, would be put down to coincidence or intuition. But in Kilwa *karamah* was quite different.

'It's something I'm still working on,' Pascal continued. 'But in short, *karamah* here is a power that's used mainly for malediction. People go to a graveyard called the Cemetery of the Forty Shaykhs – in other words, *sharifs* – and they say prayers and make sacrifices to bring down curses on their enemies.'

I was shocked. Sacrifice, actual or symbolic, plays an important part in the Judaeo-Christian-Islamic tradition, beginning with Abraham and Isaac/Ishmael; but that is sacrifice for propitiation or expiation. This was for execration, and it was about as Islamic as Baron Samedi is Christian. 'But . . . that sounds more like voodoo,' I said. 'I'm surprised it's tolerated.'

'If anything it seems to be getting more popular. People come to Kilwa from all around specifically to visit the Forty Shaykhs. I'm trying to get Ahmad to take me there and explain things.'

In a world of hardening boundaries where the lines between religions seemed, like those between nations on the map, to be ever more rigidly drawn and reinforced, where the frontier-guards of faith were getting ever more violent in their defence of perceived purity, here on Kilwa the opposite was happening – a blurring of the border between Islam and pre-Islam, between beliefs that came from over the ocean and those that dwelt in the continent across the strait. In this, Kilwa was not unique. Throughout my travels with IB I'd found Islam cohabiting with earlier beliefs, from fertility-inducing eels in Morocco to yogic breath-control in India. Besides, the evidence of what was there before lies at the very heart of Islam – in the Ka'bah of Mecca, a temple that had been revered for centuries before the Prophet's time. That is how religions work – by cohabitation, co-option, compromise; not by confrontation. But here out on the edge the cohabitation was, to say the least, eyebrow-raising. I wondered what other surprises I would come across in my travels with IB on the periphery of Islam.

★

I lay awake in the small hours, my mind crawling with questions. It was all that talk of the Forty Shaykhs, Ahmad's jinn, and those other denizens, angelic and satanic, of the spiritual compost-heap. Above all, one question wriggled around: how could *sharifs*, descendants of the holy prophet of Islam, have lent their God-given *karamah* to the unholy business of cursing? Perhaps a look round the Cemetery of the Forty Shaykhs would yield some clues . . . except that it seemed casual visits were strongly discouraged. Given the reputation of the place, I wasn't sure I wanted to go trespassing. And, come to think of it, curses weren't always unholy. Christ cursed the barren fig-tree. Muhammad cursed his own uncle: 'May the hands of Abu Lahab perish . . .'

★

The earliest known material evidence of Islam on the East African coast lies 500 miles up the coast from Kilwa, at Shanga in the Lamu Archipelago, in the form of the buried remains of a mid-eighth-century wattle and daub mosque. Here, in this deepest Islamic stratum, some sherds of Chinese stoneware were found. Just as significantly, the mosque appears to have been built inside a pre-Islamic-style ritual enclosure. The association of Islam with far monsoon trade, and its cohabitation – literal in this case – with local beliefs, seem to go right back to the beginning.

Approaching the Great Mosque of Kilwa with Ridwan the head student, it was clear that mosques had come a long way since the humble syncretic prayer-hut of Shanga. The former rulers of Kilwa had built a mosque in stone here in the eleventh century. IB's Sultan Hasan added to this, more than quadrupling the area of the old building with a multi-domed prayer hall and making it the biggest mosque south of the Sahara.

You wouldn't know it from IB's account (although to be fair on him, it isn't certain that Sultan Hasan's extension was built when he was here). The traveller was, as usual, more interested in the human action than the architectural backdrop. One day, he remembered, the sultan was coming out of the mosque when he was collared by a mendicant – that same dervish who ended up with the train of ivory-laden slaves. The dervish had realized Hasan was a soft touch: he demanded, literally, the clothes off the sultan's back. 'Certainly,' the sultan said, making as if to go to his palace. 'But I want them *right now*,' the dervish shouted (some of these holy wanderers had an insubordinate streak and saw themselves as God's anarchists). The sultan went meekly back into the mosque and changed into another set of clothes in the preacher's room. He called the dervish in and gave him his own robes then and there.

Ridwan and I poked around the mosque and decided that the preacher's room was a small ruinous chamber, a sort of vestry, in the north-west corner of the original smaller mosque. We sat there and reread the tale of the sultan's robes; I had, not for the first time on my travels with IB, the strange and pleasurable sensation of bringing a story home. 'Do you think the President of Tanzania would give his suit to a beggar?' I asked as we were leaving the mosque. Ridwan's answer was a laugh that echoed up in Sultan Hasan's domes. But then, I thought, what head of state these days would part with his Gieves and Hawkes or Georges de Paris? In a dervish-unfriendly world ruled by democrats and dictators, inaccessible in motorcades, *noblesse* no longer obliges.

We explored a second, smaller mosque: more domes, some collapsed, some still intact and inset with turquoise Persian bowls, echoing this time with the rhythmic hum of Qur'anic verses. Another student reciting in the ruins, giving voice to the book and the building. 'It was someone from Kilwa who took Islam to Indonesia,' Ridwan said as we walked from the mosque across the sand of Jangwani Bay. Another simplification, I said to myself, of a complex process. Then again, I could as well believe the claim here as anywhere. The islanders may not have been missionizing muscular Muslims; their fervour was lightly worn. But I could see faith taking ship from Kilwa and shaping course across the ocean.

It was now past mid-afternoon, and we walked on through a yellowing glaze of light, heading for a baobab. Sultan Hasan's tomb

is unknown, but here in the shadow of the great tree was a cemetery where the later rulers of Kilwa were buried. Walls of tomb-enclosures leaned this way and that, holes gaped in plaster – round ones where porcelain bowls had been prised out, rectangular ones where inscriptions had been wrenched away. Like their predecessor, the great forgotten builder of mosque and palace, the lesser rulers of Kilwa now decomposed in anonymity. I wondered what that other cemetery looked like . . .

'Would you like to visit the Forty Shaykhs?' Ridwan asked,

reading my thoughts. I was surprised by the offer and could only nod. Surprised and, I realized as we set off down a narrow path through dry and rattling brush, apprehensive.

It wasn't far. The tombs of the Forty Shaykhs lay in a clearing in the bushes. Like those of the sultans, they were neglected and nameless. They were divided into walled enclosures, one containing a score of graves, others only a few. There were some headstones; all were effaced and blank. There was also a faint sweet smell, of rotting animal matter.

'Do you know their names?' I asked. 'Or their dates?'

He didn't. 'We only know them as the Forty Shaykhs,' Ridwan said.

'So why are they so special?'

'The Forty Shaykhs were *sharifs*,' he said in his quiet, precise Arabic. 'They came to Kilwa Kisiwani. They slaughtered a sheep – a ewe. The chief of the *sharifs* wanted to eat the liver of the ewe. But a pregnant woman took it and ate it instead. The chief was so angry that he had her stomach cut open, while she was alive, and ate the liver of the ewe from the woman's stomach. Some people say he took the liver from the mouth of the woman's foetus. The woman's people started fighting to avenge her, and the fighting got so bad that every single one of them was killed . . .' He stopped speaking, eyes downcast, as if in shame at letting out a secret. But he continued, quieter still. 'People come from all over Tanzania, even from Kenya, to offer prayers and make requests. They say, "Please God, through the blessing of the Forty Shaykhs, do this for me . . ." And prayers are answered here.'

Again he stopped. I wanted to ask what people prayed for, but I didn't want to break that frail thread of trust by which Ridwan had led me here. It might be one secret, one shame too many. 'If they were so bad,' I said eventually, 'how can the *sharifs* intercede on behalf of people?'

'Because of their descent from the Prophet, may God bless him and give him peace,' Ridwan said, 'the *sharifs* are close to God. To pray here is like approaching the president through his cabinet ministers. But, yes, it is the custom that before you offer up your request you first ask God to forgive their sins.'

We stood there a little longer in the fading light, then turned to leave the clearing, that shadowed no man's land between Islam and paganism. Ridwan paused and glanced back. Then he looked at me: 'Some people say that God took away Kilwa's greatness as a punishment for the sins of the Forty Shaykhs.'

★

Nothing subverts one's perception of time and distance so much as travel. My trip to Kilwa Kisiwani seemed to have spanned weeks, not a couple of days. I could only think that this seeming elastication was the result of coming to see a few ruins on a small island – and then finding myself traversing, at great speed, an unexpected landscape of beliefs. Some islands can, like maps, express big things on a small scale. Kilwa Kisiwani was such a place, a continent in miniature that spoke of worlds far wider than the narrow compass of its shores.

On my last afternoon there I made two small discoveries that also played, in different ways, on the specific gravity of time. The first was lying in the mud down by the mangrove forest on the shore – a truncated obelisk four feet long, carved from a single stone and pierced crosswise at its thick end with two square-section holes. I knew what it was: the stone anchor, minus its wooden shanks, of an early dhow. I only found out later that it was of a type found commonly in the region of Siraf, a Persian port destroyed by earthquake in 977. At the time, all I could tell was that it was old; and yet it had a curious look of having been dropped there just moments before, a look not of archaeology but of lost property. Pascal's pipe had been enigmatic because it was an object out of place. This was an object out of time.

The second temporal distortion took place after I'd stopped to examine a ruined house on the shore near the Great Mosque. It was roofless, and its skin of coral rubble was sloughing away from the mud substructure of its walls. The wood of its finely carved doorway was grey and dry with age. 'That was the house that Chitiki built when he was digging,' Ridwan told me later. Chitiki: Chittick, the archaeologist. His house was already archaeology itself and – shockingly – give or take a year or two, it was the same age as me. For a moment I felt immensely ancient; and then perception swung the other way, and that larger ruined house along the shore, Husuni Kubwa, seemed not so many lifetimes old.

★

I needed to move on, to Dar es Salaam and Zanzibar, to look for further survivals that would give a voice to that silent palace by the sea. But even as I said farewell to Pascal and Ridwan, I began to miss Kilwa Kisiwani. To cross the narrow strait to Kilwa Masoko ('Kilwa of the Suq'; Kisiwani, that euphonious name, is simply 'of the Island') would be to return to a more mundane world, one neither blessed with recitation under porcelain-studded domes nor cursed with the horror of the Forty Shaykhs. A mundane, mainland world: unless you know you're going back, there's no departure quite as final as leaving an island; perhaps not even leaving a lover.

The skipper of the dhow managed to dispel these thoughts of finality, so inappropriate to the start of a journey: he was wearing a pair of shorts tailored from a plastic grain-sack and saying GIFT TO THE PEOPLE OF TANZANIA across the crotch. And it was good to watch the patched lateen sail swell in the breeze, to be on the move. Further out into the strait, the wind freshened, the boat heeled and creaked, and we skimmed over water marbled with light by the lowering sun; *dud ala ud*, ticks on sticks.

Kilwa Masoko – Zanzibar

'That's old Friddie over there,' the man beside me at the bar said in an Afrikaans accent that managed to be both clipped and slurred. 'He's been at the gin and tonic since ten this morning.'

Friddie looked up in slow motion. 'Got . . . keep . . . malaria away,' he said, slaloming round the syllables. He had a point. Ever since dusk had fallen over the game-fishing lodge where I was spending the night in Kilwa Masoko, squadrons of mosquitoes had been attacking my ankles. Their bites didn't itch; they *hurt*.

'OK, but the quinine's in the tonic, you old fool,' my neighbour said, 'not in the gin.'

I killed another couple of Kilimanjaro beers and retired to mosquito-netted dreams of that other Kilwa in my air-conditioned fisherman's hut.

In the pre-dawn dark next morning, the deserted market was permeated by a tang of rawhide and raw onion, smoke and dung.

Another sailing dhow would, of course, have been the proper way to travel on to Zanzibar. But there were none heading that way in the immediate future for love or money; or at least not for the amounts of either currency I had at my disposal. I was equally poor in patience. I could – should – have waited, as IB would have had to wait. To match myself to his pace was the only way I'd ever catch up, or perhaps down, with him. Instead, I caught the bus.

My fellow-passengers, squatting in the dark by the shuttered premises of the Muddy Hair Cutting Salon and nursing large and pungent baskets of smoked fish, seemed a lugubrious lot. But when we set off, things were improved by fresh dawn air and a general mood of merriment. I was partly the cause: I'd had a long loud conversation in Kiswahili with an old blind man sitting next to me, to which my only contribution was, inevitably, mmms and aaahs. The one-sided dialogue only ended when someone tapped him on the shoulder and stage-whispered to him that I was a *mzungu*.

The growing light revealed a landscape of fuzzy ridges in a uniform shade of lovat green, unrolling into the distance like a bolt of corduroy. We rolled with it for a time then, as the sun rose, pulled up in the small town of Somanga – home, it seemed, to half the fishwives in Africa. Most, in fact, were fishmaidens, of great beauty and charm. The bus was filled with their laughter, with yet more baskets of kippered sprats and, at a nearby garage, with diesel from an antique hand-cranked pump. We set off again, packed to the gills with fish and people.

Old Africa hands will probably tell you never to say, even to yourself, 'What a good road!' I did, and in less than a minute we'd run out of tarmac and taken to the bush. The effect of two and a half hours of corrugations and potholes was like being trapped in one of those vibrating slimming belts – but one designed to fit a sumo wrestler. At the back of the bus a baby yelled so loudly that we all kept looking round, even the blind man, wondering how it hadn't disgorged its lungs. In the gaps between yells, a whirring sound came from the forest we were now passing through, an insect symphony loud enough to be heard over the noise of the engine. *Waaahh-waaahh-whirrrr-waaarrgghh* . . . A pair of baboons, squatting on the verge, mooned at the bus with their leathery backsides as if in contempt for their distant, fallen cousins.

The asphalt reappeared as inexplicably as it had vanished. In minutes we were in the great terraqueous jigsaw-puzzle of the Rufiji Delta, flying over bridges. A late breakfast of *supu*, broth with a piece of fowl, spiced with limes and chillis, further restored the spirits. But the spell of the south was broken. Seven hours after leaving Kilwa Masoko, mud and thatch had given way to breeze-block and tin. Dar es Salaam, the Abode of Peace, began with a long and painful assault-course of roadworks; the southern part of the city was being slowly eviscerated in preparation for a new sewage system, and its above-ground arteries were all but terminally clogged with traffic. Kilwa Kisiwani, with its paths of red earth trodden by silent feet and its lone bicycle, seemed far more than a bus-ride away.

★

The Funduq al-Uruba, or Hotel of Arabism, in the Kariakoo district of the capital, had enticed me with its name and its cheap rates. It was a place of diasporas run by a man whose family came, like that of IB's Sultan Hasan, from Hadramawt, and it was mainly patronized by large lost-looking Somalis in lunghis, wanderers in a more recent and less happy exodus. Downstairs in the busy restaurant, the menu was littered with the usual culinary castaways – parathas and samosas, Coca-Cola and cup cakes; and the tempting 'Beef Williton'. The waiter confirmed that it was indeed 'pasty beef', so I ordered one, wondering how they could do their own take on *boeuf en croûte* (clever, that, naming it after a village just up the road from Wellington) for a mere 1,200 Tanzanian shillings. Perhaps they'd left out the *pâté de foie gras* and skimped on the *duxelles* . . . It came, a sort of sausage roll containing a smidgeon of mince. From the world of Carême and the Iron Duke, via some long-dead Tanganyika civil servant's cook-boy, to this. How are the mighty fallen! Beef Williton could be the signature dish of post-imperialism.

Next morning I stepped out into Kariakoo (another garbled memory of Tanganyika days – the area was originally settled by men of the First World War 'Carrier Corps') and pushed my way through a large market where more smoked fish, in various stages of arrested decay, combined with the scents of dust and garlic, chicken-shit and porter-sweat, a soupçon of sewer and a thousand other substances to produce an intoxicating bouillabaisse of smells. Across a park, and I was back in the diasporic city, on Morogoro Road, where Indians from Gujarat sold pumps and mopeds, and milk-white mannequins with *Boy's Own* haircuts – so dated, so ageless – sported safari suits and cravats, and the façade of Bagamoyo House was all peeling Tuscan columns and tottering balconies and skew-whiff Indian lattices. Eclectic, relic-strewn Dar es Salaam was growing on me.

Rain came on as I reached the museum, an unpromising concrete box lit by low-wattage neon, to look for relics of IB's Sultan Hasan. Yes, they said at the desk, Kilwa was on the first floor.

Upstairs, beneath a damp-stained ceiling, in a quiet broken only by the patter of raindrops and the chirp of nesting sparrows, I found the lumber room of Sultan Hasan's palace. Here were the objects that gave the place a voice. There was a resounding Arabic inscription that had proclaimed the sultan's name across that now silent, lizard-haunted court: 'Verily God is the Helper of the Commander of the Faithful, the Victorious King al-Hasan son of Sulayman, may God Almighty grant him success!' Other epigraphs spoke with bumptious optimism, of felicity that would renew itself perpetually, of bounty whose days would never end; as if the small print wasn't on the wall that said the price of gold could go down as well as up . . .

Otherwise, it was broken pots and bits of twisted metal, lost spindle whorls and kohl sticks and earwax spoons, the usual understated domestic detritus. Perhaps my visions of argosies laden with eastern luxuries had been a little too romantic. But then, among the common crockery of the age, I saw something beautiful. Even in its smashed and reassembled state, it was an object to stand alone in one of those empty niches of Husuni Kubwa. It was an early fourteenth-century Yuan dynasty porcelain flask, its slender neck and swelling body both voluptuous and chaste, its surface sparely incised with cloud-scrolls floating beneath the stratospheric blue-white of *qingbai* glaze. It was the sort of vessel you would use to imprison a very high-class jinni in, and it made China seem magically close again . . . I wondered what had happened to the poor sod who broke it.*

It was as I was leaving the Kilwa room that I did the sort of double take brought on by the familiar encountered in an unexpected setting. It was a broken slab of fine white limestone, carved in deep relief with a lamp hanging in a niche. To one side of the niche was a stylized tree; above and below it were lines of Qur'anic

---

* The last indigenous ruler of Zanzibar, the Mwinyi Mkuu, owned an Imari bowl with which he was so obsessed that he decreed that anyone who broke it would be put to death. The bowl is still intact; the decree, to the terror of the cleaning ladies who dust it in Zanzibar's House of Wonders, has never been repealed.

script – as dense and hard to read as such things always are, but I made out '. . . and he whom We grant long life We reverse in creation . . .' The verse was from the Chapter of Ya Sin, a sort of Islamic *Nunc Dimittis* read over the dead. The stone, a label said, had been found in the sultans' cemetery on Kilwa: that graveyard by the baobab overlooking Jangwani Bay. But for me the jolt of recognition set off a wave of resonances that rolled around the whole arc of the Indian Ocean's shores. These memorials were only carved in one place – the port and manufacturing city of Cambay in north-west India, 3,000 miles across the sea from Kilwa. The last time I'd seen one had been in Kollam, in the far south of India, where it had been brought up from a drowned mosque in a fisherman's net. On my earlier travels I'd looked for the tombstone of IB's host in the southern Arabian city of Zafar, a revered holy man, only to find it – another Cambay piece – in the Victoria and Albert Museum in London; for good measure, the British Museum had a Cambay slab as well, looted from Aden in 1839. Along the byways of book-research, I'd come across mentions of other Cambay stones. There was one from Sumatra that commemorated a son of Ghiyath al-Din, a wealthy scion of the old Abbasid dynasty of Baghdad who was IB's friend in Delhi and on whom the traveller dumped his infant son (IB no doubt thought the boy would be well provided for: Ghiyath al-Din bathed in a solid gold tub, he says, and his coat buttons were pearls as big as hazelnuts). This adoptive brother of the abandoned boy ended up marrying an Indonesian princess; both he and his wife had Cambay gravestones. Stones from Cambay had also turned up in Iran, and in other places as far apart as Mogadishu and Java. Dazed by distance, I almost forgot that Cambay stones are found in Cambay itself, where a businessman of Persian origin – 'the Merchant King', IB called him – still lies in a tomb carved with those same hanging lamps.

The workshops where these stones were carved must be the most successful monumental masons in history, and Cambay among the most successful exporting cities. The first Portuguese interlopers in the Indian Ocean marvelled at the city's commercial reach: 'she stretches out her two arms,' wrote the chronicler of ocean trade Tomé Pires, 'her right arm extending to Aden, her left to Malacca'. In fact Cambay's embrace was even wider, taking in Java and, as the stone before me proved, Kilwa. It spanned the centuries too: most of those sellers of pumps and mopeds on Morogoro Road were from that same industrious corner of Gujarat. To me, then, these Cambay monuments were milestones along the route of IB's Indian Ocean travels. He had visited every single land in which they'd been found. But in three cases they were also relics of the personal, human geography of the *Travels* – of a saintly host in Arabia, a Persian plutocrat in Cambay itself, a wandering Arab prince in Sumatra: a cross-section through the crowd that throngs IB's gregarious pages. All three of them had been commemorated by Cambay stones, the mortuary equivalent of Louis Vuitton or Rolex, expensive objects that proclaimed allegiance to an opulent and cosmopolitan culture.

I ran my hand over this stone that exuded associations. There was no name on the fragment to identify the person buried in the shadow of the baobab; only that verse from the Chapter of Ya Sin. 'Who', it goes on, 'will give life to these bones after they are rotten and become dust?'

*

Stone Town is one of the great landfalls, a shimmering line of palaces on the shore; and if at closer range some of the palaces turn out to be godowns or fish-suqs, and nearly all of them to be in various states of decay, it is that first and pristine view of the capital of Zanzibar that prints itself on the mind's eye and stays there alongside Hong Kong and the Grand Canal.

So too once was Kilwa Kisiwani, now tangled in mangroves. That was why I'd come here. IB had sailed past Zanzibar, an unimportant place in his day. But in the nineteenth century it became the new Kilwa, and I wanted to see the intact remains of Swahili sultanic splendour – a splendour that had lived on into my own lifetime, until the overthrow of the last sultan of Zanzibar in 1963.

On second thoughts, perhaps 'splendour' wasn't the word. Stone Town was heaving with foreign holidaymakers, all frantically shopping for spiced seaweed foot-scrub and carved chests with sprayed-on patina. But Bayt al-Sahil, the 'Palace by the Sea' of the latter-day rulers, wasn't the tourist trap I'd expected it to be. I could see why. There was a photographic display on the nineteenth-century Princess Salme, who according to an information panel 'had loped with a German trader and wrote her extremely interesting biography'. Otherwise there was little to attract visitors, unless they were into big bad portraits of sultans and knobbly ebony furniture. Except, maybe, for the palace's strategically located public *choo*, or lavatory – a magnificent squat model bearing the sign 'Thanks For Using Shanks'.

On the top floor, in the private apartments of the last sultan (who ended up in exile by another sea, in Portsmouth), ebony gave way to cream woodgrain Formica, and thrones to pouffes; a quadruple bed stood beneath a collapsing ceiling. The two ends of the main drawing-room were furnished according to the tastes of two co-wives, a sign explained. One half had pink brocade sofas and a Sputnik-era coffee table, the other a rash of resurgent, bubonic ebony and enormous and equally knobbly Chinese vases, the sort of things you would pray not to win at a coconut shy. I thought of a certain member of the dynasty I once met who was given to appearing at parties wearing a feather boa; coming as he did from such aesthetic confusion, I could sympathize. And I thought of that chaste and exquisite vase from that other palace by the sea, in Kilwa Kisiwani.

There remained one last seaside palace, the next-door Bayt al-Aja'ib or House of Wonders, finished in 1883 and now the national museum of Zanzibar. A big square block enclosed by deep verandas, with cast-iron pillars rising through its three tall storeys and an even taller clock-tower rising on its seaward side, the building is the last great expression of the Swahili-Eclectic school of royal architecture that Sultan Hasan founded with Husuni Kubwa. But it was something it contained that drew me to the House of Wonders.

I was still haunted by visions of Ahmad the witch doctor's jinn. And here, I'd heard, was an object that seemed physically to embody the world of half-repressed animism I'd glimpsed in Kilwa: a genuine jinni in a bottle. It was a potent symbol of that world – it showed how barely, in what frail vessels, were the old anarchic forces contained. Besides, like anyone who has strayed as a child into that universe of stories contained in the *1,001 Nights* and never lost the sense of wonder it inspires, I was simply intrigued to see such a curiosity. The nearest I'd ever got was the Sussex witch imprisoned in a bottle in the Pitt Rivers Museum in Oxford ('and if you let 'un out,' the label warns, 'there'll be a peck o' trouble . . .')

The bottle-jinni, I decided, would probably be in the department of *uganga,* or 'traditional medicine'. This was situated upstairs and lay through large doors carved in Arabic script with 'O merciful God, protect us from every accursed satan' and other reassuring prayers.

The exhibits took me by surprise. Living as I do in the outwardly orthodox Arab heart of the Islamic world, I was astonished to find heterodoxy not just admitted to, here on the periphery, but celebrated. Information boards spoke of Zanzibar Muslims propitiating ancestral and natural spirits at altars in caves or under trees, and of the role of the *mwalimu-mganga* or Islamic medicine man who, like Ahmad in Kilwa, performs exorcisms and – 'occasionally' – curses.* Such openness was extraordinary, the most wondrous thing so far in the House of Wonders; once again, IB would have swooned with horror. But there was no bottled jinni that I could see. There were containers with dried medicinal substances, a few nasty-looking objects that had been buried with intent to harm enemies; even 'A horn used to exorcise devils. It contains herbs and a dog's nose.' (So that's what happened to the poor dog in the world's worst joke, I thought.†) But no bottled jinni. Perhaps it didn't fit in with current notions of museology and had been banished to a box-room. It might even have been exposed as a fake.

'Ah, yes, the jinni . . .' From his tone of voice, the assistant curator might have been referring to a once-loved uncle who'd been caught doing something unspeakable. We were standing on the veranda in the thickening afternoon light. I could hear them shutting doors inside. 'It was removed. A few years ago, you see, people decided it was . . . not good for the building.'

'How do you mean?' My suspicions, it seemed, were right.

He didn't answer at first. Then he looked closely at me, and

---

* The term *mganga* is an old one. Writing in twelfth-century Sicily, al-Idrisi uses it of the witch-doctors of the Swahili coast.

† 'Your dog's got *no nose*? How does it smell?' 'Terrible.'

continued. 'They decided that the . . . the owners of the building did not like the presence of the jinni among them. Things were moving about at night.'

Now I looked closely at him – a studious-seeming man with a greying goatee and specs. If he was joking, or mad, or had watched *Night in the Museum* one time too many, it didn't show. 'And, since it was removed?'

'The things stopped moving about.' He looked at his watch. 'Please excuse me. It is closing time.'

I stood alone on the veranda for a few minutes more. To one side, the bulbous bastions of the old sultanic fort; to the other, tee-tering balconies seen through crowshitty palm tops; and before me, on the peacock-coloured ocean, a motley fleet – a couple of small freighters, a gaggle of rust buckets, canoes threading courses between them – and two big high-sterned dhows sliding over the sea on opposite tacks in a mere sigh of wind.

Someone was telling me I had to go.

*

A long journey lay ahead. The young IB, when he sailed through these waters on his first voyage to the periphery, had gone way beyond the Arab confines of the Islamic Grand Tour. Here he both tasted the freedom of the scholar-gypsy and got wind of fortunes in far lands. Later, in India, he found his fortune – and lost it. Battered by failure but always buoyed by hope, he became an Islamic Candide. After India, in his further travels on the edge – journeys on which I now planned to follow him – he would fall victim to the Sindbad Syndrome. He would be propelled no longer by conscious quest but by the momentum of all the accumulated miles and years, caught at times between lotus-eating and homesickness, meeting with marvels and monsters within himself and without; and finally returning to the narrower land he still called home, to discover there the extremes of honour and rejection, to tell his tale, and then to disappear.

How could I ever catch up with a man who was so mobile, so elusive – and who had a 660-year head start? IB's was a life of landfalls. He is a serial stranger whose true home is hemispheric, everywhere and nowhere. But he lives on in his book, the *Travels*, that rambling house of many stories. My own travels in its further reaches would take me east, through the strange sea-land of the Maldives, up IB's 'pillar of smoke' – Adam's Peak in Sri Lanka – then beyond the monsoon winds to the Hill of Souls and the Phoenix Mosque on China's southern shores. They would take me way back west, to the shores of the Saharan sand-ocean. And finally they would take me to China's Andalusian antipodes – back into what had since become a part of my own native world of Christendom and Europe; if it was my world any more.

After his brief trip to the Swahili coast and further wanderings in the Middle East, IB had made his way overland to India, arriving in 1333. He was appointed one of the four Sunni judges of Delhi and spent eight years in the post. He eventually fell foul of his eccentric and bloodthirsty master Muhammad Shah ibn Tughluq, the sultan of Delhi, and nearly lost his life. The sultan, however, rehabilitated him and appointed him to an embassy entrusted with delivering a rich diplomatic gift to the Yuan emperor of China.

Shortly after their embarkation on junks at the south-west Indian port of Calicut in the spring of 1342, disaster struck: the gift and the other envoys were lost in a storm. IB, who had lingered ashore, was the only survivor. Wisely choosing not to return to Delhi and face the sultan's music, he had spent the rest of 1342 and much of the following year roaming India's Malabar coast. Then, at some time towards the end of 1343, he had set sail on a whim for the Maldives.

As IB was aware, the people of this mid-ocean sultanate, composed of hundreds of small scattered islands and ruled at the time by a woman, Sultana Rehendi Khadijah, had been Muslim for almost two centuries. What he apparently did not know was that the Maldivians were in need of a new chief justice. As a former judge of Delhi, IB's CV was perfect.

His jaunt to the islands was to last much longer than he had bargained for and, like his mission to China, was destined to end in another fine mess.

The Maldives

The Ship of Blazing Lamps

Sparkling white sun-kissed beaches; palm-fringed islands;
the pervading serenity; all of it summarized by the famous
Moroccan traveller Ibn Battuta on describing Maldives as
'one of the wonders of the world'.

Hello Maldives, 22nd edition

Kinolhas – Malé

'You see that?' the imam of Kinolhas asked, pointing to a semicircle
of dark rocks in the shallows. 'That's the *bandar*, the old port.' So
this was IB's landfall in the Maldives at the end of 1343, on the
island of Kinolhas, eighty miles north-east of the capital island of
Malé. 'It used to be an important harbour', the imam went on,
'because it was safe in both monsoons for the *na*, the big ships, on
their way to Malé.' We were talking in English with a seasoning of
Arabic. *Bandar* and *na*, however, were from Persian. The Maldives
were cosmopolitan long before the tourists came.

I could see why they did come. Looking at the undeniably sparkling white and sun-kissed beach of the palm-fringed island, I
thought how true the advertising copy was, for once, and wondered how IB would have felt at being quoted in it. He would
have smiled at the idea of 'pervading serenity'. His eight-month
stay in the Maldives turned into one of the least serene episodes
of his travels.

IB and I had both come to Kinolhas via the Malabar coast of
southern India, he directly by dhow, I on a plane to Malé followed
by a seaplane up here to Maalhosmadulu atoll; these days we tend

43

to see countries inside-out. IB's actual landing, however, was probably the same as mine, in a type of small rowing boat called, I learned from the imam, a *boh-kura*, or 'frog-teapot'.

'These islands are around two thousand in number,' IB wrote at the start of his Maldivian chapter in a geographical introduction so necessary for a land unlike any other on earth, or rather at sea. 'Each hundred islands or fewer form a group like a ring . . . They are so close together that when you leave one island you can see the tops of the palms on the next one.' In fact the number of islands is more like 1,200. Around 200 of them are inhabited; another hundred or so are resorts. North to south, the chain of atolls (the word is the sole contribution of Dhivehi, the Maldivian language, to English) is not much shorter than the British Isles. The total area of dry land, however, is rather less than that of the county of Rutland, or about the same as Martha's Vineyard. As for the distance between islands, I was unable to confirm the picturesque claim of Mandelso, a seventeenth-century envoy from Schleswig-Holstein, that 'in some places a nimble man may leap into an island from the top of a bough that grows in another'. Generally, as IB wrote, the tops of the neighbouring island's palms are visible; but nothing more, for the average elevation above sea-level is four feet. This suggests that the name of the Maldives on Chinese charts of IB's time, Liushan, 'the *Mountains* of Liu', takes into account their submarine height as well. More recently, I'm told by someone who was present, the former British Foreign Office minister Jeremy Hanley was on an official visit to the Maldives and asked what the highest point of the archipelago was. The head of the Maldivian reception committee looked the imposingly built Tory up and down and said, 'It's you, Minister.' (If global warming isn't stopped, the Maldives may be the first country on earth to have no land above sea level.)

My own one-man reception committee, the imam, was young and dressed in a T-shirt, cut-off white jeans, flip-flops and a black micro-turban – little more than a knotted handkerchief – as a badge of office. I noticed that he also wore a small but unmistakeably Wahhabi-wispy beard. Its suggestion of dour zealotry was however belied by an open face, plump, smiling and slightly feline. One should never be misled by first impressions, I told myself; certainly not in the Maldives where, if another piece of advertising copy were true, even the sharks are friendly.

'You are welcome to my country,' the imam said, beaming, as we walked up the gentle incline of the beach. (The Dhivehi word for 'country' is used indiscriminately whether you're talking about tiny Kinolhas or a larger island such as Australia.) A few yards inland we came to the single main street, a wide straight road of sand. Set back from this behind low walls were tin-roofed cottages faced with carefully knapped lumps of coral stone. Coco-palms, papayas and big spiky-leafed breadfruit trees shaded their yards; a number of householders had placed seats strung with cord along their front walls, each designed for four or five sitters. The streets and the yards were immaculately swept and, in the heat of the afternoon, empty. So too, we found when we walked through the open door, was the house of my intended host. 'Don't worry,' the imam said when I wondered if the absent gentleman might object to an impromptu guest. 'Any visitors who come here stay with him. He was the island chief till recently, and now he preaches the sermons at Friday Prayers.' Just like IB on Kinolhas, then, I was the guest of 'pious persons'. The imam left me in the preacher's front parlour where, suddenly overcome by torpor, I fell fast asleep in an armchair.

I travelled imagined archipelagos in my sleep – a full dream-odyssey – only to wake and see that I'd been out barely ten minutes. It seemed I was still alone in the house. Outside, the street remained empty. The hush, the coral cottages took me back to Kilwa Kisiwani. But here, in a first brief wander round the the settlement and its environs, I found no ruins, no building that showed any sign of age; and no people. What had happened to the 'many mosques' IB saw here? And the cosmopolitan crowd he met – people from Arabia, Karnataka, Somalia?

And yet IB's world, if it was gone, was not forgotten. Eventually, down on the beach, I found an old man sitting on an upturned boat. There was no harm in asking . . . 'Ah, Ibn Battutah. *Yes!*' he said when I tried the name out on him – the rest was in voluble Dhivehi, with gestures towards a broad track leading through the palms. With perfect timing and his beamy smile, the imam appeared out of the greenery like a tropical Cheshire Cat. The track, the imam explained, was called Ganduvaru Magu, Palace Road. The old man's grandfather had told him when he was a boy that it was the road on which IB had lodged during his ten-day stay on Kinolhas. The information took me aback. I'd been hoping for such traces; actually to find one on this speck of land in the ocean was unnerving – like the shock Crusoe had when he stumbled on that first footprint of his future companion. And it seemed my own long-dead companion had left other traces in the sands of time, for the old man was speaking about him again. I watched him, scrawny-chested beneath a ragged T-shirt that claimed in faded letters to be 'The Look of Luxe', his face scored by years of salt spray and squinting into the sun. He seemed slightly cross, his speech accented with dismissive flicks of the hand and ending with a 'hmph!' The imam translated: 'He says the people on Fainu, that is the next island to the north, claim that Ibn Battutah stayed with *them* first, before he came to Kinolhas. But the Fainu people are liars, he says. They have no evidence. I also am sure he is right.'

On Kilwa Kisiwani, IB's name had produced blank looks. Here it had sparked off *memories* – inherited memories, perhaps, but ones that still touched nerves two dozen generations on.

I showed them what IB himself had written about his arrival: 'When I came to these islands I disembarked at one called Kannalus.' They knew the text already. And it did seem pretty indisputable: Kannalus could only be Kinolhas. But perhaps, I said, IB really had made his first footing on Fainu and had forgotten; perhaps the collective memory of the people of Fainu could be more reliable after six and a half centuries than IB's lone recollection, writing ten years after the event. My attempt at devil's advocacy got nowhere. I had to concede that the hardest evidence was in my hand in black and white.

The two of them went off to afternoon prayers. I stayed on the beach to enjoy the pervading serenity. A minute later a voice from behind startled me. 'I am thinking you are Mr Tim!' As the only potential Tim on an island half the size of Kensington Gardens, it was hard to deny. 'I am Dinakar, teacher of English, and I am very interesting in you because I am so *boring*.' I suppose it was hardly surprising that the pleasures of Kinolhas would pall; particularly if you came as Dinakar did, I learned, from the fleshpots of Andhra

Pradesh. 'And my very biggest problem is that I am pure veg,' he explained. 'Here there is nothing but tuna, tuna and more tuna.' I knew what he meant. I'd already discovered that Maldivian cuisine was composed of endless variations on the same tuna.

We went and sat on a platform of coconut logs in the shade of an enormous tree overlooking the beach. The tree's warty bole must have been a good twenty feet round – had probably been growing, I realized, since before IB stepped ashore a few yards away. I am no botanist; to me it was a BLT – a big leafy thing. Dinakar didn't know what it was either. But a group of his pupils who came to join us said the tree was called *kaani* in Dhivehi. We sat on, Dinakar grumbling about the price of aubergines, while his students furiously texted on their mobile phones. (The conversion to Islam in 1153; the ejection of the Portuguese in 1573; the arrival of marine diesel engines in the 1960s, followed in 1972 by the first tourists; the introduction of the GSM telephone in 1999. These are the important dates in Maldivian history.)

The sun was falling, the text conversations flagging, and we all left the shade of the *kaani* tree and strolled along the beach into a breeze that came from the open sea beyond the lagoon. Dinakar suggested to his students that, since a native English-speaking audience was a rarity in Kinolhas – in fact, I might be the first – we would all benefit from a story in that language. One of the older students pointed out to sea, to where waves were breaking white on a reef. 'You see that?' he said. 'We call it Beriyanfanu, meaning the Reef of Beri. Beri was married to the daughter of the chief of Kinolhas, long time past. But Beri was not a man. He was a jinni. At night he was growing very very tall and going to the graveyard.

He was digging the dead bodies and eating them. When the chief saw this he called his friend Vaadhoo Dhanna Kaleyfaanu from Huvadhoo atoll.' The rest of the group were listening closely. They all knew the story; told in a strange tongue, it cast a new spell. 'Dhanna Kaleyfaanu was a big *fandita* man . . . a magic man. He caught Beri and made him very very small and put him in a bottle. He threw the bottle in the sea, on that reef. That is why we call it the Reef of Beri.'

We stood there, watching the inaudible breakers out on Beri's reef. I'd crossed 2,500 miles of ocean but was back in that same other-land of spirits.

We walked back towards the declining sun. In front of us, a low silhouette out in the lagoon, was the island of Meedhupparu, home to the Select Resort and Ayurveda Village. Many of Dinakar's pupils would eventually commute there to work. It was perhaps two or three miles away, but to me it seemed much further. I'd passed briefly through that other other-land in the airport at Malé, the only single person, it seemed, in an arrivals hall full of couples – some so closely coupled that it looked as if the foreplay had already begun. They weren't travelling; they were being sent to a novel setting in which to copulate, to a destination. That's what made Meedhupparu seem distant – it was a destination. Kinolhas was a place.

'We found a dead woman here on the beach,' one of the students said.

'She was swimming at Meedhupparu and she drowned,' said another. 'British, like you.'

I could picture her white corpse on the whiter sand, British like me, strange as a mermaid.

*

'It is very *envying* of the Fainu people,' Dinakar said with a frown as we sat in the mosquito-filled twilight under the *kaani* tree, talking about IB and the question of where he first landed. 'They are great big fibbers.'

Even Dinakar, an outsider, had been drawn into the inter-island spat. So why did a ten-day visit by a wandering foreigner 663 years before matter so much? Admittedly, this particular wanderer went on to write himself into Maldivian history by marrying into the royal family and becoming Chief Justice of the archipelago; but this would hardly explain the passion with which the islanders defended their claim on him. The real answer, I realized, is to be found in IB's own *Travels*, a few pages before the account of his landfall. There, in his introductory notes on the thousand-island sultanate, he tells the story of that first and most important date in Maldivian history. It doesn't matter that the telling takes no more than a page or two. To Maldivians, IB is what Virgil was to Rome, or the Venerable Bede to England: he is the narrator of the national legend. All Dinakar's students knew it, just as they knew the story of Beri's Reef. The story, stranger and nastier than tales of necrophagous ghouls, is best told in IB's words:

Account of the reason for the islanders' conversion to Islam, and of the demons of the jinn that harmed them every month. I was informed by reliable persons among the islanders, such as the jurist Isa al-Yamani and the jurist-professor Ali and the judge Abdallah and a number of others, that the people of these islands were formerly infidels. Every month, an evil demon [*afrit*] from among the jinn would appear from the direction of the sea, looking like a ship filled with lamps. Their custom when they saw it was to take a virgin girl, dress her in finery and place her in a certain *budkhanah*, or idol-house, that was built on the sea shore, with a window looking on to the sea. There they would leave her for the night. In the morning they would come and find her raped and dead. Thus they went on, drawing lots each month, and he to whom the lot fell would give his daughter over to the demon.

It happened that there came to them a Maghribi named Abu 'l-Barakat al-Barbari, who knew the Holy Qur'an by heart. He lodged in the house of an old woman on the island of Malé. One day he returned to his lodgings to find her female relatives assembled and weeping, as if for a funeral. He asked them what the matter was, but they did not understand him. So an interpreter came and told him that the lot had fallen to the old woman, and that she had only one daughter for the demon to kill. At this, Abu 'l-Barakat, who was fresh-faced and beardless, said to the old woman, 'I will go tonight in place of your daughter.' So they took him that night and put him in the *budhkhanah*. Abu 'l-Barakat had performed his ritual ablutions, and now he began to recite the Qur'an. At last he could make out the demon through the window, but he persisted in his recitation, and when the demon was near enough to hear the words of the Qur'an it plunged under the face of the sea.

When dawn broke, the Maghribi was still reciting. The old woman and her relatives and the people of the island came, for their custom was to remove the dead girl and burn her corpse; but they found the Maghribi still reciting. They took him to their king, whose name was Shanurazah, and told him his story, at which the king was amazed. The Maghribi proposed to the king that he should embrace Islam, and tried to persuade him to do so. At this the king said, 'Stay with us another month, and if you can do again what you did last night and save yourself from the demon, I will become a Muslim.'

So the Maghribi stayed on, and it happened that even before the month was out God opened the breast of the king to Islam and he embraced it, he and his womenfolk and children and high officials. Then at the turn of the month the Maghribi was taken back to the *budkhanah*, where he recited till dawn, but the demon did not come. The sultan and the people came and found him reciting there, and they smashed the idols and destroyed the *budkhanah*, and the people of the island embraced Islam. They then sent word to all the other islands, and their people became Muslims as well.

The Maghribi remained with them, and they gave him many honours and adopted the school of law which he followed, that of Imam Malik, may God be pleased with him. Even today they still treat Maghribis with particular honour, on account of Abu 'l-Barakat. He built a mosque which is known by his name. I have read an inscription on the dividing screen of this mosque, carved in wood, which says, 'Sultan Ahmad Shanurazah embraced Islam at the hand of the Maghribi, Abu 'l-Barakat al-Barbari.'

Abu 'l-Barakat belongs to an ancient and noble order of dragon-slayers and demon-layers. Its membership is international, supra-denominational and, although predominantly male, open to both sexes. Proving herself the equal of St George, St Martha captured an amphibious dragon that had been terrorizing Tarascon on the Rhône. In Yemen, Abu Zayd al-Hilali killed a great serpent that had long devastated the region of Mahrah; Amadou the Taciturn performed a similar service in ancient Ghana. No less venerable personages than the Prophet Muhammad and his first four caliphs are said to have joined forces with a prince of Champa to slay a rampaging dragon in what is now Vietnam. In a precursor to the Maldives story one of these caliphs, Umar, also wrote a letter to the River Nile asking it to desist from its annual sacrifice of a virgin; the river obliged. But perhaps the most active member of the order was Shaykh Jalal al-Din Tabrizi, a tireless battler of bogeys in the Indian subcontinent. Among his most notorious victims was the greedy resident demon of a temple in Bengal, which demanded a youth to eat every day. The shaykh disposed of it with a sharp blow from his walking-stick.

Sir James Frazer, the great collector of such tales, came across yet more examples of supernatural pest control from as far apart as Norway and Japan, and there are probably dozens more out there still – for what storyline could be simpler than goody versus baddy, goody wins? Its archetype was told, no doubt, in primal monosyllables by our ancestors over their mammoth-steaks *tartare*, and what it lacks in psychological complexity (does anyone pause to ask about the root causes of dragons' antisocial behaviour?) it makes up for in moral clarity.

As baddies go, however, the Maldivian demon is one of the worst. There is something sick about him. Serial rapist, serial killer, he laughs at the sacred with his mockery of marriage; his is a dark perversion of the wedding of the sea enacted in that other watery realm, Venice. He disturbs the deepest levels of the psyche. Out in the ocean, in those bountiful waters with their God-given time-table of monsoon winds – 'azure warm seas', to quote again from *Hello Maldives*, 'with an undisturbed, exotic marine life' – lurks something vicious and unholy. Worst of all, perhaps, the demon refuses to take on a decent form such as that of serpent, dragon or bogey. As in the most exquisite horror stories, the object of our fear remains abstract, an obscure candescence skimming ever closer on the face of the deep.

I have never known quite how to react to the story. Part of me wants to take it as it is. Most Maldivians apparently do so. They are pious Muslims for whom belief in jinn is obligatory: if you accept the existence of God, you have to accept the rest of the supernatural package as well. In Christian terms, you can't have the Sermon on the Mount without the Gadarene swine. Faith, and fear, give form to phantoms. But part of me wants to hide behind the comfy sofa of rationalism, to dismiss the demon as parable or allegory, as a fairy tale. And there is another problem: despite the simple storyline, the narrators can't agree on the most basic elements of the plot.

The nearest thing to an authorized history of the Maldives, written in Arabic in the early eighteenth century, calls the hero not 'al-Barbari' but 'al-Tabrizi'. This doesn't involve a huge transformation in the Arabic script. Disregarding the dots which distinguish letters and always have a tendency to go astray, the difference between al-Barbari البربري and al-Tabrizi السربري is negligible – an extra small stalk. The geographical difference is much bigger, however. A Barbari could indeed be a Berber from North Africa, as IB implies; 'Tabrizi' suggests someone connected with Tabriz in north-west Iran. But there is an even bigger discrepancy between this and IB's account. In the *History*'s version there is no sea-demon. Al-Tabrizi merely 'showed them a huge great beast, whose head all but touched the vault of the heavens', at which the Maldivians immediately converted to Islam. A story as bare as that begs for elaboration, which in turn generates new versions. In all the apocryphal accounts I was to hear, the elaborators agreed on one point: that al-Tabrizi reduced his enormous beast to the size of a worm, sealed it in a bottle and threw it in the sea off the south-east corner of Malé – hence, the ex-Minister of Tourism told me, the excellent surfing waves there. But the tale, and the bottle, have migrated and mutated as well. A version told by the Sri Lankan Muslims has as its hero a sixteenth-century Indian saint called Mira Sahib – obviously too late, but he in turn seems to be an avatar of the great twelfth-century Persian holy man Shaykh Abd al-Qadir al-Jaylani – who walked to Malé 'on lotus-like feet' across the sea from Malabar; he packed his bottled jinni off to Sri Lanka, where it was thrown in the sea off Galle.

If and how this last spirit *mis en bouteille* is related to Beri, imprisoned on the reef near Kinolhas, not to mention their fellow-jinni exiled from the House of Wonders in Zanzibar, their literary counterpart in the *1,001 Nights* story of 'The Fisherman, the *Afrit* and the Bottle of Brass' – and even to their possible distant but *déclassé* cousins, the 'quaint spirits sealed up like flies or ants in bottles' and offered for sale by a seventeenth-century merchant of Augsburg – I confess I don't know. Nor is it clear whether the Maldivian Tabrizi is related to the Indian one, Shaykh Jalal al-Din Tabrizi, owner of the stout demon-slaying walking-stick. To show just how hard it is to know who's who and even who's when in the saintly and super-natural world, IB travelled all the way through Bengal to Assam to see the latter saint, had a long and fascinating chat with him and left thrilled to have met him – not realizing that he'd been dead for a hundred years and that the person he'd visited was not Shaykh Jalal al-Din but another holy man, *Shah* Jalal. (The Bengalis themselves confuse the two to this day.) All I can think is that a sort of narrative Darwinism is going on. The seed of a story lands, takes root, then adapts to fit the expectations and tastes of its hearers. The geography of the Maldives alone would make the islands fertile ground for this process of evolution. They are a Galapagos of tales.

All these saints and demons morphing over time and space are enough to shake one's credibility in IB as the primary source on the islamization of the Maldives. A gullible foreigner, he simply fell for the current version of a local fairy tale, one variant in that archipelago of stories. It may have the distinction of being the oldest of those variants that we have written down. But neither age nor writing guarantee truth; and what, anyway, is truth when we are speaking of monsters?

Except that this is one of those rare things: a monster for which there is solid evidence. The demon of the blazing lamps has a face, and I will look into it.

*

The archaeology of memory is hardly a precise science. All the same, I'd already turned up two unexpected finds on Kinolhas:

the supposed address of IB's lodgings, and that on-going dispute with the neighbours over where he first landed. But from what I'd already seen, my search for more solid remains of IB's time on the island wasn't going to prove so fruitful. All I had to go on was his recollection of 'many mosques'.

'That was true,' the imam said the following morning as we walked along the track where, if the old man on the beach was right, IB had stayed with his pious host, a scholar of Islamic law named Ali. No buildings stood there now. Palace Road was a sun-flecked avenue of palms, its silence broken only by dry fronds clattering in the breeze and the odd caw of a crow. The line of palm trunks was interrupted at one point by a patchwork of watermelon gardens behind fences of woven palm leaves, tended by women dressed in all-enveloping black and wielding delicate hoes.

'There used to be forty mosques on Kinolhas,' the imam said. 'Many of them were on this street, which was where the important people lived.' Forty mosques seemed a huge number for an island less than half a mile long. It suggested an urge to pray that went beyond the call of mere piety. Now there were three mosques, the imam explained, to serve a population of 500 – the Friday mosque, where he led the prayers, and two smaller ones. When I saw them later, they turned out to be recent and nondescript buildings. But the evidence of all that former praying was here. At regular intervals in the sand at the edge of the road, the imam pointed out the square stone-cased openings of buried wells; there were around half a dozen of them, each, he said, marking the site of a former mosque. Perhaps that figure of forty was no exaggeration, even if it would have made the rate of mosques *per capita* on Kinolhas greater than that of pubs in Dublin.

There was evidence of more than mosques. Back near the shore, the imam showed me the stumps of walls from a square hut-sized building, which he called a *ziyaarath* – the Arabic word for a 'visit', but in Dhivehi usage the tomb of a holy person that had become a place of visitation. It looked as if it had been demolished quite recently. 'Whose tomb was it?' I asked.

'A leg,' the imam said, grinning. I was puzzled. 'A human leg, washed up on the beach hundreds of years ago.' We walked on and came to the remains, levelled this time to the foundations, of another shed-sized structure – just a few coral stones almost indistinguishable from the coral sand. 'And this was the *ziyaarath* of Uthman,' the imam said. 'It was very famous through the Maldives. People used to come here from Malé and further. They said that if you had a fishbone in your throat and came and prayed here, the bone would come out.'

A voyage of days, perhaps weeks, depending on the wind, with a bone stuck in your throat . . . now that was faith. 'And did it really work?'

The imam smiled. 'It was all *shirk*.' *Shirk*, 'association' of something else with the One God, is a bugbear in Islam. It covers not just pagan polytheism and the Christian Trinity but also, especially for the puritan-minded, intercession by deceased holy Muslims. 'And they used to break coconuts here, like the Hindus. The government ordered it to be destroyed.' Later, he showed me a photograph of Uthman's *ziyaarath* in the 1980s, a thatched stone hut six feet tall at the apex, the tomb just visible inside. He himself stood by the open door, a smiling boy.

There is, of course, plenty of historical precedent – Byzantine iconoclasts, sledgehammering Cromwellians, rampaging Wahhabis (who in the early nineteenth century even pillaged the mosque of the Prophet Muhammad in al-Madinah) – and, if you subscribe to the concept of an utterly unapproachable, unknowable and unimaginable deity and think everyone else should do too, the destruction has a theological basis of sorts. But why had the *ziyaarath*'s much bigger neighbour – the original Friday mosque of Kinolhas, the imam told me, in which IB might have prayed – also been razed to the ground? That looked like wanton vandalism. The imam shrugged and smiled.

It was the same story throughout the island. Our antiquarian trek took us through dense scrub, along low leafy tunnels guarded by a sticky macramé of spiders' webs, ferocious mosquitoes and the small sharp teeth of screwpine leaves. We came across a large and ancient bo-tree, and a nearby depression that the imam said was the buried ablution tank of a mosque; and perhaps before that of a temple, I thought, looking at the bo-tree – the Buddha's tree of enlightenment. Every so often, the imam's sleek feline face would light up in the gloom at the discovery of another mosque, or the few stones that were left of it. If his identifications were right, I could now well believe that figure of forty. Large areas of the low jungle were also dotted with gravestones – white coral stone delicately carved with strapwork and ropework, whorls and rosettes, and the names of dead islanders; it seemed the major occupation on Kinolhas, after praying, had been dying. And nearly all the stones had been flattened or smashed. It was the reverse of things on that other, African island of Kilwa. There IB was forgotten but the mosques and palace had survived; here, the memory of IB had been preserved, passed down the generations, while the material past had been erased. The erasure wasn't merely – the phrase came to mind from somewhere – 'the injury of time'. Time had been given a heavy helping hand.

'Who did this?' I asked, looking at the ruined tombstones in the undergrowth. 'Was it Beri?' I could picture the ghoul's nocturnal ramblings, knocking over tombstones in his hunger for corpses. The imam tittered. Or, I asked, was it the tsunami of 2004? Flying up here in the seaplane, I had noticed in a few places the wreckage of resorts smashed by that other malevolent demon from the sea.

'No, it was people.' Who they were he didn't know, or didn't want to say.

We'd made a circuit of the island and were now back at the site of the old Friday mosque. I noticed a large blank tombstone-shaped slab lying in the sand – not coral, but fine-grained limestone, almost as fine as marble. There was no stone like this in the Maldives: this had been shipped in. My mind went back to the museum in Dar es Salaam, to that fragment of funerary frieze with the lamp in its niche. We heaved the slab over . . . no lamp, no niche; but a series of grooves, into which other stones would have fitted. I wasn't sure, but I suspected this was part of one of those monuments from Cambay that dotted the shores of the ocean in a great crescent from Kilwa to Java. It would fit: the sailing ships, the forty mosques, the people IB met here from Africa, Arabia, India. Once, Kinolhas had been rich and cosmopolitan, part of the Indian Ocean internet of traders, travellers and scholars.

'Kinolhas is no longer an important island,' the imam said, reading my mind. 'What do you think is the reason?'

I ventured something about sea routes changing with the demise of sailing ships. But that demise was well within living memory, the imam said. The decline of Kinolhas happened long ago. 'So what do *you* think?' I asked.

'Perhaps an epidemic. God is the Most Knowing.'

Later, sitting on the beach in the twilight with one of Dinakar's local colleagues, I heard another theory. 'It was the jealousy of people on the neighbouring islands. Kinolhas was rich and important and they didn't like it. They made *fandita*. Everyone knows this.'

★

'So what is this *fandita*?' I asked over supper. The word – an Indo-European one, I found out later, cognate with 'pundit' – had already come up twice in my short stay on Kinolhas. And suggestions of it had come up before that, in my reading on the Maldives. IB described the islanders as a physically weak people, armed only with prayers; but in his assertion that anyone causing them trouble 'quickly comes to grief' there is a hint of something darker than prayer. The Portuguese geographer Barbosa, writing in the sixteenth century, was blunter: 'They are a feeble folk yet right cunning, and above all things they are mighty magicians.' The eighteenth-century Arabic *History* is littered with references to sorcery, of people who 'died a martyr to magic'. The subject was no less topical today. I'd heard that a brother-in-law of the long-serving president of the Maldives, Maumoon Abdul Gayoom, had recently been rehabilitated and made a cabinet minister following a lengthy period of exile that resulted, it was said, from his attempt to remove the president by sorcery.

'Ah, yes, *fandita*,' the imam said, shooting a glance at our host the preacher, a small man in his sixties wearing a neatly pressed shirt and trousers. 'We must make a distinction between *fandita* and *sihr*, which is black magic and completely forbidden. But even *fandita* is pure heresy, like the visiting of tombs. People think that because of *fandita* pieces of wood, for example, have power in them. Only God has power. And the *fandita* men recite verses from the Qur'an, but they leave out parts and mix them up.' He leaned forward and lowered his voice. 'And they sometimes write things on a woman's breasts, and on her . . . *down here* . . .' he pointed at his crotch '. . . to get her a nice boy!'

I was about to ask what they wrote down there when the preacher's wife came in with a large tray of food, and the imam sat bolt upright, looking like a schoolboy caught telling a dirty joke. Our hostess arranged the plates on the table and left the room. The food was the usual theme and variations – tuna fried, tuna boiled, tuna curried, tuna smoked. Even the bread had tuna in it, and we ate our rice with coconut milk and *rihakuru*, a sort of tuna-treacle made by the prolonged boiling of tuna broth until it becomes dark brown and sticky (aficionados, I'm told, add sugar to their rice and *rihakuru*). The only tuna-less item was a small bowl of leaves, which the imam said came from the drumstick tree.

Looking at the spread, the Monty Python Spam sketch came to mind. All the same, the freshness and excellence of the main ingredient were unimpeachable. But I was wary of its consequences. 'This fish which provides their nourishment has an extraordinary and unequalled effect on their sexual prowess,' IB recalled, 'and the islanders perform incredible feats because of it. I myself when I lived there had four wives, and concubines as well. I did the rounds of all of them every day, and then spent the night with the wife whose turn it was.' Very IB, that: he boasts about his shag*fest*, then slips in that last phrase just in case we should doubt his legal rectitude – in bed as in all other matters, co-wives (as opposed to concubines) must be treated with absolute equality. Not without justice, he has been classified by one (female) American academic as a 'spermatic' traveller.

Given the effects of the diet, it must have been hard for Maldivian monarchs to implement the Advice for Sultans which appears as a preface to the Arabic *History*. In order to retain their other powers, the author urges, rulers should have sex only once a month; or, if they cannot restrain themselves, no more than once a week, on Thursday night; or at the *very* most, no more than once every three days . . . You almost expect the text to continue, 'Oh, go on then. Do it as much as you like.' It doesn't, but as if in recognition that these exhortations will fall on deaf ears, it changes into *memento mori* gear in rhymed prose, warning the sultan of the inevitable hour when he 'will pass from being lewd with every pretty palace slave, to being food for worms and maggots in the grave'.

I broached the question of the effects of tuna on sexual appetite over the masticatory digestif of areca nuts, betel leaves and lime paste with which every Maldivian meal concludes, but *dhaththa* – 'big sister', the respectful term for the lady of the house – reappeared with uncanny timing, and the conversation was swiftly steered into the safer waters of how the fish are caught. It was a subject about which the preacher was particularly knowledgeable, even if some of his knowledge seemed arcane. 'At times,' the imam explained, interpreting, 'if a fishing *dhoni* wasn't getting good catches, they would ask him to come and . . . well, do things. Also when new *dhonis* were launched.'

The two men exchanged a look. 'What sort of things?' I asked.

Once again, I noticed, the imam had his naughty schoolboy look. 'You know, saying prayers, and things.'

'Is this because he was the island chief?' I wondered whether Maldivian dignitaries had some ceremonial function, the Islamic equivalent of a mayor launching a ship with a bottle of champagne.

'No . . . It was because he was the *fandita* man of Kinolhas.'

It was an astonishing admission. Wordless seconds ticked by. 'Don't you find it strange', I said at last, 'that the man who preaches the sermons in your mosque was doing something you said is completely unislamic?'

'That was all in the past. Now it is finished.' They both smiled. 'He has . . . how do you say *tab*?'

'"Repented of his sins",' I said. I tried to find out what 'prayers and things' the preacher had employed in his former role as the island's white magician; but the confessional moment had passed.

*

Very early next morning, the imam and I walked down to the beach under a glittering vault of stars. (I'd told him not to worry, but he said he had to get up anyway to lead the dawn prayers . . . 'Why don't you come and pray with us?' No – he hadn't asked the question, in words; but it still hung there between us. It did so every time.) 'I pray God will bless your journey!' he called softly, as I scrambled into the same 'frog-teapot' that had brought me ashore. We paddled out and I looked back and saw the smile melt into the dark.

Soon Kinolhas was hardly even a shape; just a fuzzy line on the lagoon with the first grey feathers of light behind it. The engine of the *dhoni* I'd hitched a lift on grumbled to life and propelled us over the glossy black water. I looked back again, and thought of the demolished mosques, the smashed gravestones; but also of the stranger structures that had survived – the invisible structures of memory, myth and, at least until recently, magic. Perhaps there would be more of these to find. But there was one thing I wanted to find more than anything else.

There is a sequel to IB's tale of the sea-demon. 'When I arrived in the Maldives,' he remembered,

> I had no idea about the story. One night, while I was busy with something or other, I heard the people crying out aloud, 'There is no god but God!' and 'God is most great!' And I saw the children carrying copies of the Qur'an on their heads, and the women banging cauldrons and other vessels of brass. I was astonished at this, and said to them, 'What are you doing?' And they said, 'Can you not see it, out on the sea?' So I looked, and I saw something like a great ship that seemed to be filled with blazing lamps and torches. And they said, 'That is the demon. It always appears thus, once a month. But as long as we do what you have seen, it goes away and does us no harm.'

It is one of the oddest moments of the *Travels* – perhaps of all travels: the monstrous legend sails, unexpected, into shot, and we witness for a moment the meeting of mythic and mundane.

But can we believe IB? And if we can believe his eyes, can we believe his brain, his cognition? Confronted with an image otherwise inexplicable, he did the natural thing and saw what he was told he was seeing. Surely it was phosphorescence; perhaps even an actual ship, affected by some natural phenomenon like St Elmo's Fire . . . Yes, everyone on Kinolhas said, we can believe him. The ship of lamps is still seen now and then, and has a name: *kandumathi elhun*, 'that which appears on the sea'. It is not phosphorescence, or any other explicable manifestation. Nobody I spoke to had witnessed it themselves; it seemed it frequented the atolls further south. And south was where I was going.

★

Following in IB's wake – albeit in a seaplane – 'I arrived at Hululli, which is the island to which the sultana and her sisters go out when they want to relax and swim.' Hulhule today is not such a relaxing place. It has been extended, buried under tarmac, squared off at the corners and turned into Malé International Airport. Still, it is relaxed compared with most international airports, and as I walked past Customs I got a cheery wave from Mr Moosa, who on my first arrival had impounded an item from my luggage.

Now, I would never have dreamed of trying to bring into the Maldives 'dogs, live pigs, pork or any porcine product', and had even checked to make sure there were no stray hip-flasks, liqueur chocolates or Grand Marnier soufflés in the bottom of my bag (you can get as pissed as you want in a resort, particularly if you're on an all-in deal; alcohol, though, is banned elsewhere). But I hadn't thought twice about Krishna. A present from a friend in Calicut, the small brass statue had been caught smiling beatifically on the X-ray screen and seized as an 'idol for worship'. I protested that I wasn't a Hindu, that the friend who gave him to me was himself a Muslim; I promised faithfully not to worship him. All to no avail. At the time of my final departure, I was in a hurry and – forgive me, Krishna – forgot about him. But I see now, looking at the receipt, that he would have been 'disposed' by that time anyway – he was only given a fortnight's grace. So he has disappeared into that great limbo of stuff seized at airports. There are only two things that I regret losing more: a pair of nail-clippers of great sentimental value at Ottawa, and a jar of Martha's home-made marmalade at Heathrow.

I suppose it is understandable, this iconophobia. In 1153, the Islamic Year Zero in the Maldives, IB says, 'they smashed the idols and destroyed the *budkhanah*' – the 'Buddha-house'. Since then the Maldivians, in the phrase of the historian Andrew Forbes, 'have been haunted by the ghosts of their own past'. These ghosts, as we have seen in the story of the sea-demon, are especially nasty. At the same time, the reaction to Krishna did seem a little extreme. And yet, as I was soon to discover, the Maldivians hadn't done such a thorough job of smashing their own idols as they thought.

My second crossing to Malé on the airport *dhoni* felt like a homecoming after a long voyage. Malé's chock-a-block façade of brightly painted low high-rises gives the impression of an over-loaded container ship wallowing to the gunwales. If Kinolhas would have seemed unrecognizably empty of buildings to IB, Malé had gone the other way. 'Malé,' complained H. C. P. Bell, the pioneering Maldivologist, 'with its teeming population of over 5,200 souls, is far too overcrowded already.' That was in 1921. Now the figure teems at an official 90,000, and is probably more like 100,000 and rising. Somebody once worked out that the entire human population of the planet could stand on the Isle of Wight. I kept thinking of that statistic when I was in Malé. It is not a place for claustrophobes.

As I walked the few dozen yards to my hotel in Henveru, the old royal ward of the island where IB had lived, I thought again of poor impounded Krishna. There weren't many other places on earth where that would have happened; Saudi Arabia and parts of Pakistan perhaps, Afghanistan in the 1990s. IB, I reflected, had done his bit as Chief Justice to puritanize the Maldives. An enthusiastic flogging judge, he had adulterers caned and paraded through the streets, and meted out the same punishment to divorced couples who continued living together and to men who missed Friday prayers. (This strictness about praying continued: more recently, worshippers had to 'clock in' by depositing a ticket.) Out here on the Islamic periphery, IB was at his most stridently orthodox, huffing and puffing – between tuna-powered visits to all those wives and concubines – at the islanders' laxities like some mullah on Viagra.

It was sometimes too much for the poor Maldivians. When IB sentenced a thief to have his hand amputated, 'several of those present in court swooned away'. But he didn't always have his way. He was shocked to find that the island women not only failed to cover their hair, but also went bare-breasted. 'They go about shopping and so on in this state!' he fulminated. 'I tried my utmost when I became Chief Justice to stamp out the habit and make them cover up . . . but could do absolutely nothing about it.' Was he only shocked, or was he ever so slightly fascinated too? IB in the Maldives always reminds me of Noël Coward's 'poor Uncle Harry', the failed missionary. He too landed up on an island in 'languid latitudes', where he

swiftly imposed an arbitrary
Ban upon them shopping in the nude.

It didn't work there either. Uncle Harry, unable to beat them, joined them.

Now, IB's flesh was as weak as Uncle Harry's; but he indulged his weakness – with all those wives and concubines – within the admittedly generous pale of the laws of the time, while having those whose doings lay beyond that pale flogged. The mix of sweet sensuality and bitter sanctimoniousness is curious. It isn't strictly speaking hypocritical, but it does have a sort of Taliban-ripple flavour to it. The taste lingered long after IB. Pyrard de Laval, a shipwrecked French sailor who spent five years on Malé in the early seventeenth century, noted that 'The people are above measure superstitious, and addicted to their Religion; but yet extreamly given to women, wanton and riotous. There is nothing commoner than Adulteries, Incest and Sodomie, notwithstanding the rigour of their Lawes and Penalties.' Today, at least in theory, sin is banished along with booze to the resort islands; geography works in favour of this apartheid. But I only had to look at the illustration on the cover of the *Maldives Leisure Guide*, given away free in my hotel, to see evidence of the old bipolarity. In the foreground, a pouting nut-brown girl sporting a bikini and a come-hither wink; behind her, the tomb-shrine of Abu 'l-Barakat, saviour of virgins. Today, as in IB's time, the Maldives are poised between the gravitational drag of the centre, the orthodox, and the delicious inertia of the languid edge.

IB arrived in Malé at what could be called a typically Maldivian moment in its history. The previous ruler, Sultan Shihab al-Din, had been caught 'frequenting at night the women's quarters of his state officials and courtiers'. The aggrieved husbands had got together and deposed him, exiled him to one of the southern atolls, and had him quietly bumped off. (Exile, especially to the demon-haunted south, has always been a feature of island politics. Some rulers ended up with hundreds of exiles whom they kept in strategic perpetual motion, shifting them from island to island, rehabilitating and re-exiling in a frenetic game of political backgammon. The equatorial Siberia of the south was, to recoin a phrase, an archipelago of gulags.) Meanwhile the cabal of cuckolds had set up the adulterer's sister, Rehendi Khadijah, as sultana – 'Her Illustrious Majesty', as she is called in a contemporary document engraved on copper, 'endowed with sweet words, great beauty and excellent form . . . terrible in punishing, having abundance of most cruel bows and arrows . . . learned in the thirty-two sciences . . . a lion-woman who rides on excellent elephants . . . conqueror and uniter of the people of ten thousand universes . . .' This was the Swiftian world, a micro-state with cosmic pretensions, seething with whispers and machinations, into which IB found himself sucked.

By his own account, he came as a tourist of the most casual sort – 'I decided to travel to the Maldives, of which I had heard' – and then, when the islanders found out he had been not only one of the four Sunni judges of Delhi but also the one representing the Maliki legal school to which they themselves subscribed, was pounced on and inveigled into becoming Chief Justice. They got his sulky agreement only when he had wrung extra perks out of them, such as that of being allowed to ride a horse (before, only the sultana's husband, the Chief Minister, had been allowed to do so). Clearly, however, IB soon began to enjoy his life as a big cheese in a very small larder, and he set out to milk his Delhi connection for every drop of kudos.

IB also obviously enjoyed the lotus-, or rather tuna-, eating side of life in Ruritania-on-Sea. As well as the slave concubines (two of them, both Indian, mentioned by name – the Maratha 'Flower-Garden' and the Tamil 'Scent-of-Ambergris') there were the four wives: the sultana's stepmother; a direct descendant of the first Muslim sultan; an ex-wife of the late sultan, the assassinated adulterer Shihab al-Din; and a daughter-in-law of this third wife's stepfather, himself a future consort of Sultana Rehendi Khadijah. Thus entangled in the monkey-puzzle that was the Maldivian royal family tree (a tireless social climber, he would have been thrilled to find himself in Bell's 'Genealogical Table of Maldivian Dynasties') he crows, 'the Chief Minister and the people of Malé regarded me with awe'.

IB in the Maldives is, not to mince words, a swaggering, sanctimonious, self-important dick-head. And this is precisely why his Maldivian chapter is, for me, the most important part of his book page for page. The historical, legendary, ethnological and linguistic information in it is of supreme importance. But on a personal level I find out more about my dead fellow-traveller here than anywhere else. Like so many of us who go to languid latitudes and let ourselves go, IB is more nakedly himself in the Maldives than anywhere else. The pomposity, the piety, the pettiness, the sexual braggadocio all come together in a self-portrait of unintentionally devastating, grimacing clarity. The paradox is that the portrait is both intensely unpleasant and pathetically human.

After only eight months, the dystopic paradise had become a minor hell. Ever arrogant and abrasive, IB fell out with one prominent Maldivian after another. There were reconciliations, fresh fallings-out, tears. IB half-heartedly plotted a coup with the commanders of the army and navy, planning to fetch Tamil mercenaries from India, but it came to nothing (as did an attempted coup using Tamil mercenaries in 1988; history repeats itself, or rather, people do). In the end he divorced his wives one by one and sailed away, taking only a favourite slave-girl.

Passing through the atolls south of Malé, he remembered,

> we came to a small island on which there was but one house. In it lived a weaver with his wife and children. He had some coco-palms and a little fishing boat in which he could go where he pleased among the other isles. And I swear by God that I envied that man and wished that island had been mine, that I might live there cut off from the world, until the hour of my death.

The wish echoes down the centuries, that desire to be removed, like Crusoe, 'from all the wickedness of the world', to live in the small cabin of wattles on Yeats's Innisfree; or at least to spend a week in a beach villa in the Ayurveda Village on Meedhupparu. But IB shut out the siren call of the castaway life. Instead, he went on to a bigger island he calls 'Muluk', from where a ship would take him to the Coromandel coast. 'I stayed on Muluk for seventy days', he recalled, '*and married two wives there.*' There are no italics in Arabic manuscripts, but somehow the phrase calls for them.

*

It is surprising, given the six wives, the concubines, the vast amounts of aphrodisiac fish, and the absence of reliable contraception, that IB only mentions having fathered one child in the Maldives. When that child, a boy, was two years old, IB returned to Malé meaning to take him away. 'They brought him to me; but it appeared to me that it would be best for the boy if he stayed with them.' Was the toddler the wrong colour? Did he throw a well-timed tantrum? We'll never know. Yet another abandoned child, to add to IB's lost boys in Damascus and Delhi. Assuming he lived to adulthood, the child probably added his father's Berber DNA to the rich gene-pool of the Maldives.

Walking round Malé, meeting the curious, kindly gazes of its men and women, I always wondered if I was looking into the eyes of a descendant of IB. In so small and literally isolated a place, the likelihood was probably greater here than anywhere else on earth; in the absence of genetic material from IB himself, there was no way of telling. The surfing dude with the peroxide dreadlocks and broad, almost Polynesian face; the square-jawed old man with a hint of Mongoloid in his eyes – he could almost be Iroquois, or Inuit; the slender, crinkle-haired Tamil-dark girl; the boy with the brilliant crooked smile who would have looked at home in Zanzibar; the pale hatchet-faced woman with honeyed eyes, magicked here, I fantasized, from a mud tower in Hadramawt; glances from Malindi, Muscat, Malabar, Malacca and the whole arc of lands around the ocean rim. In a sense they are all IB's offspring, all part of that great creole family born of Indian Ocean wanderings.

Malé itself is as unplaceable as its people. With its seaside-coloured buildings, its old-fashioned shops that sell ironmongery or fishing tackle or haberdashery (and sometimes unexpected combinations – one shop stocked nothing but umbrellas and plaster ceiling-roses), with the tangy proximity of the sea, it took me, if anywhere, back to pre-chain-store coastal towns of my childhood – Weston-super-Mare, perhaps; many degrees warmer, but permeated with that same torpid quiet. It's hard to see how a place so crowded can seem so hushed, how it isn't in the permanent grip of gridlock and gaol-madness. But somehow it all fits in – the 500 taxis, the thousands of Honda Wave scooters, the 90,000-plus people, all conversing and moving about *sotto voce* in this humming human hive.

Trying to track down personal Battutian relics in a place so densely lived in and built on was, I knew, a near impossibility. I had one tiny lead, though. In Bell's 1940 monograph on the Maldives I'd noticed the Dilli Miskiiy – probably the 'Delhi' Mosque – on the plan of Malé, just off the eastern end of Majidi Magu, the straight main street that cuts through the middle of the island. Contacts between the Maldives and southern India have always been close, but I could only think of one link with Delhi: the Chief Justice who had been judge of the great imperial capital, and who never let the people of this pint-sized metropolis forget the fact. It was no more than a wild hunch, but I wondered if the Dilli Miskiiy had been founded by IB.

I knew I was almost there – in tiny Malé, you always are nearly there; but the mosque was proving evasive. Finding myself in yet another dead-end alley off Majidi Magu, I sought help from a man sitting in a doorway. He invited me into his house, a slot of a room where he lived with his wife and six children. A wooden ladder rose steeply to a sleeping shelf. Culinary arrangements were at the back, and sanitary ones somewhere in the dark beyond. London estate agents would have described it optimistically as a bijou studio apartment with mezzanine, and yet this was home to eight people. As the lady of the house served tea and breadfruit crisps in delicate china, two of the younger children came home from school, with immaculate uniforms and almost equally spotless English. This was no hopeless slum dwelling, but a middle-class household miniaturized by geographical circumstance.

One of the boys took me up another alley, by Megachip Computers, to a shed-like structure called the Afif al-Din Mosque. I was wondering why we were there when a group of old men in the mosque told me that this had been the site of the Dilli Miskiiy; the old building and the old name had been done away with in the late 1970s. They all knew of IB, transmitter of the national epic, but not of any connection between him and the mosque. I looked round the featureless, flat-pack building and saw my hunch fizzle away.

Malé, I soon discovered, had like Kinolhas been the victim of wholesale vandalism in the 1970s and 1980s. The remaining bastions of the fort built by the Portuguese during their brief but violent occupation in the sixteenth century had been swept away, and their cannon used for landfill; another exorcism, perhaps, of troublesome ghosts. But why demolish mosque after mosque and replace them – often using Saudi 'aid' money – with buildings that seemed wilfully devoid of aesthetic worth? The only happy ending to these tales of loss is in that of the Ebony Mosque, an eighteenth-century gem built of coral stone with pillars of dark wood, dismantled and sold off to a resort island but since brought back and re-erected. (Although, ironically, if any of the old mosques deserved the chop it was this one – built on expropriated land and there-fore, the Arabic *History* explains at length, unfit to be prayed in.) Even the sainted shrine of Shaykh Najib al-Habashi ('the Abyssinian'), visited by IB, and by generations of sultans who processed there annually at night in Ramadan to the music of the royal band and the light of hundreds of lamps, had been razed to the ground. In an area now occupied by a small park, a dusty five-a-side football pitch and a tall radio mast, there was no hint of where it had stood.

Depressed by this initial exploration, I ended up at the quayside on the north-west of the island. Here, at least, was hustle and bustle: a fish market, shops selling shark fins and sea cucumbers (the latter, dried and blackened, come in many shapes – short and fat, long and thin, ribbed, dimpled, flanged and knobbled, as if designed by an inspired dildo-maker); here, in a covered market, among betel-chewers' requisites and spices and bottles of *rihakuru*, that treacly tuna essence, were the edible relics of IB's Maldivian chapter – coconut 'honey', made from the sap of the palm, and sweetmeats also made from the sap and flavoured with jasmine-water, wrapped in plantain leaves and resembling miniature salamis. And here, moored gunwale to gunwale along the quay, was a line of *dhonis* – vagabond vessels with not a particle of the picturesque in their looks, but laden with the promise of far atolls.

There were two built relics of IB's narrative that had escaped the tsunami of vandalism. I'd been saving them up against the expected dearth of more personal survivals from his stay. The first was the tomb-shrine of al-Barbari, defeater of the sea-demon . . . When I saw it, I realized it had suffered vandalism's reverse. The little gable-fronted building, with its white walls and flagpoles and its finicky *faux*-brickwork picked out in bright blue with a matching dado,

was appropriately nautical in colour. But 'restoration' had smothered any hints of history and left the holy of holies with about as
much outward sanctity as a bus-shelter in Bognor Regis. It was also
firmly locked and, I learned later, always remained so. If I'd been
hoping for any illumination on al-Barbari – if that was even his real
name – there was none to be had here.

At first sight, the group of buildings opposite seemed to have
suffered from the same over-zealous restoration. The seventeenth-
century minaret of Malé, a small squat cylinder sitting on a big
one with a railed balcony where the two parts met, was painted in
the same yachting colours, white and blue, as the shrine; it might
have been the funnel of a steamer. Beyond it, the Hukuru Miskiiy
– the Great Mosque, founded by al-Barbari/al-Tabrizi and rebuilt
by Sultan Iskandar in 1656–7 – was almost invisible under a
glaring tin roof. But when my eyes had adjusted to the light
bouncing off it and off the white coral sand of its forecourt, I
began to make out the details of the carved masonry under the
eaves: the elegantly incurving lines of the plinth on which
the building was raised, deeply coffered walls, panels of strapwork
and knotwork and lacework like those on the smashed gravestones
of Kinolhas, friezes of egg-and-cup mouldings and vine tendrils
– motifs that had blown in from the Hellenistic Mediterranean, via
the world of Gandharan Buddhism and the monsoon, and mingled
with the geometric *jeux d'esprit* of local masons. This one exquisite
structure redeemed, architecturally, the whole of Malé. If buildings were people, then the shrine over the road would be a spoilt
child in a sailor suit, and this mosque with its metallic roof a
dowager in a builder's helmet – but a dowager still, of ancient
lineage and great beauty.

While I stood there, bewildered by the richness of the walls, the
call to prayer sounded from loudspeakers on top of the smokestack-
like minaret. Men and boys came in from the street, took scoops
attached to long poles from a rack by the door, and did their ablutions from a well in the forecourt. Peering inside the mosque, I
could dimly make out a copse of turned wooden columns, then
watched as the line of worshippers rose and sank at an angle to the
line of the building. The mosque, for all its architectural glory, was
a few degrees off true – probably, the archaeologists say, because its

saintly founder, al-Barbari/al-Tabrizi, built it on the same alignment as a destroyed Buddhist temple.

The identity of that heroic exorcist was still bugging me. IB's 'al-Barbari' was incontrovertibly called, in an inscription on the outside of the Great Mosque's north wall, 'al-Tabrizi' – the same name he has in the *History*. There was only one solution. That much older inscription about the saint – the one IB himself read on the dividing screen of the original mosque – had miraculously survived the seventeenth-century rebuild. This was one of those rare occasions when I could examine the very piece of evidence used by IB himself.

It wasn't *in situ* any longer but, like everything else in Malé, it wasn't far away. The short walk, however, shed light on the more recent Islamic history of the Maldives. Almost too much light: the Great Mosque has its gleaming tin roof, the Malé Islamic Centre a retina-numbing gilded dome hovering over a snow-blinding white building, all clean concrete lines and soaring pointed arches. The old Great Mosque was a small but rich building executed with craftsmanship. This was clearly executed with money – lots of it – and it was certainly impressive in scale and in its initial *coup d'oeil*. There was no longer any need to bang pots and pans to keep the jinn away: all the demons of the past would flee from the clanging effulgence of this golden dome. The only problem was that 'Malé's most famous architectural landmark', as the tourist brochures call it, might have been prefabricated in Jeddah or Dubai and airdropped in. It was to mosques what Hiltons are to hotels. And that was probably the point of it: the quaint, the heterodox, the peripheral, it said, were things of the past.

Over the road, behind a large mobile phone showroom, was the only bit of the old royal palace to have escaped demolition. The last of the sultans had been deposed in 1968, and his rambling complex of residences razed a couple of years later. The site is now a public park with a tatty bandstand-like structure (someone had spray-painted $EX on it); the surviving bit of palace, a modest three-storey villa, is the national museum. An old guardian snoozed in a chair on the veranda, a radio blaring in his lap.

Inside was the sort of sultanic lumber I'd seen in Zanzibar – the knobbly ebony, the flamboyant crockery. There were also thrones and palanquins and ceremonial umbrellas and turbans; and Sultan Muhammad Shams al-Din's Metzler upright piano . . . it was too tempting, but when I lifted the lid and tickled the ravaged ivories, it sounded like a smashed cembalon at the bottom of a well. The jangling noise drew an employee, a girl who brushed away my apologies with a smile but thereafter shadowed me round the exhibits.

On our way upstairs, I was delighted to see a 'portrait' of the former Chief Justice, IB – yet another addition to my collection of his many faces. This was that of a dark-bearded Arab with a thin face, looking appropriately fortyish and harassed. The painting caused me to mention my quest to my minder. After a short conversation with a young male colleague on the upper floor, keys were hunted down and a door unlocked. Inside was a small room containing a sort of canopied day-bed covered in blue chintz and furnished with bolsters. 'This', the young man said, 'used to be in the Habashigefanu Ziyaarath' – that shrine of Shaykh Najib the Abyssinian, visited by IB in the 1340s, demolished in the 1970s. But what did this odd piece of furniture have to do with a Muslim holy man? It looked more suitable for the boudoir of a Regency hostess. 'The bed was in honour of the shaykh,' he explained, obscurely. 'And you see these wooden sandals?' They lay within reach of the bed on a low stool. 'People say they used to wear themselves out and had to be replaced every few years. The shaykh was a very holy man.'

For some reason the image brought to mind a statue of Field Marshal Earl Haig at my old school: one night, a wag painted two tipsy lines of footsteps leading from the statue's plinth to the nearest lavatories and back. 'So if the shaykh was so holy,' I said, 'why on earth did they demolish his shrine?'

The young man and the girl looked at each other, then erupted in a fit of giggles. When the giggles had subsided, the man said, 'Well, history like this used to be hidden . . .' They caught each other's eyes and tittered again. 'The reason is, President Ibrahim Nasir – he was the one before Maumoon – went to the shrine one day and found two men . . . doing something bad on this bed. So he had the shrine destroyed.'

I was intrigued to know what had happened to the two men – and for that matter why the bed had been preserved; but my giggling guides were already ushering me out of the room, locking the door and steering me towards another bed. This, they said, had been brought from al-Barbari/al-Tabrizi's gaily painted shrine, for reasons unknown and therefore probably less scandalous. It was plain and rather elegant, had a white umbrella fixed to its foot, and was about the right size for a six-year-old child.

Back downstairs in the ill-lit recesses of the piano room, I noticed a stone carved with a hanging lamp in a niche – a Cambay stone! A label said it came from Kinolhas. I thought of that other, plain slab there, near the site of the fish-bone saint's shrine; this, then, must have been the headstone. It was another milestone on the monumental journey round the Indian Ocean. But I'd only been able to make out the date – AH 858, or the middle of the fifteenth century AD – when my guides called me. 'I think this is very important for you,' the girl said, pointing to a long inscribed plank high up in the gloom on the wall.

It was very important. It was that inscription from the pre-reconstruction Great Mosque of Malé that gave the name of the demon-defeater: 'Sultan Ahmad Shanurazah embraced Islam at the hand of the Maghribi, Abu 'l-Barakat al-Barbari.' Or at least that was how IB remembered the crucial phrase, ten years and tens of thousands of miles later. If he had taken notes – and he only ever mentions doing so once in his twenty-nine years of travel – he would have lost them when he fell victim to Indian pirates after leaving the Maldives; they left him with nothing, he says, but his underpants. The likelihood of his running round making antiquarian jottings in the five-day return visit to Malé he made after the pirate attack is infinitesimal. Rather, his prodigious memory retained the essence of the inscription, including that highly un-Arabic name, Shanurazah, just as it had retained the names of Maldivian islands and atolls, and of thousands of people and places scattered over a hemisphere.

And there was that name, Shanurazah, visible in the chunky script on the plank; only, I realized after some careful decipherment, it wasn't the name of the first Muslim sultan but of his prime minister, who had supervised the original mosque building. There *was* a Sultan Ahmad mentioned: Ahmad Shihab al-Din, who ordered the first reconstruction of the mosque in AH 738 . . .

the adulterous ruler, exiled and assassinated not long before IB's arrival. IB, it seems, recalled the elements of the inscription correctly but jumbled their order, creating a composite character, 'Sultan Ahmad Shanurazah', out of two men who had lived two centuries apart.

But what of the name of the hero of the tale, al–Barbari/al–Tabrizi? 'There came into this country', I made out, 'Abu 'l-Barakat Yusuf al- . . .' Infuriatingly, the surname was undotted. But that all important extra 'stalk' *wasn't* there. The likelihood of the name being anything other than 'al-Barbari' was miniscule. Weighing up this most precious piece of evidence, IB's reading was right – and better than that of generations of subsequent Maldivian scholars. I read on: 'al-Barbari, and the sultan embraced Islam at his hand in the month of Rabi' II 548 . . .' There was no mention of al-Barbari being, as IB said, from his own homeland of the Maghrib – Morocco.

Having spent so long in IB's company I was aware of the pitfalls of false memory, and more than once had come across an invention of IB's that, as Prospero said,

> by telling of it,
> Made such a sinner of his memory,
> To credit his own lie.

We've all done it. We remember what we want to remember; wishful thoughts become that bit more real with every repetition. The Barbari of the inscription might as well have been a native of the much nearer Berbera in Somalia as of distant Morocco; or, as one distinguished recent Maldivian historian has suggested, of Beruwala, long known as Berberyn, on the even nearer coast of Sri Lanka.

Does it really matter? It mattered enough to fuel a warm debate at the National Council for Linguistic and Historical Research with Miss Naseema, a member of the pro-Tabrizi camp, and her colleague Ahmad Tholal who, as I now did, belonged to the Barbari faction. Naseema wielded some formidable evidence. 'Look,' she said, 'in Dhivehi all the most basic Islamic terms – "prayer", "fast", "mosque", "call to prayer" – come from or via Persian. Now you can't pretend a Berber would have brought those words here. It *must* have been a Persian-speaker – a Tabrizi. There is nothing worse than telling lies about history!'

This shook my confidence in even that venerable piece of evidence, the wooden inscription. As with IB's telling of the conversion story, age doesn't necessarily guarantee truth. I even wondered if perhaps the carver of the inscription simply forgot to put in that small but crucial stalk. Then Ahmad Tholal showed me another piece of evidence. It was something that consigned the whole business of stalks and dots and Berbers and Persians to the crabbed realm of scholastical nitpicking.

The object is one of the strangest and most disturbing I have ever seen and touched, and it made the fate of my Krishna statuette more comprehensible still. We were back in the museum, in a small pantry-like room lined with shelves. On the shelves and on the floor below were many pieces of carved stone, mostly bits of architectural mouldings. Among these fragments were others carved with human, or near-human, faces – bland, smiling Buddhas-in-the-round, and reliefs of scary masks with blank staring eyes, caddish upcurling mustachioes, distended earlobes and low hairlines with a curious double widow's peak. Tholal explained that the two types of heads represented the two aspects of Buddhism which the islanders had practised before Islam: the conventional sort and, later on, a curious tantric variety – in this case, a bloody perversion of the Buddha's message, brought to the Maldives by priests expelled from India. 'And this second form', Tholal said, 'involved human sacrifice.'

I thought immediately of the murdered maidens of Malé. 'Do you think there's any connection with IB's story of the demon and the virgins?'

'It's very likely that there is. Look at this . . .' He showed me a coral-stone stela in the shape of a truncated, inverted cone. It too was carved with a number of those mask-like heads. These, however, were clean-shaven; their eyes had traces of painted pupils, and their curling lips, drawn back to reveal large teeth, were stained red. 'This was dug up at the north-east corner of Malé – very near your hotel in fact – at the spot that's traditionally said to be the site of the sacrificial temple.' I was squatting by the stone, feeling its rough top. I instantly withdrew my hand. 'And, interestingly, when they excavated it, it had a human skull on top of it. We sent it to Sri Lanka for testing, and it was found that it was the skull of a young girl.'

In the close heat of the room, a shiver shot through my body. 'So yes,' Tholal was saying in his gentle scholarly voice, 'there is an uncanny resemblance to Ibn Battutah's story. On stylistic grounds the piece could be ninth- or tenth-century – there's a certain resemblance to the East Javanese *rakasas* of that period. But of course, Ibn Battutah's demon is popularly associated with Rannamari, "the King of the Sea", who seems to be part of a local pre-Buddhist pantheon . . .' By now I was only half listening to him as I looked, fascinated and repulsed, into the features on the stone. If the demon of the blazing lamps had a face, then this was it.

And there was more.

'This is also a very interesting artefact,' Tholal was saying. 'It was also used for human sacrifice.'

I looked at the object, a smallish cuboid altar with a relief of a smiling, seated female deity on one side; she had a small hole in her forehead. On the top was an incised shape, rather like a broad pointed leaf – the leaf of a bo-tree? – and in the centre of this a heart-shaped recess. I could make out another small hole in the recess – connected, I realized, to the lower hole, the goddess's 'third eye' in the centre of her forehead . . . The implication dawned. Tholal confirmed it: 'You see, they used to excise the organ and place it in this hollow, and the blood would seep down and over the deity.'

I felt a hint of nausea welling up. 'You mean they'd actually put a *human* heart there, in that heart-shaped hole?'

Tholal smiled. 'In fact, the hollow isn't *heart*-shaped, as such. It's the shape of a female sexual organ. And, interestingly, the precise organ which was cut off and placed on it was the male sexual organ.'

The Maldives: land of sand, sun, sea and sexual sacrifice. But at least the maidens of Malé got their own back.

★

Over dinner at my hotel near the site of the sea-demon's shrine, Tholal regaled me with further hair-raising tales: of the man who found out his wife was a *handi*, a female jinni, when he saw her sitting on the ground cooking lunch and using her own smoulder-ing feet as fuel; of the arsonists who started the Great Fire of Malé in 1886, having rendered themselves invisible by drinking a potion extracted from the liver of a dead boy; of his own family's Indian serving woman, who went mad and died after a *handi* blew into her room one night; of the black magicians who can procure you a nymphomaniac *handi* in the very shape of the woman of your dreams.

'*Handi* to have around,' I said.

Tholal ignored this and went on in a low voice. 'You *must* have full sex with her, or else . . .'

Recalling that second sacrificial altar, I didn't want to ask about the consequences over dinner. 'But', I said, 'do you believe all this?' Tholal was a highly knowledgeable historian. He moonlighted as a radio DJ and occasional quiz-show host. And he also appeared to be an entirely rational man.

He thought for a while, then said, 'I like to think that there are things beyond what I can understand through my senses.' He looked out over the crowded buildings, over the dark sea. 'All the time I was abroad, studying in Australia, I never felt any fear. But I wouldn't walk around the islands of my own country at night.' He looked back at me. 'Only one thing unites this country. Not religion, but superstition.'

★

As I looked out to sea the following day from the spot where the demon's temple had stood – a patch of pavement next to a small petrol station – I reflected that, in those faces of stone with their reddened, curling lips, I had looked on something that had remained hidden from IB. At the same time, I doubted whether I'd ever get to set eyes on what he had seen, that spectral ship of lamps. I'd found the actual skeleton in the cupboard, so to speak; I could hardly expect the fabled family ghost to show itself too.

Into my own lifetime, drums were beaten regularly at night at the palace gate, to keep the apparition of the lighted ship away; when the practice was stopped in 1963, the islanders crowded here to the north-east shore, fearing the worst. Nothing happened. Now, the Maldivian custom has gone the way of the ancient

Athenian one of banging bronze kettles at the moment of a person's death to scare away the Furies. Today, divine reason sheds its light over Malé, from the great gilded dome of the Islamic Centre; its dark inversion has fled. The only appearance of Rannamari, the demon King of the Sea, is his annual one on posters for the Rannamari Surfing Festival – held at the island's south-east point where, in the alternative conversion story, al-Tabrizi's bottled jinni was committed to the deep. Here, according to a surfing guide I looked at, 'a couple of shifting peaks are popular with boogie-boarders'. It is also billed as the ideal spot to begin your Maldivian surfari . . . (Now *that's* cosmopolitan: a ritualized Polynesian pastime transplanted to the western Indian Ocean and expressed by an Anglo-Saxon-Swahili-Arabic portmanteau word.)

I did see unusual vessels on the water from the site of the demon's temple. But they were a flotilla of *dhonis* chartered by the political opposition, flying party flags and blaring party songs as they circum-navigated Malé. A referendum on the form of presidential elections was imminent, and this was the only practical way to campaign on a large scale, given the island's impossible streets. Open opposition was indeed an unusual sight – so unusual as to have been unthinkable only a year or two before. But it seemed that President Maumoon Abdul Gayoom, who had run the Maldives as a very tight ship indeed for close on three decades, was beginning to think of bowing out gracefully.

I wanted very much to meet him. He had the sort of trappings of potentatehood that would be fun to ogle: a large (or, relative to the dark slots in which most inhabitants of Malé live, gargantuan) Dallas-style palace on Orchid Magu, with a roof of bright blue tiles; a multi-million-dollar yacht; a stretch-limo (even more pointless in Malé than IB's horse); and, reputedly, a gold-plated lavatory. But he was also an Arabic scholar who had studied at al-Azhar University in Cairo. Most important, IB was a great collector of rulers, the richer and more potent the better, and apart from two splendidly titled but now utterly impotent potentates I'd met in Malabar – the Zamorin of Calicut and the Bibi of Cannanore – I'd never been able to emulate him. Malé looked like my best bet. Everyone knew or was related to everyone, or at least everyone who was anyone; nepotism wasn't so much rampant as inevitable. For instance,

Tholal's boss at the National Centre for Linguistic and Historical Research was the president's brother-in-law (and brother to that reinstated cabinet minister who had allegedly tried to oust Maumoon by sorcery); another colleague of his was Yumna Maumoon, the president's daughter.

I later met Yumna's sister Dunya, Deputy Minister for Foreign Affairs, in her panelled office overlooking the sea. We talked for a while about IB and his multiple Maldivian marriages and divorces. 'I'm not sure he gives a very good picture of Muslim manhood,' she said with a musical laugh. I could only agree. At the same time, I couldn't help also agreeing with IB's enthusiasm for 'the delightful company of Maldivian womanhood'. Dunya, laughing, brought to mind the traveller's recollection of the first of his four high-born wives, the sultana's stepmother: 'She was one of the best of women. So sweet was her society that, even when I married others beside her, she showed no jealousy, but would sprinkle me with scent and perfume my robes with incense, laughing all the while.' You can almost hear the sigh, as he remembers the delights of that flawed paradise.

I mentioned to Dunya my hope of meeting her father. She said she'd do her best. 'But he's very busy, with the referendum and so on.' Suddenly the laughter left her face. Without it she looked vulnerable. 'You know . . . all the foreign media keep saying he's a terrible dictator. But, he . . .' there was a catch in her voice '. . . he's only trying to do his best.' I noticed she had her father's alert, slightly protuberant eyes, familiar from all the posters and portraits. They were bright with a film of tears. I mumbled some platitude about nobody being perfect, then left, understanding a little more about how IB fell so easily into that soft, deep, dangerous web of marriages.

Days went by in which I did little but wander the alleys of Malé by day and the windings of the Arabic *History* at night, picking up the thread where IB left off. His sultana, Rehendi Khadijah, eventually had her husband the Chief Minister assassinated for daring to try and depose her. The next consort met the same fate, for the same reason. Rehendi Khadijah died in her bed and was succeeded by her less ruthless sister, who was successfully deposed by her husband; he was succeeded by his daughter, who in turn was deposed by *her* husband . . . And so it went on in a round of coup and counter-coup – or, perhaps, of patriarchal Islam struggling with the remnants of an ancient matriarchy – punctuated by exile and sorcery. Events flashed past. 'This lower world', the author of the *History* says in his Omar Khayyámesque verse-introduction,

> is but a halt where travellers stay –
> We pass here one short night, and then go on our way.

And now the referendum was approaching and there were angry mobs and rumours of arson plots that revived dark memories of the Great Fire of Malé.

The president remained busy. So I decided to continue south, in search of phantom ships. I also wanted to visit the place where IB had his last taste of paradise, the island he calls 'Muluk'. It was both a paradise of women, where he married those last two island wives to keep him in spermatic trim during his two-month stay there, and of natural bounty, 'one of the greenest and most fertile of all the islands', he recalled. The problem was that there were two possible Muluks – Boli Mulaku and Fua Mulaku, respectively Cowry Mulaku and Areca-Nut Mulaku. On balance, the second one looked more likely to me, given IB's mention of his island's fertility. Nearly all the local fruit and vegetables in the Malé market came from there. Besides, as the only atoll-less island, rearing up in solitude from the depths of the Equatorial Channel, it looked irresistible on the map. More than any other part of this sea-land, Fua Mulaku deserved the ancient South Indian description of the Maldives, 'whose great and ancient guardian is the ocean that makes the conches resound'. I pictured it as some Prospero's Isle, a haunt of Tritons. Perhaps, too, of that ship of blazing lamps.

Malé – Boli Mulaku

To sit at midnight in the prow of a boat leaving a harbour, sliding into the dark, with two hundred miles of ocean, half a dozen atolls, half a thousand islands ahead, a universe of stars above and, all around, voices murmuring in an unknown tongue – that is freedom. After days in the straitjacket streets of Malé, by some accounts the mostly densely lived-in capital on earth, I felt like a jinni out of a bottle, like Browning's Waring giving them all the slip, like Eliot's travellers set loose from the very bonds of time and self –

> You shall not think 'the past is finished'
> Or 'the future is before us'.
>
> You are not those who saw the harbour
> Receding, or those who will disembark . . .

Love and death apart, only on journeys, in the spaces between the places, can we be so free.

The squat and beamy *Sazee*, unlikely vessel for these thoughts, resembled an overgrown cabin cruiser that had seen better days. I'd found it with Ahmad Tholal's help, moored across the road from the vegetable market in that tight-packed rank of motor *dhonis*. It was taking on goods for the south, for Huvadhoo – the biggest atoll in the world and the last before my goal, the lone island of Fua Mulaku. Gas bottles, apples, nappies, cocktail snacks, sewing machines, Indian Farm Fresh Eggs, bicycles, sacks of onions, cookers, drainpipes and even a kitchen sink or two were disappearing into its hold. The skipper, Kappi ('Cap'n') Vaadhoo Zubayr, was a man of few words, none of them English; but I sensed I was in good hands. 'They are as it were half fishes,' said Pyrard the shipwrecked Frenchman of Maldivian mariners. Solid, slow, reliable-looking, Vaadhoo Zubayr was perhaps half a grouper. He had promised to deliver me, by the grace of God, to his home island that, in informal Maldivian fashion, was the first element of his name – Vaadhoo, at the far southern end of Huvadhoo. From there it was another twenty-five miles of open sea to Fua Mulaku, out in the Equatorial Channel. This suited me well, as on Vaadhoo I could pay my respects to the tomb of the sixteenth-century scholar and alleged *fandita* man Jamal al-Din, he who had imprisoned corpse-eating Beri in a bottle on the island of Kinolhas. Now, the loading complete and the *Sazee* noticeably lower in the water, we were off at last, only two days late, threading a way through the dense shoal of *dhonis*, dodging a cat's-cradle of mooring cables, off to that demon-haunted south.

Malé was soon an afterglow receding. The air had freshened, and I left the last of my companions at the prow – two old men, talking in low voices, both of them knotting and unknotting bits of string as they spoke – and went into the covered part of the deck behind the wheel-house to get some sleep . . .

I almost laughed aloud at the thought. The deck, already crowded an hour before, was now a solid mass of bodies lying this way and that with barely a space between them. They looked less like passengers than refugees fleeing a disaster, dead from exhaustion. By the light of the single small bulb that illuminated the scene, I made out the form of the kindly Vaadhoo man who'd offered me a place beside him. That place was now taken but, as the alternative was a chilly night on the forecastle, I squeezed myself into the few inches that remained beside the new arrival and prepared to pass the night in close bodily contact with two strangers.

That night I learned the hard way just how physical T. S. Eliot's metaphysics of travel, time and self could be. Through the hours of dark, the future seemed indefinitely postponed. I was no longer the free spirit that had left the harbour, but a body, trapped on both sides and by a horny foot pressed against my head and a child's fingers interwoven with my toes; for good measure I was trodden on from time to time by nocturnal visitors to the heads. Still, dawn did come at last, and some fugitive minutes of sleep. I awoke to find the back of one of my two neighbours still pressed against me. At the same moment, he turned and opened his eyes. 'Hello,' he said, 'my name's Zuraa.' Even after a night in Club-Sandwich Class, Zuraa had the looks of a Bollywood romantic lead. I felt, and probably looked, like a freshly unwrapped mummy.

Over the *Sazee*'s breakfast of weak tea and jam sandwiches, Zuraa told me he was also a Vaadhoo man, returning to his wife of four months – 'three months pregnant', he added – with a load of Indian cloth to sell to the island women. He asked what was taking me to his 'country'. Like everyone else in the Maldives, he knew of IB; he hadn't, however, heard of the traveller's two-month stay on 'Muluk' island, or of his two brief marriages there. 'But it is not strange,' he said. 'Maldives ladies are the best wives . . .' A faraway look passed over his face, the sort that in a Hindi movie would have faded into an almost-kissing dance sequence on a mountainside.

Certain though he was about the undimmed delights of Maldivian wives, Zuraa was less sure about IB's Muluk being Fua Mulaku. 'It was very difficult to land until they built a harbour there a few years ago,' he said. 'Near the shore, the sea is very deep and the waves are very big. I think Ibn Battutah's island was Boli Mulaku.' A phrase from Bell's book came back to me, about the approach to Fua Mulaku being 'fraught with danger at all times'. The ship on which IB travelled to Muluk had lain off the island for weeks on end. Zuraa was right: Fua Mulaku and IB's Muluk didn't sound like the same place at all. Not for the first time, I admitted to myself that this voyage to lonely, sea-girt Fua Mulaku might have been inspired more by the map and *The Tempest* than by the needs of scholarly research. Then again, there was that other reason, equally unscholarly but even more irresistible, for going so far south.

Of the telling of tales about jinn there is no end, the Arabs say. Mention of my quest for the ship of blazing lamps sparked off a succession of spirit stories from Zuraa. He hadn't himself witnessed the lighted ship. But he'd had a brush with another species of malevolent spirit, a *fureta*, in the form of a turtle that, while he was out raiding turtle eggs with friends one night, had turned into a fireball and flown off into the air. And he had seen glowing angelic figures hovering at night round the tomb of Jamal al-Din the jinn-bottler. 'Perhaps you will see them too,' he said. 'My house is next to the tomb.'

We sat together on the forecastle all morning, the sun swinging higher overhead and burning my legs (I was wearing a Yemeni waist-cloth and headscarf, the most comfortable clothes for languid latitudes). Bewitched by Zuraa's stories, I didn't notice. Only hunger made us move. As we queued at the makeshift galley in the stern for our rice and tuna broth, I observed my other fellow-passengers. Together with the inhabitants of the lower deck, reserved for families, I reckoned that there were around ninety passengers and ten crew on the eighty-five-foot vessel. Many had a touch of Zuraa's looks – bronze Vishnu made flesh, but with an elvish twist to the eyes. There was less variation in the faces of these southerners than in Malé, that crowded crossroads of the ocean. I was the only European: Western foreigners are rarely seen outside the hotel islands and Malé, and hardly ever aboard workaday *dhonis* like the *Sazee*. But there were a couple of groups of young Nepalese and Bangladeshi men, on their way to build resorts and looking lost – especially the Nepalese, sea-virgins who'd come straight from their landlocked kingdom to a country that was 99.7 per cent water. One of them spent the day gazing into the wheel-house, as if at the bridge of a starship.

We chugged south through the drowsy afternoon, through the shallow waters of atolls interspersed with deeper, rougher stretches of *kandu* – 'sea' proper. From a distance, one island looked much like another, a line of greenery seeming to grow straight from the lagoon. The surface of the water gave little away, except for the occasional long flat arc of a flying fish or the sudden silver seething of a shoal of sprats; once, the fin of something big and dark scythed slowly through the blue – a whale-shark, Zuraa thought. The two old men from the night before performed their mid-afternoon prayers on the forecastle, then went back to their bits of string and threads of conversation. The younger, non-praying majority smoked and joked and whiled away the hours until the sun fell faster and grew fatter. Then, as we neared the One-and-a-Half-Degree

Channel – a fifty-mile stretch of open ocean separating Huvadhoo from the more northerly atolls and classified by Maldivians as Bodu Kandu, 'the Big Sea' – the infinite subtle blues of water and ether between which we'd been travelling underwent a violent change. Sickly sherbert-lemon cloudbanks reared against a Parma-violet sky, then turned dark and bilious as the western horizon bloomed sherry-trifle pink and gold. 'I think you will vomit,' Zuraa said as we hit the Big Sea.

I could see what he meant. And the sea, they said, was bigger than usual. The *Sazee* bucked and plunged, sending up showers of white water. There were few takers for dinner, an excellent chicken curry. Not being the vomiting type, I had double rations then took myself off to the now-dark forecastle to do some demon-watching.

It may have been too rough for demons. It was certainly too wet for humans, with a boisterous wind lashing whips of spray at right-angles to our course. I remembered reading in Bell of sailing *dhonis* on their way to the southern atolls getting blown from the Big Sea all the way to Africa, and blessed the inventor of the unromantic marine diesel. The wallowing black of the sea remained empty of apparitions, and I turned in at eight o'clock, damp and chilled.

The advantage of being so tightly packed in is that you don't roll around much, even in a big swell. The disadvantage, as I already knew, is that you can't move at all, and what with the heaving of the *dhoni* and the bruising that my bones had suffered from the unforgiving deck the night before, sleep was as elusive as sea-demons. I lay there between Zuraa and a Bangladeshi builder, painfully aware of being on board in the most literal sense. Some lines by the historian al-Maqqari, a better writer of Arabic rhymed prose than he was a sailor, began to roll around in my head. I chased after them and tried to tie them down in English: 'And we began to think that in all creation/there was neither depth nor elevation,/save the sky so steep/and the sea so deep,/and no men left save us, on board,/in the belly of that ship, our grave, immured.'

*

Three a.m. The island of Viligili in the north of Huvadhoo. Sleep-deprived passengers mumble and tumble on to the jetty. A harrassed clerk lists the stuff coming out of the *Sazee*'s hold. A midnight-blue sports car with a highly optimistic spoiler (the jetty's the only paved surface on the island) cruises up and down. It stops. The driver gets out. He's got a sculpted zigzag of bristles along his jawline – a go-faster beard – and wraparound shades, worn in the dark. On and on the unloading goes. The sun comes up. Zuraa and I go wandering past big blank warehouses and slatternly sheds. We're a long way from the Maldives of the tour brochures. The unloading takes till noon.

*

I awoke as we tied up at Dhevadhoo, in the middle of Huvadhoo atoll. Exhaustion and the flat waters of the lagoon had finally brought on sleep that was more like a temporary death. Most of the men of the island were off fishing, and brisk and beautiful women took charge of the unloading. Zuraa and I joined an informal Maldivian Democratic Party meeting, attended by a few of the older or lazier male islanders, in the shade of a group of poon trees. Zuraa, like most Maldivians who talked to me of politics, was no fan of President Maumoon. 'He comes to an island,' he'd told me, 'promises he'll build a school and a hospital, gets elected, does nothing about the school and the hospital, comes back after five years and gets elected for another five years . . . This is what it has been like for nearly thirty years.' Zuraa, I realized, had lived his entire life under Maumoon. Now, though, opposition was coming out in public – in this case on swinging beds that hung from the poon branches. It was all very laid-back.

I was shown to a bed of my own – *undhoali* was its Dhivehi name, Zuraa said – where I lay flat out and swung, hearing Dhivehi voices – ' . . . Maumoon . . . Maumoon . . .' – that elided with the cooing of doves in the poon trees, listening to the creaking of the ropes and wondering if the swinging motion was meant to counteract that rocking of dry land, that sensation of *terra infirma*, experienced by the gimballed brains of these sea-borne people, these half-fishes, and wondering if, however linguistically unlikely, the word *undhoali* could be connected with 'indolence'; and then wondering about nothing more until Zuraa shook me gently awake.

*

It began as an obscure candescence a few degrees to starboard, approaching slowly over the black water, but gradually picking up speed, then resolving into a long low line – a ship, hull down, its rigging filled with blazing lamps . . .

This time I shook Zuraa awake and pulled him out on to the forecastle. 'Look!'

'What?' he said, rubbing his eyes.

'Can't you see it?' I jabbed my finger at the glow.

'Oh yes. We're nearly home.'

'I mean the lamps – *the demon!*'

Zuraa laughed. 'That's Faares! It's the next island to Vaadhoo. They're turning it into a resort. They put up those lights so they can work in the dark.'

So I hadn't seen the demon, yet; only a ghost of the future.

On the quay at Vaadhoo there was a small cluster of people and a Gladiator motorcycle. Zuraa climbed on to the bike and started the engine. I got on behind him, and we rode slowly along a long straight dreamlike street of sand lined with dim-lit cuboid cottages in gardens. We turned into a darker side road, and another darker still, then stopped by a garden gate.

'That is the Jamal-al-Din Ziyaarath,' Zuraa said, pointing to a barely visible shape ahead, a little blacker than the surrounding blackness. 'This is your house,' he said, indicating a small building through the gate – teachers' accommodation, currently unoccupied and borrowed on my behalf by the well-connected Ahmad Tholal. 'And that is my house, over there.' He started the bike again, then said, '*Don't be afraid.*'

'Of . . . ?' But he'd already gone.

I stood there for a while, looking for the hovering white figures that haunt Jamal al-Din's shrine, then opened the gate. The door of the house was unlocked, the bed inside made, and I fell into it, into the melancholy luxury of sleeping long, deep and alone.

★

The Arabic *History* tells how Shaykh Muhammad Jamal al-Din, who had fled Malé to study in Yemen during the sixteenth-century Portuguese occupation, returned to revive Islamic learning in the Maldives once the occupiers were gone. From Sultan Muhammad

Thakurufaanu, expeller of the Portuguese, Jamal al-Din 'enjoyed such honour and veneration as has never been accorded to any scholar of the land before or since. And yet, because of his great humility and love of the ascetic life, he refused to remain in Malé. Instead, he sought solitude . . . and went to Vaadhoo in Huvadhoo atoll . . . where the island chief built him a house in a secluded spot . . . He died on Vaadhoo, near the Great Mosque, and his tomb there is renowned far and wide for its divine grace.' For its *karamah*, the spiritual energy that on Kilwa Kisiwani was harnessed to power curses.

It still is today, even if the shrine with its lich-gate, locked door and tattered white flags round the tomb in the little open yard behind (I could just see in, by climbing on to a nearby wall) is a poor cousin of al-Barbari's bandbox-smart *ziyaarath* in Malé. Looking at it, I remembered IB's wish to live out his life in seclusion on a distant island. Jamal al-Din succeeded in the ascetic life of the spirit where IB failed, and always would fail.

Zuraa came and found me, and we walked the few yards to the Great Mosque. The outside gave little away. Except for a suggestion of grandeur in the raised stone plinth on which the building stood, it might have been a middling-sized cricket pavilion. We climbed up some steps to the wide front veranda. 'This is where Shaykh Jamal al-Din used to sit,' Zuraa said, pointing to a spot on the raised floor. I recalled those inherited memories of IB on Kinolhas – and then saw the richness in front of me.

Almost every inch of the coral-stone façade was encrusted with that same strapwork and diapering, crisp as a piqué shirt-front, that I'd seen on the Malé mosque. Above arched sliding double doors, the geometry of the stone surface dissolved in a writhing tangle of knotwork on wooden spandrels. Inside the prayer hall, little light penetrated until Zuraa slid open another four pairs of doors, two on each side of the building. Shafts of sunlight revealed an interior unchanged since it was last remodelled at the end of the seventeenth century: plain walls, chaste turned columns and a rich dark coffered ceiling supported on double transverse beams, one above the other, each pair of beams interspaced with a row of lacquered miniature balusters resembling a rank of chessmen. Arabic inscriptions looped the loop overhead. I didn't try to make them out. It was enough just to sit on the floor in this precious casket of a building with its criss-cross of beams — dark beams of wood, bright beams of light — and its twinkling nebula of dust motes that, no doubt, were authentically seventeenth-century too. It was an astonishing place, given that we were on a fly-spot on the map with little but ocean between us and Antarctica. This really was the edge — of Islam and, with the equator only ten miles out to sea, of the northern hemisphere. I wondered what the European equivalent might be. A Wren church, decorated by Grinling Gibbons, on the island of Yell?

Back outside, Zuraa translated a metal plaque fixed to the wall of the shrine and engraved in Dhivehi script — a system of writing based on the Arabic numerals and characters, but disjointed and running away like the tracks of crabs or sea-birds. It gave Jamal al-Din's life in brief. 'No mention of him imprisoning a jinni in a bottle on Kinolhas?' I asked.

'No,' Zuraa said, smiling. 'But let's go now. There are other things to see in my country.'

There were. For the rest of the day we explored the remains of another, older stratum that lay beneath the Islamic surface of things. On Kinolhas that stratum had been all but extirpated. As I'd already begun to suspect from Zuraa's tales of the supernatural, Vaadhoo, no less than African Kilwa, was a compost-heap of beliefs.

We began with a literal heap, found after a search along forking paths through low tangled jungle. '*O fureta!*' Zuraa called as we approached it. 'You must say that to warn the bad spirits,' he explained with a laugh — a laugh into which, I thought, obtruded a small but nervous edge. 'But don't worry. The spirits mainly come here at night. You see', he said as we climbed the miniature knoll, fifteen feet high and overhung by banyan trees, 'this is the *havitta* of Vaadhoo.' The *havitta* . . . I remembered the accounts in Bell's monograph of his early twentieth-century excavations of similar mounds on other islands. They were the remains of Buddhist *dagabas* — bell-shaped, pinnacled structures that acted as giant reliquaries. We were standing on the ceremonial and spiritual navel of pre-Islamic Vaadhoo.

Antique sanctity notwithstanding, the dangling aerial roots of the banyan trees were irresistible. We swung on them, Tarzan-style — and were immediately attacked, not by furious *furetas* but by black ants that swarmed down to nip our arms. 'Look at this,' Zuraa called, brushing the ants away as he examined the ground where he'd landed. I dropped less gracefully from my own banyan root, and saw the half-buried masonry. We scrabbled in the leaf mould and uncovered it – a stepped facing-stone from the *dagaba*'s lower course, its middle step elegantly incurving, its top riser carved with a semicircle of petals, a demi-lotus. I thought of those moulded stepped plinths on which the temples of the newer religion stood. This looked like their direct stylistic ancestor.

We continued through the jungle until we emerged from the wall of green on to a bone-white beach. Zuraa pointed out some faint lines of masonry in the shallows, and said they were all that was left of a Buddhist *vihara*, or monastery, engulfed by the waves. We sat on the sand, listening to the deep distant roar of this next Big Sea – the Equatorial Channel, surging against the outer reef of the atoll. Somewhere out there was my southern goal, Fua Mulaku. 'This', Zuraa said softly, as if trying not to break the sea-spell, 'is where we saw the turtle fly away in a ball of fire.'

By now the day was on the wane, and we left the beach by a track that followed the coast a little way inland. Some distance along this a bo-tree stood among the palms and screwpines. At night, Zuraa said, it was infested by jinn . . . I couldn't quite decide to what extent he believed in the supernatural inhabitants of his island. Now, as before, they were mentioned with a laugh; but I suspected from his underlying tone that Zuraa's was a whistle-in-the-dark sort of cheerfulness. Certainly, when I happened to scuff the sand of the path with my boot a little further along the track, his warning sounded serious enough: 'Watch out. You might be kicking dust at a jinni, and if it's an infidel one it might kill you. We're always careful when we kick things or throw things or have a piss. We warn them first.' I remembered Tholal's words: *Only one thing unites this country. Not religion, but superstition.* But where did the one end and the other begin?

I remembered Tholal again soon after, when Zuraa described the appearance of *furetas* which, although they could take on many other forms, usually had big pointed teeth and a tendency to eat people who'd offended them. They sounded like classic bogeymen, conjured up to scare children the world over . . . and they also sounded like those demonic faces Tholal had shown me on the altar in the museum, with their serrated teeth and red-stained lips. I wondered if inherited memories might go back beyond Islamic holy men, to an unholier and more violent past.

Back in the village I walked alone along the long straight street. Sounds: the sunset call to prayer; creaking of *undhoali* ropes; soft laughter from an open window; a snatch of news in English – ' . . . President George W. Bush . . .' – from another planet; a boy, unseen, reciting the Qur'an in a thin melodious treble. Twilight nuzzled the coral cottages, lamplight flooded from a shop where spangled cloth – Zuraa's, I supposed – tumbled through the brown arms of Vaadhoo women.

Down on the jetty, Zuraa was speaking quietly but urgently into his mobile, his face lit by the dim glow of the screen. 'I must get a launch,' he told me when he'd finished. 'To Hadhdhunmathi atoll.'

'But that's back across the Big Sea . . .'

'Yes. But it's a friend, stabbed. In a gang fight.'

I looked at him and knew there were yet more layers that I could never penetrate.

★

The following evening we sat on the beach, waiting for a ship of blazing lamps.

Zuraa hadn't crossed the Big Sea. The stabbing, he said, wasn't as bad as he'd feared. So we'd spent the afternoon in search of more antiquities: a tiny old mosque on the shore commemorating a visit by a saint called al-Tabrizi (which Tabrizi? I knew I'd never know, and hardly even cared any more) and an overgrown *ziyaarath* deep in the jungle with an incense burner, recently used, sitting on its wall. And now we were waiting for a pre-Islamic demon.

' "Nothing's gonna change my love for you," ' Zuraa sang when his phone bleeped and lit up. 'A text from my wife,' he explained. In Pyrard's time, four centuries ago, young lovers would send each other 'Songs, Sonnets and Verse written on Coco leaves inscribed or graven with Bodkins'. Text messages did the job today.

We sat on into the night, chased ghost-pale crabs along the water's edge, and a white figure that flitted among the palms . . .

'OK, it was one of my friends, under a sheet,' Zuraa admitted. 'I didn't want you to leave without seeing at least one jinni.'

I saw him smiling in the dark and thought how right that other old chronicler was: they are mighty magicians.

★

Zuraa had been sure I'd vomit on the Equatorial Channel. Again, I hadn't, and instead had sat drinking Milo, the Maldivian national beverage, and, as Pyrard's picturesque translator put it, 'champing Bettel, for they account this braverie'. Others, less than half fishes, had vomited; but in addition to areca nuts and Milo, the Maldives Transport & Contracting Co. speedboat was well furnished with sick-bags. So much for the Big Sea: in little more than an hour we'd slap-bang-walloped over the swell, had crossed into the southern hemisphere and entered the new harbour of Fua Mulaku, this lone low-slung leviathan full three miles long, dark as a Dreadnought and bristling with trees.

And now I lay awake in the small hours of the following night, body taut, hair on end, waiting for another bout of raps and rattles from my landlady's wardrobe.

Silence. Ten minutes. Fifteen. The tension began to ebb. I lay back, eyes still wide open, while a slide-show of the day ran through my brain. The images began with Ali, Zuraa's friend, ex-policeman, ex-sea-cucumber-diver, waiting for me on the quay in a Hawaiian shirt and shades, an anvil-headed cloud crushing the horizon behind him. Part of Ali's mind seemed to be elsewhere. I assumed he'd been busy with something more important before getting instructions from Zuraa to look after me (Zuraa, I'd noticed, had power over people). My landlady, however, a small elderly woman in bushbaby spectacles, later said of him, 'Ali is drinking, drinking, drugging, drugging, hash, brown sugar, everything.' Whatever his poison, to me he was generous and kind, and he could recite verses in praise of the Prophet in both Arabic and Urdu.

He did so as we explored the island, walking along the shore to a refrain of clattering coral clinker and roaring sea – Fua Mulaku has a reef but, as Zuraa said, it is a mere few yards off shore. Beyond it the bottom plunges sheer to full fathom five hundred, enough to bring on submarine vertigo. We saw a thatched shelter a hundred feet long where the keel and ribs of a new wooden *dhoni* curved up from heaps of sawdust – no cabin cruiser this, it was like the skeleton of an ichthyosaur. And we visited a diminutive old mosque with wooden arcading that might have been the railing of a poop-deck on a man-of-war. Here too, as on Vaadhoo, the pre-Islamic substratum would rise up now and again – in the *havitta* that we climbed, surfacing among the watermelons and cabbages of market gardens; in the ablution tank of another tiny seaside mosque, converted from the pool of an older Buddhist temple; perhaps too in a friend of Ali's we met, a victim of sorcery who had discovered that all the prophets from Adam on were in fact *fandita*-masters – 'Moses, Jesus, Muhammad, all of them . . . I've sent so many emails to the FBI, the CIA, the White House, to warn them, but they never reply. *Why*?' And to round off the oddness of the day we had fish for supper that was not tuna: *katteli mas*, a bony deep-sea fish with flesh as delicate as a trout's and an ocean tang as rich as an oyster's liquor.

An eery place, Fua Mulaku. So I wasn't entirely surprised by the rattling and tapping from inside my landlady's wardrobe, even if I was too cowardly to open it and look for the source. Whether it was a rat or – as I suspected, for the rappings were distinctly rhythmic – one of the seventy-plus Maldivian sub-species of spirit,[*] I wasn't going to let it out.

*

'Somewhere between Calabria and Corfu,' wrote Lawrence Durrell at the opening of *Prospero's Cell*, 'the blue really begins.' And, I thought, it comes to its climax here – at Riba on the south-east shore of Fua Mulaku, where Ali brought me the following morning to visit an anonymous holy man buried on the beach. Wave on ocean wave, rolling blue on blue, each ending on the reef in an orgasm of spume. I shivered, and knew for certain that this wasn't IB's landfall, his Muluk. Not unless his ship – moored here for weeks, he said – had been equipped with 500-fathom cables and anchors of adamant.

*

---

[*] As listed by Andrew Forbes, these include the *odithan*, which sails on a black grindstone, the *mul-hadevi*, which lives underground and can be heard calling '*pi-pi-pi*', and the *badi fureta*, which fires a gun with a report that sounds like the cracking of an egg.

'So you've been married *ten* times?'

'Yeah, that's right,' the little fisherman said. His face screwed up into a scrotum-grin that reminded me of the late British comedy actor Sid James. Everyone here on Boli Mulaku had told me this tiny man was the champion marrier on an island famed for marriages. At first I'd thought he didn't look as if he had it in him. But he said that he'd always found *foo jehi mas*, or 'fungus fish', highly invigorating. (This, I discovered, is a type of dried tuna whose aphrodisiac properties are enhanced by a fungal bloom.) Certain women, I thought, were probably also disarmed by his voice, a rich and sexy *basso profundo* that sounded as if it came from a much bigger body – that of the late soul maestro Barry White, perhaps, singing 'Can't Get Enough of Your Love, Babe'.

Ten marriages matched the figure IB admitted to over his twenty-nine years of travelling. I asked my informant how long he'd taken to tie and untie all those matrimonial knots. 'Oh, that was just in one year,' he said, without missing a beat. 'But some were only for a few nights.'

Boli Mulaku may have seemed on first acquaintance much like any of the other islands, with its long straight swept sand street, the sea visible at both ends, with its cawing of crows and creaking of *undhoali* ropes, but I was now convinced it was IB's 'Muluk'. A convocation of elders, sitting in the shade by the beach, confirmed that Boli Mulaku had always been a port of call for ships sailing from Malé to Sri Lanka, IB's next destination, and that their venerable tradition of hospitality included marrying their women to outsiders on very easy terms. There were now no sailing ships to call; even so, around a dozen men from other atolls had wed Boli Mulaku wives over the last few years, they said, and some of them had settled here. The genetic benefits to an isolated community were obvious; in contrast both to under-populated Kinolhas and to Fua Mulaku, which had struck me as a strange and inbred place, Boli Mulaku felt like a thriving and jolly island. And in further confirmation that this was IB's Muluk, the elders prompted one of the group to speak. 'He says', their interpeter explained, 'that Ibn Battutah ordered a mosque to be built in our country, near where the telephone mast stands. He should know. He is the oldest person on Boli Mulaku.'

I went and poked around in the undergrowth by the mast, looking for solid evidence that might, for once, back up inherited memory. As it was I found nothing. But I made other discoveries on Boli Mulaku that, although less tangible, were to me hardly less important.

So far my other quarry, the ship of lamps, had eluded me. Everyone had known of it; almost everyone had known of someone who claimed to have seen it. The first-hand sources, though, were always dead or otherwise unavailable. My time and money were, as ever, running out, and even if I wasn't going to get a glimpse of the apparition myself, I wanted to meet a reliable witness who had.

Mr Na'im, owner of the island's general store, had heard tales of the *kandumathi elhun* – he called it 'Rannamari', 'the King of the Sea', after that pre-Buddhist Maldivian deity. An apparition of a lighted ship would suddenly come into view, he said, usually accompanied by a brief but violent storm. Although he had only heard the stories at second hand, he had some useful tips on how to scare the manifestation away. 'You can say filthy words to it,' he said.

'Like what?'

'"You bastard!" and things like that. And if this doesn't work, you can put *rihakuru* on your mast. That frightens it off. You know *rihakuru*?' After weeks of Maldivian food, I knew it well. And this unexpected property of the pungent tuna 'treacle' perhaps explained the Maldivians' fondness for it. It was to them what garlic is to Transylvanians.

And so it went on, the collection of stories in my notebook, each with its own evolutionary twist. Rich material, but none of it the result of personal, ocular experience. Until, that is, the end of my very last afternoon.

News came that the island's *fandita* expert, Mr Mataris Ali, had granted me an audience. (*Mataris* is Dhivehi for 'jasmine flower'; it was also the name of the white magician's house and therefore, to distinguish him from other Alis, of its occupant.) I was still hoping to fill in the other big gap in my experience of Maldivian esoterica and learn something about the workings of *fandita*; the subject had tantalized me since my stay with the former mage of Kinolhas. Like him, Mataris Ali was a small, neat, grey-haired gentleman. Unlike my Kinolhas host, he still practised his arts and, it seemed, was willing to talk about them.

'There are four fishing *dhonis* on Boli Mulaku,' he said as we sat in his courtyard in the half-light under a breadfruit tree. I noticed that both Mataris Ali and the young islander who was interpreting for me spoke in undertones. 'Sometimes, one of the owners comes to me and says, "Can you help me? My boat's not catching much." So I go and splash three buckets of water on the sides of the *dhoni*, and I recite verses from the Holy Qur'an while I do this. Sometimes I rub a piece of wood along the side of the *dhoni* too. It comes from a tree called *kandugas*.' This, then was the 'polytheism' the imam of Kinolhas railed against. I asked Mataris Ali what power the pieces of wood contained. 'None at all. *There is no power and no strength save in God*. The wood is just tradition. And I sometimes write the opening chapter of the Qur'an on one side of a frond from a coconut palm, and a prayer on the other side – "O God, give us guidance . . ." ' His Arabic was excellent; no mangled mumbo-jumbo, this.

'And does it work?' I asked, wishing he could charm away the particularly vicious mosquitoes.

'By the will of God. If I do the writing on the palm frond and put it on the *dhoni*'s keel, it's sure to find a big shoal. A few weeks ago, one of the owners came to me and said, "My *dhoni*'s not doing too well," and I just sprinkled some water on the sides of the hull, then took hold of the rudder and pronounced the name of the Most Merciful forty times . . . and later that same day the *dhoni* caught 2,700 tuna.'

Elements of pre-Islamic belief – perhaps even of pre-Buddhist animism – lived on, I suspected, in Mataris Ali's practices. But *fandita* hardly seemed to be the wicked anti-Islamic heresy the imam of Kinolhas had implied it to be, any more than Christmas crackers were a threat to Christianity. Perhaps, though, not everyone shared my liberal views. 'Does anyone . . . disapprove? I mean of what you do?' I asked, hesitantly.

For the first time in our conversation, he himself hesitated. Then he smiled. 'I only do these things in the dark. If I did them in the daylight, yes, perhaps rumours would spread . . .' Again, he paused; then continued in a voice that was almost a whisper: 'You see, in our younger days we . . . we used to do *dirty things*.' He stopped.

I wondered what I'd uncovered; if he'd had second thoughts. I nodded silently, feeling like a priest in a confessional. 'Once, I wanted to marry someone, and another man wanted to marry her too. So I went to the man on the island who was famous for *fandita* at that time, and he told me to bring a kind of bush called *kandolu*. He did *fandita* to it, then he told me to bury it at a particular spot on the beach. I married the woman.' He stopped again; I knew there was more. 'The authorities found out about it, and they asked me, "Did you do *fandita* to someone?" And I said, "Yes." And they said, "You must go to the atoll chief on Muli" – that's the main island – "and you will be punished and exiled from Boli Mulaku" . . . Now, I remember, it was a rainy day, and I couldn't sail to Muli. So I went back to the *fandita* man, and he told me to bring the young tip of a coconut palm. When I brought one, he said, "Write the Chapter of Palm Fibre on it." '

' "May the hands of Abu Lahab perish," ' I quoted, "and may he perish . . ." ' – the beginning of the maledictory chapter of the Qur'an with which the Prophet cursed his pagan uncle.

Mataris Ali picked up the verse and continued it. ' "All his worldly wealth will be of no avail to him . . ." ' Involuntarily, I shivered; then thought of the Cemetery of the Forty Shaykhs on Kilwa. 'And when I finished writing it, he said to me, "Tie it up like they tie the shroud of a dead man, and bury it on the beach, just where the waves come in." * So I did this, and no one ever said anything again about going to the atoll chief. They just forgot the whole business.' I could hear the ping of mosquitoes in the silence. 'No one has ever asked me about these dirty things before,' he said. I hadn't asked him. He'd told me. 'Now, we have thrown them all away. And we pray that God Almighty will forgive us.'

We sat in post-confessional silence. The breadfruit branches stirred noiselessly above us. I knew the interview was over. After a suitable pause, I was about to take my leave, when I realized Mataris Ali was about the only person I'd met whom I hadn't asked about *kandumathi elhun*, the ship of blazing lamps.

The question seemed to revive him. 'Yes. I saw it once,' he said,

---

* Pascal Bacuez, the ethnologist of Kilwa Kisiwani, tells me that precisely the same practice is carried out on that island. Another link across the ocean.

the strength back in his voice. 'I remember . . . we were out fishing, and the mast was a bit damaged – it was in the old days of sail. But we decided to go on. We got far out of sight of the islands, and caught a lot of fish. Then we decided to head for home. But, all of a sudden, storm clouds appeared overhead and it started raining, heavy rain. I remember, there wasn't much wind, and the rain tasted of salt. And then a huge great ship came into view, with a lot of lights hanging all over it. And we could see a lot of men on board . . . And the strangest thing is, the ship would cross in front of us, but when it disappeared behind our sail, we saw it coming again, from the same direction as before. Again and again it came and disappeared, came and disappeared.' For a long moment, even the mosquitoes fell silent. The dark itself was listening. 'At last it went away for good, and then two huge great sharks came up from underneath our boat. They kept circling us and splashing. Round and round they went, round and round, until we were back near our country. And then all at once the rain stopped, and the sharks vanished with two big splashes, and it was all over.'

★

The seaplane climbed. I watched Boli Mulaku dip away to port, and realized I was leaving behind miraculous draughts of fish, and curses buried on the beach, and phantom ships that plied the waves for ever with no hope of landfall.

To sail away to Sarandib, as IB did, would have been a less dislocating departure. Besides, I always worried about my reliance on aeroplanes. Quite apart from the size of my carbon footprint, 'this new element of mechanical hurry', as wise old Norman Douglas wrote, 'has produced a corresponding kind of traveller – a machine-made creature, devoid of the humanity of the old'. And he was only speaking of motor cars.

I kept thinking, *I should have stayed*; I might have seen it for myself, with my own eyes . . . Then again I thought, looking down through the port-hole, if IB saw the ship of lamps, he never saw this: peacock-blue sea strewn with turquoise lagoons and studded with sky-blue reefs and emerald islands; psychedelia. I watched the scene drift by below and thought of all those memories, all those tales, tenaciously evolving like the coral reefs on which they'd taken root. Perhaps there'd be more stories, more memories to hear as I travelled east with IB.

For the moment I was overhearing the more mundane conversation, from across the aisle of the plane, of a couple of Brits working in what is called, oxymoronically, the leisure industry. '. . . and you see that long skinny island? That's the Taj Exotica. They've got a presidential suite to *die* . . .'

My mind went back to my false sighting of the sea-demon, to that island of blazing lamps where Bangladeshis were sweating to build five-star fishermen's huts, expensive simulacra of simplicity; where, later, confectioners would toil to create the centrepiece of the dessert buffet – a marzipan pig, perhaps, like the one I sampled in the resort where, before I left the Maldives, I spent a night for research purposes. For me, that was a place to *die*; not for, but in, of boredom. And my mind went back also to another island, the one IB saw and fantasized about living on, cultivating his garden and his soul; and where, with his terminally itchy feet, his Sindbad Syndrome, he would soon have died of boredom as well. I wondered if that island, too, had been turned into a resort. ('They have a tradition', wrote Captain Moresby of the people of Malé in the nineteenth century, 'that they shall one day be subjected to Europeans, the population shall diminish, and their island shall gradually sink down into the deep.' As a prediction of the worst effects of the leisure industry coupled with those of global warming, the tradition might turn out to be a prophecy.)

'. . . It's called the Rehendi Suite,' the man across the aisle was saying. 'And we're talking big bucks. Like, three thousand dollars a night.'

Three thousand dollars a night . . . What price, then, a moment of freedom in a boat at midnight? Still, it was a nice touch, naming the suite after IB's sultana, Rehendi Khadijah.

Then again, bearing in mind those husbands she bumped off, maybe nice wasn't the word.

Sri Lanka

The View from Adam's Peak

That exceeding high mountain hath a pinnacle of surpassing
height which, on account of the clouds, can rarely be seen.
But God, pitying our tears, lighted it up one morning just
before the sun rose, so that we beheld it glowing with the
brightest flame.

John de' Marignolli (*c.* 1349)

Colombo – Adam's Peak

'*Perverse and foolish oft I stray'd'*– was it my imagination, or did the
vicar look at me on that line? – '*But yet in love He sought me . . .*' A
small congregation, but all lusty singers. I caught the eye of the small
Tamil woman next to me. Shortly before, we'd given each other
the sign of peace, *namaste*-style; the elegant solution, I thought, for
those in the Church of England who recoil from handshakes. ' . . .
And on His shoulder gently laid, /And home, rejoicing, brought me.'

Sir H. W. Baker's hymn was imported, and the Perpendicular
architecture of Christ Church, Colombo, and the names of the
Ceylon Rifles officers engraved in brass on the walls, and, it seemed,
the smell – essence of C of E, relabelled here Church of Ceylon,
impregnating everything from hymn-books to hassocks. But the air
that drifted in through the open doors, heavy with heat and humid-
ity and the scent of rotting frangipani and the clangour of strange
birds and the evening call to prayer from the mosque over on Slave
Island – that was no import; nor were the three very unEnglish
thunderclaps that drowned even Father Sarvananthan's resounding vowels – ' . . . *faileth neh-vaah* . . .' The great weather-system

of the Indian Ocean was on the turn, south-west monsoon taking over from north-east, yin and yang revolving head to tail in their elemental clinch. '*Good Shepherd, may I sing Thy praise/Within Thy house for eh-heh-vaah.*' Another thunderclap, perfectly timed, the full stop of that last line.

'Have you come faah?' the vicar asked me at the door. Gouts of rain began to plop on the flagstones outside.

I sketched out my more recent travels. 'But I live in Yemen. And I was born in England, in Bristol.'

'Ah, my son is currently in Bristol, through the good offices of the Church Missionary Society. I myself was recently in Leighton Buzzard . . .' Another thunderclap. We both looked up at the sky. 'I hope you've brought an umbrellaah.'

I hadn't. I said a quick farewell and walked out into the warm wet dark. At the gate I turned and waved. The vicar, chatting to a parishioner, didn't see. I looked at the two figures, backlit in the doorway, and thought of his question. Perhaps, in fact, I hadn't come far; had come no distance at all. This displaced building with its crockets and corbels, its air of decay and decorum, its quick and its dead, was where I came from.

I made it back to the Galle Face Hotel just before the sky burst. A little later, reading IB's short but busy Sri Lankan chapter over seafood curry and Lion Stout on the veranda – with the rain now crashing off the eaves, it was like dining behind a waterfall – I knew something of how IB felt, at home in a transplanted Muslim setting. The Anglican Church may never have put down such deep roots around the Indian Ocean as Islam, but we both shared in that rare pleasure of finding the familiar against an alien backdrop.

IB's Islamic landscape here in the island he knew as Sarandib – 'Serendip' – is rich and intricate. Today, it is all but unknown to the outside world. Paradoxically, though, its centrepiece is probably the most striking feature of the island's physical landscape: Adam's Peak, 'the Mountain of Sarandib,' as IB calls it, 'that goes up in the air like a pillar of smoke'. On its summit is 'the print of the blessed Foot, the Foot of our father Adam, may God bless him and grant him peace, impressed in a black rock . . . Its length is eleven spans.' Holy footprints are by no means rare. Following in IB's own footsteps, I had seen some in the outskirts of Damascus that belonged either to Moses or the Prophet Muhammad; in southern Oman, I had inspected an outsize print said to be that of Job, and for good measure some hoofprints left by the Prophet Salih's she-camel. The Hungarian orientalist Arminius Vambery, another collector of such things, made a list of holy footprint locations that includes Shiraz, Herat, Mount Sinai and Chinese Tartary. We belong to a long tradition of trackers, for Herodotus mentions a footprint of Heracles.

The identification of the Sri Lankan print with Adam is old too, and first appears in writing in a fourth-century work by a Gnostic Copt. It was probably via Coptic Egypt that the Muslims heard of it; at any rate, early Muslims and Christians agreed that it was on the summit of the mountain that Adam landed when he was cast out of Paradise. As for the credibility of later additions to the story – one, for instance, that has Adam spending 200 years on his Peak in expiation of his sins, standing on one leg, or another that claims his other foot landed in Malabar (doing the splits across 500 miles must have been excruciating, but I've measured the little-known South Indian print and found it a fair match to the Sri Lankan one in size) – the reader may judge.

In matters of faith, of course, nothing is ever straightforward. Dissenters among the later Christians claimed the footprint was not Adam's but St Thomas's; others attributed it to a eunuch missionary from Abyssinia. And, well before the connection with Adam had been made, a fugitive Sinhala king of the early first century BC had been led to the Foot by a deer and recognized it immediately as that of the Lord Buddha. In still earlier times, the whole mountain had been sacred to a local deity, Saman Deviya. Some Hindus were convinced the Foot was Shiva's, others that it was Vishnu's. The Chinese ascribed it to Pan Gu, their candidate for the first created man. The lone voice of Moses of Choreme claimed that the print was not made by the fallen Adam, but by the fallen Satan. And, as a further addition to the cast of celebrities jostling for a foothold on the Peak, some Samaritan versions of the Pentateuch have it not as the first footfall on earth of our first parent, but as the landfall of Noah's Ark. Take your pick.

Following in these multifarious footsteps, adherents of different creeds have jostled for a place on the Peak. As a site of polyphonic prayer, it is not unique; but it seems to have escaped the disharmonies of other such sites, like Jerusalem or Ayodhya. IB's visit is a good illustration of how different faiths got on. He, a Muslim, was provided by the Hindu Tamil ruler of northern Sri Lanka with four yogis and three brahmans to guide him to the Foot through territory ruled by Buddhist Sinhalas. Whatever the differences in dogma, Adam's Peak rises above them.

And yet I had to admit that all was not love, peace and toleration in the wider Sri Lankan scene. The night before, I'd arrived in the small hours at an eerily empty airport: no shops open, only one immigration officer, no taxis or buses. At first I'd put it down to a combination of the unsociable hour and the Cricket World Cup final, in which Sri Lanka were playing Australia. It was only when the sun was well up and I at last found a hollow-eyed taxi driver to take me into town that I discovered the real reason. The Tamil Tigers'* fledgling air corps had bombed an oil and gas storage depot near the airport, and the government air defences had responded so enthusiastically that, according to my driver, 'rockets were flying along the airport road'. I took this with the usual pinch. All the same, the Colombo *Daily Mirror* later reported 'the firing on a commercial airliner by over excited anti aircraft gunners'. That aircraft – luckily they'd been bad shots – was the one before mine. Airlines had suspended services; my plane was the last one in.

The rain came down with undiminished force. But if there was anywhere designed to make one feel immune to both the weather and the war outside, I thought as I went up to bed, it was the Galle Face Hotel. Framed encomia from distinguished past guests – Scandinavian royalty, Trevor Howard, an astronaut or two – promised an absence of riff-raff. Signs gave the times of High Tea or offered gentle but pointed advice – 'Please don't smoke in bed. The ashes we clear up may be yours' – and the furniture of this 'imperial caravanserai', as Jan Morris called it, from the davenport in the bar to the bureau in my bedroom, was all reassuringly dark brown. I poured myself three fingers of Aybrook & Mason coconut arrack and sat at my window, looking out on a spectral line of palms that tossed their heads like demented dervishes, listening to the lash

---

* In full, the Liberation Tigers of Tamil Eelam (LTTE).

of the rain on the panes and the surge of surf from the angry Arabian Sea. Even the most foolhardy Tiger wouldn't go flying tonight.

You only have to turn to IB's first page on Sri Lanka to see how old the conflict is. He landed at a place he calls 'Battalah', in the territory of the Tamil king of Jaffna who ruled the northern part of the island; he it is whom IB calls 'the sultan of Ceylon'. Crossing a few pages later into Sinhala territory, the ruler IB meets is classed merely as a local potentate, 'the sultan of Kunakar'. At the time of IB's arrival in 1344, the Tamil tide was high and the Sinhala on the retreat. Now, as I write, the Liberation Tigers of Tamil Eelam have apparently been annihilated. If so, it may be the end of one of the longest power-struggles in history, one whose ebb and flow began before the start of the Christian era; but I doubt it.

IB tells two stories that show how his fellow-Muslims had found their own respected place in the religious landscape of the island. The first concerns an early Persian visitor, identified by IB as the tenth-century saint Ibn Khafif of Shiraz. It was Ibn Khafif, IB says, who pioneered the route to Adam's Peak for Muslim pilgrims. When a miraculous escape from rampaging elephants revealed his divinely favoured status, 'the infidels began to revere Muslims, inviting them into their houses to eat with them and trusting them with their wives and children; to this day they pay the utmost reverence to the memory of Ibn Khafif'.

The second story tells of another Persian from Shiraz, a certain Shaykh Uthman. An elderly man living outside the Sinhala capital at the time of IB's visit, Shaykh Uthman had been the chief Muslim guide to Adam's Peak but had transgressed the law by killing a cow.

According to the statutes he should have been put to death, IB says, but in honour of his sanctity he suffered only the amputation of a hand and a foot. Moreover, 'The sultan and people of the city revere him and go to visit him.'

IB's Sri Lanka, in the words of the co-translator of the *Travels*, Professor Beckingham, 'bristles with problems'. And the three bristliest problems, to which neither Beckingham nor any other commentator has found plausible solutions, are Ibn Khafif, Shaykh Uthman and the Sinhala capital, 'Kunakar'. There is no evidence in the many hagiographies of Ibn Khafif that he ever visited Sri Lanka. That second Shirazi Persian, Shaykh Uthman, has evaded identification completely. And as for Kunakar, no fewer than four locations have been put forward for it. My aim was to try to pin down these problematic people and places along the way to Adam's Peak, then to explore the Islamic landscape of the sacred mountain.

It would be a challenge. For a start, Sri Lankan roads and place-names have always existed in a state of fluidity. 'The ways shift and alter,' observed Robert Knox, 'new ways often made and old ways stopped up.' An English mariner detained for nineteen years by a seventeenth-century king of Kandy, Knox got to know the land-scape better than any Western foreigner before him. The capital, Kandy, he says, had two further names, both in concurrent use. (Compare the situation today: officially speaking the capital is not Colombo but its suburb of Sri Jayawardenepura – itself a recent revival of the ancient place-name of a district known for centuries as Kotte.) Even the precise physical geography of the island was long a matter of guesswork. As late as 1852, the heyday of the British imperial surveyor, a huge low-lying swathe of the Sri Lankan inte-rior could still appear on the maps as '*unknown mountainous region*'.

In contrast to all these cartographic and other uncertainties, IB gives such a minute description of the two main routes up Adam's Peak as to draw a virtual map in words. I already had in my mind's eye the sacred layout of the mountain – the pools and pathways, springs and grottoes, all associated with Muslim personages both well-known and obscure. Thus al-Khadir, who is supposed to have accompanied Moses on a quest for the Fountain of Life, had given his name to a spring below the summit, while Baba Khuzi, an unknown holy wanderer who died on the Peak from loss of blood caused by leech bites, had lent his to one of the many caves along the pilgrim route.

But was this rich Islamic landscape still in place? It may well have been in Knox's seventeenth century, when there were still plenty of 'Moors' – Muslims, that is – going on pilgrimage to the Peak. Another two centuries on, however, and the Moors are almost entirely absent from William Skeen's painstaking *Adam's Peak* of 1870. As for today, I'd been able to find out precisely nothing about Muslim visitors to the holy mountain. My only hope was to approach it via the human landscape – to meet members of the community of Sri Lankan Moors, as they are still incongruously called in English. They are a significant minority, perhaps 8 per cent of the population, and I knew I'd have no trouble meeting them if the old Sinhala saying held true: 'There is no place where the Moor trader and the crow cannot be found.'

★

There were no Moors to be seen at breakfast, but the crows were out in bedraggled force, flopping out of the palms and hopping on the rain-soaked lawns, looking beadily at the breakfast buffet on the veranda. Fortunately the Galle Face Hotel had a dedicated crow-scarer, a bow-tied catapulteer. No shots were fired: one hop too close, the catapult was raised, and the offender would skulk off. They all knew the game.

I could see the temptation. Breakfast was no mere yoghurt-and-muesli, or even bacon-and-egg, affair, but the sort of heroic feast that elsewhere had disappeared with the demise of the Edwardian country house and the imperial durbar. There was kedgeree and fruit cake and beefsteaks and curries of fish and mutton . . . 'Nothing of the same class in India', wrote Sir James Tennent in his compendious *Ceylon* of 1859, 'can bear a comparison with the piquant delicacy of a curry in Ceylon, composed of fresh condiments and compounded by the skilful hand of a native.' Rise early, breakfast on such dishes, and you're ready for anything. These are the breakfasts of epic, breakfasts of the brave – or, in my case, of the greedy – eaten with sweating brow and ending with a triumphant belch.

The calorific intake of my first morning at the Galle Face

would have powered me straight up Adam's Peak. As it was I got no further than the Islamic Epigraphy section of the Colombo museum, a Palladian-imperial pile in a park that steamed as the sun sucked up last night's downpour. At first, the exhibits weren't very edifying – just a few gravestones and other inscriptions, a few isolated names and dates. The dots in the puzzle were too far apart, too indistinct, to be joined into any sort of picture. But among these fragments there was something that caught my eye. It was another Cambay monument, found at Trincomalee on the east coast, with its motif of a lamp in a niche – another milestone on the journey of Islam round the Indian Ocean. Now, though, such a find no longer surprised me. But on my way out of Epigraphy I spotted something else permeated with the history of the ocean. Guarded by two beefy dragons in its upper section, it was a slab inscribed in three different scripts, Arabic, Chinese and another which I didn't at first recognize. The label confirmed what I remembered from my reading. This was the Rosetta Stone of the monsoon world, the trilingual inscription set up in 1410 in Galle by the Triple-Jewelled Grand Eunuch of the Ming emperor, the Muslim admiral Zheng He, commander of six voyages by fleets of treasure junks to the far corners of what the Chinese called the Western Ocean. Zheng He reached East Africa in this last burst of imperial display before China turned in on itself and severed links with the outside world. This stone was the record of his passing here and – how appropriate, in the land of Adam's Peak – dedicated in Chinese to the Buddha, in Tamil to Vishnu, and in Persian to someone (presumably the Prophet Muhammad, but the letters are indistinct) who, like those Cambay stones, embodies the light of Islam. Diplomatically, it fails to record the fact that Zheng He kidnapped the Sinhala ruler of the time.

I left the museum excited by this potent relic of ocean history, but little enlightened about Islam in Sri Lanka. Nor did I learn any more round the corner in the library of the Royal Asiatic Society's Sri Lanka branch. Going through 160 years' worth of the branch's journal, it was all too easy to forget the business in hand and get sidetracked into papers like the one on 'Mysterious and Elegant Urinal Stones' – a typology of ancient monumental squat-loos. But again, as in the museum, there was next to nothing on the Islamic history of the island.

That afternoon Mr A. Denis N. Fernando, Past President of the Society, agreed with me about the futility of pure library research. The reading had, of course, to be done in the first place. One must have some idea about where to go and what to observe. As Dr Johnson said, he who would bring home the wealth of the Indies must carry the wealth of the Indies with him. 'But in the end,' Mr Fernando said, 'you must visit the places and write what you *see*. Not like these bloody jokers who do all their research on the Internet.'

'And the most important things you see are often not the things you thought you'd see,' I said, looking round the portico where we were sitting in Mr Fernando's house in Shady Grove. Casts of heads – Gandharan, Harappan, Achaemenid, Aztec – looked out on to a courtyard and a small fountain behind which, in an artfully placed mirror, appeared a doorway into a further, looking-glass garden. We were going through Mr Fernando's antiquarian maps of Sri Lanka and I was trying not to drip curried sweat on them.

Mr Fernando was the grand old man of Sri Lankan historical geography. I liked him immediately; liked the way the solid mahogany of his face, punctuated by wayward teeth and tufts of silver whiskers missed by the razor, would be set in sudden motion by a strong opinion. Extremist Tamil claims to a land of Eelam that filled the map of Sri Lanka were 'utter bullshit'. A certain well-funded international body for whom he'd done some recent consultation work were 'glorified Shylocks who want to get you by the balls, the bloody scoundrels . . .'

Together we traced IB's route through Sri Lanka, beginning with his landfall – somewhere on the Kalpitiya Peninsula, Mr Fernando thought – and his meeting with the Tamil king in nearby Puttalam, the traveller's 'Battalah'. 'There is something important for you to see there,' Mr Fernando said.

He wouldn't let on what it was. I asked about IB's mention of cinnamon on this north-east coast, 'brought down by the torrents and piled up in heaps along the shore'. It seemed a fanciful description, inspired by Sindbad and by the legends of the spices that had dropped from Paradise with Adam's fall rather than by observation. But Mr Fernando thought it possible. Before the arrival of the Dutch in the seventeenth century, cinnamon hadn't been cultivated but had grown wild in the forests. 'It's quite plausible that rivers like the Dedura Oya would have brought down branches of cinnamon to the shore,' he said. He held out no hope, however, for my observing another famous product of IB's Sri Lanka, pearls. The king of Jaffna gave IB a generous handful of them, from the pearl-dives further up that same coast in the Gulf of Mannar. I'd had a yen to meet the pearl-fishers of Sarandib since coming across a possibly fantastical account of their method: they went down to the sea bed, the twelfth-century geographer al-Zuhri says, in coffin-shaped one-man submersibles, provided with port-holes and projecting leather sleeves. But Mr Fernando told me that pearling had died out. Rivers had been dammed, he explained, the amount of calcium entering the Gulf of Mannar had dropped, and oysters were now rare and pearls too small to make commercial fishing viable. 'Besides,' he said, 'if you go up there you'll get shot at by those bloody LTTE rascals.' I mentioned a reference in the morning paper to frequent 'claymore attacks' by the Tamil Tigers on the coast road to Mannar, and was disappointed to learn that the claymores in question were not antique Scottish broadswords but a type of explosive mine.

Eventually we got to those three most troublesome features of IB's Sarandib. On his two unidentified Persians – the early, elephant-defying Ibn Khafif and the later Shaykh Uthman, judicially mutilated but revered – Mr Fernando could shed no light. 'Kunakar', however, the Sinhala capital, he was sure was the ancient city of Kurunegala, directly on the old route from the north-east coast to Adam's Peak. I had to admit that it sounded the best candidate, in terms of both location and name. The only problem was that IB said Shaykh Uthman had built a celebrated mosque outside 'Kunakar'; in my book research I hadn't been able to find anything remotely like that near Kurunegala. 'Shaykh Uthman', I said, 'is the key to Kunakar. If we can find him and his mosque or shrine, we can find the Sinhala capital of IB's time.'

Mr Fernando stuck to Kurunegala, but I was unconvinced. It seemed extraordinary that a capital city could be, effectively, lost. And yet, add to the problem of multiple place-names that of multiple claimants to the Sinhala throne in IB's time, and the fact that the seats of power were for ever shifting as the Tamil tide rolled southward, and at periods impossible to date with accuracy because of the eccentricities of early Sri Lankan chronology – not to mention the further complication that you're dealing with a record by an outsider ignorant of local language, geography and politics – and you can begin to see how a metropolis can go missing.

The location of Adam's Peak, fortunately, wasn't a matter for dispute. But even if IB's routes up and down are rich with wayside detail, their precise bearings are less clear. He climbed the mountain, he says, by the hard but meritorious 'Baba' track, and descended by the much easier 'Mama' track, the two paths taking their names from the original papa and mama, Adam and Eve. Mr Fernando had climbed Adam's Peak by no fewer than five different routes, which he now went on to describe at length.

What with the welter of place-names and the sweltering heat, I was soon lost. Two features of Peak landscape, however, stuck in my mind from Mr Fernando's comments. The first was that 'it'll be raining like bloody hell'. The other concerned the leeches that IB said infested the mountain, and had even caused the death of that Muslim pilgrim, Baba Khuzi. 'Ah, yes, the leeches . . .' Mr Fernando said, shaking his head and grinning at the same time. 'They love the rain. You'll get leeches on your peaches!'

*

It was raining like bloody hell the following morning. I awoke at six to a crash of thunder and a sound like cats-o'-nine-tails whipping at the window, and burrowed deeper under the bedclothes. Being cosily in bed in a storm is a rarely celebrated joy, the epitome of the third of the primal pleasures of sex, food and shelter. But I was on the top floor, and I soon began to have doubts about the ability of the Galle Face Hotel's roof to provide that last pleasure. There was now a constant barrage of thunder, and one drip on the ceiling rapidly became many, rapping out a mad tattoo. By seven, water was running down the wall; by quarter past I was being rained on in bed. That, and the thought of breakfast, got me up in record time. I dodged drips on the landing, climbed over a heap of collapsed ceiling on the staircase, walked into a wedding photograph in the foyer just as the flash went – bride and groom in gorgeous Kandyan costume, bedraggled Brit saying 'Whoops, sorry' at the camera – and finally, having reported the leak to reception, sat down to a restorative mutton curry and to the *Daily News*'s dry announcement, 'Pre-Monsoon Season Begins'. If this was the pre-monsoon, what was the monsoon like?

Such a morning, with the division between the elements of earth and water temporarily suspended, seemed a suitable time to visit the Maritime Museum. It wasn't on my list of destinations, but neither was it the weather for going off in search of dead Persian saints and lost cities. Besides, Mr Fernando had told me I'd have another important but mysteriously unspecified surprise there. When the rain finally eased I made my way along the Galle Face prom to Fort, the headland overlooking the harbour of Colombo, which had served for centuries as the administrative quarter of the city. With the Tamil Tigers' current flexing of their claws, Fort lived up to its name, and getting to the old harbour front meant passing through two sandbagged guard-posts that bristled with weaponry. A soldier delivered me to the museum, appropriately housed in a seventeenth-century naval warehouse. Inside, I bought a ticket from a mournful, plump-faced man behind a desk. Wordlessly, he led me down into the dark interior of the building.

The roof had leaked here too and the floor was several inches deep in water. I waited for my guide to turn on the lights, then realized they must have been put out of action by the storm. I could just make out the main exhibits, a series of displays about celebrities who had made landfall in Sri Lanka. They began with Prince Vijaya, legendary founder of the Sinhala race, disembarking in the fifth century BC. There was a large model ship, supposedly of the period, a painting of the hero's arrival that was garish even in the gloom, and an inept but jolly statue. We had passed on to the nun Sangamitta bearing her sacred cutting from the Buddha's bo-tree when my guide spoke for the first time: 'Marriedorsingle?'

'Sorry?'

'Marriedorsingle?'

'Oh, single.' Next came the Chinese Buddhist monk Fa Xian, and then the statue of a man in a long Fagin-style coat and what looked like a giant ring-doughnut on his head. I peered at the sign: '*Ibn Batuta, The Traveller Of The Middle Ages, A.D. 1344*'. Out of respect for my taciturn guide, I smothered a laugh and tried to make out the painting.

'*Marriedorsingle?*'

'I told you, *sing* – ' In a swift fluid move like a cobra's strike, the guide's hand went for my crotch and made contact: a delicate, perfectly aimed double pat. For a few more seconds I stared at the painting of IB, scarcely believing what had happened and wondering which – IB, or the groper – was Mr Fernando's surprise.

'Sorrynotinterested,' I said, shaken.

We walked on past the arrivals of the Portuguese, the Dutch and finally the British, I as nonchalantly as I could, and reached a section in which various maritime artefacts were on show in the gloom. As I was inspecting an elephant hoist, the serpentine hand struck again, this time minus the chat-up line. I parried with mongoose-like swiftness. 'Look, I'm really *not* interested,' I said, and accelerated towards the exit, water sloshing into my boots.

The groper raced past and was back behind his desk as I reached it, looking even more mournful than before. I suddenly felt sorry for him, and bought his entire stock of postcards of the IB painting. I hoped I'd made his day, even if not in quite the way he'd wanted.

The postcard shows lateen-rigged dhows at anchor on a dark bay, black stacks of cloud, crows and tossing palms, bundles of cinnamon on the bare shoulders of porters, and IB looking lost in the middle in his big bagel turban. I'd never expected to bump into my deceased fellow-traveller in this manner. Not, for that matter, had I expected anything to go for my peaches; at least not until I got to Adam's Peak.

*

There had been another deluge the following morning. I began to wonder if my trip was badly timed and if I'd be stuck in Colombo; but, looking at the papers, it seemed that this year's 'pre-monsoon' rain was exceptional. 'Rain Reigns,' said one. 'Floody Hell!' exclaimed another. (French colonialism bequeathed baguettes and croissants; the British left good governance and bad puns.)

Now, in the early evening, it was chucking it down again, and I gladly agreed to the Galle Face commissionaire's suggestion of a taxi to the Grand Mosque. In the end it made little difference. The narrow streets of the Pettah, the suq-like quarter in which the mosque is situated, were torrents in which abandoned cars sat askew. We could drive no further. I rolled up my trousers, got out on the edge of a lake where the junction of two main roads had been, and waded up to my thighs against the current.

The mosque, unsurprisingly in these diluvial circumstances, was empty. Next door, however, a sign in Arabic on a small building caught my eye: Al-Tariqah Al-Rifa'iyyah. The Rifa'i 'Way', or sufi order, made regular appearances in IB's *Travels*. He visited its head-quarters in Iraq, and witnessed its adherents' practices, including fire-walking and fire-eating. Later, in the Maldives, he gave a banquet to some Rifa'i dervishes. Instead of singing for their supper, they put on an after-dinner display in which, he says, 'they ate coals as if they were sweetmeats'. (It is unnerving to watch this: once, during a similar display at Ahmadabad in north-west India, I saw, inches before my eyes, a red-hot coal on a dervish's tongue, and heard the 'crunch' as he chewed it with a mixed expression of pain and ecstasy.) IB's Rifa'i dinner guests were on a stop-over after vis-iting Adam's Peak. If any Muslims still climbed the holy mountain in our time, the Rifa'is would surely be among them.

The small neat room inside didn't look like the sort of place where ecstatic adepts chewed live coals, skewered themselves or bit the heads off snakes. One of them, however, was in residence despite the rain, a man in his sixties with a long grey beard. And, yes, he had climbed Adam's Peak. It wasn't difficult, he said in broken Arabic, if God was with you. In eager anticipation, I showed him my list of IB's sacred spots on the mountain – the Cave of Baba Khuzi, the Spring of al-Khadir and all the rest of them. They meant nothing to him. Neither did the names of that first Muslim pioneer of the Peak, Ibn Khafif, or of that other saintly Persian, Shaykh Uthman.

'I am sorry,' he said, 'I do not know any of these places or these shaykhs. But perhaps', he added as I stood to leave, 'I will see you later this month at Daftar Jaylani?' I had heard of it. A holy site in the jungled uplands south-east of Adam's Peak, it was the setting for an annual Muslim festival. 'We go there and do . . .' The word escaped him; he mimed drumming.

★

At last the pre-monsoon seemed to have exhausted itself. I felt absolutely no guilt about starting my journey to Adam's Peak the easy way. IB was supplied not only with his three brahmans and four yogis, but also with ten other travelling companions from the king of Jaffna's entourage. In addition, he had fifteen porters and a detachment of the king's slaves as bearers for his palanquin. These comfortable bed-like litters were treated as mobile homes-from-home. Captain Buzurg, the early writer on the Indies, describes the king of Sarandib chewing betel in the royal palanquin and pissing out of it as he was carried along ('and he didn't wipe it before he put it away,' the fastidious captain observed).

Things aren't what they used to be. I had no yogis or brahmans or bearers; only a hired Nissan Sunny with Mr Athula De Silva at the wheel. But we did pick up another travelling companion – Mr Fernando, who'd decided to come for the first part of the ride. 'Before I forget,' he said as we drove off from Shady Grove, 'a present for you.' With a significant smile, he handed me a paper bag containing Hacks cough lozenges and extra-strong paracetamol tablets. I thanked him, thinking wistfully of IB's present from his Tamil host – a fistful of pearls from the Gulf of Mannar. In the event, Mr Fernando's gift would prove more useful.

'As you can see,' said Mr Fernando some time later, 'they're all Catholic buggers like me in these parts.' We were driving north along the ribbon of development that spools out northward from Colombo. Waxy figures of the Virgin, Christ, St Francis and others stood in glass shrines at regular intervals by the road. (Only now did it cross my mind that, while they both had Portuguese surnames, Mr Fernando was a Christian Tamil while my driver, to judge by his looks and his sacred dashboard accessories, was a Buddhist Sinhala.) Gradually, the suburban ribbon frayed into a sporadic village of cottages and coconut groves, and the wayside shrines diversified. Simpering waxen Virgins were joined by saccharine Buddhas and occasional Hindu temples crawling with highly-coloured deities. The aniconic Muslims rather lost out, I thought, with their drab cement mosques.

As we passed through Chilaw, fifty miles north of the capital, Mr Fernando commended IB on his rendering of the place-name. 'His "Salawat" is an excellent stab at the Sinhala name for Chilaw, "Salawata" or its variant, "Halawata". And he was remembering it donkey's years after he was here. Remarkable . . . Ah, you see that temple?' he said suddenly. 'It's dedicated to Shiva, the god of the *member*.' He cocked his forearm and gave a merry wink. 'And thereby hangs a tale. It's very popular, you see, with ladies who can't have babies. They come here and prostrate themselves on the floor in front of the sanctuary. And there's a trap-door, you see, and they've got all these potent buggers on call, perhaps half a dozen of them, and they screw them through a hole in the trap-door and the women cry out, "Oooh! Shiva is entering me!"' He winked again, as if to assure me it was all a great joke. As a travelling companion, Mr Fernando was worth any number of the king of Jaffna's courtiers.

Another thirty-five miles of coconut groves later, we reached Puttalam, scene of IB's audience with the king. Today it is a market

town overlooking a hazy lagoon where shrimpers wade far out in the shallows. A brief inspection of the place revealed that, short of a major archaeological dig and lots of luck, I would find nothing solid to connect the place with IB's arrival. Mr Fernando, however, said that there was one link. We found it on a side-road off the southern end of the main market street. It turned out to be another trilingual inscription, obscured by a tangle of parked bicycles, a sign for a tailor's and a tree. It was not, in the scheme of things, as important as Admiral Zheng He's trilingual stone, but it gave me as much pleasure to see it, for it said, in Sinhala, Tamil and Latin characters, IBUNU BATTUTA ROAD.

I wondered if this was the crucial sight of Puttalam Mr Fernando had mentioned at our first meeting. But no; it turned out there was something more important. We left the town and headed north on a bumpy single-track road – the road that led to the old pearl-dives up on the Gulf of Mannar, north of Portugal Bay. 'We can't go far,' Mr Fernando said. 'It's too dangerous with all those claymores about. But I want you to see something of what these LTTE rogues have done.'

The road passed shimmering salt-pans where an occasional sea-bird contemplated the shallow brine. Clumps of palm-frond huts stood here and there on the landward side of the road. It was a dreary landscape, flattened by heat from a sunless sky. The only relief to the eye came in the odd roadside pond studded with lilies and herons. We passed unchallenged through a security post, between sandbags and the barrels of machine guns, then turned off at a sign that said 'Salamabad Camp'. Salamabad: the Abode of Peace.

Harith was the leader of the refugees. We sat with him by a makeshift mosque in an open space among the palm huts. The sun had put in a bleary appearance; a single tree gave a little shade. Harith's dark face, framed by a white cap and a grey beard, was eloquent of long-borne resignation. It wasn't a hopeless face; but the hope, I sensed, was not for this world. In a quiet monotone he told us the history of Salamabad. In October 1990 the LTTE evicted the Muslims from all the regions under their control. His and the other hundred or so families in this camp were from Marichchukkaddi; I'd seen the place on the map – it was further up the road, one of the old pearling settlements at the southern end of the Gulf of Mannar. The Muslims of Marichchukkaddi were given twenty-four hours' notice, and could take only what they could carry. 'We were lucky,' Harith said. 'The people in Jaffna only had two hours to leave, and they only let them take 300 rupees each . . . That was all seventeen years ago. And we're still here – more than 60,000 of us if you add up all the camps round Puttalam. The government helps us out with rations, but it's not a lot. We get bits of work now and then – odd jobs, labouring on the salt-pans. *Al-hamdu li 'llah.* Praise God.'

I asked Harith what he knew about the earlier history of his community. I wanted to look for links between him and the Muslims of IB's age. 'Our ancestors on the male side were Arabs and Persians who married Tamil women,' was all he could tell me. But it was enough to show that these people too came from that great rootless family tree, that of the Muslim merchants and mariners who wandered the roads of the Indian Ocean. But over the centuries the Middle Eastern blood had been diluted, generation by generation. Harith and the other camp dwellers who'd joined us looked Tamil and spoke Tamil. Their culture was Tamil, enriched by their old cosmopolitan Muslim heritage.

'So why did they throw you out?'

Harith laughed softly, as if the answer was obvious. 'Because we're Muslims! *Al-hamdu li 'llah.*'

★

'In this area', IB remembered, 'are many elephants. But they do no harm to pilgrims and strangers on account of the *barakah*, the blessed influence, of Ibn Khafif.' We had doubled back to Chilaw and put Mr Fernando on a bus back to Colombo (I wished he could have come further; but, he said, he was too old for leeches and other adventures). Now we had turned east, along the first inland section of IB's route to Adam's Peak. The land was, as the traveller also recalled, well watered. Our road rose and fell as it crossed rolling ridges, between which heron and coot paddled in fallow paddy fields. Here and there, clusters of neat bungalows stood in carefully tended gardens. It didn't look like country for wild elephants, however well behaved.

So far I'd found out nothing about the enigmatic person IB calls Ibn Khafif, whose sanctity tamed wild beasts. As IB tells the story, Ibn Khafif came to Sarandib with thirty sufi brethren to blaze a Muslim trail to Adam's Peak. On their way to the mountain, they got lost in the jungle and ran out of food. The ravenous pilgrims decided to catch and eat an elephant calf. Ibn Khafif tried to stop them, but they ignored him and slaughtered and roasted the young victim. 'That night,' IB says, 'when they had gone to sleep, elephants converged on them from all directions. They sniffed each man, then killed him' – all except Ibn Khafif, who alone was free of the odour of their roasted baby. One of the elephants picked him up with its trunk, took him to a village and set him down in front of its inhabitants. Amazed, they took him to their king. Since that day, IB says, all Muslims have been treated honourably by the non-Muslims of Sarandib. And so it has gone on, in general – the sectarian cleansing of the Muslims of the north by their Tamil cousins being a notable exception.

IB isn't the first to tell the story of the sage and the elephants. Al-Tanukhi, a judge in tenth-century Baghdad and a contemporary of the actual Ibn Khafif, recounted a version of it in his book of tales, pious and profane, about miraculous escapes. Most famously, Rumi, the thirteenth-century founder of the Whirling Dervishes, gave it an allegorical twist in his collection of transcendental verse stories, the *Mathnawi*. In Rumi's parable, the baby elephant stands for all victims of the greed and corruption 'that stink as strongly as onions and garlic'. Its avenging mother symbolizes the prophets and saints who protect the innocent:

> She will roam a hundred leagues in quest of her children,
> > moaning and making lament.
> Fire and smoke issue from her trunk:
> > beware of hurting those cherished children of hers!

The problem is that the hero of these earlier versions of the story has no name; IB is the only narrator to link the tale with Ibn Khafif. The story would, however, be in keeping with what we know of the ascetic saint. He wrote a treatise, now lost, called *The Book of Hunger and the Suppression of Appetites*, and he practised what he preached. Once for example, shocked at having enjoyed a nibble of an almond, he deliberately bit his tongue so hard that it bled and put him off eating the rest of the nut. At the same time, if he had indeed visited Sarandib it is hard to see how every one of his hagiographers could have failed to mention the fact.

Then again, in terms of natural history the story is not as far-fetched as it may seem. Even if the area we were travelling through didn't look like elephant country, its tame appearance was deceptive. According to a newspaper article I'd read, a herd of wild elephants were even now making night raids on a village not many miles from the road we were following. Four inhabitants had been trampled to death, and several of the flimsier houses destroyed. The report spoke of a 'human–elephant conflict' caused by farmers encroaching on the elephants' traditional jungle feeding grounds. As for acts of vengeance by elephants whose young have been killed, Rumi's bereaved mother snorting fire from her trunk doesn't owe everything to poetical exaggeration. 'Next to a rogue in ferocity,' wrote S. W. Baker in *The Rifle and the Hound in Ceylon*, 'and even more persevering in the pursuit of her victim, is a female elephant when her young one has been killed.'

It remained to find evidence of the story, and memories of Ibn Khafif, here on the ground. So far it had rung no bells – neither with Mr Fernando the scholar, nor with the Rifa'i dervish of Colombo; nor, when I tried it out on them, with the Muslims of Salamabad Camp. Now, travelling along the very road that had inspired IB's telling of the tale, I stopped several times at village mosques and asked likely-looking Muslims about Ibn Khafif and the elephants. My inquiries, pitched in simplified Arabic with Athula the driver's supplementary interpreting, met with smiles, shrugs and apologies. After mosque number three or four, I was struck by a sudden image of what I was trying to do, translated into a European context: picture a Sri Lankan popping into country churches in, say, County Waterford and interrogating parish priests and sacristans, in Latin, about a little-known Italian holy man who'd passed through a thousand years ago and whose doings were recorded only by a Byzantine traveller of the time of the Palaeologues, and you have some idea of the futility of it all.

*

' . . . So onceuponatime King geegeed here, clip-clop clippety-clop. King peepholed lady Fatimah Kuraishan – ' the narrator, a handsome woman in her late thirties who could have passed for a Persian, adjusted her slipping headscarf then smiled indulgently at the tomb of Fatimah Kuraishan; her elder sister whispered a prayer at the name of their sainted ancestress. 'King say, "*Salam alaykum!* O frabjous lady! You Queen Two? To be or not to be?" I tell you honest, golly Moses! Fatimah Kuraishan say, "Yes, by God, fritter my wig!" They live lily the pink and Fatimah Kuraishan have baby, little niminy-piminy lambsy-tivy, his name Vathimi. Now, I say,

Vathimi manned, Vathimi kinged; Vathimi Muslimed. But Queen One . . . she Buddha-woman. She bloodyhelled, she say, "Vathimi must buggerup!" I seek refuge from the accursed Satan!'

'Me too,' I said, returning her surreptitious wink and enjoying the complicity. (The story-teller's words, as represented here, are an attempt at an English impression of her 'Arabic'. It *sort* of sounded like Arabic, but it was Arabic that had been exploded and stuck back together, very roughly, with a fluent glue of nonsense. I wasn't quite sure where it was all going and yet, like you do with *Finnegans Wake*, I was getting the drift. And I certainly wasn't going to let on to big sister that the great Arabist of the family was a charlatan; not when she'd virtually invented a new language.)

'Now onceuponatime Vathimi upupped Etigala. Savvy Etigala, my dear you?'

'Yes, absolutely,' I said. 'I also have upupped it.' Only this morning I'd climbed Etigala, the great 'Elephant Rock' that loomed over the city of Kurunegala.

'Vathimi say, "Calloo, callay, have a nice day, God is most great, so on so forth." But . . .' she paused, narrowed her eyes, twirled an imaginary dastardly moustache '. . . Queen One brothers upupped, backsided Vathimi – and – *gee-whizz*!' She mimed a violent two-handed shove.

'Really? No!'

'Yes, really! I tell honest my dear you! Vathimi down down deedle-um downed, harum-scarum *wheeee* . . .' This time she mimed with one hand a slow-motion fall through the air. 'Vathimi kerplunked. Vathimi kersplatted. Vathimi buggerupped. God most high have mercy on his soul.' She dabbed at one eye with a corner of her headscarf and winked at me again privily with the other eye.

'Amen to that,' I said. But for the melancholy ending of the story and the august setting of its performance – the tomb shrine of Fatimah Kuraishan, Muslim wife of the Buddhist king of Kurunegala, mother of its martyred Muslim king, Vathimi – I would have cheered. The narrator's elder sister gazed fondly at the linguistic prodigy. Athula the driver beamed. 'Her Arabic is brilliant!' he said.

'Quite astonishing,' I replied. She had outdone even the allegedly brilliant Arabic speaker IB had put on the spot in Turkey and who, when the traveller addressed him, said coolly – and in Persian, for extra effect – 'This man speaks Archaic Arabic; I am conversant only with Contemporary Arabic.' That was quick thinking. What I'd witnessed was performance poetry.

I'd given up for the time being on my quest for the elephant-charming Ibn Khafif. Now I was on the outskirts of Kurunegala, Mr Fernando's and most other commentators' candidate for IB's Sinhala capital, Kunakar. Hill-sized outcrops of gneiss dotted the landscape, most prominent among them Eel Rock, surfacing from the ground like a giant petrified submarine, and the elephant-shaped Etigala. Without much imagination, the setting of Kurunegala could be made to fit that of IB's Kunakar, a narrow valley between two hills, with a gem-bearing river nearby. The problem was that so too could the settings of the other three suggested Kunakars – Peradeniya, a few miles south-west of the later capital, Kandy; Gampola, a few more miles further south; and Ratnapura, on the far southern side of Adam's Peak. And so for that matter could the settings of dozens of other towns across the entire river-, gem- and hill-filled region of southern central Sri Lanka. It seemed impossible to pin IB's place down. Except by looking for that mutilated fourteenth-century holy man. As I had said to Mr Fernando, Shaykh Uthman was the key to Kunakar. Fatimah Kuraishan, fascinating though her story was, unlocked no doors for me.

Back in town I found the shrine of Fatimah's son, the martyred Vathimi. It was near the foot of Elephant Rock, and had been totally rebuilt a few years earlier by a pious local jeweller over the grave at the place where the unfortunate king kersplatted. Inside, ranks of tall oil lamps smoked and dripped beside Buddhistical-looking arrangements of fresh bo-tree leaves at the base of the outsize tomb. Muhammad Rasul, the guardian of the shrine, told me in English the story of the holy murder victim. His version may have been more sober than that first one I'd heard; it wasn't anywhere near as much fun.

As he was speaking, a pair of Buddhist women with uncovered heads came in, saluted the tomb with elaborate *namastes* then added to the bo-leaves. Muhammad Rasul excused himself and went and prayed for the women, who left some coins and took away with them expressions of satisfied piety. I remarked when they had gone that it must be unusual for people of other faiths to pray at the shrine of a Muslim saint. Muhammad Rasul explained that his dead charge was regarded by local Buddhists as a minor deity. He smiled at my wide-eyed look. 'In the end,' he said, 'we're all human. We must help each other. We all pray to the same God.' In the land of Adam's Peak, it was an appropriate mission-statement.

'"Our God and your God are one and the same,"' I said, quoting the Qur'an.

'"And to Him we have submitted,"' Muhammad Rasul went on, completing the verse.

There were other Buddhist visitants awaiting the benisons of the Muslim guardian, but I wanted to ask one more question – about IB's mutilated Shaykh Uthman. Like everyone else I'd questioned – and like everyone I'd asked about IB's enigmatic elephant man – Muhammad Rasul knew nothing of the story. 'But there's an old mosque this side of Gampola,' he said. 'You may learn something there. Go in peace.' I clasped his hand, and felt the first stirrings of a sense I hadn't felt so far in Sri Lanka. It was the sense of being on the right track.

★

Notwithstanding the apparent difference in their names (both of which could in any case refer to the same person, 'Shaykh' and 'Bāwā', cf. Persian 'Bābā', being interchangeable titles, while 'ᶜUthmān' is a personal name and 'Kūfī' a *nisbah* derived from the place of origin or former residence, namely the Iraqi city of al-Kūfah) there is a certain superficial resemblance between Ibn Baṭṭūṭah's account of Shaykh ᶜUthmān, mutilated by royal decree, and the popular legend of Bāwā Kūfī (reputedly d. 1344) of Kahatapitiya (formerly known as Botalagama/Botalapitiya and also Sakkaranwatta), said to have been mutilated by a royal servant. This resemblance may lend weight to the identification of Ibn Baṭṭūṭah's 'Kunakār' with the ancient city of Gampola, *c.* 1.5 miles SSW of Kahatapitiya. Moreover, given Ibn Baṭṭūṭah's tendency to represent the voiced velar stop *g*, unknown to standard Arabic, by the letter *kāf*, his Kunakār, read as 'Gunagār', may possibly reflect the fourteenth-century name of Gampola, Ganga-śri-puram, or a local contraction of it. It is unlikely, however, that either the city of Ibn Baṭṭūṭah's text or his Shaykh ʿUthmān will ever be definitively identified.

That is the conclusion to which my 'right track' led that night, ringed about by academic rigour and hedged with mays and possiblys. It isn't very satisfactory, but it's so much easier to put it like that (easier still to say nothing at all – like Professor Beckingham, whose visit a generation ago to Sri Lanka produced not a single annotation that he couldn't have picked up in a library). So much easier than to write about the fast and tangled flow of raw reality, about sitting on the steps of Bawa Kufi's mosque in the mosquito-ridden dark while all around you people are chipping in with Arabic and English fragments of the *bawa*'s story, of how he sat here under a *kitul* palm, lost in contemplation of the far prospect of Adam's Peak, of how the king's toddy-tapper came to climb the palm and found his way blocked by the ecstatic pilgrim, whose nose he cut off in anger with his toddy-knife, only to find when he came down from the palm that the nose had been miraculously restored ('A historian trying to establish the reliability of travel narratives', Professor Beckingham wrote, 'often encounters ... *ʿajā'ib* [wonders], which are plainly impossible and which he can dismiss without qualms, except for the suspicion they may arouse concerning more plausible parts of the work'), of how the toddy-tapper ran to the king, who came to Bawa Kufi beneath the *kitul* palm and asked him what he desired most, of how Bawa Kufi wished only to have a piece of land on which he might stay, here, in contemplation of the distant Peak, even such a piece as could be encompassed by the beads of his rosary, of how the king said he should ask for more, and of how Bawa Kufi flung his rosary in the air so that the beads parted and landed in a circle a mile across that gleamed with a halo of many colours; of how the flow of wonders had continued, how, for example, a British railway engineer a hundred years ago had planned to demolish Bawa Kufi's tomb-chamber, and of how Bawa Kufi appeared to him in a dream and persuaded him to put a bend in the track ('Look! You can see down there, at the bottom of the embankment, how he made it curve round the tomb ...'); of how the wonders had not ceased, of how Bawa Kufi still appears in the dreams of those who visit him, 'the dreams of Muslims, Hindus, Buddhists, perhaps in your dreams too', an old man with a hennaed beard told me in the silence after the rest had gone, his voice breaking, offering me a cheek, wet with tears, to kiss.

I left not knowing for sure if I'd found IB's Shaykh Uthman. But I did know that I'd found a corner of IB's Islamic landscape, and in Bawa Kufi a brother to IB's *babas*, pilgrims all of them, lost in contemplation of Adam's Peak. It was a landscape that, yes, bristled with problems, but one that also glinted with wonders.

*

If Bawa Kufi appeared in my dreams that night he left no imprint on my memory. Nor, I thought as we drove the next day through Gampola – IB's Kunakar, I now felt almost certain – across the Mahaveli River and past two prominent mountains that dominated the town, had I been granted the ethereal glimpse of Adam's Peak that had so captivated the old pilgrim under his *kitul* palm.

No doubt I would see it soon, for the Peak was where we were now heading, along the back-roads and under a glowering sky. At Nawalapitiya the clouds burst; at Rambukpitiya we sprinted through the downpour for curry, an ambuscade of spiciness followed by sweat, tears and welling phlegm. After lunch the rain came and went, and each bend in the road seemed to have its own nano-climate. The tea estates began, dark and dripping, shot with viridian where shafts of sunlight hit the marching ranks of bushes. Up and up we rose along the single track, past the Lonach Estate, heading for Dalhousie. With names like these, and Braemar and Glentilt, and the chill, and the mist, you could indeed have taken a very long wrong turn to Scotland; except that the greenery was a little too yallery and the spell liable to be broken by the sudden appearance of a sign in Sinhala or a banana tree. Through this vast inhabited shrubbery moved small flocks of brightly dressed tea-pluckers, the very image – even if it should be the other way round – of the picture on the PG Tips packet; until you saw the women closer up, and noticed the premature lines, the signs of over-work and under-nourishment.

Still we rose, shrubbery turning into rockery, up through the thickening mist. Still we hadn't had even the briefest glimpse of

Adam's Peak. Athula the driver wasn't a chatty type; until, that is, the subject of cricket came up, and the alleged heinous insertion of squash balls into the Australian batsmen's gloves at the World Cup final. The topic saw us through the mist to Dalhousie and the end of the road. Above the village, by all accounts, soared Adam's invisible Peak.

Now, as in IB's time, there are two main tracks up the mountain. They are no longer called after 'Baba' and 'Mama', Adam and Eve, and from what I could work out they are not the same as IB's paths in all their details; but it is still the case that one is long and hard, the other shorter and easier. 'As for this easy track,' IB says, 'it is the one by which pilgrims come down the mountain. They look on those who go up by it as if they had not undertaken the pilgrimage at all.' Naturally I would emulate IB and his contemporaries by doing it the hard way; even if, in these namby-pamby times, the vast major-ity of pilgrims go up by the easy route that starts at Dalhousie. However, too much time and food in languid latitudes – especially in the Maldives (current maximum altitude four feet) – meant that my mountain muscles were distinctly flabby. When I added to this the fact that IB did much of his pilgrimage reclining in a palanquin,[*] I felt justified in doing it the easy way first to break myself in gently.

I knew the main Buddhist pilgrimage season was over; it ends, sensibly, just before the turn of the monsoon and the onset of the rains. But I wasn't prepared for the uncanny quiet of Dalhousie. The muted burble of a stream drifted through the mist. Otherwise all was silence. Most of the buildings were shuttered against the absence of visitors. We did however find a guest house that was still open, and I was soon sitting down with a cat in my lap, a cup of tea and a blank piece of paper.

Not for the first time, I tried to make a sketch map of the mountain out of IB's description. To see, in miniature, the land that you are going to walk over, to explore the contours in your hand, to hear the names in your head, is to possess a magical key. Ever since I first lost myself in one-inch maps of the Mendips and the

---

[*] Diyabetme, a plateau on the difficult track which Skeen in his *Adam's Peak* says was the litter-limit in his time (the 1860s) and therefore probably was since long before, lies at an altitude of 3,800 feet; in vertical terms, over half-way up – the summit of Adam's Peak is 7,360 feet above sea level. I suppose it might be argued that a Nissan Sunny to Dalhousie is the equivalent of a palanquin to Diyabetme.

Hebrides, I'd felt that the very terminology of maps – 'legend', 'symbol', 'key' itself – is to do with more than physical geography. IB's list of features on the way up Adam's Peak reads like a set of passwords that unlock a scaled-down world of Islamic legend: the Cave of the Lur, the Channel of the Monkeys, the Bamboo Pool, the Old Woman's Hut, the Caves of Baba Tahir and al-Sabik and Baba Khuzi, the Seven Caves, the Hollow of the Gnostics, the Gate of the Mountain, the Cave of Iskandar, the Chain of the Profession of Faith, the Cave and Spring of al-Khadir and, finally, the climax to which it all leads – or, if you like, the symbol with which it all begins – the Foot.

It is a landscape with a strong Persian element in its population, made up of those otherwise unknown pilgrims whose names show they were from Luristan, Khuzistan and Isfahan. But it is crossed also by the tracks of those who exist beyond national boundaries. There is al-Khadir, the mysterious 'Green Man', the prototypical wanderer, and that equally seasoned traveller of multiple identities, Iskandar/Alexander the Great – who in addition to his islamicized appearance here on the Peak also pops up at the Hindu-Buddhist-Islamic shrine of Kataragama sixty miles to the south-east as a Hindu deity called Skanda, an alias of Murugan. And there is Adam himself, figuratively and literally above all distinctions of ethnicity and questions of identity. His mountain is the Tower of Babel turned upon its head: by ascending it, you transcend the confusions of race and religion and language.

IB's Peak is also home to less congenial inhabitants. First, there are the bearded monkeys to be found in the jungles round the mountain, which attack humans, he says, and have even been known to rape them.[*] I was reasonably sure of being able to defend my life and, if necessary, my honour. In truth, I was more concerned about my peaches, and the dangers to them posed by what IB calls 'the flying leech, which they call *zulu*'. This, he says, springs

---

[*] Al-Mas'udi, the tenth-century 'Arab Herodotus', reports violations of lone travellers, both female and male, by gang-raping apes in Yemen (they seem now to be extinct). Speaking, admittedly, of a bigger and stronger species than those found in Sri Lanka, Sir Richard Burton lends his dubious weight to stories of ape rape in an annotation to the *1,001 Nights*. There is, he says, 'ample reason to be frightened. The large Cynocephalus is exceedingly dangerous . . . During my four years' service on the West African Coast I heard enough to satisfy me that these powerful beasts often kill men and rape women.'

at passers-by and sucks sometimes fatal quantities of blood. 'People therefore come prepared with lemons, which they squeeze on to the leeches, making them drop off. They then scrape the place of the bite with a special wooden blade.' Following Mr Fernando's advice, I went and bought a jar of Siddhalepa, a herbal goo more effective than lemon juice, of which the few shops in Dalhousie that were still open had large stocks. Interestingly, although it claimed to alleviate a wide range of complaints from fevers and flatulence to tonsilitis and toothache, there was no mention of its anti-leech properties in the accompanying leaflet. The smell, however, was strong enough to keep off not just leeches but vampire bats, and probably vampires too. (I can still detect a trace of it in the rich and complex scent of my boots, two years on. Also, just, the ghost of a whiff of the fine crop of mould that had grown on them after my wade through the Colombo floods. Given a really discriminating nose, I could probably relive my entire hemispheric travels from the smell-map of my boots.)

Soon after dawn the following day I awoke to an amplified temple chant and to a less melodious fanfare of farts from the lavatory next to my room. I opened the window. Outside, all was fresh and clear. On this dry morning, I realized excitedly, the Peak might even be visible for the first time. The weather seemed to be confounding expectations. I remembered Mr Fernando's forecast, that it would be 'raining like bloody hell'; I remembered the assertions of the old Arab and Persian geographers, that it rained here every day 'without fail'; I remembered Robert Byron's sola topi turning, he said, into a pudding in the relentless rain; I remembered a diary entry in Skeen's *Adam's Peak* – 'Dry clothes we had long looked upon with scorn, as tokens of effeminacy and luxury' . . . and in the moments it took to remember all this, it came on to rain, at first in an English and considerate manner; and then it pissed it down.

My landlady, Mrs V. (she said to call her that, rather than attempting the Tamil tongue-twister that was her name), lent me a walking-stick and a plastic mac. I waited for a break in the downpour then girded my loins – a red and green checked sarong in an approximation of the Mackintosh tartan seemed appropriate highland gear – and set off.

The path led gently up from Dalhousie through dripping tea gardens, then widened as it reached a large Buddha reclining in a grotto of cement. Beside this was an arch, put up in 1950, an inscription said, to mark the sacred boundary of the mountain, 'in fulfilment of a vow made to Saman Deviya by Col. the Hon. Sir John Kotewala, KBE, for the successful completion of the Laxpana Hydro-Electric Works'. The Lord Buddha, a Knight of the British Empire and Saman Deviya, the pre-Buddhist tutelary deity of the Peak: none of this boded well for my exploration of IB's Islamic, Adamic landscape.

It was good, all the same, to be walking. The anti-leech precautions seemed to be working. And even the rain was holding off. There was, however, a constant water-music composed of the soft percussion of a billion drips on a ground-bass of rushing river. That deeper roar was growing in intensity. I came to the source of the crescendo, a chasm with a series of leaps and deeps and a tumbling stream, whipping itself up into a foam. A high footbridge crossed the torrent. Beyond it was a shuttered tea-house and then a sign: ANCIENT CAVE. It seemed like a first pointer to that Battutian mountainscape that I was looking for.

The sign showed the way into a ramshackle shelter. As I entered it, a pile of cloth stirred itself in the half-light and became a young man in a grungy saffron robe. He smiled and beckoned, and I followed him down a steep path above the gorge. '*Purana gallena,*' he said, indicating the cliff-face. Having done a little Sinhala homework, I knew this was the 'ancient cave'. And there it was – with a suitably ancient hermit inside to complete the picture. 'My helper,' the hermit explained in English, as he dismissed the young man.

At first it seemed surprising that a cave-dwelling ascetic should have domestic help. But, come to think of it, several of the solitary holy men IB met had servants; so did most Christian anchorites. In fact, given that a hermit, by definition, shouldn't be popping down to the corner shop in person, a home help was a necessity. Furthermore, looking round the monk's cave I realized that in fact it was reasonably well appointed. It was somewhat cramped, and blackened by centuries of smoke, but it was just high enough to stand up in. It had a sort of sleeping-platform on which we both sat, and a pile of recent-looking newspapers, a transistor radio, an altar with a seated Buddha and a small brass reliquary, and several clocks, all showing different times. '*Mors certa hora incerta*,' I said.

'Meaning?' the hermit asked.

' "You can be dead certain the clock's wrong." '

The rain came down again with renewed and gleeful vigour. Here inside there was a cosy, paraffinny fug – the cave had heating too, and, I noticed, electric lighting. The hermit showed me his identity card (he was in fact only a little older than me; I'd been misled by his lack of teeth), a photocopy of a drawing of Adam's Peak done in the 1840s by, the caption said, 'a prince namely Wilhelm Waldimer, a Persian', and a typed appeal for donations, covered in cellophane:

> Respected devotees and visitors,
>
> This is to bring to your kind and meritorious attention that I being the chief combatant of the Rock Cave and developing same to the required standard, yet, I am only being facilitated for free electricity and other flimsiest facilities.
>
> Apart from the above flimsiest relief, I do not get as much as the required support to construct, develop and maintain the above ancient Temple.
>
> In the circumstances I would pray that the triple gems bless you for internal and eternal life when you think and be a donor to full fill the above short comings of the said Temple.

Yours in religious services,
[SIGNED]
Reverend Maskeliya Seelaratna Thero

As hermits are an endangered species and need to be protected, I happily parted with a large-denomination note. In return I received a prayer, and what the hermit called a map of the mountain. The word excited me, as I'd looked long and in vain for a detailed plan of Adam's Peak. But the 'map' was not what I'd expected. On the right it showed an epicene saffron-robed Buddha accompanied by an umbrella-bearer (how sensible, I thought, looking at the rain now cascading over the cave entrance). On the left, next to a white elephant and a quartet of celestial dolly-birds, kneeled the pre-Buddhist Saman Deviya, who in the syncretic Sri Lankan account invited the Buddha up his mountain, looking more like a pretty Burne-Jones altar-boy than an ancient chthonic deity. Each group of figures hovered on a cloud, and between them rose the object that I had yet to glimpse in actuality, the steep green isosceles triangle of Adam's Peak; or, as it should be termed in this Buddhist context, Samanala, the mountain of Sri Pada, the Sacred Foot. Up the emerald triangle zigzagged a yellow road, the way punctuated by little red-roofed cottages, up and up to a pavilion on the summit, above which floated an image of the Foot itself, inscribed with hieroglyphs and encircled by a corolla of lotus petals.

How on earth to square these Buddhist co-ordinates with the Islamic ones plotted by IB, I wondered? And yet, as the hermit led me up the yellow path with his finger-tip, stopping at each schematic cottage and pronouncing the name of the pilgrim station it represented, I had the same sensation that I'd always felt while exploring IB's word-map of the Peak – that of the slow unscrolling of hallowed ground. It must have been like this, I thought, to be taken by a fourteenth-century Christian monk along the winding ways of a *mappa mundi*, to Jerusalem. Finally we reached the top, and the Foot, and I thought, We're all on different paths to the same goal. And how not, when the ways to God are as many as the souls of the sons of men?

In another break in the rain, I said farewell to the hermit and left with his blessing. I felt I'd dropped in on one of IB's holy cavemen, but seen through a different lens, through saffron-tinted spectacles.

The mountain still refused to unveil itself. To left and right dark cliffs were streaked with waterfalls; ahead, the mist began a couple of hundred feet above. The steps steepened just below the cloud-line, but with the rain holding off it was fine walking weather, and not an ape or a leech to be seen. And yet something, I sensed, was following me . . . I turned: three dogs, caught stalking and looking guilty. 'Scram!' I said. 'Piss off!' No response, except a tentative wag of tails. 'Oh, well, if you must . . .' I whistled, and we carried on up together, the dogs alternately racing ahead and falling behind. They looked as if they had some foxhound in them. It was good to have their company. We were the only pilgrims on the Peak.

We trudged on up through the thickening cloud, up steps well made but steep. And never-ending. I took them a hundred at a time, counting to twenty in the rests; then decided that a hundred was a little too much like hard work. I tried seventy; then forty, then twenty, still counting twenty in the rests. The dogs were always in front now. They would disappear into the mist, and I would eventually catch up with them, panting, as they looked back at me with pitying expressions.

We were now in a sparse cloud-forest, a monotone montane world of grey gnarled trees and silver-grey lichen and grey-green ferns that faded into the grey-white mist a few feet from the grey path – or staircase, as it now was. A world of silence, but for my laboured breath and a barely audible harmonic moan of wind in the flimsy power line that followed the track and – *BuddhaAdamShivaSamanGod save us!* – a massive rip-roaring thump of thunder that I could have sworn shook the mountain.

In moments that montane world seemed overturned and plunged into the deep. 'Raining' doesn't do it justice. Rather, the air had become an almost solid mass of water. Mrs V.'s mac was useless. The dogs were now invisible, but I could just hear them whining. 'And I told you to piss off,' I shouted. There was nothing for it but to go on through the storm.

I passed a small waterfall and for a moment considered taking shelter under it: it would have been less wet than the rain. But by now I was so thoroughly soaked that, as long as I wasn't physically washed off the mountain, it no longer mattered. At length I reached a staircase proper, with handrails, a central barrier and a sign, 'Go Upwards On Right'. The staircase was a torrent, and I was going against the flow. A small boulder crashed past, descending dutifully on the left-hand side. Eventually I came to another cave, an overhang with ferns and roots half concealing the entrance and a murky interior in which I could just make out the three shivering dogs. Inside, we shared a sodden packet of Munchees Hawaiian Cookies. A desultory inspection of the cave revealed an old inscription in a script unknown to me, but nothing in Arabic that I could see. This could be IB's Cave of Seth, I thought; but for now it was a case of any port in a storm. I hummed 'Rock of Ages' to pass the time.

The top, it turned out when the deluge had finally spent itself, was only another hundred feet above. The rain might have stopped, but the cloud was thicker than before. Ugly barrack-like buildings were crammed into the confined space. They were all locked and shuttered. Silence swirled around us with the mist. The dogs were looking particularly wretched. 'It's your own stupid fault for coming, isn't it,' I said to them. My voice sounded unnaturally loud.

A door opened right next to me, making all four of us jump, and an unshaven middle-aged man appeared, wearing nothing but a towel. 'Hello,' I said, 'I've come to visit the Foot. *Sri Pada.*'

'*Pada* no,' the man said. Seeing my puzzled look, he motioned me into the room.

Inside was another, younger man. The small space was almost filled by the three of us and two double bunks. We huddled over the glow of a small electric ring. Abruptly, the glow faded. 'Light no,' said the older man. Again, I said I'd come to see the Foot.

'*Pada* lock,' the older man said.

'Haven't you got the key?' I asked.

'Key no. Key in Colombo. *Pada* open December.'

That was seven months off. No one had told me about this. I knew it wasn't the Buddhist pilgrimage season; I'd never suspected the whole place actually shut down – even the Foot itself. 'Can't you open it?' No reaction. 'I mean for, you know, um, *money*?'

'Key in Colombo.'

I thanked the men, these spiritual lighthouse keepers on their lonely tower of rock, and went back out into the mist.

The summit of Adam's Peak is topped with a knob of dark gneiss. I climbed the steps that led up its side, to the small square silver-painted shrine that houses the Foot. The metal doors were indeed firmly padlocked. I stood by them and prayed – for the people I love, for peace.

Over by the perimeter wall of the holy enclosure, two bells hung in frames, one large, one small. I rang each one, once; the sound was muffled by moisture and cold. I noticed that my hand was perfectly white, the little hairs on it covered in hoar-mist. Beyond the wall there was nothing but white.

Adam's Peak – Daftar Jaylani

I hadn't seen the Foot, or the view from Adam's Peak. I hadn't even seen Adam's Peak; just my own feet plodding up and down 4,800 steps, with occasional snatches of cliff and forest glimpsed through gaps in the cloud. And now, despite the idea of breaking myself in gently my legs were, in a word, knackered. It had happened in the afternoon, on the descent. The path was good, I was wet and cold, I'd taken it at a lick – and suddenly, two-thirds of the way down, what had been two reasonably muscular limbs turned to quivering columns of jelly. Only Mrs V.'s stick and 'Onward Christian Soldiers' got me back to Dalhousie. I wondered if it was the mountain god Saman Deviya's revenge for the aspersions I'd cast on his chthonic machismo. But perhaps it happened to everyone. It certainly made sense of Mr Fernando's odd gift of painkillers.

Now, three days later, fortified by good curries at a hotel outside the gem-mining centre of Ratnapura and by a graded programme of walks in a nearby rubber plantation, jelly was slowly reverting to flesh and bone. But I still wasn't up to the hotel's tempting 'Try Your Luck Gem Mining Programme', which took place in a pit in a paddy field outside the gate. 'The Gents will be wearing sarongs and the Ladies will be wearing beach wrap . . . Clients who participate will be very much muddy as an aftermath of the mining.' It sounded great fun, like a cross between a lucky dip and mud wrestling. It also reminded me of a curious coda to IB's tale of Ibn Khafif and the elephants. One day, IB says, while he was staying with the local ruler after his miraculous escape, Ibn Khafif suddenly plunged into the local river and emerged holding something in each hand. He invited his host to take his pick. The ruler chose; Ibn Khafif opened his hand and revealed three huge rubies, which he gave to the king. 'No greater deformation of Ibn Khafif the ascetic, the world-renouncer, is possible,' commented Annemarie Schimmel, the late distinguished writer on Islamic mysticism, on the episode. Moreover, it seems the anecdote was borrowed from one of the Sindbad tales.

It did indeed sound fabulous. And when, during my convalescence, I read for the umpteenth time IB's account of Adam's Peak, I began to see even that in a new and sceptical light. There was no sweat in it, let alone jellied legs. According to IB, for example, the distance from the Cave of al-Khadir to the summit is two miles — two miles, that is, of steep and at times near-vertical climbing; no palanquins here. 'The custom is for pilgrims to stay at the Cave of al-Khadir for three days and to visit the Foot every morning and evening. This is what we did.' And that is all, from a man who, thirteen years earlier and in the prime of his youth, could spend six days in bed with 'the blood almost starting under my toenails' after a level half-day's walk. IB's Adam's Peak is packed with dense, guidebook detail, and devoid of aches and pains. A gnawing worm of suspicion was beginning to insinuate that it read *too* much like a guidebook; that perhaps a guidebook — or rather a human guide, most likely the maimed Shaykh Uthman — was where that account came from. In the end, I could only hope to find more evidence on my own second ascent of Adam's Peak, the hard way.

In preparation for this I went into town to try out IB's description of the route on the unsuspecting Muslims of Ratnapura. It seemed an unremarkable town, except for the number of citizens who thought they knew me. 'James?' said a young man. I shook my head. 'Hello, James!' said another. Again I shook my head, thinking I must have a *doppelgänger*. 'You are wanting to see James?' asked an older man.

'Thank you,' I said, 'but I really don't know this James.'

The man looked surprised. He took a small packet out of an inside pocket. 'You are not knowing *James*? Rubies? Sapphires?'

'Ah . . . gems.'

A little plain white mosque stood near the town clocktower. It was locked, but I could hear what sounded like a sermon going on inside. I knocked on the door. Bolts slid back and the door opened to reveal a young man with a wispy beard. He regarded me dubiously. I greeted him in Arabic; his expression changed to one of welcome. 'Come in, my brother! Come and meet the brethren!'

The brethren, all half a dozen of them, had the same wispy non-cut of beard, and shiny eyes. Something about them told me they would know nothing of the mystical, sufistical *mise-en-scène* of IB's Adam's Peak. I was right. They knew of the Foot itself – 'The Buddhists control it now,' their leader said, not looking as if he thought it a great loss – but had no inkling of the rest of the sacred landscape of the Peak. Similarly, the story of Ibn Khafif and the elephants meant nothing to them.

'So many of these old myths are just superstition and *shirk*,' the young man who'd let me in said gently. *Shirk*, 'association', particularly of holy men, with God: that puritan bugbear. 'You have heard of our organization, the Tabligh?' I had. So these were the missionaries; the reformers who'd got the cold shoulder back on Kilwa Kisiwani, I recalled. 'We are here to inform the faithful of Ratnapura about the true path of the Prophet of God, peace and blessings upon him.' They hadn't exactly picked up thousands of disciples, I noticed.

'Your Arabic is excellent,' their leader said. 'How long ago did you embrace the religion of truth, brother?'

Put on the spot like this, the only thing to do was to come clean. 'Um, well, actually, in denominational terms, I'm more a sort of *cousin* than a brother, so to speak. A follower of al-Masih, the Messiah, peace and blessings be upon him.'

They all looked deeply concerned. After a long silence, the first young man pulled out a hundred-rupee banknote from his pocket. 'Look at the date on this,' he said. It was 2003. 'Now, if you tried to pay today with currency a hundred years old, who would accept it? It's the same with religions.' The brethren were nodding vigorously in assent; the speaker warmed to his theme. 'Christianity is outdated currency. It's been superseded by Islam.'

'I agree', I said, 'that if I took a silver rupee coin from a hundred

years ago to buy something in a shop, it would probably be refused.'
More nodding of assent. 'But there are people who appreciate old
currency – not to mention its silver content – and will pay many
hundreds, perhaps thousands of times the face value for it.'

I was saved from any further parrying of parables by noon
prayers, and left with heartfelt but I think hopeless prayers for my
right guidance.

★

The following day I walked to the Maha Saman Devale, chief
temple to the *genius loci* of the mountain of Sri Pada. It was only
six level miles there and back, but I still couldn't quite believe that
my legs had regained their old solidity and I wanted to test them.
Some syncretic part of me also needed to propitiate the aboriginal
guardian deity of Adam's Peak before the tough ascent from the
Ratnapura side, especially as I'd found out nothing about
the Islamic landscape of the route, not even from those Muslims
of the town who were – in Tablighi eyes – mired in *shirk* and
superstition.

On three altars in the central shrine of Saman's temple sat platters
of fruit – pineapples, wood-apples, limes, papayas, bananas, coconuts
– and others with artfully arranged bo-tree leaves. With matter-of-
fact grace, chanting white-clad priests took the offertory plates, one
by one, into an inner sanctum behind a painting of a winsome
Saman and his white elephant. The supplicants, the donors of this
greengrocery, squatted and looked on, their hands in attitudes of
prayer. The idea of offering fruit to a mountain-god was delight-
fully primeval. Then again, so are Harvest Festivals.

I had no offering. But perhaps my presence had been noted on
high. Afterwards, as I stood with one of the priests on a terrace and
mentioned that I'd already climbed Saman Deviya's mountain but
had still not actually seen it, he said simply, 'Look.'

And there it was, at last, a luminous triangle riding like a silver sail
above a deep green rolling sea of jungle.

★

'*Yuck* . . . What do you call them in Sinhala?' I asked Dharmawardana,
my guide to the hard route up Adam's Peak. We weren't far into

my second ascent of the mountain, and already he was having to de-leech me.

'*Kudella*,' he said, flicking off the last of the uninvited drinkers from my bare calf. He used his fingers; no nonsense with lemon juice and wooden blades.

'*Kudella*,' I repeated. A charming name for a revolting creature. I'd forgotten to apply the Siddhalepa, and had sprouted a small crop of them – luckily, nowhere near my peaches – in an abortive attempt to find a way up to a creeper-hung cave high above the path. They were each an inch or more long and, not yet tumescent, about the thickness of a stout bootlace.

The idea of finding a cave, or some other feature, with an Arabic inscription that might fix the co-ordinates of one of IB's sites was highly appealing. The trouble was, almost every flattish surface within reach of the path had been written and rewritten on in various scripts and at various stages in history, and from what looked to be very ancient history up to the most recent times (later, Dharmawardana showed me his girlfriend's name, inscribed lovingly by him in red paint on a concrete step). But I had yet to find anything at all in Arabic, let alone a sign pointing to the Cave of Baba Khuzi or any of his Muslim fellow-hermits. Now, looking at my blood-streaked legs and recalling that martyr to leeches, I asked Dharmawardana if there was any danger of the bites getting infected.

'*Kudella*, cobra, spider, elephant, wanderoo no problem on this path.'

'How do you mean?'

'*Sri Pada*,' he replied, looking up into the cloud ahead. 'No problem for pilgrim.' We were under the aegis of the Noble Foot. *They shall not hurt nor destroy in all my holy mountain.*

Already in the semi-cultivated lower stages of our climb, as we followed the gorge of the Kalu Ganga up through patches of cinnamon plantation and stands of *kitul* palm, we'd encountered some of the rich and peaceable wildlife of Adam's Peak. A muscular lizard, five feet long, had crash-landed from a tree and streaked across the path in front of us – some kind of monitor, I guessed, although Dharmawardana called it a 'wild crocodile'. Further on, a flurry of leaves overhead revealed a trio of wanderoos in a jack-tree – IB's

bearded rapist apes . . . Dharmawardana called out in imitation of their whooping cry, but they remained looking mutely down at us like Victorian aldermen in Dundreary whiskers. As the last of the cultivation gave way to jungle we came across a giant squirrel bouncing noisily from branch to branch above, and more troupes of wanderoos that bounded through the forest trees unseen, but for an occasional glimpse of slender limbs. Dharmawardana laughed at the idea of them being dangerous. There was, however, an exception to the list of eirenic mountain creatures. Higher up, I tried calling out to a gang of *rilava* macaques but was immediately silenced by my guide. 'No!' he whispered. 'They attack. I am frightened.' I wondered if IB had confused the two species.

I trusted Dharmawardana's judgement. He knew the montane jungle well from his work as a postman delivering letters on foot to isolated hamlets in its lower reaches. He also worked as a pilgrim guide in the season. (The incorruptible guardians of the Foot, he said, were his friends; I was hoping he'd be able to get me a private viewing.) There was only one thing that annoyed me about him. In our 6,500-foot climb, much of which he did shirtless, and all of it in flip-flops, I never saw so much as a pinhead of sweat on his stringy body. 'I am small,' he said when I pointed this out, 'and cool.'

I'd first met Dharmawardana a few days before in his home village of Palabaddala in the foothills of the Peak. The place, he told me, was famous for a miracle that took place there long ago. A poor woman arrived in the village, a pilgrim to the Peak, with no other food than some leaves that she'd scavenged from the jungle. Opening her meagre lunch-pack, she was astonished to find that the leaves had turned into rice and vegetable curry – hence 'Pala-bat-dola' or Palabaddala, the Place of Rice and Vegetables. Skeen, hearing the same tale 150 years ago, identified the village with IB's 'House of the Old Woman'. The identification looks plausible. Palabaddala is, and feels like, IB's description of the place as 'the end of the inhabited parts'.

On my arrival in Palabaddala, attempts to identify other IB sites had got nowhere. The courtyard of the village's Saman temple, where I'd been trying to interrogate the priest, wasn't the most auspicious place to find out about Islamic holy sites. Even more of a problem was the lack of shared language. Only as an afterthought, I asked if anyone spoke Arabic; a pointless question in an all-Buddhist settlement – except that one of the villagers present suddenly smiled and motioned to me to follow him.

'*Ahlan wa sahlan!*' Mrs Pereira exclaimed. '*Fawq al-ayn wa fawq al-ra's!*' My saviour's wife, who had worked for twelve years in the Gulf as maid to a judge's family, could not only welcome me 'upon eye and head', as the saying goes; she could rattle away in fluent if sometimes ungrammatical Arabic, with her husband looking proudly on. She found me Dharmawardana and, now my legs were finally back in shape, the two of us had set off this morning. '*Fi aman Allah!*' she called after us: go in the safe-keeping of God. So odd, I thought, this Islamic benediction, coming from a Sinhala Buddhist with a Christian Portuguese surname. And yet, given that we were heading for that patch of common ground, Adam's Peak, not inappropriate.

In English conversation Dharmawardana was no Dr Johnson, but he was keen to improve. His main items of mountaineering equipment were a Sinhala-English dictionary and a small Indian-produced book of chat-up lines, both of which he perused while zigzagging up the path in the lower, easier stages of our climb.

In the few weeks since the end of the pilgrim season, however, the jungle had begun to reclaim the path, covering it with leaf mould and blocking it with fallen branches, and even sure-footed Dharmawardana had to watch his step. Now and again we had to avoid the webs of enormous black and yellow spiders that spanned

our way – no gossamer creations, these, but strong and springy barriers. ('More than once in riding,' Tennent remembered in his
Ceylon, 'I have had my hat lifted off my head by a single thread.')
Off the path, as I'd found in my failed attempt to get to the cave,
the undergrowth was impenetrable.

We passed an empty open-sided rest hall for pilgrims. Shortly
after, Dharmawardana pointed to an overgrown side-track and said
it led to something I should see. Looking at the dense verdure, I
decided on a major application of Siddhalepa. As I rolled down my
right sock, I found we'd missed one of the earlier leeches. It was
now the size of a large English garden slug. Dharmawardana dealt it
a sharp flick; I watched it lope off, dazed but sated, towards the
nearest foliage, its head still delicately petite, its body engorged with
a generous dram of my blood. Fifty yards along the small track we
came to a spring, the water trickling slowly out of a rock-face and
down into an ancient-looking cistern built of finely dressed stones;
beyond the cistern was a cave-like overhang. It was a very Battutian
ensemble of features. I checked the text: there was indeed a cave by
a spring, but clearly much nearer the summit. That was still a long
way away.

The site of the pilgrim hall by the turn-off, Dharmawardana said,
was called Lihini-hela. 'I show why,' he said. A little further on
along the main track, he led me a few yards over to the right.
There, fenced off by a few spindly sticks and a strand or two of
rusting barbed wire, we came upon a stupendous precipice. 'Lihini
was beautiful girl,' my guide said. 'She fall here. Now I call her.'
With all his might he yelled across the chasm, '*Lihini akkaaa!*'
Several seconds later, the echo bounced back from a great grey
sounding-board of cliff a thousand yards away. 'Her spirit answer,
"*Ennaaa!*" meaning, "Coming!"' We called her once again,
together, and again she answered back across the gulf.

My legs were now their old selves again, and by imitating
Dharmawardana's zigzag ascent I fell into an easy rhythm of climbing. As on the Dalhousie track, the concrete steps were numbered
at every hundredth stair. As the total mounted, I began to wonder
whether the difficulties of the path were exaggerated. But soon
after step number 3,600, cement gave way to stone blocks in
various states of disrepair. Many had been prised apart by roots,

others washed away entirely. The higher we got, the worse the path became. And there was now almost no respite from the upward angle. A few delicious flat yards, where we stepped across the new-born Kalu Ganga – a foot-wide trickle here, a broad estuary where it flowed into the Arabian Sea – left me pathetically grateful. The head of a col gave us another few level paces. Dharmawardana called it 'Elephant Pass', and pointed out a track through the jungle crossing ours at a right angle, along which the beasts came on an annual trek north. Not long after, the canopy of trees and clouds parted, and there it was above us – the steep cone of the Peak with a gleam of silver temple on its summit. From here, on a still day in the pilgrimage season, Dharmawardana said, you could hear the temple bells.

That glimpse gave me a burst of upward energy. It was immediately dissipated by the news that we were barely half-way to the top, and by the realization that the path was getting even worse. On we slogged, labouring up a staircase of rocks and roots, at times an entirely arboreal ladder, where a moment's inattention would have meant a sprained ankle or worse. Eventually the forest cleared once more, and we were on a plateau composed of enormous flat boulders riven by deep splits. This was Diyabetme, the furthest limit to which litter-bearers would climb. A stream meandered through the fissures in a series of bubbling waterfalls. Some low bushes were draped with long tatty hanks of cotton yarn. 'Lord Buddha mending his clothes here,' Dharmawardana explained, 'so pilgrims leaving threads.' This place, he also told me, was on the watershed. We ate our picnic lunch – cold rice with boiled jack-fruit – where the waters parted, heading on one side for the Arabian Sea and on the other for the Bay of Bengal.

Here, as all along the way, I continued my exploration of the more accessible cave-like overhangs and undercuttings; but there were no Arabic inscriptions, nothing that could have served even tentatively to triangulate the sacred mountain with IB's word-map of it. Soon, however, we came to something that seemed to have come straight out of his book. It was a bald and near-perpendicular mass of rock, into which two successive flights of steps had been cut. I carefully counted eight, then ninety-seven steps (Skeen made the figures nine and a hundred, noting that 'a hundred different people may count them, they say, but their numbers will always differ'). 'The people of old', I read in IB's account when we reached the top, 'carved into the mountain a sort of staircase by which one can ascend, and fixed into the rock stanchions of iron on which they suspended chains for those climbing to hold on to.' In places there was a newish-looking iron handrail. But on the opposite side of the steps a line of clearly ancient holes had been cut into the rock; surely, I thought, for upright posts. Other early writers on Adam's Peak ascribed its chains and other ironmongery to Alexander the Great. IB himself mentions a Pass of Iskandar. And when Dharmawardana told me that the beetling outcrop we had just climbed was called Dharmaraja-gala, 'the Rock of the Righteous King', I wondered whether I had stumbled on, or up, that very feature of IB's topography; whether its Sinhala name commemorated the Macedonian monarch who in popular Perso-Islamic legend was a paragon of righteousness. 'Look,' said Dharmawardana, 'Dharmaraja, praying to Saman.' There, incised in the stone at the head of the stairs, was a kneeling male figure, his hands joined in salutation above his head, pointing to the invisible summit.

From here on, more of IB's co-ordinates began to fall putatively into place. Not long after the Rock of the Righteous King there was a short descent with a house-sized boulder on the left, furry with moss, and, below it, a deep and cavernous recess, overgrown and impenetrable. Was this IB's Cave of al-Isfahani? His next feature, an unnamed spring, might have been the source of a small brook called by Dharmawardana Poddu-gangula-oya, the Stream of the Little Waterfall, which emerged from a rock and flowed into a dam. A pump-house raised water from here to the summit.

That summit had been wrapped in cloud since the one glimpse we'd been granted. And now we ourselves crossed the cloud-line. For the first time since my original, sodden ascent, I felt the chill. The short trail of Battutian discoveries also went cold. And as we plodded and scrambled on, ever upward, I kept thinking that my attempts to see IB's landscape on the ground were themselves veiled in a mist of supposition; that the only indisputable features of his scenery were the mountain itself, and the Foot; that I was indulging in a pointless exercise in evocation, orienteering by a forgotten Islamic map whose topography would, inevitably, remain as elusive as the vapours that swirled around us. It was like using Coleridge as a guide to Xanadu.

The mist thickened as we reached the pilgrim station of Heramitipana, the place, Dharmawardana explained, where you raise your *heramitiya*, your walking-stick, and pray to Saman for the strength to do the last and hardest part of the climb. Many pilgrims had also stopped here for other reasons: Heramitipana stank of human shit, and rats rustled in the piles of detritus from thousands of last season's picnics. Three hangar-like rest halls loomed out of the fog among the ghostly and twisted forms of cloud-forest trees. From one of these a crow swooped down to snatch a rat, which it devoured back on its perch. Death-squeals echoed through the desolation.

It wasn't a place to linger in. A short descent took us down into a depression. I looked again at IB's text: taking the Rock of the Righteous King – if that was the same as IB's Pass of Alexander – as my last fix, the depression looked distinctly like his Hollow of the Gnostics, 'close by the gateway of the Peak' . . . and there, rising in the mist, was indeed a gateway, the counterpart to that concrete votive gate on the easy side of the mountain. It was a *makara torana* or 'dragon arch', such as I'd seen at Buddhist temples elsewhere in Sri Lanka – a cement archway in which two composite monsters supported a roundel containing a seated Buddha – and it was clearly of recent construction. At the same time, I reflected, one element of sacred topography that was likely to remain stable while hermits came and went, and pilgrim halls collapsed, was the limit of the temenos, the holy boundary of the Peak.

We walked on, up through the dragon arch, as if entering the illuminated initial of a bestiary. Another sudden break in the cloud: this time the silver temple glinted against a deep blue slash of sky, almost vertically above us and yet still unattainably high. The perspective was dizzying, like Pozzo's *trompe l'oeil* ceiling of Sant' Ignazio. I half expected to see a foreshortened Adam caught in his fall from Paradise, surrounded by hovering saints and baroque Bodhisattvas; and then the cloud closed in again.

The light was fading and our ears were popping as we reached the base of the rock cone that crowns the Peak, the path up this side of which is called Ahasgawa – 'Lifting-sky Climbing', in

Dharmawardana's translation. This was the supreme challenge for the pilgrims, who would haul themselves up this final, almost sheer stretch in fear of their lives; that is, until 'Walkers, Son & Co., Engineers, Ceylon' dynamited a path and installed concrete steps and handrails, according to a plate at the bottom of the staircase. The steps were no doubt less meritorious, but also something of a relief; especially, I realized, when we got to a section that led round and up a corner of rock, fearsomely exposed and called Hulang-kapolla – 'Wind-gap', Dharmawardana explained, trying to subdue the riffling pages of his dictionary. An unbroken blast blew here, and a bird shrieked up past us with a Doppler glissando, like some fragment torn from the air itself. 'Now wind is not bad,' Dharmawardana called through the gale. 'Sometimes you go like this –' and he went on all fours.

Perhaps fortunately, the drop below us was invisible. For this, I realized, was the surest point in IB's co-ordinates so far. 'There are ten stretches of chain . . .' he wrote, 'and the tenth is called "the Chain of the Profession of Faith" because when one reaches it and looks down, one is overcome by terrors and recites the Profession ['*There is no god but God!*'] from fear of falling.' I read the passage to Dharmawardana, and he immediately began to scrabble in the undergrowth beside the path – and revealed, ingrown with roots, a tangle of rusted links: a chain! I scrabbled too and we found more, here and higher up, in different sizes and shapes, some links as long as ten inches, a few S-shaped, all in different states of decay, some all but rusted through. They might have been of any age or ages; they were all links with a past that began before Walkers, Son & Co. and went back via IB to that enigmatic Alexander and a vanishing-point in the fog of pre-history.

We reached the top ten hours after we'd set out, to a well-timed parting of the clouds. It disclosed the twin summits of Bena-Samanala, the lower and demon-haunted sister of the Peak, rising beneath us like a gaping whale, barnacled with jungle, from a sea of mist; and then the sinister black conning-tower of Kunudiya; and beyond that, the setting sun.

Adam's Peak may not be, as IB and many of the old geographers thought, 'one of the highest mountains on earth'. But up in this crow's nest, riding on an ocean of cloud, it felt like it.

*

Next morning there was no cloud. The clarity was disconcerting – as if you'd gone to the seaside and found the sea drained dry, revealing range on range of submarine mountains that receded in gradations of grey. As the sun edged up behind us, there was a single distant glint of gold: 'Maha Saman Devale,' Dharmawardana said – the main temple of the mountain god, from where I'd had my first sight of the Peak. Soon the Peak itself appeared, or rather the isosceles triangle of its silhouette, projected on to the range behind Bena-Samanala. 'Look!' Dharmawardana whispered. 'The triple-James shadow!' But for me its mystical significance was lost in a wider world of colours and dimensions that were deepening in the warmth of the rising sun, until the nearer summits seemed so close and clear that by some trick of perspective you could have reached out and touched them.

Rustlings from immediately below diverted my attention from the sublime to a moraine of trash that the recent pilgrim season had left hanging on the lip of the Peak. It was home to hundreds of cavorting rats. I suddenly remembered the two new words of Sinhala I'd learned the night before: *pusa*, 'cat', and *miya*, 'rat'. The guards, the same two as on my first ascent, had given us a mound of rice and dhal in their little room, and we'd turned in early to sleep while our hosts watched TV. I was just dropping off when there was a muffled cry from Dharmawardana, up on the top bunk, and *miya* shot down the wall and under my bed. I felt it would be bad manners to mention this to our hosts, but they'd seen the intruder too. There ensued a good twenty minutes of poking and prodding, until at last *miya* was prised from the last of its hiding places and *pusa*, a small grey tabby, called in to deliver the slow *coup de grâce*. With a fine delicacy of feeling for the veg-etarian majority, *pusa* devoured *miya* out of sight, under my bed; but not out of hearing. When the squeals, growls and crunches had finally ceased, I turned to the wall again – and was joined by *pusa*, who snuggled into my neck, smelling of freshly killed *miya*, and purred herself to sleep. I hadn't the heart to eject her; nor to complain to our hosts who, justifiably proud of their now un-broken electricity supply, kept the TV on at full volume into the small hours and five high-wattage bulbs burning all night, thus enticing most of the local fly population to do their bit towards this Guantánamo of sleep-deprivation.

And now, the trials of the night behind us, we looked out over a world awakening into shape and colour, iridescent with jungle greens and blues. The old Arab geographers hadn't exaggerated much when they spoke of Adam's Peak being suffused with a sheen of light the colour of peacock feathers. And though I had yet to hear the birds one of these authorities said lived there, 'the size of doves, variegated in colour, that sing the praises of God in Arabic and Syriac', I realized that another, later geographer was right – Purchas, who thought it 'no marvell, if sense and sensualitie have heere stumbled on a paradise'.

But did IB look on this same prospect? The more I thought about it, the more the doubts multiplied. After the final chain, that terrify-ing Chain of the Profession of Faith, he says, you have a *seven-mile* walk to the last pilgrim station; and then that apparently easy twice-daily four-mile round trip to the Foot. I'd already looked at the text every which way, played with readings and timings and distances. Now, *in situ*, the only conclusion I could reach was that IB had subjected the whole orography of Adam's Peak to gross deformation. What he had seen from afar as 'a pillar of smoke' became, in his distorted close-up view, a broad steep-sided plateau.

Now, there was always the possibility that he'd forgotten the shape of this, one of the world's most memorable mountains – up there in profile, if not in elevation, with the Matterhorn. If so, it wouldn't be the first time I'd diagnosed a sort of spatial dyslexia in him, an impressive, at times astonishing ability to recall the elements of a scene but not the relationships between them. And yet, even if we let him off on this count, there was still that lack of sweat, that lack of fear. Climbing up that final chain, IB lets slip, 'one is overcome by terrors', not 'I was . . .' I began to wonder once more whether his whole description of Adam's Peak might be second-hand; whether in fact I'd been following a trail of phantom footsteps.

If I was right and IB hadn't climbed the Peak, then why would he claim that he had? For those who leap to his defence in moments of doubt, the usual whipping-boy is his editor Ibn Juzayy, ever ready with an interpolation and perhaps not above turning a second-hand account into a first-person one. Then again, IB himself is not beyond suspicion. Perhaps the best that can be said is what the French critic Alain Niderst once wrote, that travel books sometimes have to tell lies in order to tell the truth; or, in this case, that you could hardly write truthfully about Sarandib for a fourteenth-century Muslim readership without making Adam's Peak its centrepiece and, moreover, that you could hardly write about the Peak at second hand – in travel, unlike descriptive geography, it is the personal experience that validates the journey. Travel books are the literary equivalent of pilgrimages.

If IB didn't get to see in person the goal of this particular pilgrimage, the Foot, then neither did I. The key really was in Colombo. As Dharmawardana and I said our various prayers together before the padlocked doors, I realized that my double ascent added up, in vertical terms, to not far short of half an Everest. I also realized something else: that, whether I'd been following IB's actual foot-steps or not, he had led me somewhere I hadn't expected to go – back beyond Odysseus, beyond Noah and Gilgamesh, to the very first landfall, the very first footfall in the history of travel. And whether a vague five-foot-long depression in a rock is an actual human footprint or not, whether you prefer Adam or an upright ape to be your ancestor, it is a potent allegory, that giant step. It is the genesis of the human journey, the spot from which all these journeys of ours spin out.

Some travellers have to lie in order to tell the truth. Others have to fail to see what they came in search of in order to find what they were really looking for.

*

Only scattered sounds and images remain from our descent. A noisy rustling in the cane-brakes; wild pig, Dharmawardana thought. A dry clunk then a rasping blast of noise as a cicada fell on my head from a forest tree. And, just below the top of Elephant Pass, a thrill-ing sight: a sinuous metallic streak of indigo – a cobra, crossing the path a few feet in front of us, spinning his own silent journey through the jungle. When Adam fell, they say, some of the spices of Paradise fell with him. So did the serpent.

We trod the sinuous way, down and down to the cinnamon groves, the first cock-crow, the first faint sound of a lorry labouring through the tea gardens.

'*Subhan Allah!*' said Mrs Pereira in her excellent Arabic. '*Huwa yusa'id al-nas fi 'l-jabal.*' Glory to God! He helps people on the mountain.

*

At the Rest House in Balangoda, a small town twenty miles south-east of Adam's Peak, evenings passed slowly, measured in Lion Lagers and mosquito bites. My room was a touch gecko-shitty and my style somewhat cramped by the notice on my door, which not only stipulated that guests 'shall be dressed pleasantly and well behaved at all times' but also warned that they 'shall not use their rooms for any immoral purpose'. Otherwise it was a fine establish-ment that offered facilities not to be found in Hiltons and Novotels, such as Bed Tea, Servants' Meals and an elderly and cadaverous waiter who could discourse on the relative literary merits of Bram Stoker and Mary Shelley. And all for less than three pounds sterling a night. I'd therefore trusted the manager's judgement when he urged me not to waste my money on an autorickshaw to the jungle site of the Muslim festival at Daftar Jaylani, but to go on the bus. It was advice I soon regretted taking.

'Oh, that's all right, thank you very much,' I said to the woman who'd offered me her seat (*Lord*, I wondered, *how old does she think I am?*), 'I enjoy standing.' I enjoyed standing for about thirty seconds; by the end of which a sudden last-minute influx of passengers left at least five hanging out of the door and the crush inside so tight that only my sweaty fingertips had a hold on the bar, while my feet had moved further and further back until I stood at a mad balletic angle, held up only by the bodies of my fellow-travellers and with my crotch pressed into the kind woman's shoulder. Worse, I was in the inescapable embrace of a skeletal old man, whose stick-like arms were clamped round my neck and, I noticed with horror, covered with swollen, ashen lumps. He looked like a Lazarus who'd been left too long. I spent the next hour wondering if the bubonic plague had erupted in rural Sri Lanka, and glimpsing fragments of roadside ditch between the top of the window and the jackfruit breasts of a hefty woman feeding a hefty baby, before being spat out, shattered and sweating, at the turn-off to Daftar Jaylani.

In the company of an excited group of Muslim passengers from the bus, I walked along the lane that led to the site of the festival and soon revived. Every few seconds a minibus or autorickshaw overtook us, packed with more Muslims, chanting and clapping. I thought back to Adam's Peak, thirty miles to the north-west, to the padlocked Foot, the bells muffled by mist. It too had resounded to festive chants until the turn of the monsoon had ended the Buddhist pilgrimage season. But to Muslims, the mountain seemed now to be permanently off-season. The Islamic identities of its sacred caves and holy springs, recorded by IB, were forgotten. I had tried to carry on the record where IB left off and, except for a few guesses, had failed. I suppose I was, in Lévi-Strauss's estimation, a thoroughly modern traveller, 'chasing after the vestiges of a vanished reality'.

Is it a loss to the sum of knowledge if the location of a cave some unknown Persian gave his name to 700 years ago has slipped from human memory? It is, if Tim Robinson is right in his *Stones of Aran*, one of the richest records of place ever written: 'If we think of all the placenames humanity has applied to the surface of this planet as constituting a single vast fingerprint, can we neglect even its most minute particularities in trying to identify ourselves?' That fingerprint is the cumulative mark to which that first trace, Adam's footprint, leads.

Then again, to have pinpointed all those places would have been satisfying; but I wondered if the satisfaction would have been ultimately empty, like that of working out a tricky equation – a 3-D sudoku, perhaps, with the added dimension of time, but still no more than an antiquarian puzzle. The content, the meaning, would only have been there if the sacred caves and holy springs had still been sanctified in the minds of living Muslims, had been inhabited, if not by hermits, then at least by memories. Those hallowed places had been deconsecrated by oblivion; unless – and this was my hope – I could turn up some recollection of IB's sacred landscape among the thousands who converged on Daftar Jaylani for one of Sri Lanka's biggest Muslim festivals.

The tens of thousands: men, women, children, of all ages from totterers to teenagers, from greybeards to babies at breasts, camping under trees, umbrellas, awnings, overhangs, milling, sitting, sleeping. Like the boat people of the Maldives, they might at first glance have been refugees – and then you noticed the smiles, the excited chatter, the gaudy toys and fizzy pop, the fizz of expectancy. The atmosphere was more rock-concert than refugee-camp.

Joined by a small herd of bullocks – sacrificial animals, one of the bus passengers explained – we climbed up a flight of shallow steps hewn in a great outcrop of rock (it bore more than a passing resemblance to that possible Pass of Alexander on Adam's Peak), then entered the sacred confines of Daftar Jaylani through a gateway; no dragon-arch, this, of course, but topped by two-dimensional Islamic domes. The path then descended, passing a rest hall and kitchens before skirting cliffs and the open outer part of a mosque built into a cavernous overhang. The press of pilgrims increased; families were camping in the mosque itself, and on ledges in the cliff-face above. People looked at me with benign curiosity – and I suddenly realized that, among this mass of humanity, I was the only person who was neither Sri Lankan nor Muslim.

The way continued through the holy campsite and the cliffs receded a little, but the rate of pilgrims-per-square-inch seemed only to increase, while the sky was invisible behind impending rock and a forest canopy of green bunting. And then, abruptly, the path, the people, the world, it seemed, came to an end: sky and earth opened up in a sheer drop and the sort of view you seldom see with your feet on solid ground – dark jungled lowlands interspersed with cultivation and framed, perhaps twenty miles to the east, by a range of low smoke-blue hills, while twice as far and more to the unframed south, so distant you could sense the beginning of the curve of the earth, was a sparkle of ocean.

It was this view, they say, that the twelfth-century Persian mystic Shaykh Muhyi al-Din Abd al-Qadir al-Jaylani spent ten years contemplating. Now you might expect a whole decade of Jaylani's life, even if it was a decade short on happenings in the usual sense, to deserve at least a mention in the extensive writings on him. But, as with Ibn Khafif's elephant episode, the sources are silent. The biographers do however agree that Jaylani spent twenty-five years engaged in *siyahah*, spiritual travels, apparently in the deserts of Iraq; for eleven of these years he was entirely lost to the world. During that period, according to the late Mr Aboosally, hereditary guardian of Daftar Jaylani and author of a slim but fascinating book on it, it is probable that the mystic shaykh travelled further afield, 'physically or metaphysically'.[*]

In fact, the association of Jaylani with this secluded corner of the Sri Lankan highlands goes back unbroken only to the late nineteenth century and the visit of a *sayyid*, a descendant of the Prophet Muhammad, resident in the southern Indian city of Calicut. This gentleman had made it his life's quest to find Jaylani's secret spiritual retreat. Quite how he lit upon this then almost inaccessible spot in the jungle isn't altogether clear, but it seems to have been partly a

---

[*] Jaylani allegedly made it further than Sarandib, and in time as well as space, for he also paid several visits to northern Nigeria in the eighteenth century and to various other periods and places on the Islamic edge. His fame is even more widespread, as witnessed by his appearance in the incantation of Ahmad the witch doctor on Kilwa Kisiwani.

matter of divine inspiration and partly success in what I'd failed to achieve on Adam's Peak – the discovery of some very old Arabic inscriptions. One of these is the tombstone, dated AH 715 (AD 1315), of a certain 'dervish of Muhyi al-Din' – apparently a sufi disciple of Muhyi al-Din al-Jaylani. To hang a whole tradition on so thin a thread is impressive; the more so when you admit that the inscription could equally well be read as 'the dervish Muhyi al-Din' without the crucial 'of' – in other words, that the name was the dervish's own. But it is in the nature of faith to spin cables from cobwebs.

In a little office near the tomb of the fourteenth-century dervish, I drew my usual blank with Islamic sites on Adam's Peak. The only one still known was the Foot itself, and there, the trustees of Daftar Jaylani said, Muslims were no longer allowed to perform their prayers openly. The name of Ibn Khafif meant nothing to them. It was the elephant story that – at last – rang a muffled bell. 'Elephants, snakes etcetera are never hurting visitors to Daftar Jaylani, because of the *barakah* of Shaykh Muhyi al-Din,' said Mr Iqbal, one of the trustees. I thought of Dharmawardana's comment on the similarly harmless animals of Adam's Peak. But here, it seemed, the defences against wild animals weren't only spiritual, intangible ones. Another trustee, Mr Rifaideen, opened a draw in a desk and carefully unwrapped a cloth. In it were some round black seeds, a dried leaf and a stick eight inches long.

'These are from the Mal Madara tree,' Mr Rifaideen said. 'It is down at the bottom of the cliff. Once upon a time Shah Madar, one big Indian shaykh, was cleaning his teeth with a *miswak* – you know?' I nodded: *miswak* is the Arabic name for a tooth-stick. 'He finished cleaning and threw it over the cliff. At the self-same time, down below, an elephant was molesting a girl. The *miswak* hit the elephant on the head and he ran away. The Mal Madara tree grew from the *miswak*. All these things from the tree keep you safe from elephants, snakes etcetera. You would like to take?' I was touched by the offer, I said, but couldn't in honesty claim that my need for anti-elephant talismans was great. It was enough to see them.

Did the story contain an echo of IB's tale of Ibn Khafif and the elephants? Or was it the other way round? Then again, IB reported the existence of 'an ancient tree at the base of the mountain . . . They tell untrue stories about it, one being that whoever eats one of its leaves will regain his youth.' There was something going on in all this, if I could only see through the fabulous trees into the historical wood. It didn't necessarily matter that the visit of the tooth-stick saint had, they thought, taken place two centuries after IB's time. Shah Madar was supposed to have lived to the ripe old age of 383. Besides, I'd learned that identities and dates of protagonists were the least important elements in the transmission of such stories.

There was *something* going on; and I realized what it was when I went through the names of the four villages IB passed through on his way from Adam's Peak to the lowlands. The last of the upland villages, he said, was 'Atqalanjah, where Ibn Khafif would spend the winter . . .'

'Ah, that is totally clear,' said Mr Manaf, the director of finance. '"Atakalan" is the old name for this self-same area, i.e. Atakalan-pattu, the area in which Daftar Jaylani is situated.'

Perhaps both Persian saints, Jaylani and Ibn Khafif, spent time here during their physical or metaphysical travels. I certainly don't wish to nullify the whole hagiological basis for one of Sri Lanka's biggest Muslim get-togethers. But I suspect that what is going on is that two famous names have been grafted on to some long-forgotten wandering holy man – that of Ibn Khafif by his patriotic fellow-Shirazi, IB's mutilated Shaykh Uthman; that of Jaylani by nineteenth-century sufis to whom, as to their fellows on the other edges of the Islamic world, he was the paragon of early Persian mysticism. All this mythopoetical matter, these stories of elephants, rubies, tooth-sticks and ten-year retreats are, like those of jinnis in bottles, legends in search of heroes, and Jaylani and Ibn Khafif are characters in search not of authors but of actions. When I brought the subject of the Maldivian sea-demon up, I wasn't surprised when the trustees all asserted that Jaylani was the true protagonist of the tale. He is an Islamic Heracles, and he will never tire, however many labours he may be given.

Heraclean labours were going on in the kitchens. We feasted, along with all the other pilgrims, 'at Jaylani's expense' – with a little help, the trustees admitted, from some wealthy Muslim businessmen. The logistics were challenging: next time you fret over Christmas dinner for twelve, think of a festive lunch for twenty thousand plus. Thanks to the volunteers manning the cauldrons and a non-stop supply of sacrificial bullocks falling to the butcher's knife, a constant flow of palm-frond platters passed along the human chain of pilgrims, piled high with rice and dhal, gravy, tripe and meat. To the accompaniment of a ladies' choir chanting mixed Arabic and Tamil praises of the Prophet's daughter, Fatimah, in the nearby cave-mosque, we piously stuffed ourselves. As at the religious festivals-cum-picnics of the old Italian south, *si mangia per divozione*.

The rest of the afternoon I spent visiting the holy attractions. Daftar Jaylani resembled an *al fresco* cathedral, its multiple chantries and crypts dotted about the little valley that hung above the precipice. The valley bottom lay between three towering masses of rock, called in the Tamil tongue of the Muslims Kappul-mala, Sorangam-mala and Jinn-mala: the Rocks of the Ship, the Cave and, furthest away from the precipice, of the Jinn. The various 'chapels' were located in and around the first two outcrops. High up above were the living gargoyles of this inside-out minster, macaques that lived among the buttresses of cliff and peered down from the pinnacles.

On the strength of his Arabic, picked up as a migrant worker in Saudi Arabia, the trustees appointed the portly, goatee-bearded Muhammad Rizvi to show me round. He was in charge of one of the cave-chapels, but only a shawl over his shoulder marked him out from the rest of male humanity here; like almost all of them, he wore a blue checked sarong, a white shirt and an embroidered cap. The female pilgrims were demurely but brightly dressed. There wasn't a face-veil to be seen, and headscarves were of the most diaphanous.

We began at the 'high altar' – the main cave-mosque, which was fronted by a screen of open arches. In the inner depths of the huge overhang, white-capped youths had taken over the relay of praises, now addressed to the Prophet and Jaylani. They formed the words with mantra-like concentration. Further out, a crowd of women and children queued to feed two smoking braziers with incense sticks. Others waited to pour oil into tall and dripping lamps of bronze. They then took strips of green cloth, torn off a rapidly shrinking roll by the imam of the cave-mosque, and passed them over the heads of their children before returning the strips to the imam with a few coins. The imam mouthed a quick prayer then handed the strips and coins to an assistant, who tied them to the lamps. For a while Muhammad Rizvi and I were conscripted into the tying process. It was all the rough equivalent, I supposed, of lighting votive candles – and the exact equivalent of what I'd seen Buddhist worshippers doing at their own shrines. I thought of the Tablighis I'd met back in Ratnapura, for whom these practices would be a screaming heresy. Then I looked at the fervent faces of the votaries, and knew that the puritans were fighting a losing battle. However unorthodox their practices were, the faith of these women was as powerful, as pervasive as the smoke of incense and the smell of lamp-oil; and they had numbers on their side.

We got away in a lull and climbed some rock-cut steps that led up a cleft in Ship Rock. The cliff did indeed look like a rounded stern – 'of the ship of Dhu 'l-Qarnayn Iskandar', Muhammad Rizvi explained. So Alexander of the Two Horns had made it here too; and in illustrious company, for some older pilgrims sitting by the path pointed out what they called 'Hebrew letters from the Torah, written by Solomon, on whom be peace'. I couldn't make the characters out as they were too high up. How the Solomonic and other graffiti, some clearly Arabic, had been written so far up the sheer rock-face was mystifying; but not to our informants, who assured us the cliff grew a little every year, like a tree. To round off the A-list of Islamic celebrities, Muhammad Rizvi pointed down to the fenced-in spot from where I'd first seen the abyss, and explained that it was called the Station of al-Khadir after the mysterious proto-sufi, who had prayed there and still apparently did so when no one was looking.

Muhammad Rizvi's own small cave-mosque was dedicated to Mira Sahib, a celebrated South Indian holy man. It had been walled off and provided with a vinyl floor-covering in tasteful tones and with reproduction tapestries of holy places (this, I suspected, was the sort of look my reverend Buddhist host on the far side of Adam's Peak was aiming for with his cave-temple improvement campaign). I had to admit that neither the plump Muhammad Rizvi nor his cosy cavern fitted my notions of Islamic troglodyte eremism. But we had one last cave to visit.

It was a dark opening in the scarp of Sorangam-mala: rock the colour of raw steak, a tunnel disappearing into the cliff and, framing it, a carved surround painted green and bearing Arabic words in gold – *He Is Now As He Was* . . . God, that is, and was and will be. Or did it refer to the man in purple with a green turban sitting on a skin in the tunnel entrance? He might have been my age, or seven times as old. A white beard and grey hair hung down to his chest, but his face was curiously unlined, and he sat straight-backed in the half-lotus position, his left hand playing with a rosary, his right arm resting on a sawn-off crutch (a prop for meditation, I later learned), swaying very slightly, slender and supple as a youth. A luminous half-smile flickered across his face, at once nonchalant and knowing, as if he'd been through it all, seen through it all, time included.

For a very long moment we looked into each other's eyes. Whatever it was that he was seeing, it was images of Baba Khuzi, Baba Tahir and the other anchorites of IB's Sarandib that passed through my mind and projected themselves on to this undatable face.

Muhammad Rizvi broke the moment: 'This dervish, Abd al-Jabbar Bawa, has been sitting here for thirty-five years.'

Is that all? I thought.

The dervish made a tiny motion with his head. I squatted in front of him. He took my hand and gripped it hard. Still looking into my eyes, his breathing changed to sharp, deep intakes followed by low rumbling exhalations. The inbreathing deepened, the rumbles turned to growls, and I felt my own respiration drawn forcibly into his rhythm – then found myself falling, falling into a clouded sky. Panic; then I saw not sky but eyes, sightless whites, looking not out to the world but in, into the dervish's own head. I fought against the rhythm of his breath, saw the eyes swivel outward like those of a doll. Abd al-Jabbar Bawa, smiling, released me. As I was led through the portal, I turned and saw him spitting – emitting a silver stream from his mouth into the face of a young man in a denim jacket whose expression changed, in the instant that I witnessed, from shock to beatitude.

The tunnel led downwards and narrowed, then opened out into a broad low chamber dimly lit by tapers. Here was a column of people, half-seen shapes edging along a flickering line of light and, sharp in the cool of the cave, a sweet-and-sour tang of sweat. Muhammad Rivi steered me away from the people and towards an opening that was all but invisible, dark on dark. It led into a further corridor, little more than a crack of triangular section along which we squeezed, my stout guide puffing with the effort, making for a gleam of daylight.

My first impression of Jaylani's meditation cave was how small it was – about the size of a double bed. And then all other impressions fell away: there was a flimsy grille, only lately installed, Muhammad Rizvi said – adding, with sublime understatement, that the drop was 'a little dangerous' – and, beyond it, the nothing of the abyss. I turned away in reflex, back to the solidity of the rock. We were standing on a flat boulder stuck horizontally into a vertical fissure in the sheer cliff-face, with another, more massive boulder wedged into the fissure above us to form the roof of the cave. Then I turned back to that thrilling, terrifying view, the better part of a thousand square miles bounded by those smoke-blue hills and the flash of sea. I was monarch of it all – for about a second; and then I was a microbe in a crevice in a pebble on a beach of an ocean on a planet in one of many universes. And then what?

The vertigo is both literal and ontological. Perhaps it was too much for the other pilgrims. For ten minutes we sat there alone, hearing only a deep aeolian melody, wind in rock. Jaylani, they say, sat here for ten years. To contemplate this double prospect, of infinite creation and infinitesimal self, ten lifetimes might be a beginning.

Back inside the bowels of the cliff, I edged a little way along the line of candles, then got the jitters. With thousands of tons of rock above and below and dozens of bodies behind and before, the bus from hell fresh in my mind, and a fearfully narrow squeeze ahead, I chickened out of seeing heaven on earth. The bottleneck led into Ghar Bab al-Jannah, the Cave of the Gate of Paradise, from which Jaylani had passed each night in the last hour of darkness through a supernatural adit to pray the dawn prayer 3,000 miles away in Mecca. The mystical aperture,

Muhammad Rizvi told me, allowed the faithful to catch a glimpse across the Arabian Sea of the far Islamic holy land. This, then, was why they crowded in here and ignored Jaylani's meditation cave: rather than making for the cerebral destinations to be seen across the abyss, they were on the nearest most of them would ever get to that physical journey to Mecca that every Muslim dreams of making. 'Poor thing,' an elderly woman sighed, looking at me on her way out. 'You didn't see Mecca!' I didn't need Muhammad Rizvi's translation.

And what of Muhammad Rizvi, who had been to the actual Mecca? Did he believe in the miraculous telescopic property of this hole in the rock? I didn't ask him. Faith, like ignorance, is a delicate fruit; touch it and the bloom is gone.

It needed another act of faith, and also one of gymnastics, to make out the final sight on our tour of Daftar Jaylani. I must have lacked the necessary suppleness of either body or soul; I seemed to be almost standing on my head, trying to spot the impression on the underside of the enormous slab of rock that lay atop Sorangam-mala, capping the fissure that plunged down to Jaylani's meditation cave. 'No,' I said, 'I can't see it.'

To me it didn't matter much whether I could see the print or not; and it didn't matter much more whether it had been made by the foot of Adam, as Muhammad Rizvi told me or, as perhaps more reliable authorities maintain, by that of Jaylani.* The very fact that people thought it was there rounded off the realization that had been slowly impressing itself on my mind all day, ever since I climbed the rock-cut steps at the entrance to Daftar Jaylani: that instead of preserving mere memories of the Islamic landscape of Adam's Peak described by IB, the Muslims of Sri Lanka had preserved the landscape itself – and moved it here, complete with inhabitants living, dead and supernatural, thirty miles to the south-east. The steps, the gateway, the caves, the praying-places, the

---

* Or even, certain Buddhists have claimed, by the Lord Buddha. The lower courses of an aborted modern *dagaba* make a circle on the rock nearby: for a few years in the 1970s, Daftar Jaylani threatened to become a precursor of the bloody Hindu-Muslim shrine dispute that centred on Ayodhya in northern India. Here, though, the Buddhists bowed out under the weight of Islamic evidence around them, made weightier still by a wise ministerial decision to block the building of the stupa.

neighbouring mountain of the jinn, at least one dervish-hermit, Adam, Iskandar/Alexander, al-Khadir the wandering Green Man, and for good measure Solomon and Jaylani – they were all here, suspended over a view of staggering sublimity and finished off with that stamp of authenticity, a holy footprint. The mountain, so to speak, had come to Muhammad.

*

It seemed appropriate, in this mobile land- and timescape, sanctified by the presence of Jaylani – or Ibn Khafif, or both, or neither – and by living Muslims of largely Tamil blood known in English as 'Moors' (as if they'd come from north-west Africa) and in older Sinhala usage as 'Yon' (as if they'd descended from the 'Ionian' Greeks who followed Alexander into India) that my own identity should end up lost in translation. Word had gone round that the man with the headscarf and the blue eyes was a Pakistani *bawa*.

The old travellers like Burton had put on disguises and never felt comfortable in them. This surprising identity just attached itself to me, and I felt at home in the rather Battutian persona of a wandering mystic. I enjoyed the sticky handshakes, smiles and calls of '*Bawa! . . . Salamu alaykum, bawa!*' with which the pilgrims greeted me; even if it was all a long way from the more familiar sensations of spiritual homeliness I'd experienced back in Christ Church, Colombo.

Later that afternoon I called on the other dervishes-in-residence, a group of authentic *bawa*s belonging to the Rifa'i order who spent the festival season in their small green-painted headquarters beyond the kitchens. Here they evidently kept alive the tradition of gruesome rituals described by IB. Their leader, Abd al-Salam Bawa, sat beneath a wall hung with winking fairy-lights and implements of self-torture – daggers, skewers and spikes. With these the dervishes would wound themselves in a holy frenzy of drumming and chanting, anaesthetized by their faith and by the blessing of their founder, Ahmad al-Rifa'i, a disciple of Jaylani. The thaumaturgic rites were billed for this evening, the last of the festival. I was looking forward to them: the *pièce de résistance* of the Sri Lankan Rifa'is was said to be the hammering of metal spikes into the top of the skull.

In my unexpected role as a visiting *bawa* of dubious antecedents, I wasn't sure how warm my reception would be, but Abd al-Salam Bawa expressed what I assumed to be his approval by taking hold of my head, pressing his lips against each of my ear holes in turn, blowing very hard, twice, and pronouncing the profession of faith into each of them, then offering me a cigarette. His standards of dervishhood, however, were clearly high. 'Abd al-Jabbar Bawa?' he said with a laugh when I mentioned the dervish of the cave. 'He may have been sitting outside his cave every day for thirty-five years, but he goes home to his bed every night!' I wasn't disillusioned. Why should one not be a flexi-time hermit, commuting to illumination? I could picture his wife waving him off with a cheery 'Have a nice day at the orifice, dear.'

For some time we discussed mystical breath-control and saintly miracles. Then, as Abd al-Salam Bawa was showing me the shell of a coco-de-mer – 'just like the one Shaykh Muhyi al-Din Jaylani crossed the sea in on his way here'* – a motley group of dervish reinforcements, among them the Rifa'i I'd met way back in flooded Colombo, suddenly marched into the room in a tangle of hair, beads, beards, drumming and incense smoke. They processed round the small chamber, greeting each of us with arm-wrenching double-fisted handshakes, piercing looks and equally piercing yells of '*Ilm! Ilm!*' – the Arabic for 'Knowledge! Knowledge!' – then, just as suddenly, marched out. Hard on their heels came a young couple with a baby for Abd al-Salam Bawa to dandle and bless. In my new guise of itinerant mystic, I felt I could hardly refuse when my own benedictions were also solicited.

*

The night air was thick with heat, sweat and suspense. The pace and volume of the drums and tambourines and chanting voices had been growing in a long, slow climax, the crowd swelling until the pressure of bodies and anticipation were almost unbearable. Boys had climbed every available wall and tree, women and small children were crammed into the front rows, and every eye was on a red

---

* A feat of maritime miniaturization outclassed by St Costanzo, who more than once was spotted cruising the seas off Capri in a walnut shell.

carpet spread before the drummers. Upon it, honed and gleaming, lay the instruments of mystical masochism. One of the Rifa'is came and extracted me, with difficulty, from the crowd, and led me by order of Abd al-Salam Bawa to a place in the front of the stalls, to witness as closely as possible the bloodletting to come. (For a ghastly moment I'd wondered if they expected me to show my mettle as a *bawa* and put in a guest appearance with the spikes . . .)

The rhythm of the drums was on the edge of frenzy. Inside the green room, I could see the first celebrant of the gory rites composing himself with prayers, about to come on stage. And then there was a tiny, tinny clang, hardly audible in the crescendo of percussion – and a pebble dropped from the corrugated iron awning above the drummers and fell, noiseless but visible, on to the carpet. The climax was now approaching its peak; someone came and gave a signal to the lead drummer; and the rhythm fell apart, fell silent, to be replaced by a low hum of talk that spread through the crowd and in which I could make out the whispered word, 'Wahhabi!'

The trustees had perhaps erred on the side of caution in stopping the spectacle. Later in their office I pondered aloud, and a little flippantly, whether the offending pebble had maybe come not from the hand of a Wahhabi puritan but from one of the supernatural denizens of the nearby Rock of the Jinn. 'The jinn are good compared to *those* people!' one of the trustees said, with a rueful smile.

I wondered how many of 'those people' had been present. Not many, on the evidence of that single pebble cast against tens of thousands of pilgrims. Perhaps those myriads were indeed all howling heretics; but I doubt whether the stone-thrower was without sin.

*

I went to bid farewell to Abd al-Salam Bawa. He was sanguine about the cancellation of the ritual. These things happened, he said; there would be other times, by the will of God. 'Tell me,' he asked as he released my hand, 'what is your *tariqah*?' My sufi order; at least, that is the common gloss on a word that also means a way or course or line.

A tricky question. For a moment I thought of telling him I was an independent. But it wasn't strictly true. 'I follow the *tariqah* of Ibn Battutah,' I said, and went out into the night pursued by slightly puzzled blessings.

Leaving Sri Lanka, IB followed a route that is in parts hard to follow, punctuated by more or less brief visits to places and people along the way. First he spent a while on the Coromandel coast of India, then made a very short return trip to the Maldives. On the way, his ship was plundered by pirates; he lost all his possessions, including some notes of inscriptions he had taken more than a decade before (this is his only reference to keeping written records during his travels).

From the Maldives IB sailed to Bengal, travelling inland up the Meghna River to pay his respects to a celebrated local holy man. Resuming his eastward progress, his ship called in somewhere on the coast of present-day Burma, where he describes a people 'with mouths like those of dogs' called the Barahnakar. Opinions vary as to who they were, but they share a number of characteristics with certain groups in the Nicobar Islands, who appear to have migrated from an earlier homeland on the Burmese coast.

The precise details of his onward itinerary continue to be blurred in places, but IB undoubtedly passed through the Strait of Malacca. Here he called on the ruler of the recently islamized sultanate of Samudra, on the north coast of the island to which it gave its name, Sumatra. From here he sailed on by way of a land he calls 'Tawalisi', ruled by a king of the same name or title; he visited the king's daughter, governor of a port called 'Kaylukari'. This lady, an accomplished warrior who could speak a little Turkish and write Arabic script, caused one commentator to say that this part of IB's voyage is to be found in 'the Marine Surveys of the late Captain Gulliver'. Others have proposed real provenances such as the Celebes and the Philippines. There is evidence, however, to suggest that the princess was indeed a genuine person and that her fiefdom was situated either on the coast of Champa in what is now Vietnam or, conceivably, in some outpost on the coast of Borneo belonging to the Javanese-based empire of Majapahit.

It is not unlikely that this whole problematic section of IB's itinerary eastward from Bengal has suffered from an unsuccessful attempt at abridgement by his editor, Ibn Juzayy. However, with IB's landfall at the Chinese port of Zaytun (Quanzhou, in Fujian province) in the summer of 1346, we are back on solid ground.

China

To the Mosque of the Phoenix

In autumn, when the wild geese
Fly out to sea,
The ships of the foreigners come
Sailing in to Quanzhou.

Xue Neng, ninth century AD

Hong Kong – Hangzhou

'I know just how they feel, those crabs,' Martin said with a shake of his head. We were watching a man picking them one by one out of a basket and deftly trussing their struggling legs tight by their sides with twine. Another man then lined them up in rows in a glass-fronted cabinet on the pavement. Here and all along Hong Kong's Wing Lok Street, they stared out in their immobile thousands, all knees and eye-stalks, waiting – how long? – for the pot. I looked at Martin. 'I mean I've just flown all the way from London,' he said, 'on Emirates, economy class.'

Of all the lands on the edge of IB's world, I'd been hoping most of all that it would be here, in China, that Martin would be able to slip away from his commitments as a painter and a father and join me on the road. We'd followed IB round India together. Since then, I'd missed my old friend's world-worn wit, and his ability to see, and draw, the marvellous in the ordinary – 'to show beauty', as Stevenson said of Whitman, 'in common things'.

Here, though, on Wing Lok Street, common things were a rarity. As well as all the crustacean bondage, the street was lined with pungent and peculiar smells from shops selling other edible or medicinal creatures, more or less dead, or their parts, dried, salted or otherwise preserved; even, in one case, fossilized, although I was mystified about the nutritional or pharmaceutical value of dinosaur teeth. Looking at it all – and what was *that*? a pickled stag's penis, of course – and knowing that these were only the outward signs of strangeness, I realized why I was so pleased to see Martin here. Other than the ground beneath our feet, just about everything else seemed alien. Even the sky, far above us between vertiginous walls of building, had a slightly lemony tinge, as if it belonged to a different planet.

Martin laid out his drawing kit on a ledge by a shop that sold sun-dried reptiles. "I've got this theory', he said, 'that however quickly you get to somewhere, by plane or whatever, you still need the same amount of time you'd have taken to get there slowly, over-land, to get into the place properly.' He peered into a small bottle of home-brewed oak-gall ink. 'To acclimatize, culturally and so on.'

We were planning to be in China for less than a month. According to Martin's theory, we'd be leaving physically before we'd mentally arrived. And this, I reflected, was why IB would always be the better traveller; not because long hard authentic low-carbon journeys were good *per se*, but simply because of the improved acculturation the extra time gave him. We've swapped acculturation for acceleration.

Then again even IB, who took twenty-one years – not Martin's twenty-odd hours – to get here from the Far West, had problems. 'China,' he wrote, 'in spite of all its good qualities, did not please me. My mind was always in a state of great commotion because of the overwhelming presence of infidelity there. Whenever I left my lodgings, I was so perturbed by the many reprehensible sights I saw that I would stay indoors unless it was absolutely necessary to go out. When I saw Muslims, it was as if I had met my own kith and kin.' 'Infidelity' might be better translated as 'unislamicness'. It is short-hand, like my squashed lizards and pickled pizzle, for all the rest of the otherness. The Prophet Muhammad famously told Muslims to 'Seek knowledge, even if the journey take you to China.' His China, too, is shorthand. It is not just the geographical land, but every place in which Islamic norms are overturned. Here, in his geographical and cultural antipodes, IB could see over the edge of his world, and what he saw made him queasy.

The best way to deal with culture shock is to brace yourself and jump in. At lunchtime, Martin and I were the only non-Chinese in a vast eating hall near the waterfront at Aberdeen. It was the size of a couple of decent ballrooms and was packed with families and middle-aged couples. Our food came – for me, tripe dumplings with a pleasant tang of digestive juices, rubbery-crunchy deboned chicken feet, and a salad of cucumber and what the English menu called 'floating bladder' and which, I believe, was jellyfish. 'Aren't you having the puppy-dogs' tails?' Martin said, trying to concentrate on his beef with green pepper.

Constrained neither by squeamishness nor by Islamic dietary restrictions, during our travels in southern China I ate, and generally enjoyed, a selection of dishes the mere idea of which would have had IB reaching for the sick-bag. They included fried snake, stewed toad, jellied sandworms, a peculiar if islamically unimpeachable soup of fishes' lips, the *haram* double whammy – something like savoury pink blancmange, partially set – of pig's blood soup (the blood of all animals is taboo to Muslims); and, by the lake in Hangzhou, a real chopstick challenge – preserved ducks' tongues, which inspired a stream of badinage from Martin (' "What's up, Doc?" . . . You must be quacked to eat those . . . Ah, there'll be a hush on the lake tomorrow . . .'). I don't mind having missed dog – along with pork, one of the horrifying foods IB specifically mentions – but I still regret not trying Emu's Stomach Baked in Pot, one of the dishes at our hotel in Guangzhou, or the intriguing Essence of Kangaroo spotted by Martin in a Hangzhou deli.*

And yet, despite my culinary bravado, I could empathize with IB in his alienation. Here we were both *gharib* – strangers, in Arabic, both from the cognate *gharb* (the west) and literally disoriented whether we liked it or not. Here, again, I was to know the meaning of that fragment of ancient Arabic verse that had haunted me since I left Morocco with IB a decade earlier: *Wa kullu gharibin li 'l-gharibi nasibu* – 'All strangers are to one another kin.'

*

IB's Chinese landfall, probably in the late summer of 1346, was in the Hong Kong of his day – Quanzhou, four hundred miles up the coast to the north-east, where he made straight for the leaders of the city's wealthy and welcoming community of foreign Muslim merchants. Martin and I planned to follow him there. First, though, furnished with an introduction from a mutual friend, we headed for our Hong Kong equivalent of IB's hosts. They lived up on the Peak, a sort of cross between Mayfair and Simla in which the elevation of one's house is an expression of one's wealth and status. The taxi driver was visibly awed as he took us up, past discreetly guarded condominiums and the gates of increasingly inscrutable mansions, ever higher, then on to a zigzag private drive. 'It's like being a pinball,' Martin said as we switchbacked upward.

---

* It's probably a terrible cliché to go on like this about the weirdness of food in southern China. I should point out for reasons of cultural balance that the Chinese have never had a monopoly of such things – that snake broth, for instance, was regularly served in Spain well into the nineteenth century, or that cats stewed in sherry were once a fairly common dish in Bilbao. Perhaps strangest of all was the old south Italian practice of feeding scrofulous children with the flesh of puppies suckled by human wet-nurses (human-suckled dogs were also once favoured in Hawaii, but for everyday eating).

'And I think we've hit the jackpot,' I said as we drew up before the muted grandeur of Taikoo House. It was a house fit for a taipan.

'Some people call me that,' Chris Pratt said, with a smile that was not altogether self-deprecating. The title 'taipan', meaning 'top class', was given in colonial times to the bosses of the big old foreign trading companies of Hong Kong, and especially to the bosses of the biggest two, Chris's company, Swire, and the even more venerable Jardine, Matheson. Before 1997 it was often said that the taipans wielded more real power than the governors appointed by the Crown; in the Conradian era a hundred years and more before that, Swire had printed its own money. The taipans were successors in spirit to the nabobs of the Honourable East India Company. But they were also heirs to the merchant princes of that earlier age of ocean trade in which IB travelled. Chris, whose mercantile empire included Cathay Pacific Airways, the China Navigation Company and fabulously valuable swathes of Hong Kong real estate, was a direct economic descendant of IB's mansion-building King of the Merchants in Cambay, of his shipping tycoon and China trader Mithqal of Calicut, and of Sharaf al-Din of Quanzhou, that fourteenth-century Hong Kong, whose powerful financial tentacles extended west via the north Indian credit markets to his native Persia.

Taikoo House, built in the 1940s, was almost an ancient monument by the standards of a city that was for ever reconstructing itself. A fire crackled in the drawing-room grate, books lined the library walls, and the savour of roasting lamb (no pigs' blood soup here) drifted in from the kitchen wing. Best of all was the Olympian view from our bedrooms, down on to the skyscrapers of Central and across the strait to Kowloon; except that, for much of the time, Hong Kong was cut off by smog.

Later in our stay we called on Chris in one of those skyscrapers, where we found him in his thirty-fifth-floor, dual-aspect office. Pointedly, perhaps, it looked up to the soaring Bank of China, and down on the smaller Jardine, Matheson building, a box with row on row of identical round windows.

For some days Martin and I explored the city, ascending each evening to the splendours of Taikoo House and the generous hospitality of the taipan. So too had IB lived in China, a spectator of scenes of 'infidelity' who could take refuge in the familiar comforts provided by his wealthy fellow-Muslims. But I realized that the similarities between his China and ours ran deeper. It wasn't only that IB's Quanzhou, like Hong Kong, was a vast seashore caravan-serai, packed with merchants and money and mediating between an ocean busy with shipping and an industrious hinterland. Yuan-dynasty China as a whole, like the post-Mao People's Republic, thrived on an open-door policy that not only pushed exports but also welcomed foreigners and their capital in.

The Mongol Yuan, Genghis Khan's offspring who in 1260 seized northern China from their indigenous predecessors, the Song, and eventually expelled them from the south nineteen years later, were by no means the first rulers of the land to encourage overseas trade on a big scale. As early as the eighth century, commerce with the west flourished, and particularly with the Islamic world. 'Here is the Tigris,' the caliph al-Mansur is reported to have said as he stood by the river of Baghdad and watched the silks and porcelain unload-ing, 'and nothing bars the way between it and China.' But it was under the Yuan that the barriers really came down and the door swung open to its widest extent.

With the building of new barriers in the fifteenth century by the isolationist successors of the Yuan, the Ming, the machinery of Old World trade went out of kilter, like clockwork that had lost a cog. A new world-system developed, revolving round Europe and, later, its newer satellites across the Atlantic. Today, once more, the Chinese barriers are down. The wheels of commerce are turning on their old axes, and Arab visitors to China come home again with breathless impressions. 'Its harbour is one of the greatest in the world,' IB said of Quanzhou. 'No – it *is* the greatest! I saw there about a hundred of the largest type of junk, and countless smaller ones.'* A neighbour of mine in Yemen, unloading his latest shipment of elec-trical goods, told me he bought them in Yiwu, near Shanghai. 'It's the biggest suq in the world,' he said. 'Half a million shops!'

It's all very well to point out parallels between IB's China and ours. But I wanted to look for points of convergence – for places he'd

---

* Not only the Arabs were breathless. Marco Polo said that for every ship that went to Christendom laden with pepper, a hundred went to Quanzhou.

been, sights he'd seen. The first of these I hoped to find up the Pearl River in Guangzhou, and while Martin drew Hong Kong street scenes I looked into appropriate ways of getting there. IB's great junks, the supertankers of his day – 'like enormous halls,' a Song writer said, 'their sails like pieces of cloud suspended from the heavens' – were long gone; the taipans' steamers had done for their punier descendants. Now I found that even the Pearl River hydrofoil service to Guangzhou had been temporarily suspended, and booked us on a swift and deeply inauthentic train that left the next morning.

'So you're going to *China?*' said my neighbour at dinner that night, a British woman long resident in Hong Kong, as if it were somewhere far away and unbearably exotic. 'How fascinating!'

It wasn't the first time I'd had that reaction from an old Hong Kong hand; what they called '*China?*' I'd been studiously calling 'the Mainland'. I nodded, and realized that Martin's theory of acculturation didn't go far enough. Evidently you could spend years living bang next door to a whole country, a continent, and still be mental oceans away.

★

On the Guangzhou express, I turned over in my mind the further implications of Martin's Brain-Lag Theory, and saw that they might go some way to explaining how IB could have made such an almighty cock-up of parts of his China chapter. The errors are gross enough to have made several eminent commentators wonder – as have other scholars in the case of Marco Polo – whether IB went to China at all.

Some of the mistakes are forgivable. For instance, if you hadn't actually observed the process of porcelain manufacture you might indeed get it into your head, as IB did, that it contained the ashes of coal. You might also believe it possible to travel all the way from Guangzhou to Beijing on inland waterways (in fact it was almost possible in IB's day, except for a shortish portage in the mountains of Fujian). And you might very easily, with all the -zhous and -jings and -fus, garble a place-name or two. But it was sheer fantasy for IB to claim that while he was in Khanbaliq – the Mongol name for Beijing – the Yuan emperor, supposedly killed in a recent battle with a rebellious cousin, was interred amid solemn festivities, along with live slaves and impaled horses. The emperor in question, Toghon Temur, died in his bed – admittedly in the far north, having been deposed by the Ming – no less than twenty-four years after IB's visit. As for the grisly Mongol obsequies with the entombed slaves and horses *en brochette*, the last recorded time these had taken place was forty years before IB was born. His southern China is flawed yet plausible. But the further north he claims to go from the familiar world of balmy ports and fellow-Muslims, the foggier his observations get, until in the Yuan capital he ends up groping in the dark.

I find it hard to defend IB against the charge of what used to be called 'tipping one the traveller' – in short, lying; except by saying that his ignorance of China beyond the cosy coastal cliques of co-religionists would have been almost total, and that if he did go to Beijing he would have been in the position of someone trying to make sense of a few bits of a thousand-piece jigsaw puzzle – and a Chinese puzzle at that – without ever seeing the picture on the lid. I once spent a couple of days in Beijing as an even more than usually idle tourist, and remember little but a very large public square, a succession of very large old buildings, and the fact that in my moodily lit hotel room I opened a little sachet thinking it was part of my bedside tea-making kit and found it to be a minibar-chargeable condom. Of the bigger picture, of Tiananmen, the Forbidden City, even of the name of the Chinese leader, I would be in ignorance without the BBC and the *Blue Guide*. I could further point out in mitigation that other western visitors to China got into messes quite as fine as IB's. Consider the goodly but gullible thirteenth-century friar, William of Rubruck. He undoubtedly made it to the court of the Mongol ruler, but could still in all seriousness repeat the story of the Chinchins, a race of kneeless hopping humanoids who are enticed by alcohol – their name comes from their habitual drinking cries (and yes, 'Chin chin!', or more correctly *qing qing*, is the origin of the English toast beloved of majors in golf club bars) – and then bled while inebriated, their blood being the source of an excellent red dye . . . I forebear to mention again in this context Marco Polo, who lived in China so long, he says, and still got so much wrong.

Chinese scholars have in recent years given IB that most generous gift, the benefit of the doubt. They accept his visit to Beijing as fact, and quote from the *Yuan History* to show that, even if Emperor Toghon Temur didn't engage the rebel in person, there was indeed a serious uprising in 1345 led by an alleged son of the emperor's predecessor, his paternal uncle. Few of the people of Beijing, they say, let alone clueless foreign friends, would have known what was going on. They explain IB's 'funeral' festivities as the usual New Year celebrations, and his account of the emperor's burial – which IB, in any case, doesn't claim to have witnessed in person – as a mangling of reports that Toghon Temur was at that very time building a tomb for his father. Back home a decade later, IB or his editor titivated the account of the interment with the only details on Mongol burial rites available in Morocco – those fascinating but anachronistic impaled steeds and immured slaves.

This is all very persuasive. Moreover, it's easy to forget how hard it is, today, to get things as wrong as IB did. The dangers of superficiality posed by almost instant travel – the dangers Martin implicitly warned of – are made up for by the depth of detail available at the speed of light down an Internet cable. We skim the surface in our travels; and yet we can fact-check deep down without going any further than our computer screens.

All this instant information is an excellent thing, of course. It is also fatal. There is no excuse today for gross errors of fact. But the

Wonders and Marvels of the old travellers are now almost extinct; the Chinchins have gone the way of the woolly mammoth. Perhaps travel books, which make at least a partial state of ignorance their point of departure and journey slowly towards an elusive sort of knowledge, will go the same way too. Information technology could do to the literature of journeys what photography has done to the portrait in oils. It certainly will, if people ever start to think of information and knowledge as the same thing.

So, to return to the question, did IB really go to Beijing? I could see no way of answering it myself, nothing that I could add to what the Chinese scholars have said by trying to follow IB's Beijing ramblings on the ground. But I could at least follow him up the coast to Hangzhou. All but the most crazed of his critics agree that his journey thus far has a ring of truth to it. I wanted to listen *in situ* for that ring, for echoes, however faint, of one man's footfalls long ago.

IB visited three great cities on the coastal bulge of southern China. The first was that great port city of his day, Quanzhou, which he and other westerners called 'Zaytun'. In Arabic, this happens to mean 'olives', but it comes in fact from the Chinese word for another type of tree, the *citong*, a kind of catalpa planted in the city in large numbers; the name further mutated in English into that of the city's most famous export, 'satin'. From Quanzhou/ Zaytun IB then doubled back westward to our current destination, Guangzhou – the old English Canton, which IB refers to both by its Persian name, Sin-Kalan ('China the Great'), and its Arabic name, Sin al-Sin ('the China of China'); both of these commemorated its status as the Chinese city *par excellence* in the earliest age of trade with the Islamic world. The third and last city was Khansa, Polo's Kinsay, versions of the name of the sea-port of the old Southern Song capital properly known as Hangzhou.

Given this plethora of place-names, one might be forgiven for thinking IB had visited not three cities but a decapolis. I'd always found the multiple names confusing, and their current Chinese versions tended to lapse into a hypnotic and unhelpful mantra, 'Guangzhou, Quanzhou, Hangzhou'. It so happened, though, that these three cities were home to the three mosques that are said to be the most ancient in China. It was their names that had become my mnemonic for our destinations: the Mosques of the Lion, the Unicorn and the Phoenix.

★

Perhaps, I wondered as we crossed the imperceptible border between the Special Administrative Region and the rest of China, those references by Hong Kong hands to '*China?*' were simply a concomitant of Britishness, of the semi-detached mentality that makes Great Walls of party walls. There seemed to be no immediate difference on the other side, unless it was that the industry was heavier and the pollution thicker. We were in a floating world where factories loomed out of the vapour; a Whistler world, Martin said – not a nocturne, but an aubade for a day that never quite seemed to dawn. From Hong Kong to Hangzhou we hardly saw the sun, and when we did it was as a wan blob suspended in smog. I kept thinking that it all had a peculiar beauty, that the grisaille had its own minutely varied palette; then I would remember that it was the ugly by-product of human activity. Strange, how one's reaction would depend on knowing if the scene was natural or artificial. The view's the same, and nowadays, increasingly, Nature herself is man-made.

After all the grey, the White Swan Hotel in Guangzhou was a shock. Christmas was coming, and tinselled sleighs laden with spangled gift boxes were parked in the lobby. A passing waitress in Santa get-up (minus the beard, and the trousers) flashed us a smile. 'Brilliant,' Martin said, 'whoever sold Christmas to the Chinks!' The view from our fourteenth-floor room was not so festive. Beyond the gentrified environs of the White Swan, Guangzhou was all grey elevated roads, tangled here and there into noodle junctions, and grizzled tower blocks receding into the ubiquitous grey-out. 'It looks like a carcass that's been picked over,' Martin said in his gloomy, where-have-you-brought-me-now? tone of voice that I knew well from our Indian travels. I had to admit that I was wondering if anything of IB's city of China the Great, with the fine temples and mosques and banquets that he described, could possibly have survived in this grim metroscape.

As it turned out, the White Swan's luncheon buffet – everything (and I had everything) from snails through Double Boiled Rabbit and Beef Wellington to chocolate profiteroles – was of banquet proportions. And it was Martin who alerted me to another, entirely unexpected Battutian parallel before we'd even ventured out. The big dining-room overlooking the Pearl River was full. Surprisingly, at least a third of the lunchers were middle-aged American couples – WASP-looking types, each couple with a Chinese baby. I caught fragments of conversation:

' . . . there's a sweet little park in the centre of town – can't wait to take our new little one there . . .'

' . . . How old's yours?' 'Eight months.' 'Isn't he cute!'

'Looks like the Chinese have added another item to their list of exports,' Martin whispered as the same thought came into my head. 'And just in time for Christmas.'

'Baby doll!' exclaimed a fat woman on the next table, coochy-cooing an astonished infant. The child was undeniably doll-like; but was it a baby, or a doll? Elsewhere, less effusive couples ate in silence on either side of high-chairs, looking as if they were wondering what they'd taken on.

'Remember what they used to say,' I whispered back to Martin. '"A puppy isn't just for Christmas." I hope the same goes for babies.'

In the lift, a thoroughly nice New England couple had a Chinese toddler with a deformed hand. No doubt, I thought, he and the other adopted children were unwanted or orphans, or the wrong sex, or in some other way surplus to requirements. No doubt – faint infant squalls sounded from every other room along our corridor – the Americans would cherish their ready-made offspring. And no doubt middlemen were making a buck or two facilitating adoption. It was this that made me feel queasy about the whole business.

'Have you got the IB translation?' Martin asked when we were back in our room. I handed it to him. 'Yes, here it is,' he said, finding the page. He read out a sentence I'd forgotten, or rather dismissed from my mind as fantasy: '"The Chinese sell their sons and daughters, and it is not thought shameful among them."'

Of the more conventional exports of Guangzhou, IB particularly mentioned its ceramics, sent from here over the ocean 'and all the way to our land in the far west'. The potters' market, he says, was vast; the city as a whole was 'one of the finest for bazaars'. To our surprise, when we reached the old neighbouring market quarter of Qingling, that was what we found. 'It's just like a suq!' Martin said as we entered a wonky grid of narrow streets hidden within the unpromising urban mess. I left him drawing in an alley and went to look for pots – only to be diverted by the other products on sale. They were ones IB would have classed as prime manifestations of overwhelming infidelity.

The covered market of the apothecaries outclassed Wing Lok Street in Hong Kong. There were shops that specialized in dead beetles or dried millipedes. One woman sold nothing but the shells of tortoises, and was keen that I should buy one. But, I mimed, what do I *do* with it? Eat it? Drink out of it? Grind it and snort it? Wear it as a skullcap? Or a codpiece? We parted with much laughter and mutual incomprehension. A nearby market selling smaller livestock seemed innocuous at first, with its poultry – there were some strapping hens, but I looked in vain for IB's 'cocks as big as ostriches' – and tanks of turtles and eels and cages of rabbits. But I soon passed from the edible to the inexplicable. Another woman shopkeeper had several big plastic bowls outside her premises, each seething with thousands of small brown scorpions. As I squatted there watching their endless attempts at mass break-out, a thin old woman came and squatted by me, took a tin can and a pair of chopsticks out of her handbag, and began selecting her wriggling victims with a connoisseur's eye, dropping them one by one into the can. Again, I resorted to dumb show with the proprietress: What on earth do you do with them? She led me into the dim recesses of the shop, showed me an electric rice-boiler and indicated that you pour in water, add scorpions, brew them up, and drink the broth . . . To my eternal shame as a culinary adventurer, I passed on scorpion soup.

After this nothing else surprised me; not even the edible pussies. They were crammed into cages near the duck department, and all had something of the alley-wise look of Hogarth's famous cat. (Come to think of it, there was something Hogarthian about Qingling as a whole – hellish and jolly at the same time.) Round the corner was a street of small dogs: pugs, pekes, poodles and dachsunds . . . I remembered IB – 'they eat the flesh of pigs and dogs' – and imagined poodle soufflé and sausage-dog sausages.

But the animals here looked groomed, even pampered. This must be the lap-dog market, I thought. But one could never be sure.

I found Martin back in his alley, and we wandered through the failing afternoon light; a sooty light, thick with smoke along the busy roads beyond the bazaar quarter. At a junction on the busiest road, where cars were jammed bumper to bumper under a visible pall of fumes, an old blind man sat on a box with a cymbal strapped to one leg and a wood-block to the other, holding a three-string fiddle. As we watched he threw back his head and sang, sliding up and down the fingerboard and the pentatonic scale, vibrato voice and portamento strings filling the filthy air with the catch of Cantonese and with a pathos that washed away the ugliness, singing his heart out – could the phrase have been more true? – by the rush-hour road.

*

The cherubic abbot of Guangxiao si agreed that his Temple of Glorious Filiality could be the one described by my traveller – 'a huge temple in the middle of the city,' IB called it, 'with nine gates . . . It was built by a certain king who declared the city and its dependent villages and gardens a *waqf* [a religious endowment] for its upkeep.'

'Guangxiao si was indeed first built by a king,' the abbot said. 'It was the palace of the Nanyue king, the last of the southern rulers under the Han dynasty.' The nine gates, he explained, would have been in keeping with palace design, although the layout had changed since IB's time. I asked about dates. 'It was a local aristocratic family who donated the palace as a temple,' the abbot said. 'That was in the third century.' So it was already an ancient monument when IB was here. On the scale of Chinese history, we were both fly-by-nights.

As we walked round the temple's enormous precinct the abbot sketched out its subsequent history. He also pointed out items of antiquarian interest – a twenty-foot mini-pagoda built in the seventh century to enshrine the hair of a founding father of Chinese Buddhism; two further ancient small pagodas of gilded iron; various old and significant trees. Apart from these objects, the main buildings of the temple – the great halls with their quiffed roofs and their reddy-gilt Buddha figures – looked as if they'd been recently restored, and with more than just a lick of paint and gold leaf. I wanted to know how the temple had fared in the Cultural Revolution.* But the abbot elided the traumatic events. 'Guangxi si fell into decay during the Qing dynasty', he said, 'and was largely rebuilt from 1986 onward.' The rosebud lips smiled; I didn't ask about the eighty missing years between the end of the Qing and the post-Mao re-opening of doors – of temples, as of trade. The silence had its own eloquence.

I'd first caught sight of the abbot, his shaven head topped by a mitre, as he presided at a ritual in one of the main halls. During the ceremony I was thinking how gormless IB had been to refer to a place like this, crowded with gilded Buddhas and Bodhisattvas, as a *kanisah* – a church or synagogue – when I realized that I, too, had almost as foggy a notion of what was actually going on. With the voices of the monks straying in and out of sync and the seemingly aleatoric booms, bangs, taps and tinkles of percussion instruments, I might for all I knew have been at a performance of a Steve Reich chamber opera. In fact the ritual, the abbot now explained, was

---

* The main Buddha statues, I found out later, had been completely trashed, the Red Guards foreshadowing the Taliban in their ferocious iconoclasm.

designed to elevate to heaven the spirits of every single creature that had ever existed on land or sea. This Atlantean task of intercession had been going on, he said, for more than a thousand years.

If IB witnessed the same ceremony, its cosmic import eluded him too. He was more interested in services provided to the living. The temple, he says, offered board, lodging and physic to the blind, the halt and the lame, the aged, and to widows and orphans. Today, the abbot said, the endowments that paid for all this are gone, but the Guangxiao Temple still runs a small clinic. There must be plenty of takers for it, I reflected, thinking back to the gauntlet of beggars that we'd run to get here: the road leading to the temple was lined with the leprous, the palsied, the cretinous and the simply decrepit. In these free-market times, charity had been privatized. None of the unfortunates made it past the main temple gateway, which was guarded not only by human doorkeepers but also by four outsize statues of demons – one with a sword, another wrestling with a dragon, a fey but probably highly dangerous creature with a parasol, and a figure with a quiff and a small guitar that looked like a hellish Elvis.

The abbot excused himself to go and elevate a few more departed souls. As the morning went on and living souls multiplied in the temple precinct, Guangxiao si took on a fairground atmosphere. Joss-sticks were selling like candy-floss at the more popular shrines, and a crowd of visitants were trying to toss coins into the intricate apertures of the small Pagoda of the Sage's Hair. 'Do you get to win it?' Martin wondered as he sat down to draw the scene.

I went off to explore further. It struck me that not the least of the temple's attractions was its colour. Here in the middle of a monochrome city were the parsley-greens of trees, the spinach-green of roof tiles, the dull saffron of monkish robes, the brazen yellow of polished brass, and the whole rich red end of the spectrum – crimson velvet cushions, poinsettia-red lanterns, statues in half-lit halls whose smiles glowed with rufous gold, lacquered columns of a shade that an Arab would call 'gazelle blood', and the russet and ruby and peach-pink and plum-purple of fruit piled high on altars in cornucopious epergnes. (In between these grander offerings was the occasional saucer of peanuts, presumably the *ex-voto* of a less well-off worshipper. We all know what you get if you pay peanuts – but what if you

pray peanuts? Perhaps in divine eyes they're the equivalent of the widow's mite.) Clashing with this pleasing colour-scheme were displays of gewgawful souvenirs and the brash leisure wear of the milling faithful. Martin, when I found him, pointed to a typical example of the latter, modelled by a girl sitting on a nearby wall. She amply filled a pink velour tracksuit, and had a momentarily enigmatic inscription embroidered in bold silver letters across her splayed backside – 'JUI' said one buttock, 'CY' the other; and then she stood up and made sense.

It was good to see IB's temple at a time of such busy and colourful renaissance. But *was* it IB's temple? Sir Henry Yule admitted in his book on early Western travellers to China, *Cathay and the Way Thither*, that he could not identify the place; later commentators on IB have followed him. I felt strongly, however, that the temple was the Guangxiao si. Too much history had happened for IB's nine gates to have survived; but it was big, old and central enough, and its founder was a king. All the same, strong feelings aren't the same as solid survivals, inscribed and stratified. I could never be sure.

Before we left the temple I bumped into a survival even more tenuous but who, in his very transience, was as much a part of IB's China, of his world, as buildings and inscriptions. He was a Tibetan Yellow-Hat lama and shouldn't have been where he was, he said, because of 'government regulations'; but he'd adopted the habit of the Chinese monks, and was learning Chinese. From a pocket in his robe he produced a tattered envelope of photographs – of the lamasery he'd entered back in his homeland, twenty years before, at the age of eight; of himself and fellow lamas in snowy courtyards; of a group of gleaming buildings at the end of a glittering valley. Guangxiao si, he said, was a half-way house. He was on his way west to found temples and seek knowledge, and he thought the journey might take him to America. I remembered Fa Xian and the other old westward-wandering monks; and IB – hardly a monk, but a secular, eastward pilgrim, seeking knowledge in China. The lama gave me a photograph of himself, standing and staring straight into the camera. It is in front of me now, and I sense that what it caught is less a moment in the past than a look into the future; that he is gazing not at the lens, but along the road. I wonder where he is.

*

Mosques in China can be tracked down by smell: the rare smell of roasting mutton. IB commented on the scarcity of sheep in China; mutton-starved, mutton-chop-whiskered expats in Victorian Hong Kong set up a Sheep Club to ship in animals from Australia and India; the roast lamb at Taikoo House was also a special delivery from Down Under. But on Guangta lu or Smooth Pagoda Road, especially on a Friday, you can go mad on mutton. Muslims and mutton go together like Mary and her little lamb, and the savour of grilling sheep on Guangta lu is as emblematic of Islam as that of bubbling shishas on London's Edgware Road. I got wind of it and, with Pavlovian immediacy, was wafted home. (Which home? My favourite childhood food was lamb chops from Mr Jay the butcher, grilled by my favourite aunt in her Belling. Olfactory memories of

Arabia and Somerset commingle in China: *l'Islam, c'est l'Occident de l'Orient* . . . But unlike Professor Lévi-Strauss, who made the discovery in a fit of ennui in Karachi while simultaneously feeling out of sorts with Paris, for me it is a pleasurable sensation.)

Naked dead sheep dangled all along the street on racks – as if, in a fit of absent-mindedness, they'd hung themselves up instead of their overcoats. White-capped Uighurs stoked barbecues placed at regular intervals along the pavement. One could go on a mutton-crawl; one could go completely bo-peep on mutton. Later on, we headed for the Nur Bustan Islamic Restaurant. The menu was entirely ovine and occasionally alarming, with dishes like 'Hand Scratches Mutton' and 'Burnt Pepper Sheep Feet'.

'Makes a change from lamb and mint sauce,' Martin said. 'And what's this – "Mutton With Toothpicks" . . . ?'

'Haven't you heard of it? It's a new time-saving invention.'

The waiter was hanging over us. 'Come on,' Martin said, 'we've got to make a decision.'

'Yes, *revenons à nos moutons.*'

'Hmm . . . I used to be a glutton for punishment. Now I'm a glutton for mutton.'

'Don't stint yourself – you know, no holes baaa-ed. I think I'll go for the "Sheep In Wolf's Clothing".'

'And I'll start with a little "Lambsy-Tivy" . . .'

The waiter, who fortunately didn't understand a word, was still hovering. We discovered, at some length, that every single item on the menu was as apocryphal as our two last inventions. The only dish available – an unctuous hash of mutton on a thick trencher of Uighur bread drenched in garlic and ginger gravy – appeared, eccentrically, to have no name, so we christened it 'The Lost Sheep'.

First, though, as Friday Prayers were approaching, we explored the building on account of which all these *halal* hecatombs had died. Its old legendary name, the Lion Mosque, seems to have fallen out of use; IB referred to the place, already venerable in his day, only as the congregational mosque. Officially it is known as Huaisheng si, the Cherish the Sage Temple; but everyone calls it Guangta si – the Temple, or Mosque, of the Smooth Pagoda. The feature in question is a minaret of two stages, a tall fat cylinder with a shorter thin one on top, in all over a hundred feet tall and a thousand years old. The 'smoothness', meaning the unpagoda-like lack of eaves, dragons and other protuberances, is not enhanced by a rendering of streaky grey cement; the shape is strange and, if vaguely Central Asian, unique. I could only liken it to a closed parasol planted in the ground, handle-up. Martin perhaps more accurately compared it to a lavatory brush in its stand.

Apart from this mysterious tower behind a blank brick wall, there was nothing to be seen from the road. But a discreet entrance gave on to a series of seven gates surmounted by bold and beautiful Chinese inscriptions – the loveliest framed by dragons rampant and, I later learned, in the hand of a Ming empress who confirmed in it the right of the Muslims of Guangzhou to pray here in perpetuity. Unable to read the inscription, however, I might as well have been in a temple as a mosque. The architecture of white-grouted black brick and thickly glazed green roof tiles, like that unspecific word *si*, 'place of worship', was multi-purpose. The last of the gateways was a cuboid structure of red stone, topped by a two-tier roof with the usual upward-sweeping eaves and called, according to a sign, The Building For Looking At The

Moon. The name seemed as intensely Chinese as the shape, until it dawned on me that there was probably some link with the workings of the Islamic calendar and the need to sight the new moon which marks the beginning of its months.

Beyond the seventh gate, carefully pruned trees, cloud-scrolls carved on low stone walls, and the continuing curliness of roof-lines all contributed to the sensation of being in the wrong sort of *si*. I recalled the Hindu-temple-like mosques of Malabar, and the Buddhist-inspired mosques of the Maldives; but nowhere had Islamic architecture gone quite as native as it had here. Only that strange smooth tower, devoid of chinoiseries, suggested that you were in anything other than a temple; at least, until you entered the main prayer hall. Here, idols, altars, incense, fruit, flowers, braziers, mirrors, vases, gongs and all the other impedimenta of a temple were absent. The only interior decor was the Word of God: a big mural Qur'anic inscription in Arabic that looked speeded up, sini-cized, as if the characters had been dashed down with an ink-brush and inspiration, not slowly inscribed with reed pen and perfect proportions. All else was white and bare. Islam, after atheism the ultimate faith of minimalists, travels light, without the priestly baggage of reliquaries and statues and thuribles; without even a priesthood. You could see how it had got so far.

There were already a few worshippers here, sitting and chatting in their Friday best. As the meridian approached the number grew, men hurrying across the courtyard glancing at watches with an oh-my-ears-and-whiskers look, women entering in headscarved and gregarious groups and heading for their own part of the mosque. A handful became a hundred, then half a thousand, and as the air of expectation thickened the call to prayer sounded – a summons that I've heard forty thousand times and more and never answered, that here in this alien city brought a lump to my throat. 'When I saw Muslims, it was as if I had met my own kith and kin . . .' I knew what IB meant. And even if I didn't answer the call, I felt at home on the sidelines of Friday Prayers.

The young preacher up on a balcony was in a white robe and turban that wouldn't have looked wrong in a fourteenth-century miniature. The sermon was in Mandarin, but kept slipping into Arabic for quotes from the Qur'an and the Hadith. Given the phonetic gulf between the two tongues, it was the sort of feat demanded of bedtime story-tellers doing 'Goldilocks', but so deftly ventriloquized that I had to look about now and again to see if there weren't in fact two speakers. Most of my attention, however, was taken by the worshippers – now, I guessed, in four figures, for they had spilled out of the prayer hall and filled every inch of the court-yard and colonnades. Many of them were Turkic Uighurs, internal migrants from Xinjiang, here in search of jobs and bringing, along with the savour of mutton, the ruddy look of the far cold steppe in their young-weathered faces. A small minority looked like native southern Chinese. I wondered if any were descendants of the Middle Eastern merchant venturers of IB's age, sinicized like the script in the prayer hall; I also wondered how I'd ever get to find out. And there was another, bigger minority – of modern-day Middle Easterners, with faces that might have come from Arabia or the Levant, Persia or Anatolia; unplaceable, diaspora looks from lands as far apart as Sind and Barbary.

In the Yuan age, in the months of April and May, when the native Chinese of the southern seaports would sacrifice on coastal hills to propitiate the sea goddess Lin Mo and ensure a favourable monsoon and profitable trade, the Muslims of Guangzhou would climb their Smooth Pagoda, which then doubled as a riverside land-mark, and make the same petition to their own more abstract deity. Their prayers, it seems, are still answered. The Pearl River no longer flows beneath the Smooth Pagoda, and the junks no longer make their autumn landfalls at the time when the wild geese take wing. But the same old current of commerce still sweeps across the ocean, bringing men and money from the Muslim heartlands.

After the prayers were over I talked to some of those men. One of them was a compatriot of IB's, a Moroccan buyer of TVs and fridges. And there was a small crowd of Yemenis, young traders and students, dumbfounded by the dialect of their homeland coming from the mouth of an Englishman in China. One of them was frowning at me . . . then the frown unknotted: 'You live in the old Cattlemarket in Sana'a, don't you! I live round the block, by the Blacksmiths' Suq!' Slowly his features dawned on me, a face seen on the street 4,500 miles away, and we laughed and embraced. IB was to have a similar encounter. All strangers are to one another kin.

And there'd been another stranger. He'd passed through a month or two ahead of me, they said . . .

He always was a little ahead. He'd been looking for traces of Burhan al-Din the Lame in Alexandria – the holy man who first foresaw IB's travelling future – not long before I did; a few days before me, he'd been waiting on a jetty in Oman for a boat to Masirah Island. And then, after a couple more second-hand sightings, he had disappeared. For the past seven years or so I'd been wondering if he really existed in the usual sense – or if he was what is vulgarly called a ghost (and if a ghost, whose ghost?). But now our paths had nearly crossed again in Guangzhou. One of the mosque-goers later sent me a photograph of him. I look at it, and wonder where he is now. He is, like IB, a wiry Maghribi, although a native not of Tangier but of Tunis. He has broad cheekbones, a closely clipped moustache and a full Islamic beard with a touch of grey; is probably, as IB was in China, in his early forties. He wears a T-shirt and baseball cap, and carries a prodigious rucksack that looks too heavy for a ghost to carry. He is following IB on foot and makes me, with my planes and trains and boats and motor cars, feel something of a fake, for he is putting Martin's theorem of deceleration and acculturation into practice.

IB, who never walked anywhere if he could help it and nearly always had a slave or two to carry his bags, would have thought him an admirable example of *tawakkul*, putting one's trust in God, and totally mad.

★

IB's world of travel, trade and faith was alive and thriving in twenty-first-century Guangzhou. But I still wanted to find some more personal memento of his passing through; something like the photo of the walking Tunisian. It isn't quite as crazy an idea as it sounds: 'Whenever I returned to one of their cities that I had visited before,' IB remembered, 'I always saw my picture and those of my companions, painted on paper and put up on the walls of the market. We would all inspect each other's pictures, and find them to be perfect likenesses.' The portraits were painted, IB says, to keep tabs on foreigners; they were an early step on the road to the passport mug-shot and the retinal scan. If only they'd survived . . . The riddle of his appearance still haunted me, and I still knew nothing more of it than that he was bearded and probably thin.

. What of the Middle Eastern expats IB met in Guangzhou, the ones who stayed on and might have left mementos – or even descendants? He only mentions one by name, Awhad al-Din, originally from Sinjar in northern Iraq, a wealthy merchant who put him up for his two-week stay. The name meant nothing to the mosque official I spoke to on a return visit to Guangta si; not surprisingly. Then again, the official was an indigenous Guangzhou Muslim whose own ancestor came, he thought, from the Middle East in Yuan times. It was a tantalizing crumb of information, but it was as much as he knew.

We were drinking tea in the portico of the prayer hall while Martin worked on a pastel of the Smooth Pagoda. The official's Arabic was good, and talk turned to the state of Islam in Guangzhou today. 'Religion is strong here,' he said. 'It wasn't before, but we've had migrants coming from the north, Uighurs. They've brought the Message with them, the *tabligh*. Including all the incomers, there are now about 80,000 Muslims in Guangzhou.' I remembered the Tablighi missionaries getting short shrift in Kilwa, and their earnest but ineffectual brethren in Sri Lanka, and was surprised that the puritanizing revivalists should have had success in China, of all places; moreover, that they belonged to the restive Uighur population of Xinjiang. The mosque official noticed my surprise. 'We worship in freedom,' he said.

And so they do, it seems – within the courts and halls of Guangta si and the other mosques around the city. I remembered seeing only two overt policemen at the outer gate during Friday Prayers. No doubt, however, if a single toe went outside the line, if the political genie showed the tiniest hint of leaking out of the bottle, the two policemen would turn into two thousand before you could say '*Allahu akbar*'.

What the mosque official told me of the Uighur proselytizers sparked off a moment of illumination: I saw the Mosque of the Smooth Pagoda as a meeting place, not just of individuals in the here and now but of the two continuing historical currents that had brought Islam to the Far East, one across Central Asia, the other over the Indian Ocean. This was where the terrestrial and maritime Silk Roads came together. The Uighurs bringing their mission and their mutton and the Arabs buying their fridge-freezers and flat-screen TVs were all part of a human ebb and flow that went back to IB and beyond, back to the first Islamic century.

Silk Roads are now Microchip Motorways. After we left the mosque I looked in Guangta lu for presents for my friends back in Yemen. I didn't have to look far. Right next door to the Smooth Pagoda was the perfect gift: a palm-held gadget with a screen that displayed in scrolling text the Holy Qur'an, an entire Arabic exegesis of it, and prayers for all occasions, plus an audio recitation of the whole lot, an Anno Hegirae-Anno Domini converter, and a device for finding the direction of Mecca, all for about £10. The various other gizmos on display included, for the lazy faithful, electronic rosaries that 'told' themselves in a tinny voice, '. . . Glory to God Glory to God Glory . . .'

The shop doubled, of course, as a mutton butcher's.

★

In unexpected ways, I was finding out a lot about IB's China and how it was now resurgent. But I still longed for relics, for something or somewhere that held more intimate memories of IB's visit. There was one slim possibility.

Over half IB's account of Guangzhou is taken up with '*An Amazing Anecdote*':

> When I was in China the Great, I heard of a certain venerable shaykh there who was more than 200 years old. They said that he neither ate nor drank nor excreted and that he had no sexual relations with women, even though he was still perfectly able to do so. I was told that he lived in a cave outside the city and that he spent his whole time in performing devotions. I therefore made my way to the cave, and found him at its entrance. He was thin and had a very ruddy complexion. The effects of his ascetic practices were visible in his countenance, and he had no beard. I greeted him, and he took my hand, sniffed it, and said to my interpreter, 'This man is from the end of the earth, just we are from its other end.'

The antique anchorite then revealed an astonishing piece of information. A few years earlier, IB had stopped off at an island while sailing down the west coast of India. There he found a yogi at a Hindu shrine, surrounded by idols, who intimated by signs that he was in fact a Muslim, made a coconut fall by shouting at it, and then gave the traveller ten gold coins. The Guangzhou hermit now asked IB if he recalled the meeting on the island. 'I said, "Yes," and he said, "I am that man."'

Having made this disclosure the hermit entered his cave. IB waited a while for him to emerge again, then followed. Inside, the hermit was nowhere to be seen. One of his followers was there, however:

> He gave us a bundle of paper money and said, 'This is your hospitality gift. Now go.' I said to the man, 'I will wait for your shaykh.' But he said, 'If you were to stand here ten whole years you would not see him, for it is his custom never to allow anyone whom he has let into one of his secrets to set eyes on him again. Do not think, though, that he has departed from you. Rather, he is present with you.'

IB was not the only one to have a strange experience with the hermit of the cave. His host, Awhad al-Din, had been to see him too, had been hypnotized into believing that he was in a vast palace, and had fallen sick for months as a result. The hermit was a master-mesmerist, Awhad al-Din explained; the 'follower' whom IB met inside the cave was none other than the hermit himself. As for his religion, it was rumoured that he was a Muslim, but no one was sure.

As a zero-waste celibate bicentenarian yogic-Islamic syncretic troglodyte hypnotist who flits across Asia with no visible means of support giving money away, the hermit of Guangzhou is one of the more troublesome characters in the *Travels*. IB's book, this house of many storeys, has a few lunatics in the attic about whom the commentators have kept an embarrassed silence, and he is one of them. He shouldn't, though, be written off as a fiction. For a start, not many people would dare to make him up. Moreover, in India I'd learned that traces of the island shrine might still exist, and had spent a lot of time trying to get to the place in question, Anjidiv; my way had been barred by the immovable might of the Indian Navy, who were developing the island as a base. Now, I thought, I might have better luck with the cave outside Guangzhou.

It was one of the longest of my many long shots. But I had to try. The hermit embodies one of IB's great unspoken themes. He shows how the apparent accident of the double meeting is in fact no such thing; how both travel and life – for which travel is so close a metaphor as to be almost a homologue – follow clear paths that run beneath the trackless and chaotic surface of events. The hermit is, in short, a reminder of the workings of Fate, and his cave – like the Cave of the Seven Sleepers, like IB's own tunnel of mystical retreat that I ran to ground in Delhi, like Jaylani's transcendant cave above the abyss in Sri Lanka – shadows forth the deeper shape of things.

★

When I found the cave – it's called the Cave of Melting Rock, and is high up on White Cloud Mountain – there was no hermit to be seen. Only some rather good *feng shui* in the form of a pool in the rock immediately outside: dragons live in caves and like to pass over water as they come in and out.

The way up was jolly. White Cloud Mountain is a very large public park, and as it was a Sunday *le tout* Guangzhou were out for a breath of relatively fresh air. The broad asphalted paths, winding up the mountain through willow-pattern forests, were full of promenaders and t'ai chi fans and joggers – some of them trotting backwards up the mountain – and players of *jianzi*, a sort of combination of badminton, soccer and ring-a-ring o'roses in which you kick a shuttlecock round from one to another in a circle. There was even a lone karaoke singer belting out that Sinatra-inspired hit, 'Mai Wei'. The paths were unnaturally clean, disfigured neither by so much as a sweet-wrapper nor even a fallen leaf. One was exhorted by signs not only to refrain from 'throwing sundries, spitting and scribbling', but also to 'Stop And Gaze At This View' and to visit 'The Pavilion For Listening To The Soughing Pine'. And just as Nature did what she was told here, so did the citizens of Guangzhou, who gazed and listened and refrained from throwing sundries in their tens, perhaps their hundreds, of thousands.

Martin and I were the anarchists in all this order. For a start we were much too tall, and must have looked to the short Cantonese like a pair of bearded Smooth Pagodas. Then, at a tea-house half-way up and under the fascinated gaze of a dozen pairs of eyes, Martin imbibed from the slop-bowl. Finally, further on, I forgot myself and swung from a low and irresistible branch. It proved to the onlookers what they'd suspected all along – that Martin and I were in fact yetis. Amid much polite giggling, we posed for group photographs with the human park-goers. It was good to give others pleasure simply by existing.

We elicited directions from various joggers and *jianzi* players – once, even, from a lance-wielding kung fu master with Fu Manchu moustaches and a gaggle of teenage pupils – and got to Nine Dragon Spring. Here, according to a helpful leaflet, dwelt the proto-anchorite of White Cloud Mountain more than 2,000 years ago. He was shown carved in relief, flying along a stone frieze on a crane, in company with a later Tang-dynasty hermit wearing a cloak of leaves and a procession of subsequent sojourners on the mountain, monks, poets and scholarly recluses. None dated to IB's Yuan era; but the frieze proved that the mountain was the favourite retreat of Guangzhou's more eccentric inhabitants. It was exactly the sort of place where IB's hermit would have lived. And according to my map, a spotty photocopy from Dr Kerr's 1904 *Guide to the City and Suburbs of Canton*, we were almost at our goal. The path, now stepped, rose steeply.

And here it was. Inside, beyond the perfectly placed dragon's pond, was an equally perfect cave, carved out of the mountain with perfectly spaced pillars of rock left to support the ceiling. It was all so perfect, in fact, that I tapped the rock to check it was real. There was not only no hermit; there were no vibes, no insights. The glimpses from the cave were not of the workings of Fate, but of suburban Guangzhou tower-blocks seen through the white cloud and yellowish smog. On the mountainside directly above was a large tea-house. 'Very convenient for your caveman,' Martin said. 'I can just see him nipping up here for a lapsang souchong.'

Later on, Mr Wei Wei, one of the park managers, did his best to demolish once and for all the carefully built structure of my faith. 'The Cave of Melting Rock', he said with the sort of smile you might put on to admit to a child the terrible truth about Father Christmas, 'is recent and artificial.'

★

He did his best, I reflected as the Guangzhou–Quanzhou (or, as I also thought of it, the Lion–Unicorn) plane taxied to the runway; but he didn't quite succeed. In Dr Kerr's comprehensive Canton guide I can find no other plausible site for the hermit's grotto than on White Cloud Mountain, and no other caves anywhere near Guangzhou. Moreover the mountain, I'd discovered, had been the place for mystic and artistic types since the days when Egypt still had pharaohs. Granted, the cave I saw did look brand new. But there *was* a cave there more than a century ago on Dr Kerr's map, above Nine Dragon Spring: 'the Bed of the Genii', he labelled it. Caves aren't in the habit of disappearing. Mr Wei Wei knew of no others on the mountain; he himself was too young to have memories of anything before the Cultural Revolution, that self-inflicted attack of amnesia. To me the only possible explanation was that the Cave of Melting Rock was in fact Dr Kerr's suggestively named Bed of the Genii, enlarged and beautified. After all, the whole of White Cloud Mountain, with its pedicured footpaths and picturesque prospects, bore witness to a mania for improving on nature. There only remained that small matter of the further leap of faith, back 500 years from Dr Kerr . . .

' . . . Radies and gentermen,' said a voice that cut into my thoughts, 'this is a non-smoking fright.'

Now, though, we were on our way from the misty hypotheses of White Cloud Mountain to the more solid ground of Quanzhou. There, at least on paper, I'd already tracked down one of those foreigners whose ships, the poet said, made landfall when the wild geese took wing. Like that figurative wild goose, the hermit, but in a far more explicit manner, this man revealed the deeper structure of IB's apparently haphazard journey.

Twenty years before his own landfall in Quanzhou and nearly 6,000 miles to the west, IB arrived in Alexandria. He was less than ten months into his travels and intending only to go on the Mecca pilgrimage, probably with a little higher jurisprudential study on the way, and then to return home to Morocco. So far he was a perfectly standard Islamic Grand Tourist. In Alexandria, however, he got to know a man who would redirect the course of his life – and the literature of travel. This momentous person was 'the learned ascetic, the pious and humble Burhan al-Din the Lame' – the saintly man whose traces both I and the mysterious Walking Tunisian had sought. One day, IB remembered thirty years later,

> He said to me, 'I see you are a lover of travel and of wandering about the world,' and I said, 'Yes, I am,' even though it had not at that time even crossed my mind to penetrate into such far lands as India and China. Then he said, 'You must visit, God willing, my brethren Farid al-Din in India, Rukn al-Din Zakariyya in Sind, and Burhan al-Din in China and, if you make it to them, give them my greetings.'
>
> I was astonished by what he said; but the idea of travel to those lands was thus projected on to my mind, and my wanderings did not cease until I had met the three persons he had mentioned, and had delivered his greetings to them.

This was only the first of two occasions in Egypt when the young traveller's fate was disclosed to him by a sufi shaykh. For IB, much of the next three decades would be spent working out that fate.

There was a problem, however. Of the learned and pious Burhan al-Din the Lame, this figure of supreme significance to IB, who gives his wandering life and book their whole geographical structure, I'd found not a trace. I'd searched for him both on the ground in Alexandria and, for more than ten years, in the crowded biographical literature of IB's age, and not come across so much as a whisper of his name. I admit I'd long wondered if he was a figment of IB's imagination, a literary device to point himself on his way. He seemed more insubstantial even than the hermit of Guangzhou. Not long before I left for China, however, I found him.

He made a brief but intriguing appearance in an obscure dictionary of saints compiled by one Ibn al-Mulaqqin at the end of the fourteenth century. Burhan al-Din the Lame, it said, was a sufi who used to recite the whole Qur'an every day and night. He made his living from winding yarn into balls. His wife had a covered basket from which he could produce objects even when onlookers were certain it was empty. That was all: a short record of a life that was a mixture of piety and conjury – the sort of life lived by the hermit of Guangzhou and by the dozens of other godly showmen to whom IB was drawn throughout his travels. Not a momentous life, perhaps; but at least, it seemed, a real one.

Burhan al-Din the Lame, holy winder of yarn, gave IB the thread to follow. I'd been led too in those book-travels to the third of his far-flung brethren, his Chinese namesake Burhan al-Din of Quanzhou. There he was, in the Fujian volume of Chen and Kalus's *Corpus d'inscriptions arabes et persanes en Chine*; not, as it happened, in either of those languages, but on a Chinese tablet in the old mosque in Quanzhou, and transmuted into 'Bu-lu-han Ding'. This sinicized Burhan al-Din, a note said, also had an entry in an old Chinese history of Quanzhou, which said he arrived in the city in 1312 or 1313, was in charge of the ancient Unicorn Mosque, and died at a very great age in 1370. The compilers of the corpus didn't make an overt link with the Burhan al-Din of IB's *Travels*. I felt sure, though, that he was IB's man, 'one of the pious shaykhs' of the city, who ran a sufi hospice in its suburbs.*

It seemed too that in Quanzhou, now a smallish city in Fujian province, there might be human survivals from IB's age. According to the notes in Chen and Kalus's book, Shaykh Burhan al-Din had

---

* IB says Burhan al-Din was also China representative of the Kazaruni *tariqah*. The Kazarunis were not so much a standard sufi order as a sort of mystical marine insurance company, based in Persia and with offices across Asia, from Anatolia to China. Those covered by their policies enjoyed the double advantage of paying their premiums in arrears, and only if they escaped danger: threatened by storm or shipwreck, merchants and ship-owners would pray to God for salvation, vowing alms to the Kazarunis if they survived. The alms would then be paid to representatives at the major ports. The order ceased to be active in the seventeenth century, but I hear there is still a nominal head of the Kazarunis living comfortably near Isfahan.

left descendants, known from his title as the Xia – the 'Shaykh' – family. One of these, Burhan al-Din's grandson Xia Wennan, sailed with the eunuch Admiral Zheng He as interpreter. Most exciting of all, when the compilers were at work on their book in the 1980s, members of the Xia clan were still to be found in Quanzhou, living among the ruins of the same old mosque in which their ancestor's name appeared on that ancient tablet . . .

My journey with IB had been set in motion by my friend Hasan, a direct male descendant of the traveller's host in Yemen. In the Levant and in India, I'd met other descendants of people IB met and stayed with on his journeys. I'd never dreamed that such human relics might have survived in China. But, in Quanzhou, it seemed more than a possibility.

The plane touched down. Xiamen Airlines, an announcement said, hoped that we would be frying with them again.

*

'What are they saying?' Martin asked as he laid his pastel boxes out on Luoyang Bridge. Rosy-faced women in conical straw hats were waddling past, trousers rolled up to their thighs, each lugging a yoke of oozy baskets filled with oysters. Almost every one of them threw a look at Martin and me, then a very audible comment.

Wang Feng smiled down at the granite pavement. 'They are saying what fine noses you have,' he said. I sensed that 'fine' was the diplomatic version. I could picture IB getting similar comments from the Fujianese. Not long after his visit, an indigenous pro-Ming writer lampooned some foreign Muslims killed in the collapse of a building: 'Their elephant noses are now flat, their cats' eyes no longer shining.'

The young and scholarly Mr Wang (whose *nom d'*email was 'Ratty', 'from *The Stories by the Side of the River*'), had been given the task of guiding and interpreting for us by the Maritime Museum in Quanzhou. As he'd suggested, Luoyang Bridge, a long low line of granite that crossed the estuary north-east of the city as it had done since well before the time of IB's visit, was the perfect scene to keep Martin busy. It began beside an elegant tapering column and traversed the water in an interplay of rhythms: of cutwaters, of sejant lions on the balustrade, of oars in sampans down below

– 'they row standing up', as IB noted – and of receding rows of paired stones planted in the mud, inverted Vs on which oysters congregated. (Just as you can go mad on mutton by the Smooth Pagoda, you can go crazy with oysters in Quanzhou.) It was perfect, provided Martin could rise above comments on his nose and problems with pastels. 'I've brought the wrong colours,' he sighed. 'As usual.' I could see what he meant. In the muted morning light, the whole scene – water, mud, stone, sky – was a study in dull pewter. It was intensely beautiful, intensely Chinese in a way we'd both begun to think had disappeared; as if a Song dynasty wash drawing had come to life, or never died.

Another rhythm broke in, an audible one – the far faint whump of a bass drum. It was joined by an exploratory rattle on a snare drum, then by the parps and farts of brass warming up. Suddenly the distant music took off, extraordinary in the morning air of rural Fujian: tiddle-*pom* tiddle-*pom* tiddle-*pom-pom-pom* . . . the Radetsky March.

'I think it is a funeral,' Wang Feng said.

By the time we got to the nearby village of Bridgend (I forget the Chinese name), the rehearsal had broken up. The band were wandering among the village butchers and fishmongers and their attendant cats and pugdogs, wearing shakos and frogged and epauletted tunics in red and green and looking like survivors from Austerlitz. Later, however, we watched the funeral procession. The Radetsky, at a lick, was joined by firecrackers thrown at the feet of us onlookers. It was all most unfunereal; at least until the bereaved came past – 'for mourning apparel the infidels wear white capes', as IB noted – weeping loudly round the catafalque and counter-pointed by a quartet of wailing shawms while, far ahead now, the strains of old Austria-Hungary faded and died.

Back on the bridge, Martin had by now become inured to the aspersions cast on his nose, so we left him happily pastelling and set off back into town. On the way I asked Wang Feng about the slender conical column that rose on the riverbank. He explained that it was supposed to ward off typhoons. As we drove back into the city, the elegant obelisk remained in my mind. So too did that enigmatic word, 'typhoon'. It is as encrusted with associations from the ocean world I'd been exploring as 'monsoon', and at first sight it seems to have arrived in English by a similar route – from the Arabic *tufan*, a great flood, via the Indian subcontinent, where it designates a storm, by way of the Portuguese *tufão*. But what of the ancient Greek Typhon, a monstrous creature that whips up hurricanes? And *t'ai-fung*, a dialect word from over the strait in Taiwan meaning a deadly wind? If and how the three terms are tied up, no one has ever worked out. It is a word freighted with meanings. But in a place like this, frequented by tycoons from far away as well as by typhoons, such multiple possibilities of origin aren't so surprising.

Reading the Arabic inscriptions in Mr Wang's Maritime Museum was the *post mortem* equivalent of meeting those multinational wor-shippers at the Smooth Pagoda. The Muslims of Quanzhou IB mentions are all of Persian origin; here were tombstones of his century, and not just of Persians but of Turks and Bukharans and Khorazmians and Arabians – even a Yemeni from Hamdan, a mountainous region north of my adoptive home and far from the sea. The diversity went beyond graves, and beyond Islam. Here too were a statue of Vishnu, a relief of Mani, a slab engraved in Gothic script, and the carved and inscribed remnants of Zoroastrians, Nestorians and Latin Christians, all living and trading in Quanzhou under Yuan rule. 'In the lanes and streets of Quanzhou,' wrote the poet Bao He back in the time of the Tang dynasty, 'strangers come together from across the entire world.' They stayed on and, along with the local population, multiplied. By IB's time the city with the greatest harbour in the world also had one of the greatest populations – at around half a million, perhaps seven times that of London.

Wang Feng and I made our way to the world's former greatest harbour. It is to the west of the city on the Jin River, and far enough inland from Quanzhou Bay to be reasonably safe from typhoons. We stood on the quayside watching the river slide past, yellow with silt and thick as potters' slip. Here, at the far end of his world, IB made his Chinese landfall; here landed the merchant venturers of the west whose tombstones I'd seen – landed and never left; here Marco Polo took ship with the Mongol lady Kokachin, betrothed to the Khan of Persia; here Admiral Zheng He set sail with his treasure junks to bring to the Yongle emperor ebony and ivory and giraffes and the obeisance of kings from the end of the Western Ocean; here embarked another young scholar called Mr Wang, whom I'd recently bumped into in my book-travels – the tantalizing Wang Dayuan, a traveller on his way to India, Sarandib, Persia, Arabia, the Swahili coast, Egypt and, in the far west, IB's home town of Tangier, all of which he described in his *Summary Information on Foreign Lands* of 1350 . . . in short, the Chinese mirror-image of IB.* And here, today, where IB saw a hundred junks of the largest size, were a few shabby fishing boats painted in peeling green. Here, where the treasures of a quarter of the globe once came ashore, they were unloading sprats and crabs and moribund eels in slimy plastic crates.

But in Quanzhou dreams of argosies come true. Back in the centre of town, we emerged from Shoe Alley on to West Street, a road busy with motorbikes, cycle-rickshaws and salesmen's cries. Towards its western end was a line of dark trees with twisty trunks, their branches severely pollarded. 'These are *citong* trees,' Wang Feng said. 'The ones that gave the city its name for the Arabs and Europeans, "Zaytun".' (Strange how words go travelling, I thought; as early as the eleventh century, silk weavers in Muslim Spain were producing glossy fabrics and calling them *zaytuni*, 'satin'.)

---

* The symmetry is uncanny, even down to the doubts of scholars as to whether Wang Dayuan really made it to Morocco. He tantalizes me because only bits of his work have been translated from the original. What further treasures there must be in a book by a man who can compose a hundred-stanza poem describing a piece of coral found south of Kelunpu (Colombo); who can write of the witches of Champa whose heads fly off at night and go looking for human excrement to devour!

Behind the trees was the garden of the Kaiyuan Temple, and beside the temple a modern and undistinguished building. Inside this, high and dry in the flow of time, was a Song-dynasty junk.

It wasn't one of those giants that IB saw; they could reach 300 feet and more in length. But it was the real thing: an almost complete cedarwood hull found in the preservative mud of Quanzhou Bay downstream from where we'd left Martin, seventy-five feet long even with its prow missing. It dated, Mr Wang said, from the mid-1270s – a lifetime before IB stepped ashore here; about the time young Marco Polo got to Xanadu. I looked down into the hull from above and remembered IB's account of the unique construction of junks. The interior of the hull, he said, was divided by 'enormous baulks of timber fastened by huge nails three cubits long . . . and on top of which they fix the lower decking of the ship'. And there were the baulks, bulkheads forming thirteen watertight compartments. Later in our stay, we went to visit a shipwright at Chongwu, a little way round Quanzhou Bay from where the Song junk foundered. He still used the same form of construction for his hulls, and followed the same shapely lines; and we delighted each other when I tried out on him IB's term, *zaw*, for a middling-sized junk – 'Ah, *zao*, this is what I am building!' Ships, no less than living things, have their own genetics, their family features, for 'The Junk and the Dhow, though they look like anyhow,/Were the Mother and the Father of all Ships.'

More evocative still of the great days of Quanzhou than the junk, however, was its cargo. It was stored in an upstairs room and still had its original labels of consignment, written on little dockets of bamboo. There was sandalwood and aloes-wood, areca-nut and tortoiseshell, mercury and cinnabar. There were cowries from the Maldives, peppercorns from Malabar, Arabian frankincense and 'dragonspit' – ambergris, from the whale-haunted waters of the ocean itself. A whole material odyssey. These products from across the ocean world hadn't, of course, come from their diverse places of origin aboard this one small ship. Rather, they were evidence of that vast network of trade and transshipment that made the ocean small. I remembered looking out to sea from the palace at Kilwa Kisiwani, 7,000 sailing miles away on the Swahili coast, and picturing China just beyond the horizon.

And there were other objects from the ship that made the scale human once again. Who had owned the chess set from which that pawn had come? Who had worn that battered straw hat? . . . It might have graced the head of one of those nose-admiring oyster-wives down on Luoyang Bridge.

*

'Do you not see that the ships run their course through the ocean by the grace of God, that He may show His signs?' The Qur'anic verse was as clear as the day it was cut in the hard Quanzhou granite in 1310 – the year the mosque was rebuilt, according to an inscription over the entrance. The Mosque of the Companions had been founded three centuries earlier; not as early as the ancient and no longer extant Unicorn Mosque, but old enough for IB and me. More remarkable than its age, however, was its appearance. Of all the Yuan-dynasty imports into Quanzhou, this was the biggest – an entire Near Eastern-style building, complete with an *iwan* vaulted entrance and vestigial stalactite pendentives. The city records mention that it also had a minaret, and another feature extraordinary in China (*pace* 'Kubla Khan') – a stately dome; they both collapsed at some time in the seventeenth century. Even without these, it looked stranger here than a gothic church in Colombo – as strange as the pagoda at Kew. And in it was something of supreme importance for me.

'Here it is,' Wang Feng said. We were standing by a granite slab incised, this time, with Chinese characters. '"From the land to the west of our land,"' he read, '"from the Tashi land . . ." "Tashi" is the old name for the Persians and Arabs. It comes from the name of the Tajik people. " . . . from the Tashi land came . . ."' I followed Wang Feng's finger down the characters; it was like watching an expert tracker at work. The marks told of another mosque and of how a certain A-ha-mo – 'Ahmad' – had neglected his duties and let it fall into disrepair, until the Muslims were encouraged to complain – '"by . . ." ah, this is your man, ". . . *Bu-lu-han-ding.*"'

I touched the characters that contained the name of Burhan al-Din. To me they were haphazard arrangements of strokes, as inscrutable as runes, visually ungraspable – except for the 'Ding', which resembled an anchor with a missing shank. But they were proof to flaunt in the face of scholars like Ferrand, the historian of Arab geography who doubted IB ever went east of Sarandib. Perhaps not proof positive; but then, when I'm dead too, who of you who read this will be able to prove I went to China? No, this inscription was enough to vindicate IB. It is the touchstone of his travels east, the landfall of a trajectory that took off way back in Alexandria with the prophecy of that first Burhan al-Din, surnamed the Lame.

What about that other trajectory, the one that links the name on the stone to living flesh and blood? We asked around for Bu-lu-han Ding's descendants, the Xia family, who had clung to this mosque until a generation ago, camping out in its ruins. But they'd been relocated, tidied away when the place was renovated in the years after the Cultural Revolution. There were a few of them left, but no one knew where. Quanzhou's material Muslim heritage was preserved; the human chain, the link between people and place, was broken.

★

It was Dr Ding, Director of the Maritime Museum, who turned out to be my missing link with IB's age. Ding Yuling was even more charming than her name. As I remarked to Martin, it was a name that rang a bell; but a bell with resonances beyond those of unseemly puns. There on her card was the one Chinese character, of all the thousands, that I could recognize – that broken anchor that said 'Ding'. And just as the Xia family had taken their name from an element of an Arabic title – 'Shaykh' – so had the Dings. 'They say our surname is from someone called "Shams al-Din",' Dr Ding told me. The hairs on my neck stood up: Shams al-Din was IB's honorific. 'But you should meet one of my older cousins to hear the details.' She arranged for me to visit the Ding ancestral temple, outside Quanzhou in the village of Chendai.

Although he'd scattered his seed across a wide swathe of Asia, Shams al-Din Muhammad Ibn Battutah of Tangier wasn't, it seemed, the progenitor of the Ding clan. The sainted grandsire, however, was a worthy representative of IB's world. In a glassed-in portico at the Ding temple, Dr Ding's elderly and birdlike cousin showed me the portrait of his ancestor of twenty-three generations back: 'This is him: Zhan Si Ding!' Nobody seemed to know where Shams al-Din Tughanshah came from; but that was his unsinicized name, and he had arrived in Quanzhou a century or so before IB. To me 'Tughanshah' sounded Seljuk Turk, which could mean a provenance anywhere between the eastern Mediterranean and the Pamirs. Looking at the portrait of the big middle-aged man, I thought I detected a Central Asian cast to the features; but then, how lifelike was it? Unlike the portraits of himself that IB saw, this was a copy many times removed from the sitter's lifetime – perhaps no more than the graphic equivalent of a Chinese whisper. Still, he was depicted with a *gravitas* appropriate to the patriarch of a family that Mr Ding said was now 60,000 strong.

With the next portrait in the gallery we had leapt forward to the following century, and four generations, to the time after the Ming revolution and the resulting fall of the Yuan. By then, little more than twenty years after IB's visit, the China he saw had been transformed. Under the Yuan, Muslims of foreign origin had ranked second in dignity and wealth to the Mongol rulers. Over half the Yuan governors of Quanzhou had been Muslims; Muslim merchants had been the biggest taxpayers in this fabulously wealthy city.* But the rise of the Ming in the 1360s led to the persecution of the privileged *semuren*, or 'foreign population'. In 1366 there were massacres of Muslims in Quanzhou; after 1368 the victorious Ming regime banned all maritime communications. The door to the sea was opened briefly once again, early in the next century, for the splendid political armadas of Admiral Zheng He to sail out; and then it slammed shut. Another hundred years on, and Zaytun/ Quanzhou is mentioned by the Arab navigator Ahmad ibn Majid, along with a clutch of other places now lost to geography, only as a place of hearsay. It had slipped off the edge of the charts. Meanwhile, prudent Muslims like Shams al-Din Tughanshah's great-great-grandson had fled the towns and turned from trade to agriculture. They cultivated their gardens and made themselves as Chinese as they could.

The portrait of that descendant showed features that were already, appropriately, somewhat sinicized. It was a process that continued gradually along the line of pictures in the portico, and then accelerated into a large hall at the back of the temple. Here, rows of images done by hand from photographs showed deceased twentieth-century Dings, their faces indistinguishable from any others you might see in Fujian. The acculturation looked complete, the assimilation total. Revolutions, whether of Ming or of Mao, were only secondary cycles within the greater evolutionary wheel whose relentless turning flattened noses and ironed out all other differences.

I found also that the Islam of the Dings had undergone a similarly inexorable evolution. In the entrance to the main hall at the centre of the temple court Mr Ding pointed out the *basmalah* – 'In the Name of Allah' – carved in Sino-Arabic cloud-scroll script above a frieze of gambolling dragons. There was also a *shahadah* – 'There is no god but Allah' – in squared Kufic that had taken on the angular form of Chinese seal-script. Inside, the decor was tastefully opulent, with light percolating through lattices on to lacquered columns and carved console tables, on to sealing-wax red and dusky gold. Facing us was a large bronze jardinière containing joss-sticks, an altar bearing a vase

---

* The biggest of the big, the merchant Folian, is on record as having died leaving eighty ships and the equivalent of 13,500 litres of pearls – enough to fill a small swimming pool. Has a zero has crept in? Maybe not.

and a mirror and, behind them, an arched niche. It resembled the *mihrab* of a mosque, the bare alcove showing the direction of prayer. Here though, in place of the emptiness that pointed to an ineffable deity, the niche was filled with tall rectangular tablets, each carved with gilded characters on a green background. Mr Ding pointed to the central tablet, taller than the rest.

' "Zhan Si Ding" !' he read. 'Please note the green of the background. Green is the Islamic colour.' He then took me through some large framed inscriptions that hung on the side walls. They were honours boards, recording the names of Ding family members who had passed the civil service examinations on the Confucian classics and risen to become prominent mandarins. It was all inordinately strange – a sort of cross between a family crypt and a prefects' common-room, furnished like an up-market opium den and then given a token Islamic twist.

I asked Mr Ding the question that had been on my mind since I'd seen the Arabic script in the entrance to the hall. 'Would you consider yourself a Muslim?'

Mr Ding smiled and blinked through owl spectacles. 'No, I myself am not a Muslim. But I understand Islam, because I am head of the Islamic Association here.' A non-Muslim head of the Islamic Association . . . I was beginning to wonder if some vital nuances were being lost in translation. 'Of course, we do not burn symbolic money here,' Mr Ding went on; I remembered watching visitants at the temple in Guangzhou stoking a furnace with sackfuls of 'banknotes', offerings to appease the ancestors. 'And we do not bring pork into the building.'

Back in the portico, things became a little clearer. Mr Ding showed me the family history, published a few years earlier. It had a page or two of English summarizing the Chinese contents, and in this was the recurrent phrase, 'the Ding family of Hui nationality'. Hui – in full, Huihui guo, 'double-return religion' – denotes return to God and submission to Him and is the equivalent of the Arabic *islam*, 'giving oneself up' to God. Here though, 'Hui' had become a signifier of ancestry, of some generalized 'Muslim' ethnicity. The symbols and taboos of the ancestors' faith were worthy of respect, but the true reverence was to those ancestors themselves.

With this partial clarification, however, my mental map of how our world overlies IB's had just become more complex. Throughout my travels with him, I'd been looking not only for material relics of his age but, more importantly, for the human links. Here I'd found those links not only preserved and cherished, but worshipped with incense and prayers. Elsewhere – in Kilwa, the Maldives, Sri Lanka – I'd discovered how Islam had formed a crust on top of earlier beliefs, and how those beliefs had a habit of bubbling up to the surface. Here the opposite had happened. Islam was only a buried memory. I looked again at that nebulous *basmalah* that proclaimed the Name of God. In the beginning was the word; in the end, it's all that's left.

How wrong I was.

*

Imam Husayn Ding squeezed my knee to emphasize a point. It was a very Arab gesture – but then, he'd spent six years in al-Madinah, studying the language of the Prophet of Islam in the city where he is buried. We were nattering in Arabic on the steps of the mosque of Chendai – situated, with wonderful incongruity, bang next door to the Islamic ancestor temple.

Imam Ding was about thirty and, I couldn't help thinking, had a faintly Middle Eastern look to him: a slightly more prominent nose, rounder eyes than most Fujianese. I wondered if it was a case of Shams al-Din Tughanshah's genes bubbling up along with his faith, or if it was the effect of those six years' residence in Arabia. (It does happen. I was sure Martin's eyes had narrowed since we'd arrived in China; in his case, though, this may have been the result of squinting all day at sampans and mudbanks, for he was still on the Luoyang Bridge.)

I'd just sat in on the imam's Arabic class – mostly children, and some headscarved women, all Dings, repeating their *ba bu bi* just as they do at literacy classes in the Moroccan antipodes. He was a good teacher – firm, kind, giving. 'The number of students is limited to seventy,' he said. 'You see, there is a fear about the influ-ence of Islam. In fact most of them are hoping to work with the Arab traders who come here. But I have my hopes too', he added with a gentle smile and another knee-squeeze, 'for the *da'wah*.' The 'summons', the call to make that double return to God.

Husayn Ding called the afternoon prayer, then I joined him inside the mosque. The congregation was small – some women from the Arabic class in their own purdahed-off section, and a few men; but the summons was getting heard. While Husayn led the prostrations, I sat out in the lobby of the prayer-hall. Here on the wall hung a photo of the Ka'bah and, written beside it in what I recognized as the imam's hand, a saying of the Prophet: *Seek knowledge, even if the journey take you to China.*

★

The juxtaposition of buildings – mosque, ancestor temple – and of Dings – Dr Ding the scholar, old Mr Ding the guardian of the ancestors, young Imam Ding, still younger Dings hoping to work with Arab businessmen – epitomized the Muslim history of southern China. In them the old cycle of travel, trade and religion, of acculturation and reculturation, keeps turning. And on a hill on the other side of Quanzhou I found the completion of a cycle.

In the eastern outskirts of the city is a small but prominent knoll called Lingshan, the Hill of Souls. Martin, under the influence of a soporific lunch of clam stew, oyster omelette and beer, eaten under a tree at the bottom of the hill, soon dropped out and stayed on a bench to sketch. Wang Feng and I continued up the path. 'According to *Fujian Annals*,' he said, 'Prophet Muhammad sent four sages to bring Islam to China. One went to Guangzhou, one to Yangzhou in Jiangsu province, and two came here.' The path became a broad staircase. 'That was in Wude regnal period, at the start of Tang dynasty, AD 618–26.' It sounded impossibly early. Would Muhammad have had time to dispatch missionaries across Asia when he was still fighting the pagan Meccans and dealing with the Jews of al-Madinah?

We reached the top of the stairs. Whatever the date, it was a remarkable place. A horseshoe-shaped colonnade, more than Doric in its severity, had been sunk into the hillside. In the open centre of the horseshoe was a plain and elegant pavilion, its sweeping stone roof raised on four more columns and, beneath this, the ogival ends of two tombs. All was of glittering granite that stood out with dream-clarity against a dark, almost black backdrop of trees. There was no other colour, and none of the waxen prettification that weighed heavy on almost every other historic site I'd seen in China. The Two Sages, it seemed, had slept untouched through war and revolution, up here on the Hill of Souls.

Like the legend of elephant-taming Ibn Khafif in Sarandib, the story of the anonymous sages almost certainly simplified a longer and more complex history, that of Islam's arrival in China. But it also materialized it, provided relics to touch; and perhaps, I realized when I looked at a pair of granite incense burners, one at the head and one at the foot of the tombs, it provided the rootless Muslims with adoptive ancestors to venerate. Both incense burners contained the stubs of joss-sticks. I sniffed them: they'd been burned recently.

Wang Feng called me over to the colonnade and showed me a granite slab bearing crisp Chinese characters. 'This inscription was placed here in 1417,' he said, 'by Admiral Zheng He.' That other great Muslim traveller, the one whose path I'd crossed in Sri Lanka. There, his landfall was marked by that trilingual inscription in the Colombo Museum. This stone was still in its original place. It commemorated the admiral's safe return, Wang Feng said, from a voyage to the Western Ocean and the Arabian Gulf – to the homeland of the Two Sages. '"He came here,"' Mr Wang read, '"to offer incense."'

Yet others had offered their fragrant thanks in this place. In the apex of the horseshoe was another inscription, this time in Arabic. The script was wayward, but just legible enough for me to make out that the occupants of the tombs were 'two men imbued with *barakah*' – with blessed influence – '. . . and if calamities arise and people are powerless and perplexed, they seek refuge with these two and make a mutual vow to visit them . . . and thus they return safely'. The inscription was dated AH 723 – AD 1323.

It was a numinous place; a place where voyages and trajectories ended, where circles closed . . . and linked, too, for it took me back without warning – to Bristol, of all places, back to the English city of my birth and to the surprising medieval-oriental chapel attached to my childhood parish church, another holy place where prayers were made before the ships set sail from the harbour down below, where thanks were given for safe returns. That chapel was built around the year IB left his home town, a year or two after this Arabic inscription was set up here on the Hill of Souls. And it was one of the points – for what journey has just one beginning?

– where my own voyage through this world of landfalls and homecomings had begun.

We went down Lingshan by another path. Round the flank of the hill we passed hundreds of much more recent tombs, copies of the tombs of the Two Sages, but each with the broken-anchor character at its foot. The Dings, in death, had returned to the very beginnings of Islam in China.

★

Before we left Quanzhou I met one last member of the Ding clan. Yusuf Ding owned the harbour where IB had landed, and a clutch of factories, and real estate in Hong Kong. He put on a banquet in which we drank bumpers from gilded goblets and sang his company song. After an inspirational number of 'dry bottoms' (as the toast goes; 'chin chin' seems *passé* even in China) I improvised a solo version of the song in English; luckily, 'Ding' is not a difficult word to find rhymes for. After dinner we cruised Quanzhou in an open-topped Porsche. Back at his hilltop villa I tried to teach him 'Chopsticks' on a gilded grand piano; he tried to teach me mah-jong, and let me win a pleasing sum.

In Yusuf Ding the old Muslim mercantile tradition of Zaytun lives on.

★

'Before I do anything else,' Martin said when we were installed in our hotel room in Fuzhou, 'I'm going to go and have a massage.'

The oystery, estuarine damps of Luoyang Bridge had got to his back, never Martin's strong point. I couldn't help thinking, though, that with massages – in China no less than anywhere else – one thing might lead to another. The first person we'd met when we stepped out of the back door of our hotel in Guangzhou was a stocky, frizzy-haired woman who greeted us with, 'Massage? Sex? You wan'? Is nice?' and a broad unhappy smile. She wasn't the last; although, as Martin observed, the prostitutes tended to go for him while I got the beggars.*

---

* We never heard the old-fashioned poetic invitation extended to my friend Kevin Rushby by a rickshaw-pedalling Chinese pimp in Penang: 'Missah, you wan' suckee, or fuckee?' Missah's Missus was sitting next to him at the time.

'Enjoy yourself,' I said over the top of the hotel directory. This heavily tooled volume said that 'sauna center provide you sauna and steam room and several services you will be enjoyed . . .' The services listed were all perfectly innocent ones such as ear-picking, but no doubt there were extra-curricular activities on offer too. I thought back to the sauna wing of our Quanzhou hotel and the besuited harsh-voiced businessman I'd seen scratching his crotch in the doorway; he didn't look as if he needed his ears picked. And I thought of what IB wrote about special services in Chinese hotels: 'If a merchant wants to take a concubine, the hotel keeper buys him a slave-girl . . . The price of slave girls is cheap.' This IB puts under a heading, '*On their way of preventing depravity among the merchants*'. (A touch hypocritical? Not according to the letter of the Islamic law of the time – a law of which IB himself, the legal scholar, took such pleasurable advantage: to *buy* a slave-girl for sex is perfectly permissible, to *pay* a girl for sex is depraved. There is no hypocrisy. QED.)

In a way, the present-day arrangements made sense. In a hotel you have a restaurant, a bar, a laundry, a coffee shop; why not have a knocking- (or, I suspect in most cases, only a frotting-) shop?

Another need is supplied: we give you a bed, we feed and water you, we jerk you off, or whatever. The more Chinese hotels we stayed in, the more I realized this was the case. It must be utterly passionless. There was no temptation, no turn-on – certainly not for me nor, I think, for IB. China is one of the rare places where he spent some time but doesn't mention his own (perfectly permissible, of course) sexual experiences.

Martin was back much sooner than he'd expected. He seemed a little flustered. 'I didn't realize it was *that* sort of place. I mean, they even had this notice that said, "Venereal Disease Will Not Be Tolerated" . . .'

'I think they're all those sort of places,' I said. 'You get your massage, but you get the other stuff as well. Willy-nilly.'

Martin groaned.

Later, while he was fixing his pastels, I had my own small experience of twenty-first-century concubinage, or at any rate hostessage. I'd gone off in search of an early beer. In the big empty hotel bar, the only other customer was a studious-looking girl with spectacles and very creditable English. After the usual introductions, I asked Patricia about a small scarlet-faced deity sitting behind the bar among the whisky bottles. I'd seen him before, or a bigger and more ancient version of him, in a sort of sentry-box shrine by Luoyang Bridge. In both manifestations he had a beard and looked very cross, like an angry garden gnome.

Patricia was beginning to explain that the deity's name was Guanggong, 'Redface', and that he was very popular, when I realized she had no drink. 'I'm so sorry. May I tempt you to a beer?'

'Thank you,' she said in a tone that could have meant Yes or No. 'Excuse me, please.' She rose and left the bar. I wondered if I'd offended her.

Some minutes later her place was taken by an elegant woman in a slinky cheongsam – split, I couldn't help noticing, to the moot point between thigh and buttock. She gestured languidly at Redface. 'They like Guanggong', she said, 'because he attracts money.' My new companion had very creditable English too; but it was a strange conversational opener.

'What a coincidence,' I said. 'I was just talking about Guanggong with . . .' – the realization hit me just in time – '. . . with *you!*'

Patricia's transformation had been swift and startling. Cinderella wasn't in it. I was red-faced now.

I had another beer; she preferred water. Conversation wilted. Except for us and the barman, the bar remained empty. I asked for the bill. It came, also swift and startling. 'Good Lord!' I exclaimed. 'I see what you mean about Redface attracting money.' Patricia smiled and hoped she'd see me later, when the karaoke got going.

★

Fuzhou, on first acquaintance earlier that afternoon, had not been a lovely city. Entering its industrial outskirts on the bus from Quanzhou, we watched a grey disconsolate scene grind past. After a long silence, Martin spoke, as if to himself. 'It could almost be Watford . . .'

'But as somebody once remarked,' I said, 'it's a hell of a lot further away.'

On second acquaintance the following day, things didn't improve much. Unlike Watford, Fuzhou had an eighth-century pagoda in its town centre; but the tower was marooned in acres of ugly buildings and construction sites. 'They ought to start a PLO,' Martin said. 'A Pagoda Liberation Organization.' A group of building workers downed tools and stared at us in astonishment as we walked past.

Overhead, the sun was invisible behind the opaque greyish-white substance that masqueraded as air. It wasn't so much a pea-souper as a rice-congee smog, and the citizens of Fuzhou were obliged at regular intervals to expel its congealed residue from the bottom of their lungs. The streets were loud with the sound of hawking; the ground glistened with pavement-oysters. Martin asked me to remind him why we were here.

The reason sounded dreadfully flimsy. During his stay in the city of Qanjanfu, IB says, on the way from Quanzhou to Hangzhou, he was introduced to another arrival, an Arab like himself. 'I looked at him for a long while,' IB remembered,

and he said, 'I see you looking at me as if you knew me.' I said, 'Where are you from?' and he said, 'From Sabtah.' I said, 'And I'm from Tangier!' And he greeted me a second time and wept, so much so that I ended up weeping with him. I said, 'Have you been to India?' and he said, 'Yes, I've visited the sultan's seat, Delhi.' And when I heard this I remembered who he was. I said, 'You're al-Bushri, aren't you!' and he said, 'Yes, I am!'[*]

It was Burhan al-Din the Lame, the yarn-winding mystic of Alexandria, who first set IB on the road to China. It would be a fair guess to say that, in China, it was al-Bushri – a native of Sabtah, now the Spanish colony of Ceuta and just twenty-five miles from IB's home town – who pointed the way back west. It is after IB parts from this poignant reminder of his native land that he writes of his severe bout of culture-shock, of the unbearable strangeness of China. For the rest of his Chinese travels his heart is elsewhere. From the time he left Tangier it had taken him more than twenty years and 900 pages to get here. He was back home in three years and fourteen pages that are little more than a blur of place-names. (And then he was off again . . . but I mustn't get ahead of him.)

'Qanjanfu', I said, summing up these thoughts for Martin, 'is the turning point, so to speak, of IB's travels.'

'Then why are we in Fuzhou,' Martin asked, 'and not in . . . what's it called?'

'Qanfanju. I mean Qanjanfu. Well, it's because Qanjanfu doesn't seem to exist. I mean, I think IB got his –zhous and his –fus in a twist . . .'

'Don't we all.'

'. . . and Qanjanfu is in fact Fuzhou.' It could hardly be anywhere else, I explained: a big city with a port for sea-going ships and a prominent Muslim population between Quanzhou and Hangzhou.

Martin, I could see, was unconvinced by all of this. More

---

[*] Sir Henry Yule, commenting on this meeting in *Cathay and the Way Thither*, mentions a similar anecdote told of Marshal Keith, an eighteenth-century Scots nobleman in the Russian service. Keith was negotiating with the Turkish Grand Vizier on the Black Sea coast following Russo-Turkish hostilities in 1739. 'The venerable Turk's look of recognition drew from the Marshal the same question that Al-Bushri addressed to Ibn Batuta, and the answer came forth in broad Fifeshire dialect – "Eh man! aye, I mind you weel, for my father was the bellman of Kirkaldy!"'

worryingly, so was I. We were in Fuzhou because of a brief encounter that might have taken place here ten lifetimes ago . . . The mists were closing in over IB's Chinese journey, and ours.

There was one last island of relative solidity, in Hangzhou, the city of the Phoenix Mosque.

★

'You are like two ancient sages,' Nancy said, beaming at us through her spectacles.

It was a change from being like two Himalayan yetis. But it was hard to know how to respond. 'More like Gilbert and George,' Martin murmured.

Nancy was another studious-looking woman with excellent English, enlivened in her case by the odd malapropism. She was older than my hostess in Fuzhou, however, and if she possessed a slinky cheongsam she never slipped into it for us. But in any case Hangzhou was too cold for thigh-revealing silk.

'Perhaps, later on,' Nancy said, 'you would like me to show you some genuine Chinese antics?' She smiled suggestively. Even Martin had no answer to this. Maybe I'd misjudged her . . . 'Such as porcelain and old carvings?'

'Oh, I see,' I said. 'Very kind of you, but we are on a bit of a budget.'

Time was running out as well as money, and Hangzhou was big. IB said it took three whole days of travelling to cross it, and described it as the biggest city on earth. This was no exaggeration; it only lost the title five centuries later, to Victorian London. We'd therefore decided it would make sense to engage a guide. Lai-lan – 'because I show you the *lie* of the *land*!' – sounded perfect. She preferred 'Nancy', however; I think we mangled her tones.

We delivered Martin at Nancy's suggestion to the Pagoda of the Six Harmonies. Like the obelisk by the Luoyang Bridge it was an apotropaic structure, designed in this case to subdue the notorious Qiantang Bore that surged seasonally up Hangzhou's river. The pagoda, though, was no dainty spire but a miniature mountain of a building 200 feet tall. Martin felt he would soon need some relief from painting such a large object, and said he had a yen to draw animals.

'It is always a pleasure', Nancy said, 'to look at oily portraits of animals.' She wrote Martin a note in Chinese saying, 'Please take me to the zoo'. (I nearly asked her to add, 'put me in the yeti enclosure, and feed me three times a day'.) No doubt, she said, some kindly cab driver would deliver him. 'In the meantime, we will go and injure ourselves on West Lake.'

Ever since the days of the Tang, West Lake has been the place to enjoy – or did she mean 'endure'? – oneself in Hangzhou. IB did it in style. Almost incredibly, given that he had lost the rest of his embassy – including the stupendously valuable diplomatic gift and all the returning Chinese envoys – in a shipwreck on the Indian coast and had taken more than four years over the journey, he was still posing in China as an ambassador from the sultan of Delhi. Perhaps it is a piece of retrospective self-puffery. Whatever the truth, he charmed himself into the hospitable circle of 'the great amir Qurtay'.

This person has been identified by Mongolists as a high provincial official called Quratai. Just when his own veracity has been established, however, IB goes on to stretch our credibility with an account of the celebrated Rope Trick, staged by Quratai for his amusement. In this most elaborate version of the illusion the conjuror's assistant not only climbed a rope hanging from the sky but was also bloodily dismembered, then reassembled, before the gaping spectators.* In contrast, IB's description of the water-borne entertainment Quratai put on is easier to believe in. The mock battle in which decorated boats shot fruit at each other, oranges versus lemons, is almost too whimsical to be invented, and perfectly in keeping with the tastes of Yuan-era Hangzhou. And then, IB says, there were 'musicians who sang in Chinese, Arabic and Persian. The amir's son particularly liked the Persian songs, and he told them to repeat a certain verse. They did so many times, until I was able to memorize it. It had a beautiful melody, and it went,

> My heart I gave to care,
> I sank in sorrow's flood,
> Until I stood in prayer,
> And turned for strength to God.

Although IB didn't realize it the verse, which he quotes in the original Persian, is by the great poet Sa'di of Shiraz. For me there is something about this scene, this song, that has that academically unrigorous yet clearly audible ring of truth.

I'd already seen, and heard, the unexpected but enduring influence of Persia on the music of southern China. In Quanzhou, we had been to a concert at a tea-house in an old Confucian temple. The music itself was indescribably strange: a Trobriand Islander would have grasped as much of *Wozzeck* as I did of this song-cycle

---

* On the Rope Trick, see *The Hall of a Thousand Columns*, pp. 182–5. I wonder if the nineteenth-century Moroccan version of the trick reported in Wilfred Scawen Blunt's diary was originally inspired by IB's Chinese chapter.

in the Fujianese dialect. But some of the instruments were familiar. There was a lute which could have come straight from the arms of one of the coy singers who appear on Persian lustreware tiles. And there was a type of oboe that had even retained its Persian name, *sunai* (though minus the troublesome rolled *r* of the original *surnai*), as well as its shape. I could picture such instruments accompanying the Persian hit IB heard on West Lake.

Nancy couldn't arrange a Rope Trick, she admitted when I went through my wish list with her, or a Battle of the Fruit; nor could she sing Persian poems. 'I can recite Chinese poetry,' she said. But as we floated over West Lake in a boat that resembled a college barge, a relentless amplified commentary (' . . . on the right you can see the Pavilion at the Heart of the Lake, formerly known as the Pavilion Where the Herons Flap Their Wings . . . now you can see the restaurant where President Nixon dined in 1972 . . .') left no space for poems. The day was cold and damp. The lake, the sky, the surrounding hills were barely distinguishable from one another, lost in a monochrome wash of grey. The lake looked bored with itself, as if it had been contemplated, painted, versified about and whimsified over for too many centuries (' . . . the Pavilion of the

Reflections of My Heart . . . the Autumn Moon on the Lake, which is one of the Ten Prospects . . .')

And then, in a gap in the tour-guide's litany, Nancy recited a poem about the lake that made sense of it. It was, she said, by Su Dongpo, an eleventh-century poet-governor of Hangzhou who enlarged the lake during his term of office. I remembered the name: Su Dongpo was one of the Song-dynasty poets who had lived on White Cloud Mountain. The original was in a lilting iambic. 'It is hard to translate,' Nancy said. (When isn't it?) 'But it means something like this:

> Shimmering water at its fall
> Sunny day best
> Blurred mountains in a haze
> Marvellous even in rain
> Compare the lake to the beautiful woman Xizi
> She looks just as becoming
> Lightly made up or richly adorned.'

It was equally hard to translate this muted scene back into the water-extravaganza IB saw. There was, however, one memory of that opulently frivolous age. We tied up beside it at the west end of the lake – an enormous barge, copied from a Song imperial design, Nancy said. Its superstructure was a pair of sweeping-eaved pavilions, its hull a gilded dragon with a head as high as a house and an expression on its face – as well it might have, finding itself adrift in the twenty-first century – of gape-mouthed astonishment.

We walked back round the lake, back from golden dragons into the monochrome present. Monochrome, that is, except for splashes of colour among the willows – one was a girl in a long orange off-the-shoulder number and goose-pimples, sitting on a bench, another a woman in a mauve ball gown shivering in the boreal mist at the water's edge – brides, Nancy explained, waiting to be photographed. 'Marco Polo also mentioned weddings on West Lake,' she said. The brides looked as if they had bloomed in the wrong season. The warm ocean world that I'd been exploring seemed a long way away.

That evening Martin and I discovered more evidence that the

opulence IB saw in the world's biggest city – a city of extravagant display that the Chinese of his time called 'the Melting-Pot of Money' – is still to be found. Near the shore of the lake was a Bentley showroom that might have flown in from London's Park Lane. Round the corner there was a Vacherin Constantin shop; I went in and gingerly asked the price of a chronometer that was displayed in splendid isolation in the window. It cost the equivalent of £10,000 and yes, they said, they sold well.

We visited a large chemist's to make some more modest purchases. The place was packed with shoppers and Christmas decorations. As I waited in the queue for the check-out holding my tube of toothpaste and a banknote, I realized for the first time how surprising the currency was. IB, too, had been surprised: 'They buy and sell with bits of paper! Each note is the size of the palm of one's hand, and is stamped with the stamp of the ruler . . .' I hadn't thought about it before, but the ruler's stamp of our age was very strange indeed; stranger than the Queen on coins in Hong Kong. For here in my hand was a portrait of Mao Zedong, a man whose lifespan had coincided for fifteen years with mine, and yet who seemed to belong to a time way back beyond the Yuan, when the outside world was kept at bay by the Wall. And here we were on a street with a Starbucks, a Pizza Hut, a McDonalds and two KFCs, listening to a Chinese girlie band singing a disco-beat version of 'Silent Night'.

Come to think of it, that was probably today's equivalent of Persian hymns on the lake.

★

Equivalents were all very well. But I still wanted to look for some final, tangible survival from IB's world, before the eastern trail went cold.

The Phoenix Mosque, the Friday mosque IB mentions, was the place. The phoenix had lost its 'head' – another Building for Looking at the Moon – to a road-widening scheme in the 1930s; old photos show a portal dripping with Arabic calligraphy, a stack of curling roofs above. But its wings were still intact, formed by long porticos, together with the main prayer-hall that is its body. The exterior of the hall was topped by three stubby pagodas. Inside,

I found myself in a tall brick chamber. The pagodas concealed three very un-Chinese, highly Middle Eastern domes. Like the mosque in Quanzhou, this structure still looked foreign 700 years after it was built – as foreign as a Starbucks or a song by Sa'di. I sat there in the chilly half-light, peering at a leaflet about it – 'Muslims from home and abroad praying', one of the captions read – and wondering at which spot in this chamber IB had prayed on the two Fridays he spent in Hangzhou.

I went to look in the mosque's Hall of Tablets, housed in one of the wings, in case any of the few people IB mentions by name in Hangzhou were to be found among the score of old Arabic and Persian tombstones that had survived. I wanted to look too – a wild, mad stab – for a stone bearing the name of the fellow-countryman IB bumped into, al-Bushri. God knows where he ended up; he was no more than a needle in the haystack of history. But he could have just as well ended up here as anywhere, here where the Maritime Silk Road finally petered out.

To be honest, though, it was less a case of me hoping to find him than of him haunting me. Like the hermit of Guangzhou and the two Burhan al-Dins, al-Bushri has wider implications. Much wider even than China and India: at the far end of another continent, a full 8,000 miles to the west, IB's chance meeting with him would have a sequel. At the time, all we see is the surface, the coincidence in the chaos. The deeper structures of journeys, lives, histories, remain invisible.

I examined the stones in the dim damp cold; rain fell audibly outside. Persians, Turks, Arabs, hard to decipher as ever, all from IB's fourteenth century; but no one I was looking for. And, of course, no Bushri. '*Listen to advice*,' said an Arabic verse on a gravestone, in a script that was clearer than all the rest:

> Our time upon the earth is short.
> Not so our time beneath it.

To be honest, I'd had enough of slabs of stone, of stabs and long shots, enough of the cold and the dead and the hard-to-read. But before I left I went to an office along the phoenix's wing to pay my respects to the living imam.

Imam Ma took me aback. It wasn't that he looked as un-Chinese as the domed prayer-hall of his mosque. If he looked like anyone – small compact figure in a well-worn suit, high-bridged nose (like mine), intricate wrinkles (also, increasingly, like mine), growing smile about to break into some gleefully embarrassing remark – he looked like my father. I blinked hard and the vision went.

The reality was almost as strange. After the usual compliments I happened to ask Imam Ma about his family name. It is one of the most common Muslim surnames, and happens to mean 'horse'.* Was I right in thinking it was another of those abbreviations from Arabic, like 'Ding' and 'Xia'?

'That is correct,' the imam said. 'It is usually a shortened form of "Ma-ha-mo", which is the Chinese form of "Muhammad". But in our family it is different. We do not know exactly who our ancestor was, but we think he was an Arab, because his surname was "Ma-li-ki", that is, "al-Maliki".'

Again, I was taken aback. The Malikis are one of the four Sunni schools of Islamic law. Such badges of jurisprudential allegiance were often worn by scholars of the law in addition to their other surnames. And the Maliki school is virtually confined, now as in IB's day, to north-west Africa. The likelihood of Imam Ma being descended from a Maghribi compatriot of IB was overwhelming. Perhaps he was a descendant of that scholar of law, al-Bushri al-Maliki of Ceuta . . . perhaps of Ibn Battutah al-Maliki and of some hotel concubine . . . . . .

The dots might as well go on for ever. It was a flight of fancy. But then, this was the Phoenix Mosque.

'Have you noticed', Imam Ma asked as I said farewell, 'that you and I have the same nose?' He beamed and squeezed my hand. 'Muslim noses!'

---

* Nancy tried me with a Chinese tone-twister that includes all the four words transcribed by the single Latin digraph, *ma*: '*Mother* rode the *horse* but the *horse* was *slow* so *mother swore* at the *horse*.'

West

I arrived at the town of Sijilmasah . . . where I stayed with the jurist Abu Muhammad al-Bushri. It was his brother whom I had met in China, in the city of Qanjanfu. How far apart the two of them were!

Ibn Battutah, *Travels*

Embarking on a junk at Zaytun (Quanzhou), IB began his long but sketchily recounted westward voyage. On the way to his first stop-over, a return visit to the Sumatran sultanate of Samudra, his ship had a close encounter with what the crew called a rukhkh. Some commentators have cited this episode as an example of the alleged untrustworthiness of IB's eastern travels. At no point, however, does he himself identify this 'roc' with the giant bird of legend. Rather, he depicts it as a natural phenomenon, perhaps the sort of looming cloud formation associated with the arch-squalls common in the China Seas.

From Sumatra IB's account of his itinerary is severely attenuated: by sea to south-west India, southern Arabia and Hormuz, then by land through Persia to Baghdad and Damascus. Here, his path crossed that of another traveller from the east – the pandemic later known as the Black Death (on which see the Damascus chapter of Travels with a Tangerine). After visiting the plague-ridden cities of Jerusalem and Cairo and performing the Mecca pilgrimage, perhaps for the seventh time, IB decided to return to his native land. The journey took him back to Cairo then on to Tunis; from there he sailed in a Catalan vessel to Tilimsan (Tlemcen) in present-day Algeria, touching at Sardinia, then went on by land to the Moroccan capital, Fez.

Following a visit to Spain (see the Andalusian chapter, below), IB set out southward over the Sahara in February 1352, heading for the Western Sudanic empire of Mali. At this time, Mali was an extensive and wealthy state that controlled the major sources of the world's gold. Trade across the Sahara meant that the desert, far from being a blank on the map, was a sphere of communication comparable to the Indian Ocean.

The trans-Saharan route IB followed was later abandoned. I planned to pick it up at its southern terminus, Walata, now one of the remotest settlements in Mauritania.

West Africa

A Trip to the Music of Time

> He began to play. Never had he heard so harmonious a
> sound. Bala Faséké had only to stroke the keys of the balafon
> with the sticks for their sonorous wood to emit notes of an
> infinite softness, notes as bright and pure as gold-dust. In him
> the instrument had found its master. He played with all his
> soul, enchanting the strange inhabitants of the chamber. The
> dozing owls, their eyes half-closed, began gently to sway.
> The eyelids of the severed heads of the nine defeated kings
> began to flicker. The great serpent, resting his head on the
> brim of his jar, seemed to listen too . . . Bala Faséké watched
> with satisfaction the effect of his music on the denizens of
> this macabre room. But he knew full well that the balafon he
> was playing was unlike any other. It was the instrument of a
> master-sorcerer.
>
> *The Epic of Sundiata*, related by Mamadou Kouyaté

Dakar – Walata

'So you're following Ibn Battutah to Walata,' said my neighbour in
the St-Louis taxi in his exact Arabic. His thin face broke into a grin.
'That's where he talked about them having girlfriends!' He winked
at me – an 'enjoy yourself!' sort of wink, as if I was on my way
to the stews of Babylon.

I doubted whether the evidence of IB's text promised much in
the way of sexual gratification, even if the traveller himself was
shocked by the goings-on in Walata. The men and women of the
town, he wrote with quivering pen, form *friendships* with each other
. . . One day, for example, soon after his arrival there on 17 April

1352, he went to call on the judge of Walata, Muhammad ibn Abdallah Ibn Yanumar, and was invited into the dignitary's sitting-room. 'I found him with a young and exceedingly pretty woman,' he remembered. 'When I saw her I held back and made to go out again, but she laughed at me quite shamelessly. The judge said to me, "Why are you going out? She's my friend!" I was amazed at this, he being a jurist who had been on the Mecca pilgrimage.' Horror was to be piled on horror. Calling later on another worthy citizen who had spent time in Morocco, IB found the man's wife *in flagrante delicto* – sitting on a bed with an unrelated man, the two of them chatting away while her husband looked on unconcerned. 'I said to him, "How can you let such a thing happen, you who have lived in our country and know what is customary in religion?" And he said, "Among us, friendship between women and men is regarded as a good thing and is totally acceptable. No suspicion attaches to it, for our women are not like the women of your country." I was astounded by his silliness, and I left the house and never went back. He invited me several times but I did not even reply.'

Unless you happen to be a member of or sympathizer with the 'moral' police in Saudi Arabia or some other kindred body, you are no doubt astounded by the silliness of a man who regularly bought or was given women for sex, a man who abandoned wives and children across Asia, ranting at the immorality of an innocent chat between two consenting adults. Needless to say, by the looking-glass logic of his own ethical universe, he was absolutely right to rant. I admit that like the judge's friend I laugh at him shamelessly.

I wondered if I'd have an opportunity to do any anthropological field-work with the friendly ladies of Walata. 'Do men still have female friends there?' I asked my neighbour.

'I think not. These days we call Walata "the City of the Righteous",' he said, switching off the grin and looking pious. When pressed, however, Muhammad – a grocer in my immediate destination of St-Louis, the old colonial capital of Senegal and Mauritania, but originally from a village within striking distance of Walata – admitted he'd never been there. 'It is very far away,' he said, 'on the edge of al-Sahra al-Kubra.' The Great Desert, the Sahara.

We sat in silence for a while, staring at the featureless scrubland of north-west Senegal through which the road from Dakar to St-Louis passes. It was a preamble to that void that began not far to the north and stretched away unimaginably to the east, where Walata lay on the shore of an ocean of sand. 'You were right to come this way,' Muhammad the grocer said eventually. 'Ibn Battutah's route through the desert from Morocco is impossible now. The wells are forgotten. You'd need several vehicles, and back-up, and GPS.'

'I know,' I said. 'My problem is that the only GPS I've got is Ibn Battutah.' Muhammad laughed. There were of course other problems with IB's desert route, like time, and money; and, above all, that newfangled nuisance of borders. From where we were, for example, Walata now lay across an upstart boundary in Mauritania, a state – of mind, it seemed, as much as of reality – that was less than three years older than me.

Bloody borders. IB, if he can, must be laughing shamelessly at us: at the lines in the sand, the tribes with flags, at the whole business of visas and frontiers and men in uniform peering at passports in god-forsaken dumps; at the spectacle of his own people and the Polisario Front scrapping over the Western Sahara; at the sad fact that following his original route to Walata today would mean crossing no fewer than four international frontiers – Morocco-Algeria, Algeria-Mauritania, Mauritania-Mali and Mali–Mauritania – and that in any case his caravan would have come to a shuffling halt only fifty miles into the journey, since the first of these frontiers has been tight shut for fifteen years. If he were with us now, IB would shake his head at the map and exclaim, '*Al-dunya li 'llah!*' – the world belongs to God. But then, who owns the oil and the uranium? That is the question.

I'd thought long and hard about following variations on IB's currently unfeasible route from Morocco; and then I'd realized that what I was looking for – the physical and human relics of his age – were almost by definition not to be found in the great absence of the desert. Someone else could fill that gap in the map; someone more patient, more foolhardy and richer than me. I would head straight for IB's goal, the empire of Mali.

★

Like Kilwa, the island city-state on the other side of Africa where this journey began, Mali was a sub-Saharan Eldorado. There is that other nice symmetry, too: Kilwa is in *al-sawahil* – the Arabic 'coasts', the Swahili lands bordering the ocean – and Mali in its singular, *al-sahil* – the Sahel, the 'coast' of the desert. 'Mali' itself is a garbling of 'Manding', the name of a people long established in the Sahel. In IB's time, however, the name also described an empire the size of continental Western Europe that cut across seven states on today's political map.

As with all the best empires – the British empire, which just sort of happened, excepted – Mali had a heroic founder, Sundiata, born into that age of nascent empires (the Mongols, the Mamluks, the Sultanate of Delhi), the early thirteenth century.* IB says it was he who first embraced Islam. This may be true for Sundiata's immediate family. But Islam had been crossing the desert for centuries before, coming with the caravans just as it had sailed to China with the merchantmen; God moves in mercantile ways. And, as ever, the long and patchy process of islamization was tidied up and recast as legend. The Maldivians had their virgin-hungry demon from the sea; ancient Ghana, a precursor of the empire of Mali, had a serpent similarly mad about maidens, and its own Islamic St George. Elsewhere, there were miraculous blindings of pagan sorcerers and wonderful showers of rain in the midst of droughts, all in answer to the prayers of pious Muslims. As a result there were the usual smashings of idols and conversions of courts and nobles. 'But', wrote the geographer al-Bakri of one such West African conversion in the eleventh century, 'the common people of the kingdom remained polytheists.' As in all the other lands of its periphery, Islam cohabited merrily with what was there before. It has continued to do so.

For the growing empire of Mali, Islam was a matter of commercial *realpolitik* as well as of piety. Sundiata and his successors, even if the borders of their realm were more nebulous than today's sharp boundaries, were not immune to the advantages of controlling minerals. By the end of the thirteenth century they had taken over the sources of the three most lucrative ones: salt, mined in the desert in the far north-west of the present-day Republic of Mali, and of

---

* The *Travels* calls him 'Saraqjata', or in some copies 'Marjata'. Both of these are known to the bards who recite his epic and for whom he is 'the hero with many names'. The –diata/-jata element present in all of them means 'lion'.

vital importance to the saltless Sahel; copper, from what is now central Niger; and gold, from the north-eastern corner of modern Guinea. The last of these was practically useless in Mali itself, where barter was the general rule (when money was needed, lumps of precious salt were used, and Maldivian cowries for small change). But with the help of the yellow metal and of Mali's fellow-Muslims across the Sahara, the empire entered a literal golden age.

Again like that other golden African kingdom, Kilwa, Mali both fuelled and fed off the growing appetite for gold specie in the Islamic world and Christendom. In terms of quantity, however, it far outstripped the exports that passed through the island state. It has been estimated that at its height in the first half of the fourteenth century, that booming age of monetarization through which IB travelled, Mali was supplying as much as two-thirds of all the fresh gold going into the world's money markets. Since it all went through the hands of Muslim middlemen in North Africa and Egypt, it made sense to have good politico-religio-commercial relations with the Arabs beyond the sands.

The most brilliant PR consultant could not have devised a finer advertising roadshow for Mali than the Mecca pilgrimage in 1324 of Sundiata's great-nephew, Mansa Musa.* On his way to the Arabian holy city, he doled out lucre so liberally that his fame reached Christendom: his picture appeared soon after on European maps and remained a feature of them for more than a century to come, an enthroned black Croesus fondling an enormous golden orb, with something of the barbaric allure of the future oil shaykh. It didn't matter that he temporarily depressed the price of gold by flooding the market, or that he doled himself out of pocket and had to borrow heavily in Cairo on his way home. In the racially tinted view of the Arabs – whose official correspondence with the emperor regularly began with a prayer that God would whiten the faces of the Blacks on Judgement Day – he had made black, if not beautiful, then at least glamorous. More important, he had shown them that Mali meant business. And he had even managed to spread some useful commercial disinformation by perpetuating an old yarn about gold 'growing', in impenetrable cannibal country,

---

* *Mansa* is the Manding term for the supreme ruler.

like carrots. (Presumably the best sort grows in clumps of two dozen: twenty-four-carrot gold.)

It has to be said that the trend of Mali's economic graph-line has been downhill ever since. The decline began with the drop in world gold prices that took place in the reign of Musa's brother, IB's host Mansa Sulayman. These days the region still exports a small amount of gold, but it is little more than a cottage industry. Now, on my way to the empire of Mali's northern outpost of Walata, where the Sahel is lapped by the vast sand sea, I was looking forward to finding out what remained of the glamour and the greatness.

*

That afternoon I sat on the windy veranda of my hotel room at the northern tip of St-Louis, in a banging of shutters and a clattering of palm fronds, thinking what a confusing place it was. A *baguette*-shaped island in the Senegal River, from across the water it had resembled a stunted Zanzibar. From the inside, balconies and peeling pastel paint made it more like a low-rise Havana. (I see now in the atlas that St-Louis is roughly equidistant from Havana and Zanzibar – and recall the surprise of seeing a knub of land out in the Atlantic on the in-flight TV map as my plane entered Senegalese airspace, and realizing it was *Brazil*.)

It was also strange to be on the road again minus Martin. In anticipation of the gap I'd brought Palgrave's *Golden Treasury*, which went some way, as its Dedication hoped, to sweeten solitude. So did a bottle of Famous Grouse, which for once I had an excuse for drinking as much of as possible: by all accounts the bottle would have cost me a fine, and possibly a night in gaol, at the Mauritanian border. At length Palgrave palled. In my state of Scotch-induced introspection, I began to wonder – not for the first time – if I was a wimp not to have had a go at IB's trans-Saharan route. After all it was, in the phrase of Bovill, the historian of Saharan commerce, 'among the oldest highways in the world'. It was also one of the most challenging.

From Sijilmasah, an oasis town in the lee of the High Atlas, IB trekked south in a merchant caravan. After twenty-five days and 500 miles of fairly easy going they arrived at the half-way point of Taghaza, a squalid spot 'with brackish water and the greatest number of flies on earth' – but of immense importance: here were the salt mines that supplied most of the Sahel with the indispensable mineral. They were worked, IB says, by slaves of the Massufah, a Berber tribe who roved this part of the western Sahara and piloted the caravans. Here the traders travelling with IB bought slabs of the valuable rock salt before moving on. Ten days more took them to the only well between Taghaza and Walata, another 500 miles further south. From this halt a Massufah scout was sent ahead on a swift camel across the most fearsome stretch of sand desert. His mission was to summon a reception party from Walata, who would rendezvous with the caravan four days' journey north of the town and replenish their exhausted water. 'But at times the scout perishes in this desert,' IB wrote,

> and the people of Walata have no news of the caravan's approach, with the result that many or all of the people in the caravan themselves perish. There are many demons in that part of the desert, and if the scout is alone they sometimes make sport of him and lure him off his course, so that he loses his way and dies. For there is no road to be seen, nor any tracks to follow, but only sands blown hither and thither by the wind.

No. I wasn't a wimp to skip that; I was sensible. But now, rereading IB's account, I realized that the wilderness was by no means a vacuum. There would be plenty of features left from his landscape apart from the wind and the sand. Most of them I'd be happy to miss. As well as brackish water and flies, lice were so abundant, IB says, that people had to wear repellant necklaces containing mercury. There were also venomous snakes. One of IB's fellow travellers was bitten on the finger, but cured himself by killing a camel, slitting open its belly and keeping his hand overnight in the dead beast's stomach, then chopping the finger off.* There was

---

* The idea is old. The cosmologist al-Qazwini quotes Pliny on the efficacy against poisons of a certain type of lump found in camels' stomachs. It should be minced up and mixed with vinegar before being swallowed. Is there also a link with the old Greek practice of sewing up the sick or wounded in fresh ram-skins, or with the American traveller Stephen Bodio's experience of a Mongolian fever cure – being wrapped, mummy-wise, in raw horseflesh and bin-bags?

the ever-present risk of running out of water. IB says that the Massufah nomads when caught short will hunt down an addax, cut out its maw and drink the juices squeezed from its tripe.* And then there were IB's *shayatin*, 'satans', those sportive spirits of the waste, sirens of the sand sea that entice the wanderer to his doom.

But there were other features of IB's Sahara route that I wished I could experience. There were the desert truffles he says were plentiful in the wilderness around the salt mines. Some of these, the geographer al-Bakri wrote, grow to such a size that hares make their forms inside them; another geographer, al-Idrisi, claimed in the book he wrote for his Norman French patron that *chameau aux truffes sahariennes* was the finest dish on earth. There was the airy joy of boundless spaces to which even IB, rarely a lover of scenery, was not immune: 'This desert is luminous and radiant; one's chest expands in it and one's soul delights.' And there was Sijilmasah, city of embarkation for the caravans.

Beyond praising its dates, IB has little to say about a place familiar at least by repute to his Moroccan readers. Or rather, he has little to say in the *Travels*. Elsewhere (and it may surprise some readers to learn that there *is* an elsewhere, when the *Travels* has been thought of up till now as his only known work; all will I hope be made clear) his more effusive self describes Sijilmasah as a city the verdant vault of whose palmy heaven is aglow with galaxies of ripening dates,† but also as 'a battleground of dust, the victims of whose scorpions die unavenged'. Others praised it as a Saharan 'port' of the first order. For Abu Hamid of Granada, it was the haven of caravans from which 'they travel in the desert as it were upon the sea, with guides to pilot them by the stars or the rocks'. The metaphor of the ship of the desert is an old one. Another native of Granada who used it was the poet and architect al-Sahili, who navigated the Sahara in the splendid pilgrim-convoy of Mansa Musa and whose tomb IB was to see in Timbuktu. He recalled the long night-marches of the dromedaries,

---

* If there are no addaxes conveniently to hand, the tried and tested Arabian method reported by Wilfred Thesiger (now he wouldn't have wimped out of IB's Sahara crossing . . .) is to thrust your camel-stick down the throat of your mount and slake your thirst on camel's vomit.
† There is sometimes a Joycean touch to the more picturesque prose of IB's age. Compare with this the 'heaventree of stars hung with humid nightblue fruit' in *Ulysses*.

Shaping their course over the thirsting dunes,
Across deep dale and billowing sandy height,
Like ships upon a sea of mirages,
Pitch-blackened by the dark and tarry night.

Sijilmasah was a place of departures. But it was also the landfall of caravans returning with gold and slaves, hippopotamus teeth, addax-hide shields and all the other exports of Bilad al-Sudan, the Land of the Blacks. As for the intervening Sahara, it was seen not as a barrier, but as a high road free from human hindrances. Providing one followed the desert highway code, it offered an easy passage. 'Ghana and Mali', wrote IB's exact contemporary al-Umari, 'are joined to Sijilmasah by long stretches of wilderness and broad desolate deserts' (note, not 'separated from' but 'joined to'). Sijilmasah was also joined to the wider world. An annotation, for instance, on an early fourteenth-century Italian map reveals that the West African information on it came from a Genoese merchant living in Sijilmasah and trading with Walata and Guinea. Looking east, a letter found in the waste-paper dump of a Cairo synagogue mentions a Jewish merchant of Sijilmasah doing business in Gujarat. And then there is IB's glimpse from Sijilmasah of an even further orient, of his host's brother in China, in which the traveller puts a girdle round about the earth – or the known half of it, at any rate – in forty words.*

---

* The quotation is on p. 226, above.

To end up staying on the far north-western edge of the Sahara with the brother of a man you'd bumped into first in northern India and then again in south-east China, particularly when they were natives of a place a day's journey from your own home town on the Europe-facing coast of Morocco, would seem to intimate once more that travel, if nothing else, is subject to some sort of intelligent design. It also proves another point: 'How far apart the two of them were!' IB says of the Bushri brothers. Eight thousand miles, give or take. But they were almost on the same latitude; and more importantly, in a world where nation spoke to nation largely through the mixed medium of commerce and Islam, they were on precisely the same wavelength. Seen from the distance that time gives us, from a world fractured by frontiers, the two brothers on their shores of sea and sand were closer in a sense than IB could have known.

Sijilmasah, viewpoint of these panoramic prospects, is now a mass of unremarkable rubble. In the post-Black Death economic slump whose early effects IB witnessed, fewer caravans left its gates. The rulers of Mali and Morocco began to lose their revenue and their grip; the roads to Sijilmasah became unsafe as central government gave way to tribal anarchy, and when trade revived, it went by other routes, further to the east. I could have gone to Sijilmasah, but I knew it was a dead end, one of those abandoned dwelling-places that haunt the old poetry of the Arabs:

> I stood where once their dwelling-place had been,
> And stained the stones with tears:
> 'Where are they now? Speak, ruins, speak to me . . .'
> Words fell on stone-deaf ears.
> But then a voice cried from the wilderness,
> When I had wept there long:
> 'You might as well weep blood, o heedless one!
> The caravans are gone.'

*

Next morning another communal taxi took me towards the Mauritanian frontier. The road passed through a scene that was, if anything, more featureless than that of the day before. If anything . . . It was pretty close to nothing. The only sights to be seen were the carcases of cattle, biltong-on-the-bone rotting into the roadside dust, each leaving a long last curving V-sign of horns raised against the cruel land.

The other passengers provided a distraction. A tall, effete and Parisian-francophone black man had paid for both front passenger seats. Not only his speech and his cash but also his clothes, a sort of designer safari suit in brown linen, marked him out as an alien. Every few minutes he drew a small camera from a mock-lizard case and took a photograph of the nothingness ahead. Most of the rest of the time he spent applying hand-cream and lip-balm. Beside me sat a veiled and silent Moor. He reminded me of the veiled cameleer on the famous Catalan Map of the 1370s, drawn a few years after IB's death, riding through the desert towards Walata and the Midas-king of Mali. Now and again the veil slipped and revealed a thin, appraising mouth that smiled, almost imperceptibly, as his narrowed eyes scanned the surroundings – for likely slaves, I couldn't help thinking.

I was filled with forebodings about the Moors of Mauritania. A recent reread of Mungo Park's travels hadn't helped. Park had a generally jolly time among the Learishly-named blacks further south – the Feloops and the Serawoollies, and rulers such as King Daisy of Kaarta and the Dooty of Sai. Detained by the Moors, however – and in the very region I'd be passing through to Walata – he found them 'a subtle and treacherous race' and 'the rudest savages on earth'. After Park, mild Victorian orientalists, searching for lost Arabic manuscripts in the same area, had been murdered for obscure motives, and probably for no motives at all. This was all comfortably in the past. But in recent months a group of French tourists had been killed, and a platoon of Mauritanian soldiers beheaded, by a group that styled itself 'the Organization of al-Qa'idah in the Islamic Maghrib'. To round things off, the head of the Mauritanian army, General Muhammad ould Abd al-Aziz, had lately found out that he was going to lose his job and had toppled the country's newly elected president in a coup. As the frontier – the Senegal River – approached, I felt I was heading for a land haunted by brooding, Bowlesian horror.

The good thing about pessimism, if you're at heart an optimist, is that you know things won't be as bad as you think; and if they are, then heigh-ho off with my head. Mauritania was no exception. I wasn't decapitated or otherwise physically harmed. But I've never been to a country where the atmosphere of fear was quite as thick, where it had such a pantomime obviousness to it. IB had a desert and its demons to contend with. I had human nuisances.

Those on the Senegal bank of the river were the usual shakers-down and rippers-off, calèche-touts and currency-pimps, pitching like a swarm of flies. But they could be swatted away with a few well-aimed Arabic curses. Those on the Mauritanian side, a short ferry ride away, were more sophisticated, and able to try it on in Allah's own language. 'Perhaps you would like to give me something for helping you?' the immigration officer said softly. The stamp hovered over my open passport.

'I'm sorry?'

'A donation – however much you like – to the immigration police benevolent fund . . .'

I was feeling far from benevolent: as soon as I'd arrived, the border post had shut down for a lunch-break worthy of an old-fashioned London publisher. 'You must be joking! You've just kept me waiting three hours.'

I could tell from the look on the man's face that this wasn't in the script. He was momentarily stunned, then rallied. 'Three hours is nothing. Sometimes, it can be a *lot* longer . . .'

We went a few more rounds, and then I threw a sly mention of 'my *very old friend* Mr _____, Consul of the Islamic Republic of Mauritania in Dakar', whose name I happened to recall. It was hardly a knock-out, but I'd caught him off guard and the stamp went reluctantly down.

Outside I found my tall and epicene fellow-passenger from the taxi. Waiting together for another ride on to the Mauritanian capital, Nouakchott, I discovered that he himself was a Mauritanian citizen of mixed Wolof and Arab blood but had lived in Paris for twenty years. He made a living by selling the *bijouterie* of his native land at private, and I imagine exquisite, parties. As we were talking we suddenly and simultaneously had the sensation of being listened in on, and both turned round. Where a pavement stall-keeper had been sitting behind a scattering of cassette tapes, there now squatted a uniformed man. I caught sight of a badge that said, in Arabic, 'National Security'.

'*Je pense*', said my friend in an almost inaudible hiss, '*qu'il est un espion!*'

'*Monsieur, vous avez raison,*' I whispered back. '*Mais, malheureuse-ment pour lui, il n'est pas dans le . . . la couverture profonde.*' That sort of sounded right for 'deep cover'.

A battered Mercedes drew up touting for Nouakchott passengers. We came to an agreement with the Senegalese driver over the price, and paid up front. The 'cassette-seller' rose and sidled over to the driver. Soft words were spoken, and a banknote went into the uniformed pocket. '*Oufff, l'Afrique,*' my friend exclaimed at this blatant piece of extortion, rolling his eyes. '*Je souffre, psychologique-ment!*' He flourished a silver cigarette case and added, for my anglophone benefit, 'P'squeako-logically!'

We picked up two more passengers, a prosperous-looking Senegalese couple, and set off. The Nouakchott road passed through low rolling dunes, rose-red in the declining sun, dotted with hamlets of long low tents interspersed with shed-like structures of concrete blocks. (I didn't yet know it, but I'd already seen almost all Mauritania had to offer in the way of scenery.) Occasionally a figure appeared, draped in the *darra'ah*, the statuesque robe of the Sahara, standing on a dune and looking like a senator who'd lost his way to the Forum. I was beginning to wonder what the point of Mauritania was, other than filling up a space on the map, when we reached the first checkpoint. Our passports were scrutinized, and the driver and the Senegalese passengers summoned. I saw them hand over banknotes.

'What was all that about?' I asked when they were back.

'We have to pay because we're Senegalese,' the driver explained, as if it was the natural order of things. The scene was repeated at the next checkpoint. So far, the point of Mauritania seemed to be highway robbery in uniform. In the hundred miles between the frontier and Nouakchott there were seven checkpoints, each one a mini-frontier. They included one, sixty miles into Mauritanian territory, that called itself a DOUANE. I thought of IB, crossing the borderless, robberless desert.

Night had fallen by the time we reached the final checkpoint before Nouakchott. So far my passport seemed to have protected me from this arrant banditry; not so here, the driver thought.

'*C'est trop compliqué*,' he said, shaking his head. But my Parisian-Mauritanian friend had a solution. He asked me to give him my bag. Mystified, I passed it to him. He pronounced a dramatic '*Bismi 'llah!*' then, after flourishing his right index finger, 'wrote' with it on the bag from right to left. I didn't catch the invisible Arabic, and asked what the words were. '*Al-Shaykh Muhammad al-Hafiz*,' he explained. 'Shaykh Muhammad, may God have mercy on him, was a great sufi leader in Mauritania.' The process was repeated with the Senegalese woman's mock croc handbag, her husband's manbag, and with other items thought to be at risk.

We drew up at the complicated checkpoint. No one came. We waited. Then we drove off gingerly, expecting angry cries, perhaps shots in the air. Still no one came.

Perhaps they'd all been inside the guardhouse glued to the coup leader General Muhammad ould Abd al-Aziz's latest Alice-in-Wonderland oration on the necessity of combating corruption and promoting democracy.

*

'Old Maggie Thatcher . . . Old Maggie Thatcher!' None of the bus passengers admitted to being the owner of this peculiar name.' . . . *Old Maggie Thatcher!*' We all looked at one another; I searched in vain for a baroness in a twin-set. Then my eye fell on the *billet de passager* in my hand – 'Nom: Timasi ould Maquitacha'. This exotic person, this Franco-Moorified 'Timothy son of Mackintosh', was me . . . and so, I realized, was Old Maggie Thatcher. I raised my hand, grinned like a fool, and got on the bus.

The persons on the stickers that adorned the windscreen of the vehicle were no less exotic. Windscreens in Senegal bore the images of prominent sufi marabouts and the odd Che Guevara. The Nouakchott-Aïoune bus had a more motley team: Zidane, Drogba and a couple of other African footballers on the wings; a cartoon cowgirl at full back, wearing a pink stetson and hot pants and thrusting out her bulging butt with the word 'ST-OP' written across the cheeks – a public health message, perhaps?; and, at centre forward, above the motto 'Never Die', the smiling face of Osama Bin Ladin.

I had no regrets about leaving Nouakchott as soon as possible. Like IB's Sijilmasah, it was a battleground of dust, and it seemed from the window of the bus that the suburbs were already losing. If the whole place got buried overnight in a sandstorm, I thought uncharitably, who would notice?

Uncharitable thoughts were in the air. At the first checkpoint out of town we picked up a pair of lost-looking tourists, a young Russian couple who had been held up there. As they climbed on to the bus I caught a comment from the commander of the checkpoint, a thug in shades: 'Perhaps the al-Qa'idah lot will cut their throats, ha ha ha!' For an evil moment I sympathized with the operatives of al-Qa'idah – those who decapitated soldiers, at any rate. The Russians disappeared to the back of the bus, and I didn't see them again. Nor, indeed, did I see any other non-African foreigners during the rest of my time in Mauritania.

Motion can in itself be a balm for troubled minds, and as we bowled eastward uncharitable thoughts were left behind. Perhaps there was something uplifting in the road we were travelling, the 'Route d'Espoir'. I hoped so, as I intended to follow it via an overnight stop in Aïoune ('Springs') to its terminus 800 miles away in Nema ('Blessing'). From there I planned to make it north to the edge of the void, to Walata. Despite the nominal optimism of the road, however, the land it passed through looked pretty hopeless. It was composed of sand in two colours – a sort of peach blush, and a colour that could only be called 'sand' – that stretched away, undulating gently, in every direction. It was sparsely punctuated by acacias and tamarisks, but bore a healthy crop of the poisonous shrub known as the Sodom apple. After not many miles the first and more interesting colour of sand disappeared. It crossed my mind that in the unlikely event of some Moorish Smetana composing a tone poem to his homeland, it would be music of such minimality that it would make Philip Glass sound like Wagner. As if reading my mind, the driver put on a CD of a chanting woman; hardly a melody, but a long linear saunter with a few quarter-tone deviations, as if the shortest way to the end of the song was as near a straight line as possible.

Scattered herds of cattle, camels and asses roamed in search of the bumfluff of grass which was the fourth vegetable sight to be seen. As before, the occasional *darra'ah*-draped human figure posed in the wilderness like a lost Roman, and the odd hamlet of tents and shacks flashed past. Most of the settlements had names that were borrowed from elsewhere – Umm al-Qura ('the Mother of Villages', an epithet of Mecca), Tafilalt (the area of southern Morocco in which Sijilmasah is situated), al-Quds ('Jerusalem'), Dar al-Salam (an epithet of Baghdad as well as the capital of Tanzania) – as if the country were a *tabula rasa*, an America that could only be filled by plagiarizing other people's place-names. Beyond these settlements the lone and level sands stretched on without end.

At least the checkpoints were less objectionable than before. They doubled as pray, pee-'n'-tea stops (the Mauritanians, like their neighbours in the region, are obsessive sippers of viscous mint tea, poured and repoured until it builds up a good 'head'). They also gave me a chance to observe my fellow-passengers, who went the whole gamut from hawk-nosed Arabs to flat-nosed Negroes. Most of the men wore the *shash*, the combined turban and face-covering (the turbo-veil?). All the women were amply proportioned and clothed in loose covers of floral chintz, which gave them the look of animated Colefax & Fowler sofas.* Many of them affected long slender toothsticks with which they toyed incessantly, like vamps with cigarette-holders at *un cocktail*.

The day wore on, and the road. Towards the middle of the afternoon my optic nerves, frayed by the ceaseless beige, were finally able to feast on a few small patches of green sorghum. This, I guessed, was the 'Zone Agriculturelle' that appeared on maps of the country. Soon after, more relief – relief to the eyes, relief on the map – came in the form of a distant range of hills. 'There are flat lands at the top of them,' said the man sitting next to me in reverential tones, 'and crops, many crops.' I looked with longing towards this unlikely Shangri-La.

On and on, eastward into the falling night, in and out of sleep along an unending headlamp-lit avenue of Sodom apples.

★

Next morning, the air of 'Springs' stung with flying sand and hell-fire sermons, the latter broadcast by competing cassette-sellers. I

---

* Writing of the nomad women of the Sahara, IB says, 'They are the most perfectly beautiful and elegantly proportioned of women, on account of their snowy whiteness and their fatness. Never have I seen women so fat in any other land. They feed on cows' milk and husked millet.' Mungo Park also admired these ladies. 'A perfect beauty', he wrote, 'is a load for a camel.'

found a sand-blown, fly-blown eatery and ordered food (it seemed pointless to think of it as 'breakfast', since in my experience so far all Mauritanian meals had been identical – rice soaked in fat and speckled with bits of goats' innards; luckily it is a diet I'm quite fond of). The food-bringer, a black boy, asked if I wanted *hors d'oeuvres*.

I looked at him. The phrase was so preposterous in this place that I wasn't sure I'd heard it right. '*Hors d'oeuvres?*' The boy nodded. My mind whirled with oysters and asparagus, Parma ham and plovers' eggs, caviar, prawn cocktails . . .

The *hors d'oeuvres* were fragments of carrot and cucumber that speckled the rice along with the bits of caprine vital organ.

The bus of the day before must have offered safety in numbers. In the shared taxi on the Route d'Espoir from 'Springs' to 'Blessing' checkpoint nastiness resumed. At one my baggage was minutely examined, in slow motion, with special attention paid to a packet of Turkish chocolate biscuits. At another, I answered three differently phrased requests for a 'donation' with 'I do not understand you' in my most lapidary Arabic, uttered through gritted teeth. 'You'd understand if we kept you here, wouldn't you!' said the commander with a horrible leer, before finally letting me go. As it was, I'd been there half an hour.

Once again I apologized to the other passengers for the delay. Once again they asked me how much I'd paid. My answer was the same: not a single *ouguiya*.

Whoever had come up with 'Blessing' as the name of the town where the Route d'Espoir comes to its bitter end in the dust must have had a dark sense of humour. But there was one blessing in Nema: a *bikab*, or 'pick-up', was leaving for Walata early the following morning. For the time being I trudged out to a rather up-market hotel that had been built on the edge of town in the days before terrorism and tinpot dictatorship had dashed the hopes for tour groups. The kind man who ran the place removed an elaborate nest built by mud-wasps, like a seal, across the crack of the door to my room. He then swept out a small drift of sand that had accumulated inside. Someone – probably from some team of EU election monitors – had plastered bilingual stickers over the bathroom tiles and, I found, at strategic spots throughout the hotel. They said, '√ *Na'am, sawti muhimm!* √ *Oui, mon vote compte!*' I thought of the cheery message later that evening when the hotel man and I sat in the echoing dining-room and watched the General's latest speech on the importance of combating corruption and promoting democracy . . . *Oui, mon vote compte!* Except that, for the General, one's vote counted for precisely naught. I picked up the remote control and zapped him.

The following morning, as I was walking into town through the flying grit, a man in striped pyjamas suddenly rushed at me, bawling and waving his arms. From his semi-coherent shouts I made out that he wanted me to walk on the other side of the road.

'Why?'

'"WHY? *WHY?*"'I thought his eyes were literally going to pop out of his head. 'You are a foreigner . . . You do not ask "*Why?*"!'

In the face of this blinding logic I crossed the road. A man with a donkey fell into step with me. 'Don't you know you mustn't walk past that gate?' he said in a fearful whisper. 'It's the local security headquarters.' I thanked him for letting me know. Having been ranted at by a man in pyjamas, I'd naturally assumed it was the local lunatic asylum. I laughed; then felt an unexpected feeling, as physical as a fist in the stomach. I wondered what had hit me, then knew: in this strange sad land, with its corrupt soldiery, its cowed citizenry and the added frisson of bloody terrorism, it was fear. In all my travels with IB it was the first time I had felt it.

The sensation dissipated in the slow-motion bustle of Nema suq. With all the robed figures flapping about in the low-level sandstorm of the streets, there was something parodically Oxonian about the scene – gowns in an Encaenia of dust. The early departure was of course a phantasm. The Walata pick-up was busy picking up goods for that isolated outpost. So I settled down to wait, receiving oh-no-a-Martian looks from passers-by. Once it became known that I could speak Arabic, however, a number of braver people engaged me in conversation. None of them had been to Walata; several referred to it, like the St-Louis grocer, as 'the City of the Righteous'. All spoke of it as if it existed on another plane of being.

I hoped it was a higher plane. Nema, and all the rest of Mauritania that I'd seen, was deeply mired in what the old philosophers called *alam al-kawn wa 'l-fasad*, the world of coming-to-be and passing-away, of existence and corruption.

*

Seven hours after the pick-up was meant to leave, I was still sitting in the suq. But at least there was one consolation – poetry; not Palgrave, but the live Arabic stuff. There we were, squatting in the dust, reciting songs of travel; travelling by the vehicle of verse if not in that more prosaic but as yet fictional pick-up. I quoted Imam al-Shafi'i on the five advantages of travel:

Arise and go a-roving if you're in the mood
To earn the money, and the manners, to live well,
To feed your brain, to free your mind from cares that brood;
Not least, to meet with other men whose minds excel.

Here, at the end of the Route d'Espoir, al-Shafi'i's sentiments sounded trite, if not perverse. I suppose I'd been feeding my brain, if nothing else; but the mental diet in Mauritania so far was worm-wood and gall.

'Have you heard the other version?' one of the listeners asked. 'About the seven *dis*advantages of travel?' I hadn't. He rearranged the folds of his robe, fiddled with his veil, and recited. When he'd finished we all laughed – grimly, in my case. Even though my West African travels had hardly begun, those seven disadvantageous boxes were already black with ticks. My companions rose, but before they left I asked the reciter to dictate the verse. To pass the time, I then subjected it to the assault and battery of translation:

The Seven Trials of Travel

Don't ever go a-roving, O my friend, if you'd
Escape the seven circles of the traveller's hell.
The first's a haunt of homesick thoughts and solitude,
The second's where your fears for far-off family dwell.
The third's a den of thieves, the fourth's the latitude
Where rogues rip off an unsuspecting clientele.
Then come the hells of lonely nights and nasty food.
The last, and worst: the Hades of the Bad Hotel.

I was still tinkering with the translation when a boy came over and told me that the Walata pick-up was going to leave without me.

*

My first impression of Walata, landfall of the caravans from Barbary, was that I couldn't actually be there. 'Walata is excessively hot,' IB said – and he should have been a good judge, having just spent two months crossing the Sahara. But in the sudden stillness after the motion of the pick-up I heard my own teeth literally chattering, like those wind-up ones they sell in joke shops. *Bard qaris*, al-Saduq called it later on: pinching cold. Mind you, he said, IB was right, as it often reached fifty in the summer.

My second impression of Walata was of how nice the men in uniform were.

The four-hour journey, clinging by the finger-tips to a spare wheel lashed to a precarious Chimborazo of groceries, had flown by, propelled by the conversation of one of my fellow-travellers. He was a small thin man, completely veiled in black and further hidden by dark glasses that stayed on even when darkness fell. As we went north from Nema into the night our talk was to pass through many fields and end, for the second time this day, in the magic meadow of poetry.

'I was in Damascus,' said my veiled companion. I'd just mentioned that I was on the trail of IB; it was a strange response. 'I went there to Friday prayers at the Umayyad Mosque, and Ibn Taymiyyah was preaching –' *Ibn Taymiyyah*? I twigged: he was quoting IB, verbatim. Damascus seemed so long ago to me; but the mosque was clear in my memory, swimming in light that bounced off gold mosaics. '"In the course of his sermon he said, 'Verily does God descend to the heaven of this lower world of ours, just as I myself descend now . . .' And he took one step down the staircase of the pulpit!"'

For a while my companion mused on the theological horror of an abstract Deity physically walking down the staircase of the Seven Heavens, as if He was on some celestial Broadway set. Like IB, he was a good Maliki who saw Ibn Taymiyyah, spiritual ancestor of the Wahhabis, as a crackpot.

'"He had something wrong in the head,"' he said, again quoting IB.

'"Consider creation,"' he went on, now in the words of the Prophet Muhammad, '"and do not consider the Creator. For minds cannot attain Him, nor sight encompass Him."' Another clear memory surfaced: of hearing those same words, in another pick-up, in another desert, on the far side of Africa, east of Edfu and ten years back. I looked at this invisible man, sitting on a bag of vegetables and weaving strands from our places and our pasts, mine and IB's, and had an almost irresistible urge to pull away the veil.

We had by now ascended a little pass, up to a broad and featureless plain; another plane, physically at least. My friend moved on to less elevated matters – the tribal affiliations of IB's Massufah guides, and the traveller's visit to Walata, which still caused what he called 'difficulties in interpretation'. But up here on this level heath our speed increased, and most of his words were lost to the wind. I wrapped my own headcloth veilwise against the chill and desiccating air.

A sunset prayer stop; then on, more slowly, in the darkness. My friend was audible once again, and I asked him about an idea that had been forming in my mind: to go direct from Walata to IB's other desert-shore destination, Timbuktu. The distance looked manageable. 'Until recently there was no problem,' he said. 'You could do it by camel in not much more than ten days. But now the way is infested by smugglers, thieves and terrorists.' The latter he described as 'Salafis', a term for puritans of an extremist bent. 'No ordinary citizen dares to go that way any more. The Salafis are very dangerous.' The border-guards of faith were a bigger obstacle than those who patrolled the political frontiers.

A thirteenth-century geographer records a scene in which a travelling scholar in the IB mould calls on the governor of Sijilmasah. 'In front of him on the ground were a number of leather mats. They were covered with the heads of rebels who had taken to brigandage and to preying on travellers on the desert road. The governor was beating a rhythm out on the ground with a wand of ebony as he repeated this couplet:

> Be not surprised that heads should answer us
> in place of words,
> When we despatched to them our questions
> on the blades of swords!'

Nowadays it's the brigands who do the beheading.

To change the depressing subject, I mentioned my poetical interlude in the suq in Nema. My veiled companion laughed. 'They call Mauritania "the land of a million poets", and I suppose there's some truth to it. You see, poetry is the only record of our past. There's nothing else to preserve it.'

I could see what he meant. Ahead was the darkness, the oblivious desert.

In the long silence that followed, some lines took over my head.

At length they came out: '"So long as men can breathe, or eyes can see,/So long lives this, and this gives life to thee."'

'What was that?'

'It's by one of our poets. It goes something like . . .' But I thought better of inflicting the violence of translation on the sonnet; of casting the moth's wing into the crucible. 'He's speaking about his beloved, and saying that even though her beauty will fade and she will die, she'll live on and be beautiful for ever in the words of his poem.' It struck me as slightly mad to be talking Shakespeare in Arabic with a veiled man crossing the Sahara on a sack of onions.

There was the beginning of another silence; the triumph of the word started to look small against the tragedy of time.

'*Li 'llahi darruh*,' said my friend.

I smiled. It is the highest literary compliment: 'To God is his milk.' Less literally, perhaps, 'Such divine outpouring of eloquence.'

Maybe the triumph of the word wasn't so small. And in the further silence that followed I thought of the ephemera IB had preserved, in words that may have lacked the milk of human eloquence but that were no less enduring than poetry. Those scenes in Walata materialized in my mind – IB's hesitation, the girl's laughter, IB's bluster; the other man's superbly barbed retort on Moroccan womanhood. Scenes of no consequence, preserved as long as eyes can see, like some small and spiky fossil in a matrix of words . . . Words, words, words. In the face of the void they're all we've got.

And then Walata itself materialized, a few blurred lights; then the low dim shapes of houses crouching in a hollow, hunkered down against the desert. The last people for a thousand miles.

*

By the time I'd experienced the discreet, and astonishing, charm of the gendarmerie of Walata and registered my passport, my veiled fellow-traveller had gone. If I were to see him again, I wondered – not unlikely in a place that is only the size of a biggish village – would I recognize him? (I remembered al-Bakri the geographer saying of these enwrapped Sahara men that even their own mothers didn't recognize them; but perhaps that was *without* their veils.) There may have been one sighting.

The Auberge de Bon Acueil – and probably, I now realized, the niceness of the gendarmes – dated back to the happier days of an EU-backed project to promote tourism. My room was in a single-storey caravanserai-like courtyard in which a small dune had formed, blocking some of the doors. The place was rumoured to have showers; they proved as fabulous as the City of Brass. I made do with a bucket and scoop (which, being a technophobe, is all I have at home) in a bathroom haunted by half-seen scurrying forms and by the rich, malted scent of vintage turds.

The family who owned the place, however, made up for the lack of facilities. Bathed and presentable, I was invited to their room. It was lit by a large TV screen and filled with a soporific fug of char-coal. One side of the room was occupied by an enormous bed, or sleeping-platform, on which lay the recumbent forms of children and a couple of reclining women. At their invitation I went and reclined with the ladies; we chatted while the man of the house squatted on the floor fanning the brazier for mint tea – and I realized I was in one of those scenes that had so shocked IB.

Talk subsided. For a while we watched the General on his cease-less campaign to promote democracy and combat corruption; then switched to another channel and the more credible scenario of Jean-Claude Van Damme combating a gang of cannibal zombies.

Back in my cell in the courtyard there was neither warmth nor electricity. I lay in bed shivering ('Walata is excessively hot . . .'), reading Milton by candlelight; reading of the winter wild and star-led wizards on the eastern road.

Outside, on the way to the loo, there was a canopy of stars, hard, solid, glittering like the ceiling of a cave of ice.

*

'No,' said Bati ould Baba next morning, wagging an indisputable finger. 'No! This is all wrong. And why? Because Ibn Battutah did not come here to Walata. Most definitely *not*.'

I stared at Walata's most revered citizen, head of the family that had guided the town's spiritual life for more than a thousand years – Bati ould Baba ould Mbwi al-Mahjubi al-Husayni, chief of the clan of al-Mahajib, 'the Concealed Ones', descendant of the Prophet of Allah through his grandson Husayn – and I thought, If anyone here knows anything about Walata, it should be Bati. And then I thought, If IB didn't come here, why the fuck did I?

Bati gazed back at me. Although I'd just got him out of bed, his eyes were bright and clear, chips of crystal set in a face hacked out of jasper. The elegant eyebrows were jet-black, the beard white and patriarchal. Bati, ascetic, adamantine, might have sat for El Greco as a Desert Father – as St Anthony himself, still fresh after a night battling demons.

I wasn't sure if I wanted to argue; but I had the evidence in my hand. 'I can well understand your doubts, sir. But Ibn Battutah's account of his visit is here in black and white. He mentions some of the most prominent citizens of Walata by name.' I read: '"Among them were its judge, Muhammad ibn Abdallah Ibn Yanumar, and his brother Yahya, the jurist and professor." Ibn Battutah goes on to say that he visited the judge in his house.' I didn't mention the judge's girlfriend. For whatever reason, IB seemed to be in enough hot water already.

'I do not know of these people whom Ibn Battutah claimed to have met,' Bati replied tartly. 'The prominent men of Walata at the time of his alleged visit were from *our* family, al-Mahajib.'

So there was the reason . . . But could it be possible to resent a literary snub for 650 years? Yes, evidently: Bati sat there regarding me in petulant silence. Seeking a safer subject of conversation, I asked about the unusual name of Bati's family. He softened a little. Al-Mahajib, 'the Concealed Ones', he explained, were so called because their lineage was originally kept secret. The reason for this was that the founder of the line in Walata, one Yahya ibn Musa, known as al-Kamil, 'the Perfect', was a ninth-century scion of the line of Shi'ite imams persecuted by the Abbasid caliphs. 'At the height of the persecution', Bati said, 'in Baghdad in the days of Harun al-Rashid, our ancestor Yahya saw his blessed forebear the Prophet of Allah, peace and blessings upon him, in a dream.' Harun al-Rashid, Baghdad, a dream . . . this was *1,001 Nights* territory. 'The Prophet said to him, "Go to the Valley of Light, to the Black Mount, where there is a well with white stones."' For years Yahya travelled in search of the spot, until at last he found it. He picked up three of the white pebbles that lay by the well, and then he threw them in, one by one. When he threw the first, the water rose in the well. When he threw the second, blood rose and covered the land. With the third, 360 wells were revealed, although some accounts say the figure was 313. He then said to the idolators who were in the place, "If you will follow Islam, stay. If not, go." And they embraced the religion of truth at his hand, and stayed.'

Blood and water, dreams and prophecy, a miracle and a conversion: this was where *Nights*-land shaded into that Islamic dawn of broken idols and defeated dragons. And here before me was the man whose ancestor had led the local pagans to the light. I could sort of see why he was annoyed about IB, whose *Travels* doubles as a *Debretts* of the Muslim world, leaving his family out.

I wondered how the legend related to the real landscape. 'So where is this place – the Black Mount and so on?'

'The Black Mount?' Bati smiled. 'We are on it.'

I looked out of the door of Bati's tiny room into the ochre court-yard beyond – one of several that tumbled down the hillside in a confusion of crooked planes and passages and perspectives and staircases, of half-seen rooms with walls of mirrored cupboards, of wandering goat-kids and pigeons that broke the silence with slow soft wing-beats in the dusty air. It was a haphazard citadel, perched above the huddled town, looking over the Valley of Light towards the void; a citadel as envisioned by the conjuror's eye of M. C. Escher. Bati's family history had just added another dimension to it all: time, a deep millennium and more of it.

There were more dimensions, political ones. Bati fixed me again with his glittering eyes. 'The truth is that the whole purpose of Ibn Battutah's so-called account of Walata was to claim that it belonged to the emperor of Mali. In fact it belonged to *us*. And it still does – to us Arabs, to al-Mahajib.' He permitted himself another small smile. 'It was the same fifty years ago, at Independence. Again, at that time, certain people wanted Walata to go to the new state of Mali. But no. It is *ours*.'

It was fascinating to watch IB getting drawn, retrospectively, into latter-day wranglings over political boundaries. But I couldn't help beginning to wonder if Bati was, in a word, batty. It was all too vehement, too personal.

As well as bats, however, there were books in Bati's belfry (and in his house: the cell-like room in which we were sitting was empty but for narrow twin sleeping-platforms either side of a floor of fine white sand; but a doorway led into a dark interior chamber in which I could make out the shapes of chests and stacked volumes – Bati's library). He quoted from memory the entry on Walata and his family in *Taj al-Arus – The Bride's Tiara* – the eighteenth-century encyclopaedic dictionary, and another one from a biographical work on sub-Saharan Islamic scholars. And Bati dismissed me with one last literary mention of his forebears, more potent than prose – a poem by a scholar of Timbuktu, 'a contemporary', he added with one last small smile, 'of your Ibn Battutah. "If you'd go wandering in the land/In search of righteous men of noble name . . ."' It went on, unsurprisingly, to say that you need go no further than Walata, and the pious and learned family of al-Mahajib. 'How could Ibn Battutah have failed to mention these great ones?' Bati asked rhetorically. 'No . . .' the moving finger wagged once more, 'No! *Ibn Battutah did not come here.*'

I left convinced of the possibility that IB had erred by cutting Bati's ancestors dead in literary terms. To claim further that the traveller had never come here at all was, however, an argument *ex nihilo* – and one fuelled, moreover, by a sense of family pride that smouldered down the centuries. But how to find solid evidence of IB's visit?

From up on the Black Mount, Walata gave little away. It was an undistinguished jumble of flat rust-brown roofs that covered the hillside and petered out on the fringe of the broad valley. But down inside its stepped and crooked wynds and silent sand streets, it began to reveal itself. The walls of the single-storey dwellings were plastered with a gingernut-coloured mix of mud and cowdung; they were blank and secretive. But at the entrance of each house there was a layer of icing – a square whitewash frontispiece relieved by ochre cartouches and geometric borders, and usually flanked by further large medallions in which the favourite shape – I don't say 'symbol', as I think there is no symbolism to it – was a figure of four knob-ended arms of equal length that a herald would call a cross pommellé. These elaborate frames contained heavy doors protected by benippled metal bosses that might have been inspired by an Amazon's breastplate. The whole effect was both splendid and gay, barbaric and sophisticated. And when one of these doors was ajar you could glimpse the courtyard within, cut by a diagonal shadow-line, the sun perhaps catching another ochre cartouche made up of self-reflecting meanders, a Troy-town map of false turns and dead ends, of hooks and eyes and key-patterns. It would be pleasing to think that these laborious labyrinths were a graphic record of the wanderings that had led here – of the search of Yahya the Perfect, say, for the Black Mount. But I felt the designs probably came from a more basic impulse, the wish to fill an empty space; and a lot of free time.

There was little human activity – no market, only one or two near-empty shops, and hardly any people out and about; just an occasional child, or a *darra'ah*-shrouded shape glimpsed at the end of an alley. Once I saw a woman in a doorway with a small girl. She pointed me out to the child. I waved, and the girl screamed and screamed while the woman laughed. 'She thinks you're going to kill her!' she called after me. (I like to think I now perform some useful function, along the lines of, 'Come on dear, eat up your couscous, or Blue-Eyes will come and get you.')*

One of the shrouded figures revealed himself as Sidi, who had been a tourist guide in the days when there was a need for such people. Sidi was tall, thin and lugubrious. His wife, in contrast, was big and jolly. When Sidi introduced me to her in his courtyard, she was wielding a hefty pole, laying into a pile of millet in a large mortar – as it turned out, to make IB's '*daqnu*, which is water and pounded millet mixed with a little honey or curdled milk', and which he was given at a village on the Niger downstream from Timbuktu. Here, they still knew it by the same name.

I asked Sidi if there were any other similar recipes in Walata. IB, at a reception hosted by the Malian governor of the town, was given a drink made with coarse-ground millet and curdled milk, different from *daqnu* but unnamed by him. It didn't inspire his enthusiasm. '"Is it for *this* that the Black got us to come here?"' he whispered to his Berber companions. 'They said, "Yes. Among them it is the height of hospitality." On hearing this I realized that no good was ever to be expected from them.' Sidi recognized this

---

* Apropos of which IB, shortly after leaving Walata, makes what was long thought to be the first ever written mention of couscous. The palm however now goes to the anonymous author of a recently discovered twelfth-century Maghribi cookbook.

different beverage immediately. 'He was talking about *sangitti*, which is the traditional drink of Walata.'

Later, we sat on Sidi's sleeping platform and had a tasting session. Unlike IB I preferred the *sangitti*, which had the comforting smoothness of invalid food, to the more lumpen *daqnu*. But I could see what IB meant: at an imperial governor's reception, one doesn't expect to be offered nothing but thin cold porridge. It must have been a gruelling experience.

Following the heavy cereal intake, we reclined on the bed. Sidi issued instructions to one of three unexplained black boys who squatted on the sand floor of the room. The youth quickly brewed up a pot of foamy and digestive tea. He was as obedient as a household slave – which, this being one of the few parts of the world where the institution of slavery still thrives, may well have been exactly what he was. I didn't like to ask; but my suspicions seemed to be confirmed shortly afterwards when Sidi said, 'He makes a lovely cup of tea, doesn't he . . . Why don't you take him away to Arabia with you?' In these lean times, running a three-slave household must have been hard work. Going by his expression, the boy was keen on the idea; having looked into the practicalities of twenty-first-century slave-owning some years before, I wasn't, and there the matter ended. But it was a very Battutian moment. At the village on the Niger where IB was given *daqnu*, he was also given a slave-boy. ' "This is your hospitality gift," ' his host said. ' "Watch him in case he does a runner." ' IB must have heeded the advice. Back home in Morocco he says, 'The boy he gave me is still with me today.'

Sidi's boys didn't look as if they'd bolt. They were too absorbed in a TV programme called *American Gladiator* which their master had just selected with his remote control (it's things like that, I thought, that'll end up putting slaves out of a job). Sidi and I reclined on the dais while the boys squatted beneath us, all of us engrossed by two men preparing to do battle with giant foam-rubber clubs. 'Karl, I know you've been taking a cer*ee*bral approach,' the compère was saying, 'r*ee*searching all the different types of combat for this very impressive weapon . . .' Other images began to appear in my mind, broadcast down the centuries by IB: '. . . for these people live a life of luxury and leisure, all of them trying to outdo one another in the number of slaves they own . . .'

Over the next couple of days I wandered Walata in Sidi's gloom-
ily knowledgeable company, but learned nothing more about IB's
visit; except to hear, from a younger scholar of the town, another
vehement denial that the visit ever took place. Like Bati, this man
roosted in a small cell with a lot of books. He was furious about the
girlfriend business. 'How could Ibn Battutah have said such things
when the pious men of Walata looked at none but the women of
their own households, when their lives were lived between house
and mosque? Explain this!' I had no ready answer. But the man's
next comment seemed to overshoot the bounds of rational debate.
'In any case,' he spluttered, 'the place Ibn Battutah claims is Walata
is in Nigeria!'

Argument only took us to an end as dead as Walata itself. In IB's
time the whole point of the place was that it was on the way – to
Morocco, to Europe; to Mali and the gold of Guinea. Now it was
ingrown, intellectually inbred, fascinating but pointless, legendary
to a few outsiders but forgotten by most, on a hiding to nothing but
the desert. And just as it was a dead end on the map, it was a cul-
de-sac in time, bursting with bottled-up anger about a few priggish
remarks in a 650-year-old book. It was all a salutary warning of the
danger and the power of words. Then again if one's experience of
the outside world today were shaped by images of foam-rubber
gladiators, cannibal zombies and cloud-cuckoo dictators, fourteenth-
century slights might seem that bit more real.

In my search for more solid realia from IB's century, Sidi took
me to the edge of Walata, to the dead end of the dead end – the
town's graveyard. It lay on the sand-blasted slope of a hill and had a
fine crop of headstones of varying degrees of ancientness and
crookedness. For some time I looked fruitlessly for inscriptions
and dates; all the slabs seemed to be blank. Eventually I found a
single stone that was inscribed. The epitaph was more interesting
than I could have hoped for:

> THIS IS THE SEPULCHRE OF HIM BY WHOM
> THE KNOWLEDGE OF THE *SHARI'AH* WAS DISSEMINATED
> BY MEANS OF JURISPRUDENCE & LOGIC
> OF LITERATURE & THE SCIENCE OF TRADITION
> WHO DURING HIS LIFE COMPOSED

ONE HUNDRED VOLUMES & TEN
WHO VISITED THE TOMB OF THE CHOSEN PROPHET
& TO THE HOUSE OF GOD PERFORMED
THE GREATER & THE LESSER PILGRIMAGES
CHIEF OF ALL JUSTICES
WHO BY HIS EQUITY OBTAINED A LASTING NAME
MUHAMMAD IBN YAHYA MAY GOD BE PLEASED WITH HIM

If there was a date it was invisible, buried at the base of the stone by the accumulation of centuries. But every line spoke of IB's age of travel and wide-ranging scholarship. 'Muhammad ibn Yahya . . .' – perhaps a son of IB's jurist and professor of Walata, Yahya ibn Abdallah Ibn Yanumar, and named after his uncle the female-friendly judge Muhammad?

★

'Ah, yes, Muhammad ibn Yahya,' said al-Saduq, recognizing the name on the stone immediately. 'He, like Ibn Battutah, wrote a travel book, *The Hijazi Travels*. It was published some years ago.' I asked when this travelling author had lived. 'He died in 1330,' al-Saduq said. I did a quick calculation: probably fifty years too early to be IB's jurist's son. Perhaps an uncle? '1330 *hijri*, that is,' al-Saduq added.

'*Hijri?*' Anno Hegirae, not Anno Domini? Al-Saduq smiled and nodded. That was almost within living memory . . . AD 1912, give or take. A couple of years before my father was born. Time just didn't seem to behave normally in Walata.

Al-Saduq was, like Bati, an elderly scholar. He too looked as if he'd been hewn from something harder than flesh – bog-oak, perhaps – but on a much bigger scale, and made even more magnificent by a gleaming sky-blue robe. With his slow and stately movements, the effect wasn't ascetic but hieratic. I could see al-Saduq playing the part of his Hebrew namesake, Zadok the Priest. Also unlike Bati, descended from the Prophet, he belonged to the Tulbah – hereditary learned clans of Saharan tribesmen mentioned by IB. He spoke with a quiet authority that needed no vehemence to enforce it.

'You need have no doubts,' he said when I mentioned Bati's

demolition of my whole reason for coming to Mauritania. 'Ibn Battutah was truthful. He visited Walata and reported what he saw. We will return to Bati later. First, let us read Ibn Battutah's text.'

I'd forgotten to bring my copy of the *Travels*, but al-Saduq had his own. It was fetched from an inner library-chamber by a young man – 'My little brother,' al-Saduq said. Clearly by a different mother, as there must have been at least forty years between them. With generations like that, it was no wonder that time had a tendency to foreshorten here. You could get back to the fourteenth century AD in a generational hop, skip and jump.

While the brother was looking for the book, I wondered what edition it would be. Perhaps, in this isolated city of learning, it would even prove to be an otherwise unknown manuscript . . . But al-Saduq's copy of the *Travels* was a printed one, and so badly printed that it was half-illegible. It didn't matter. I knew the words and, besides, it was the very same grotty Lebanese edition that had first got my feet itching for the long road that had brought me here. As on the Hill of Souls in Quanzhou, I had that sensation of parabolas concluding, of circles completing – and linking, for here was the text back in the place from which it was born. I cradled the book as if it had been a precious incunabulum.

I read aloud, and we retraced the desert journey. Al-Saduq provided oral footnotes on IB's times and distances, on the salt caravans and the demons of the sands – still encountered, he said, 'and God is the Most Knowing'. Here the young brother spoke: 'Yes, yes, this is true! I have seen the demons! We were out at night in a region to the north-east of Walata, travelling by camel through the part of the desert called al-Ary.' Was this a place-name or a common noun? *Al-Ary* would mean something like 'the Bareness'; a dark Mussorgskian vision formed of night in the bare desert. Whatever, it tallied with the area that was infested by the alluring spirits of IB's account. 'I heard distant voices, like singing,' al-Saduq's brother went on, 'and then saw lights playing on the horizon, in a place to which no human ever went. I wanted so much to go and see what was there! But my companions stopped me. They said the sounds and lights were made by *shayatin!*' Satans. He looked at me with starey eyes, as if he hadn't ever quite got over that demonic allure.

I shivered, and read on. Al-Saduq identified IB's *ruhbah*, the 'broad space' in which his caravan had deposited its goods: it was the same place in which my pick-up had unloaded. I wasn't surprised. Walata, this dead-end town, had already entered its long, slow period of fossilization when IB was here. But it was the human co-ordinates of the town that I was most interested in. At last I reached the passage in which IB called on 'the judge of the town, Muhammad ibn Abdallah Ibn Yanumar . . .'

Al-Saduq held up his hand to stop me. 'Here there is a scribal error; or perhaps Ibn Battutah's memory failed him a little. The first letter should have the two dots above it, not below. It is a *ta*, not a *ya*: not Yanumar, but Tanumar. The pointing of the word is also a little at fault. The accepted form of the name here has always been "Tannumra". It is perhaps not a matter of wonder that IB or the scribe got it wrong. It seems to be an old local word; at least, no one knows now what it means. But it was the nickname given here to Yahya ibn Musa, known in Arabic as "al-Kamil" . . .'

Yahya the Perfect. 'You mean the ancestor of the so-called Concealed Ones?'

'Yes. The original forebear of Bati. His alternative family name is Ibn Tannumra – our traveller's "Ibn Yanumar". The judge with the girlfriend is Bati's direct ancestor.'

Al-Saduq's craggy face was split by a grin. To prove his point he showed me the lineage of a nineteenth-century forebear of Bati, clearly displayed on the title-page of a biographical dictionary this more recent ancestor had compiled. There among the earlier generations was 'Muhammad the jurisprudent, son of Abdallah . . .' Further back was 'Yahya the Perfect, nicknamed Tannumra'.

'Bati, you see,' al-Saduq said, 'is trying to protect his ancestor from dishonour.'

I laughed. Bati was a genuine piece of human Battutiana, even if he was in denial of the fact. He'd led me to believe that he was angry because IB *hadn't* mentioned his ancestors; the real reason was the exact opposite. Bati wasn't exactly batty; but perhaps it was a little enthusiastic, protecting the reputation of a grandsire who was a contemporary of the Black Prince. Those scenes in the *Travels* that I'd seen as of no consequence had, on the contrary, had chronic repercussions in the spot – perhaps in the very spot, the rambling family house on the Black Mount – in which they had taken place.

It was good to see IB provoking such strong feelings across the centuries, to watch the doctored local annals being trumped by a traveller's tale.

I thought of my anonymous veiled friend from the journey here, of his comments on poetry as the memory of the past. Prose, too, is proof against the years. When all the triumphs of words are added up, the sum isn't so small.

*

I left Walata in the back of the same pick-up that had brought me, heading back for Nema and the world of coming-to-be and passing-away. Where the houses petered out I turned and looked north, past the town and into the desert, and thought, Should I have tried that other road? But no; the caravans are gone.

As I turned back a flash of movement caught my eye. It was a rider on a tall high-stepping camel. Hardly an unusual sight, here; but for a moment it was as if that cameleer from the Catalan Map had made it across the centuries as well as the Sahara. I squinted through the dusty light, and saw that the rider was veiled in black; then saw a glint of dark glasses. He raised a hand in salute. I waved back, then turned my head for a last brief look at Walata; but it had disappeared into its hollow. Then we rounded a bend and the rider was gone too.

Nema – Niagassola

Al-dakhil mafqud wa 'l-kharij mawlud. I toasted myself over a glowing log with the Malian border guards, and the old Arabic jingle kept going round in my head. It summed up the settled Arabs' attitude to the desert of the nomads, and mine – Walata excepted – to Mauritania. 'He who goes in is forlorn; he who gets out is reborn.'

I'd already wiped most of the post-Walata memories from my mind. A few remained. There were the rams on the bus from Nema, travelling as unaccompanied baggage to their fate in the approaching festival. One by one they were crammed, kicking and baaing bitterly, into sacks labelled with the recipients' names; the sacks were tied up, leaving the heads of the *moutons enragés* sticking out, then put in the luggage hold. The *chef d'escale* gave a receipt to each consignee: '*Reçu bagages – 1 Mouton – Nouakchott*'. We were held up by a late-boarding *mouton*. When the hold was opened to admit him, I saw the bagged rams moving around inside in a sheepish sack-race.

At 'Springs' I got off to pick up another bus to the Malian border. It came seven hours after it was meant to (obviously the fashionable margin for lateness in Mauritania I thought, remembering the Walata pick-up); seven hours spent in a state of catalepsy on the cold concrete floor of the bus office. Time forelengthened, a series of numb, numberless fractions. Eventually the *chef d'escale* joined me on the floor, and the only thing left that still possessed the power of motion was a huge and Kafkaesque cockroach that kept ambling through my field of vision.

Around midnight I went out for a pee and bumped into a veiled man who asked me what had brought me here. 'Walata,' I said, not wanting conversations.

'So you were following Ibn Battutah.'

I nodded, then went back to my sleepless concrete bed.

The bus came in the dead small hours. It was only half full. I bagged a double seat, wrapped myself in my headscarf and snoozed, miraculously undisturbed by checkpoints, all the way to the border and rebirth.

Borders may be one of mankind's more idiotic inventions, but I'd never been so pleased to see one as here. My passport came back with a word of welcome and a Malian stamp, first light revealed itself on the eastern horizon, and an expression surfaced in my memory from someone else's Arabic *Travels*: 'And when the negro night began to smile with dawn of day . . .'

The smile broadened as we drove south. Soon after the town of Nioro I saw the first baobab. Compared to the enormous hollow specimen IB noted on this road – 'I was amazed to find that a weaver had set up shop inside it; there he sat, plying his loom' – this was no more than a sapling, a bao-baby. But with every southward mile the trees waxed bigger and older – old enough, I realized, for their individual lives to have spanned both IB's and mine. And thinking of lifespans, I realized something else: that IB and I, who had both gone east at twenty-one, were nearing the end of our travels together in our late forties, with less than a year between us. Despite the intervening distance, we'd kept in step.

Patches of millet appeared and multiplied. Scattered huts of thatched mud became hamlets, then villages. The millet patches became fields; granaries sprang up in the villages, miniature houses with doors high up. There was a water-hole – water! – and then another. A flock of birds flashed up into the sun, a twinkle-hoofed herd of goats fled from the bus, a boy on a bay horse cantered bareback along the verge. The land relaxed, revived, grew richer, redder, greener, warmer, softer; more human. I remembered a comment I'd heard from an elderly Arab gentleman in Yemen, surveying a similar scene: 'Ah, this land! It only takes a kiss to make it pregnant . . .' I was watching the rehydration of a continent. Forty miles before Bamako came the miracle of a flowing stream with cattle wading in glorious mud; nearer still to the city, a landscape of low hills and rivulets and jungly dells. And then in the scruffy suburbs of the capital came the first prospect of that great African stream – tired and low at this time of year, crawling round tufted river-islands, but flowing all the same – the Niger.

It might have been the death of IB, I remembered, looking down into the shallows from the Pont du Roi Fahd. One day on his way to the then Malian capital he went and squatted by the river 'to fulfil a need', as the Arabic euphemism puts it, when 'one of the Blacks came and stood between me and the water. I was amazed at this shameless lack of manners . . .' It was when IB was grouching about this to his companions just after that one of them pointed to a huge log-like shape in the mud: the churlish man had in fact been keeping an eye on a lurking crocodile. (IB was lucky. Another travelling scholar died on the Nile in similar circumstances. His last words, complete with case-endings, were, '*God is Most Great! I am eaten by a cro-*')

Nearer to the bus station our progress slowed in traffic and, not for the first time, the two big questions that hang over IB's journey to Mali began to revolve in my mind. The first was the Why of the journey. Why, after already clocking up more miles than any previous known wanderer in the history of travel, did he set out on a 4,500-mile loop round the western half of the Sahara and its southern 'shores'? He had completed the itineraries to India and China predicted by the two sufi seers back in Egypt, a quarter of a century earlier. The Malian journey, without even the excuse of predestination, is one of the more puzzling parts of his travels.

The favourite explanation of the commentators is that he was on an embassy, or engaged in commercial espionage, on behalf of Sultan Abu Inan of Morocco. IB, now the celebrated world traveller, was in the sultan's entourage immediately before he left for the desert; he was summoned back to Fez by sultanic command at the end of his Sahara journey. There are sound reasons why the journey might have been an official mission. Ever since the famous PR pilgrimage, via Cairo, of the old emperor of Mali in 1324, Malian exports had been slipping away from the Moroccan route and travelling out north-east, via Egypt. More recently, the Black Death had struck a blow to commerce in general. And on top of this, Morocco was weakened by war, both civil and external, and its currency debased. The sultan needed more Malian gold and IB, the hypothesis goes, was sent to try and get it. It is a tempting theory; but given that IB was an inveterate puffer-up of his own importance, one might expect him to have dropped some hint of the great mission. Perhaps he was under a sultanic gagging order. If so, then the theory is unlikely ever to be proved.

Another possibility had come to mind. As a social climber, IB was in a class of his own: he was the equivalent of those obsessive mountaineers who set out to scale the highest peak in every continent. Much earlier in the *Travels*, he lists the Seven Great Kings of the World: the sultans of Morocco (of course), Egypt and India, and the four Mongol cousins descended from that dynamic dynast Genghis Khan – the Khan of the Golden Horde, the Chaghaday Khan of Central Asia, the Ilkhan of Iraq and Persia, and the senior cousin, the Yuan Emperor of China. IB, almost certainly uniquely, had succeeded in meeting them all – except the Yuan Emperor who, he claimed, was dead. (Could *this* be why he 'killed off' poor Emperor Teghon Temur twenty-four years before his time, like a mad collector destroying what he cannot possess?) The powerful and wealthy emperor of Mali would have been an excellent candidate for the position of Eighth Great King, and made up for that missing Chinese monarch.

But there are two simpler explanations for the journey to the

Land of the Blacks. First, that IB was already planning his book and was conscious of its potential significance as a panorama of the Islamic world; he was therefore visiting the last important corner of the *ummah*, or world-wide community of Muslims, that he had yet to see. Second, and most simply of all, the Sindbad Syndrome – the malady of Baudelaire's '*vrais voyageurs . . . qui partent/Pour partir*'.

Then again, who ever went on a journey for only one reason?

The other question on my mind, along with the Why of the trip to Mali, loomed even bigger. It was the Where . . . But for the moment all questions evaporated in the heat of arrival. My wits were focused on the business of bags, and on dealing with a dandy-ish man mutely soliciting donations, whose business card declared him to be 'Président de l'Association Malienne des Couturiers Sourds'. Deaf couturiers made a change from the immigration police benevolent fund. I liked Mali already.

★

All the ambrosia of Olympus, all the ale of Valhalla and the amrita of Vishnu-land was distilled into my first draught of cold Bamako beer in the bar of the Hotel Yamey. It took away the last lingering taste of Mauritania.

There was another antidote to that sad, sere land. The barman switched the TV on. It showed a row of large sitting men, and a group of large standing women in gorgeous draperies and turbans, smiling, and slowly, gently jiving. The camera fixed on one of the women, her eyebrows painted high and quizzical above a pair of kohl-rimmed almond eyes, her lips plump and purple as ripe figs – she might have been a Nubian queen on a state visit to a pharaonic fresco – and she began to sing, addressing the seated men in power-ful descending recitatives. It was all very ceremonious, beautiful and strange. Then the camera moved to the accompanist, and I sat up: he was playing an instrument that resembled a large xylophone, but with a double rank of calabashes suspended under the wooden keys and diminishing proportionally to them in size. He struck the keys swiftly and lightly with a pair of padded sticks, releasing from the wood sounds that were both percussive and liquid, a fluid and resonant plinking, a riff that rippled and charmed like the dancing women. It wasn't only physic to the ears after those desiccating chants and desert winds of Mauritania. It was the sound that had summoned me here, and it was the first time I had actually heard the voice of the balafon.

It was all to do with that other question, the Where of the journey. IB spent eight months in what he only ever calls 'the City of Mali', the capital of the empire. Other than nearly dying from eating undercooked yam porridge soon after his arrival, he seems to have done nothing of note during that time – except to watch. A seasoned observer of potentates, he thought very little of Mansa Sulayman, 'a miserly monarch from whom no big gifts can be expected', and even had the cheek to accuse him to his face of stinginess: 'You have given me nothing! What will I say to other sultans about your behaviour?' The emperor's interpreter, whom IB calls 'Dugha the Dragoman', must have been a master of paraphrase to cope with such an outburst; he was also the monarch's ritual bard, remembrancer, counsellor-in-chief and spokesman (IB notes correctly the Manding term for the post, *jeli*, usually rendered in English by the French word *griot*), through whom all communication with the emperor had to be made. As IB himself often did during his stay in Mali, we will return to Dugha the Dragoman.

IB has pages of notes on the Malian court, which he observed with an eye sharpened over a quarter of a century as an obsessive royal-watcher. All the glittering ceremonial is there: the ranks of nobles and warriors and doctors of the law; the spears and spurs, pavilions and parasols, ivory and gold, trumpets and drums and robes of Alexandrian *zardkhanah* and Byzantine *mutanfas*; the lesser imperial *jelis* declaiming rousing odes to the emperor through hornbill masks; the tethered talismanic rams that ward off the Evil Eye; the obeisance of petitioners, prostrating themselves and scattering dust on their heads in a Sudanic kowtow.

IB had a few criticisms of the Malian court. He thought the bird-masked bards comical, for instance, and at least in his book disapproved, as he had in the Maldives, of the fashion for young women to go about topless – including two of the imperial princesses who, he notes, 'were endowed with full breasts'. Born into another time and place, prurient, priggish, royal-obsessed IB would have made a fine tabloid hack. To be fair, he also found much to

admire in the Land of the Blacks; not least their practice of shackling slow learners to make them memorize the Qur'an.

Along with all the gems in the anthropological treasure chest, there are some amusing baubles, such as tales of talking locusts and, especially, of the cannibals who were said to infest the gold-bearing regions. White men like himself, IB maintains, are safe from being eaten as they are regarded as 'unripe'. Black females are favoured, and the tastiest morsels are the breast and the palm of the hand.* And all of this – the priceless data, the dubious tales, this full-length portrait of the greatest of the vanished sub-Saharan imperial courts – all this would have been lost in the midden of oblivion without IB. As so often, his is the only first-hand eye-witness account.

He only omitted one detail. For me, trying to follow him on the ground, it was the most important of all: IB forgot to say where the City of Mali was.

Earlier scholars of Manding history identified it on second-hand textual and traditional evidence with a village called Niani, on the Guinean left bank of the Sankarani, a tributary of the Niger that forms part of the border with present-day Mali. There is no doubt

---

* There may be something in this. Robert Louis Stevenson was informed by Moipu, 'an incurable cannibal grandee' of the Marquesas, that his favourite cut was the human hand.

that Niani was the chief royal settlement at various periods in the empire's history. But so too, at other times, were other places. Hunwick, one of the most distinguished names in Manding studies, couldn't pinpoint the site of IB's city any more exactly than 'on the left bank of the Niger from Bamako to about as far as Niamina' – a distance of a hundred miles. Meillassoux, another eminent Manding scholar, basing his careful calculations (as do all the others) on IB's information about travelling times, came up with a possible site on the upper reaches of the Gambia –400 miles due west of Hunwick's best guess. More recently a third scholar, Conrad, could be no more precise than to say that the Malian metropolis was 'ambulatory and peripatetic'. Faced as I had been in Sri Lanka with a lost capital city but, this time, with 80,000 square miles of West Africa in which to search for it, I'd admitted defeat long before I'd arrived.

There is of course no reason why IB should have known or cared where he was, in terms of degrees and minutes, for those eight months. If he was in the habit of packing an astrolabe, the fourteenth-century GPS, he never mentions it. Still, it would have helped to know where I was going . . . Or was it better *not* to know? Conrad quotes a French antiquarian who was warned a century ago by his Manding informant that 'The day the whites arrive at [the City of] Mali will be the end of the world; the sacred places will be known to all the curious people, who will come to disturb the repose of the spirits.' These spirits, the informant added, were 'all the more powerful and jealous because they once animated kings'. More recently Mamadou Kouyaté, the bardic transmitter of the *Epic of Sundiata*, put it more bluntly:

Never, ever try to penetrate the mystery which the land of the Manding hides from you. Never, ever come to disturb the eternal rest of the spirits. Never, ever come to dead cities to interrogate the past, for the spirits never pardon.

Interrogating the past was what my journey was about. It looked as if my Malian researches were doomed.

And then, in the same source that issued that second, chilling warning to the curious, I found something that pointed me in what looked like the right direction.

To read the printed version of the *Epic of Sundiata*, the story of the king IB mentions as the founder of the line of Mali's emperors, is to listen to the voice of a twentieth-century Homer or *Beowulf*. It is a cracking tale, and it has everything – irresistible destiny, triumph over adversity, superhuman strength, a journey into exile, an arch-villain, a scheming queen mother, witches, battles, magic, strange and sublime language, and a grandeur that makes it seem much bigger than its actual novella size. And as I read it I kept hearing resonances of IB. Not only are the pictures of Malian high society in the *Travels* and the *Epic* strikingly similar; you even come across the odd identical turn of phrase. 'No one', says Mamadou Kouyaté in the *Epic*, of the young hero Sundiata, 'could draw his bow.' 'No one', says IB of a famous Malian noble warrior he visited, 'could draw his bow.'* It is thrilling to hear the voice of local memory and the traveller's tale echoing in unison down the vault of time. What interested me most in the story of Sundiata, however, was the voice of the Sosso Bala.

As Mamadou Kouyaté says in the epigraph to this chapter, the Sosso Bala was unlike any other balafon. It may have resembled previous balafons in outward appearance, even down to the use of the integument of the eggs of a certain spider to cover the sound-holes of its calabash resonators. But this balafon belonged to Soumaoro Kanté, the blacksmith-king of Sosso, a sorcerer who like the Carpathian Wizard could take on sixty-nine shapes ('He could turn into a stick, a stone, even a wisp of straw!' an elderly Manding gentleman told me) and killed his victims by fiendishly inventive devices that included a poisoned hammock. The king of Sosso had a tower with an upper chamber lined with human skin and guarded by a serpent in a jar, three owls and the nine severed heads of the rival kings he had vanquished. This chamber contained the sorcerer-monarch's fetishes and, in the place of honour among them, anointed daily with the blood of sacrifices, stood his balafon, the Sosso Bala.

One day, while the king was off hunting, a bard called Bala Faséké Kouyaté came, like Childe Roland, to the dark tower. He

---

* It is possible that Mamadou Kouyaté's version of the *Epic* has borrowed details from the *Travels*. I doubt it; but if it is the case, it would be the sincerest form of flattery.

climbed to the upper chamber and, before its ghoulish guardians had stirred, began to play the sacred balafon. The effect was worthy of Orpheus. The heads and the owls and the snake all listened, entranced. Even the king of Sosso, who had flown here white-hot with rage and ready to kill the intruder when he heard the distant notes of his balafon, was captivated. He could not kill a player of such magical virtuosity as Bala Faséké; but he forced him to become his bard, his *jeli*. It was the *casus belli*, for Bala Faséké was the *jeli* of Sundiata.

The war was long and bitter. Still in his teens, Sundiata was already a famous warrior whom the *Epic* compares to Alexander (lame as a child, he had come into his own when his mother had told him to fetch some baobab fruit and he had brought her a whole tree). At first the hero and his myrmidons fought the mage-king of Sosso and his blacksmith army without success. Then Sundiata discovered the way to overcome his opponent – with the spur of a black cock. A single scratch, and the king's powers fled like ghosts at cock-crow. He and his army threw themselves into headlong flight. Sundiata razed the city of Sosso, 'rampart of the fetishes against the word of Allah'. It became the sub-Saharan Babylon, a thicket of thorns frequented in the daytime by partridge and guinea-fowl, haunted at night by the howls of hyenas.

Sundiata brought his bard, Bala Faséké, back home. And with him he brought that marvellous instrument, the Sosso Bala, chief fetish of a pagan sorcerer-king, now chief war-trophy of a victorious Muslim monarch. It was paraded in triumph before his ecstatic subjects; it became not only the model to which all other balafons were tuned, but a symbol of the harmonious unity of the empire Sundiata went on to win.

It still is. For, as I found out from a monograph on Manding music, the Sosso Bala has survived, guarded in a Guinean village by the Kouyaté descendants of Bala Faséké Kouyaté and the line of imperial *jelis* he fathered. What is more, it is still to be heard, played at the two great Islamic festivals by the head of the Kouyaté clan, who bears the title Balatigui, 'Lord of the Balafon'. The very idea of such a personage and such an ancient instrument is bewitching. It is as if not only Drake's Drum, but also Drake's Drummer had survived, the post passed down the centuries.

But what has all this got to do with IB and the lost City of Mali?

Along with the trumpets and drums of the Malian court, IB not only mentions balafons but gives a short description of them, 'musical instruments made of calabashes and reeds' – clearly, he couldn't have inspected the keys, made in fact from a rosewood-like timber called *béné* – 'which are struck with sticks and produce a marvellous sound'. Later, he mentions a particular balafon and a particular player. At the climax of the ceremonies for each of the two Islamic festivals,

> Dugha the Dragoman comes with his four wives and his slave-concubines, who number about a hundred. The women are dressed in fine raiment and wear fillets of gold and silver adorned with gold and silver balls. A stool is brought for Dugha, and he sits down on it and plays the instrument of reeds and small calabashes. As he does so he chants poetry in praise of the sultan, recalling his military expeditions and other deeds, and his wives and concubines chant with him.

Professor Charry, author of the monograph on Manding music, had already come to the conclusion that struck me when I first read the Sundiata epic: that IB's Dugha the Dragoman, chief hereditary *jeli* of the Malian emperor, was very probably a descendant – and not many generations removed – of Bala Faséké, that Orpheus of the fetish-tower. Charry had also learned that Dugha and the current Lord of the Balafon, although separated by 650 years, belonged to the same family. But it seemed to me that there was a further conclusion to be drawn: that the royal instrument IB heard Dugha playing on the day of the festival was the Sosso Bala itself – the very instrument that is still played on festival days by Dugha's descendant.

This is why I sat up at my first sight and sound of a balafon, on the TV in the bar of the Hotel Yamey. As I listened to it, as that striking woman with the quizzical eyebrows declaimed and rippled on the screen, the prospect of seeing the archetype of balafons, the Sosso Bala, grew more thrilling; and of hearing a sound, an incorporeal survival from so long ago. It would be like witnessing the raising of a ghost.

There were a number of ifs: if my theory about IB hearing the

Sosso Bala was right; if the Sosso Bala was the real thing; if I could get to its resting-place in the village of Niagassola across the border in Guinea, a country notoriously difficult to travel in; if the Lord of the Balafon was at home – and At Home – and if he was amenable to a curious stranger setting eyes and ears on an object which, it seemed, still retained a degree of numinosity close to that of a fetish; and, not least, if I could get to it in time for its second biannual airing. The Feast of Sacrifices – Tabaski, as they called it here – was almost on us.

If . . . then I might get to hear the music of time.

★

We headed south-west out of Bamako, between the invisible Niger and the foothills of the Manding plateau. The road passed through tawny scrub dotted with patches of woodland and clumps of mangoes. Now and again the slope of the plateau cropped out into a mass of creamy rock with a nutmeg-coloured top, like an egg-custard. Other rocky eruptions took the form of plinths for absent colossi; one was capped with a boulder shaped like a tam-o'-shanter.

Twenty-five miles from the capital we came to a long straggling village called Siby. On the skyline was the most striking rock formation so far – a giant half-arch like a flying buttress. 'The Arch of Kamadjan,' said Lamine, my driver. Kamadjan Camara, he explained, was one of the two closest friends of Sundiata. The army of the Manding had mustered here at Siby under their leadership before the attack on Sosso. 'Kamadjan showed Sundiata how strong he was by throwing his spear at the mountain and making the arch,' Lamine said, as if it was a perfectly natural thing to do. We had entered the landscape of the *Epic*.

I noticed that, where the shops in the village had signs, their owners were Camaras. Lamine confirmed this: 'They're all Camaras in Siby.' The idea of a whole village bearing the same surname as the local thirteenth-century hero was remarkable. In fact, I realized, being the product of a deracinated Europe, it was miraculous. The British equivalent would be going to Tintagel and finding everywhere from the pub to the bed-and-breakfast run by Pendragons.

As we turned off the metalled road a sign caught my eye. It was written in a script composed of shapes like lollipops and TV aerials,

and tricked me for a moment into thinking it was a very early form
of the angular Kufic script of Arabic. I could make no sense of it.
Neither could Lamine, even though he said it was the script used to
write the Manding language of the Mali empire, of which his own
tongue, Bambara, is a form. 'The writing is called "N'ko",' he said,
'which means "I say".' What a delightful addition to the catalogue
of interesting scripts, I thought: cuneiform, hieroglyphs, Linear-B
– and this Woosterish exclamation.

Off the main road the landscape tallied with the mental image of
it that I'd formed from IB's account. There were fields of calabashes
like giant peas out of 'Jack and the Beanstalk'; others of millet; villages shaded by ancient trees, where stately women with calabash
bowls on their heads and babies on their backs strode through fairy-
rings of thatched mud houses. Not a satellite dish, not a scrap of
plastic waste obtruded on the scene. With our Land-Rover and its
attendant cloud of red dust, I felt we were a gross intrusion – and an
anachronism, for other than us there was nothing in the whole
place to fix the century. Looking ahead, we might have been
motoring down the red road back to IB's time.

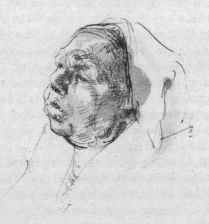

Lamine produced a cola nut from his pocket. It looked something like a large freckled kidney-bean. He broke off a piece for me.
Crunchy and earthy at first, then mealy and astringent, after a
period of slow chewing it brought on a barely perceptible but

pleasant sensation of lift; just the thing for a journey in the heavy heat of the riverain plain. Lamine was also just the man for the journey. With his goatee beard and his pork-pie hat, he had the looks and the demeanour of a laid-back jazz musician; but along with the cola, he fed me fragments of heroic tales and titbits of early Manding history. Yet it was Lamine's own history that I found most interesting, for it took me back into the parallel landscape I'd been straying in and out of on my peripheral travels with IB – that crep-uscular zone between the light of Islam and the darkness that had preceded it.

Lamine's grandfather, he said, had been a *maître-fétichiste*. He had been able to identify certain trees that were inhabited by good spirits and, just as important, to avoid those infested by evil ones. From the good trees he had gathered bark and leaves, reciting Qur'anic verses as he did so, and then used these materials to com-pound amulets and protective washes; the supernatural equivalent of anti-dandruff shampoo, I supposed. Neither Lamine's father nor he himself had learned these skills. 'But', he said, 'I carry these pro-tective things along with my prayer-cap and prayer-mat.' The latter two items, I'd noticed, he was assiduous in using.

I asked him if he saw no conflict of interests between Islam and what, to put it bluntly, was animism. 'God', he said, 'is the Creator of everything. I don't use evil things. But I don't see why I shouldn't use good things. *Ça, c'est ma logique.*'

Such intersections between Islam and pre-Islam could lead into even odder turnings, however. Lamine said that there are certain fetish-masters who make *boliw* – from what I can make out, amor-phous or vaguely anthropoid or zoomorphic lumps made of faeces, blood and other substances (somebody ought to put one in for the Turner Prize). The fetish-men have long confabs with them, 'and then they say that this or that will happen, *"in sha Allah"*!' I goggled at the idea. 'The God of the *fétichistes* is ours too,' Lamine said. It was all extremely pragmatic and accommodating; the purists would have apoplexies.

We passed through a village of the Doumbia clan, descendants, Lamine said, of another of Sundiata's lieutenants, and drove on through the flatlands. Although we hadn't seen another vehicle, the feathery grass on the roadside verges was powdered with brick-red dust. The Niger – the Djoliba or 'Great River', as everyone here calls it – was still invisible. But you could sense it, not far away across the levels, could feel and smell it in the stickiness of that all-penetrating dust.

The old imperial capital of Mali may be lost; not so its emperors. Just as there are Camaras and Doumbias there are also Keitas, the numerous progeny of Sundiata, and it was to their current 'capital' village of Kangaba that we were now heading. Kangaba was as old as Sundiata. Off a shadow-barred avenue of big gnarled trees, Lamine showed me a monument, a concrete gateway painted in ice-cream colours that commemorated in French and N'ko Sundiata's promulgation in 1236 of the Manding Charter, following his defeat of the King of Sosso. As a spectacle, this Malian Runnymede was singularly uninteresting.* In the village itself, however, was a far more notable memorial.

Wherever the political capitals of Mali might have been, it seems that its spiritual centre was always in Kangaba – not just its Runnymede, but also its Canterbury. Here, I'd learned, was a structure called the Kababolon, a sacred house rumoured to contain ancient copies of the Qur'an, perhaps brought back from Mecca by Mansa Musa after his celebrated pilgrimage, perhaps by his brother Mansa Sulayman, IB's emperor. No one seemed to know for sure. Lamine had never been to Kangaba and couldn't enlighten me. All he could tell me was that the name of the sacred house, Kababolon, meant 'the vestibule of the Ka'bah'. It was another instance that suggested, like the supernatural tunnel from Jaylani's jungle cave in Sri Lanka, that the thousands of miles from the edge of Islam to its centre in Mecca might be miraculously compressable. And even if the Kababolon's name turned out to be figurative, I was at least hoping to find out more about – perhaps even to see – its shadowy contents.

For a building of such significance it was at first sight disappointing. It was a perfectly standard-looking small thatched mud hut,

---

* Unlike the Charter itself, which includes much for the social anthropologist, and plenty of sound advice – Article 21, for example: 'Do not chase the wives of your neighbour, your friend, your protector, your chief, or of a fetish-master or a marabout.' There is also some remarkably honest historiographical philosophy, like Article 17: 'Lies which have survived and resisted contradiction for a period of forty years shall thenceforward be regarded as truths.'

distinguished only by some primitive designs on its walls, made up of blue dots – a snake, a fish and a triangle. A donkey stood in the narrow patch of shade cast by its eaves and brayed lustily as we approached. The hut gave nothing away on closer inspection. It began to intrigue me because of its ordinariness.

Mr Morifing Keita, whose small shop looked on to the sacred house, couldn't tell me anything about the putative relics within. My questions about antique Qur'ans – asked gingerly, as I remembered those dire warnings to people who interrogated the past – were answered with a shrug. At least Mr Keita, surrounded by his stock-in-trade of tea, soap, torch batteries, *spirales anti-moustiques* and not much else, looked the part: a good six foot three with bloodshot eyes and dressed in a gold-braided robe, my first scion of the mighty Sundiata almost crushed my hand as he shook it in parting.

Turning a corner, we emerged into a broad open space – and there, before us, was what looked like *another* sacred house. Again, it was a thatched hut with dot drawings on the walls; but this one was almost twice the diameter, perhaps twenty feet across. Beside it was a round earthen platform. Hut and platform were shaded by a gigantic silk-cotton tree, its columnar trunk rising from a deeply buttressed bole. The scene was flooded with late-afternoon shadows. I reached in my bag for my little-used camera; then stopped myself. For some reason, I didn't feel inclined to take a photograph of this place.

'You were right', said another Mr Keita later, when the sun had fallen, 'not to photograph the Kababolon.' We were sitting on the floor of a room that might have been a wizard's workshop. It was festooned with bundles of dried leaves, hanks of fibre, and cobwebs. Most of the floor space was taken up with braziers, calabashes and bottles containing coloured liquids, all under a thick layer of dust. The horn of a large antelope oozed with black gunge in one corner, a stack of files and books tottered in another, and beside the door stood a row of percussion-lock guns that looked as if they'd be as lethal to the shooter as the shot. In the middle of all this, on a balding goatskin, sat Namankoumba Keita. His appearance was the opposite of the warrior-like shopkeeper's – small, slight, dressed in a T-shirt and baseball cap; but as the son of the late chief of the

Keitas' chief village, and himself likely to be elected soon to the chiefdom, Nama was as worthy as any member of the prolific clan to be considered heir to Sundiata and to IB's Mansa Sulayman. Even his other roles, as chief medicine-man and hunter of Kangaba, the paraphernalia of which surrounded us, had heroic precedent: Sundiata, too, was learned in the arts of the chase and in the science of medicinal plants.

I sensed I'd gained a few points by not having taken that photograph. I felt them ebbing away with my next question. 'Why', I asked, 'is the Kababolon so important?' Nama smiled but didn't answer. 'Is it because of what it contains?' He smiled more broadly; I was rushing, like a fool, into a perilous interrogation of the past. 'I mean, I've heard it may contain ... . manuscripts, from the period I'm studying.'

His brow creased. 'What it contains is so sacred that I cannot tell you its exact nature. Few are permitted to enter the house; I am one of them. I know what is inside it.' He was silent again for a while. 'Let us say that Sundiata, *mon grandpère*, was himself descended from the nephew of Bilal. Of the celebrated Bilal, the Companion.' I nodded: Bilal was a black freedman and companion of the Prophet Muhammad, and the first muezzin, or prayer-caller, in the history of Islam. 'This nephew inherited from his uncle a certain relic of the Prophet, peace and blessings be upon him. That it what the Kababolon contains. I cannot tell you more than that.'

Nama's tone made it clear that there was no point in pressing. Of course, there was no reason why there shouldn't also be manuscripts from IB's time in the sacred house. But short of breaking into it and incurring God knows what vengeance from men and spirits, I would never find out.* I had another question, however: about that smaller house, the one Lamine and I had first mistaken for the Kababolon.

Nama smiled again. 'That is the fetish-house of Kangaba.'

'The *fetish-house*?' If Kangaba was the Manding Canterbury, then this was like having a working druid temple on the cathedral close.

'Yes. You see, when my *grandpère* founded this village, his

---

* One can never be too careful. I later found the ancient mosque of Ségou-Koro, also shaded by a giant silk-cotton tree, to be doubly guarded – by the spirits of cats, and by a supernatural swarm of bees (Bee-elzebub?), which are said to attack infidels who approach the place with malicious intent.

number-one slave said to him, "Master, we need a fetish-house to protect the village," and my *grandpère* said to him, "You go ahead and build your fetish-house, but I'm going to build a house for Islam." That second house is the Kababolon.'

'So what's in the fetish-house?'

'Fetishes.' Nama smiled.

Lamine spoke. 'People came here and brought Islam, and our kings went to Mecca and brought back Islam, but the people kept their own beliefs as well.'

It was the way things were, and are; not the all-or-nothing of the puritans and the politicians: 'You're either with us, or against us.' There were the two sacred houses, coeval, parallel, round the corner from each other, pagan and Islamic; although I couldn't help thinking of the impenetrable Kababolon and its hermetic contents as a sort of Islamic fetish-house. Like that pair of adjoining buildings I'd seen in China – the mosque and the ancestor temple – they showed how beliefs learned to live together out here on the edge. And just as strange as the proximity of beliefs was the closeness of centuries: the way Namankoumba Keita spoke of the doings of his *grandpère* as if they'd taken place a generation ago, not three-quarters of a millennium.

The next occurrence heightened the impression that Nama inhabited some kink in time. Lamine asked whether I minded if he had a 'consultation' with our host. Of course not, I said, wondering what it would entail; not realizing that Nama, in addition to his other skills, was a practitioner of the ancient science of psammomancy. Taking a small leather bag from beside his goatskin, he poured some fine sand from it on to the floor, then swiftly stroked it into a pattern with his fingertips. 'What do you see?' he asked me.

There was a vague suggestion of a dome and a minaret. 'A mosque?'

'No. This is Solomon, peace be upon him,' he said, touching one of the fingertip impressions, 'and this is Gabriel, and these are other prophets and angels.' He then began a soft incantation in which I could make out nothing other than Lamine's whispered name. During this *sotto voce* chant, Nama kept erasing and reworking the designs in the sand, smiling as if to himself. And another image came to me from the *Sundiata Epic* – of Nama's *grandpère*, 'pouring sand from his fetish-bag, tracing mysterious signs; tracing, effacing, beginning again . . .'

I don't know what riddles Namankoumba Keita discovered in the sands, for they were revealed in Bambara. But the last pronouncement was made in French: 'And, Monsieur Lamine, you will get lots of money from Monsieur Tim.' In this, if nothing else, the oracle was correct.

A tinny noise insinuated itself into the room, growing in volume. It was Nama's mobile, vibrating next to him on the goatskin and emitting a strange but somehow familiar sound.. He answered and spoke a few quiet words; I tried to think where I'd heard something like that ring-tone before – an instrument of some sort, a voice descending the scale, declaiming, recitative-fashion . . . It was the same style of singing that I'd heard from that splendid woman on the television, singing to the balafon backing. Nama put his phone down. 'Excuse me,' I said, 'but your ring-tone . . .'

Nama laughed. 'You like it?' He pressed a series of buttons and the voice sounded again. 'It is my personal *jeli*, my Kouyaté *jeli*. And you can also hear the *ngoni*, that instrument; and a rattle – it is a calabash with cowries in it . . . Listen, my *jeli* is saying to me, "*Be like your noble father! Be like your patient mother! Be noble and patient like them!*" '

I pulled the *Travels* out of my bag and translated what IB wrote about the *jelis* of Mansa Sulayman, reciting before him in their hornbill masks. ' "I was told that their poetry is a kind of admonition, in which they say to the ruler, 'On this seat sat such-and-such a king, and such-and-such, and they performed such-and-such good deeds, so be you like them and do good that will be remembered of you when you are gone!' . . . I was informed that this has been their practice since before the coming of Islam, and that they have persisted in it." And you still do,' I said, looking at the flashing mobile.

We left Namankoumba Keita to prepare for his next consultation. He prayed that I would see the balafon of his *grandpère*, if God willed it, and I took my leave of him, my mind reeling at the magnificent unison of ages that had come from a small loudspeaker.

In the torchlight in my tent I saw that everything – my bag, my clothes, my boots from the Ibn Battuta Mall – was covered in a thick adhesive layer of red dust.

Even now, this section of my diary is red round the edges, red with the dust of the land of the Manding.

★

The seven old men sat opposite us on the ground, sage-like, silent. They were in different stages of decrepitude and wore slightly different versions of the local homespun robes. One had a conical leather hat adorned with cowries. But they all wore the same faint and distant smile; all nodded slightly, like those eighteenth-century porcelain mandarins.

'Remember,' Lamine whispered, 'don't ask them anything directly.' He'd already primed me; besides, I knew the score from IB – in his day, too, everything was done via spokesmen. These greybeards of the village of Kela were among the spokesmen *par excellence* – not the personal Kouyaté *jelis* of the imperial family, but the Diabaté *jelis* who, every seven years, assembled on that earthen platform under the spreading silk-cotton tree by the Kababolon in neighbouring Kangaba. There they recited the *Mansan Jigin*, the entire history of the Manding from before the empire to the present. To Lamine I made a small speech in my execrable French, in which I praised the old gentlemen as luminous examples of the living patrimony of history, as *maîtres de la parole*. Lamine, himself a cousin of the Diabaté clan, recast this in Bambara that sounded far more eloquent than the original. The message was then relayed to the greybeards – entirely unnecessarily, as they were sitting a few feet from us – by a middle-aged man who was acting as their spokesman and earpiece. On hearing the spiel for the third time their features suddenly became more serious, and there was a slight increase in the oscillations of their heads. But the masters of the word remained silent.

The middle-aged intermediary replied to my speech. Lamine translated: it was customary to give the Diabaté *jelis* cola 'to open their mouths'. The cash equivalent, five thousand francs, would have the same effect.

The money changed hands. The *jelis* remained silent as ebony carvings. Their intermediary spoke again. 'Every seven years, the

Diabaté *jelis* assemble by the Kababolon in Kangaba,' said Lamine, translating. 'They recite the *Mansan Jigin*, which is the entire history of the Manding from before the empire to the present.'

It was good to hear my data confirmed. 'I have some specific questions', I continued, 'that arise from the text of Ibn Battutah's *Travels*.' I was keen to know what had happened to the bird–masks of the old *jelis* and, in particular, to find out more about IB's emperor, Mansa Sulayman. Namankoumba Keita, who had been full of the praises of Sundiata and of his famous and generous descendant Mansa Musa, could tell me nothing about Musa's less celebrated brother. 'The Blacks dislike him', IB said, 'because of his avarice.' It seemed that the tight-fisted potentate had been written out of history. I wanted to hear the official line from the court historians. The old gentlemen in front of me were, after all, in the words of the *Sundiata Epic*, '*les sacs à parole*, without whom the names of kings would fall into oblivion, who by the word give life to the deeds of kings'.

The answer came back from the middle-aged spokesman: 'Any other information will be released by contract.' For money, in other words, Lamine explained.

For a time we talked about talks, about francs, the three of us circling the subject in a waltz of words while the seven sages sat out the dance as silent and stately as Trappist abbots. Their gravity was slightly undermined by a hen and her brood of chicks that kept careering round them, and at one point I nearly got the giggles when I noticed that the youngest ancient, a dumpy man who looked as if he too wanted to break into a grin, could have passed as a photographic negative of the late Goon, Sir Harry Secombe. It soon became clear, however, that my already dented finances would take a serious battering from any further inquiries, and that there was no guarantee that I'd learn anything I didn't know already.

I closed with another speech: I myself was the *jeli* of IB, and my task was to take his words back to their origin; it was enough for me to have done this, and to have met the most distinguished and venerable *jeli*s of the house of Diabaté. The message was passed on with the usual palaver; again the oscillations increased perceptibly. We left. Not one of the old men had uttered a word.

As Lamine and I drove away in our jinn-like cloud of red dust, I remembered that – of course – one of the whole points of being a *jeli* was to make money from one's rhetoric. On the day of the festival, IB recalled, 'the king ordered a gift to be given to Dugha the Dragoman, and a purse was brought containing two hundred *mithqal*s of gold dust'. That was what he got from stingy Mansa Sulayman. The Diabatés hadn't done so well out of me. Still, Cfa 5,000, or about £6, wasn't bad for half an hour of eloquent silence.

The problem was, none of this boded at all well for my planned festival-time meeting with Dugha's descendants, the Kouyatés. It looked as if it might break my paltry bank. Moreover that festival, Tabaski, was fast approaching. But at least the Guinean border was approaching too, and I'd saved a few days by not going through the rigmarole of geting a visa at the Guinean embassy in Bamako. 'Don't worry,' they'd told me at the agency where I'd hired Lamine and his car, 'they'll give you one at the border.'

It was some of the worst advice of my travelling life.

*

'*Tu es entré dans la Guinée sans visa.*'

I didn't reply. There was no way of denying it. My passport disappeared into the khaki pocket.

I looked into the dark pools of Lieutenant Diawara's aviator sunglasses, desperately fishing for signs of a smile. There were none. Even in the humid fluvial air of Siguiri, my lips felt like oven-dried sandpaper. I heard Lamine swallow hard beside me.

I could just make out the eyes, roving from side to side in their lean sockets, scrutinizing, but never meeting mine. '*On peut te mettre*', Lieutenant Diawara said, '*en prison . . .*'

Whether such a thing as an iced enema exists I don't know. But at that moment I felt I'd just been administered one. *En prison*: it sounded so much more horrible in French. That '*On*' was superb as well – the pronoun of faceless power, the rhetorical equivalent of aviator sunglasses. Please God, I thought, not a Guinean prison.

The sense of doom had been gathering since our lunchtime arrival at the frontier. It was a most lackadaisical set-up, a piece of string tied across the red road between two twigs and – the Guinean secret weapon, this – a small flock of sheep lying comatose in the dust beside it. The sheep only began to move at the third blow of Lamine's horn. Sensible people without cars – everyone except us, that is – walked round the end of the string. The young officer in charge of the string was laid back too, in a T-shirt and a bead necklace. They didn't have a visa stamp here, he said. There was hardly any call for one on this back road. But all we had to do was to drive on to the town of Siguiri and report to the police and they'd give me one, *pas de problème*. He noted down various details from my passport in a grimy ledger. As he did so, I saw that on each hand he had several large rings – and a small extra finger. The vestigial digit of his right hand wobbled as he wrote. Lamine slipped him a *pourboire* from our petty donations fund; the officer gave my passport back and left his hand out to be shaken. As I took hold of it I distinctly felt the extra finger. It was smooth and cool and had a slight give to it, like a ripe gooseberry. Just as distinctly, I felt the first stirrings of apprehension.

Fifty miles down the road, in Siguiri, the smile of Mali had vanished. People here were not only poor – where in all these places are they not? – but they'd also given up trying to hide it. Poverty was as thick in the air as dust. Hope, and happiness, had fled, and left a void as empty as the shelves in the shops. And here was Lieutenant Diawara sitting on a chair under a tree, in shades, in the shade, in the courtyard of Siguiri police station. (Beware the shaded men in too-clean uniforms; beware and beware them when they are shod in flip-flops.)

'*Oui*,' he said, almost apologetically, '*en prison . . . Mais*,' he continued, after a perfectly timed pause in which a succession of images passed through my mind – clanging doors, clanking chains, dungeons swarming with rats and mad-eyed murderers and Ebola viruses – '*je pense qu'il y a une solution.*' The eyes still roved from side to side, appraising, never alighting. The tip of a tongue flicked out and back between thin lips. It was moist, I noticed, and very pink. '*Mais il faut payer* beaucoup *d'argent.*'

Did I see through the obscure glass a faint creasing round the eyes, the first flicker of a smile? '*Monsieur,*' I said, '*vous êtes trop gentil.*'

★

A few details remain from the days and nights of my detention, while initial negotiations over the sum were under way, in the Hôtel Tamtam: the look of fear and fascination on the face of the first whore, a girl with a heavy jaw and big tits, when she discovered me – '*Toubabou!*' White man! – on the cracked veranda; the sawn-off shotgun hanging by the till in the bar; the morning body-count in the yard – not dead but deep in alcoholic coma; the marooned Malian journalists doing a piece on tourism in Guinea (!) with whom I passed a morning drinking Scotch and tonic; a massive full moon like a truckle of Double Gloucester, hauling itself up through the dust and smoke of Siguiri; my room with its kicked-in door and waterless bathroom (the Great River was just down the hill) and big pink bedstead, theatre of dreams – lurid nightmares of labyrinths and, once, of my impending death. (IB remembered a dream he had on this journey, one that caused him to recite the funerary Qur'anic Chapter of Yasin every day of his life thereafter. It must be our age, IB's and mine; the relentless approach of the climacteric. *And who will give life to these bones after they are rotten and become dust?*)

In all this, the *Golden Treasury* was a mixed solace. It was good to contemplate Marvell's garden – 'What wondrous life is this I lead!'; not so Vaughan's vision of 'Time . . . like a vast shadow'. For me that shadow was cast by Lieutenant Diawara, and he had the power to make it as long as he wished. Eventually, however, the resourceful Lamine recruited the owner of the hotel – 'Chief of the Chamber of Commerce of Siguiri, one of the most puissant and celebrated notables of the city', according to this gentleman's *jeli*, himself the Head of Electricity for the town. We all trooped off to the police station to determine how much *beaucoup d'argent* was.

The little court convened in an upper room where an underling made swirls in the dust on the chairs before we sat down. Lieutenant Diawara still wore his dark glasses. The Chef de la Chambre said nothing but looked notable, puissant and large. The Commissaire of Police of Siguiri Prefecture, a man with a mournful, basset-hound face, sat in the judgement seat. The President of the Republic – who for some years had been, like his country, hopelessly sick and paralysed – smiled down from the wall, the face in the photograph faded half-way to a *toubabou* white.* A pamphlet lay undisturbed in the dust on the desk – *Le policier, ami des enfants* (*mais pas*, I thought, *des toubabous*).

The damages were announced: half a million francs for my *infraction*, and another half a million as a 'fee' to move round the prefecture. My jaw went into free fall . . . and then I heard Lamine whispering, '*Guinean* francs'. About £120. It was only a little more than my visa would have cost back in Bamako, and for the extra I got a letter from the Commissaire of Police permitting me to travel '*pour voir le Sosso Bala*'. I didn't ask for a receipt (I never do; who would pay?).

Merely to see the name of that venerable instrument filled me with fresh excitement . . . The only problem was that the festival of Tabaski had come and gone. My hopes of hearing the voice of history were one with the smoke and dust of Siguiri.

*

The night was busy with stars, and crickets, and with the hum of human voices. Djigui Kouyaté's smile appeared out of the darkness. 'Come,' he said. 'It is time.'

That afternoon, bats out of hell would have eaten the dust of our departure from Siguiri. We'd got to the turning for Niagassola, home of the Sosso Bala, in no time, and were soon rolling across red country that gleamed with the white of cotton bolls. Patches of fallow land, cleared by recent burning, were planted with the stumps of termite mounds that recalled Paul Nash's blasted forests of

---

* He faded from life itself a week later, after twenty-four years in power. At the time of writing, his successor, leader of the 'National Council for Development and Democracy' (who installed himself, in time-honoured developmental and democratic fashion, in a military coup), languishes in Burkina Faso, having been shot by the commander of his own bodyguard.

the Western Front. There were tan cattle and dun villages – those same fairy rings of thatched mud houses that sprouted like dumpy toadstools all across the land of the Manding (Manding, unlike the modern map, knows no frontiers). Here and there a tangle of woodland bordered the track and spiced the dust with the heady perfume of pandanus. The dust alone would have been heady enough after those days spent in Lieutenant Diawara's web – days that had seemed weeks, for it was a web woven to entangle time itself. But beneath the exhilaration was the knowledge that, like the voodoo priest who keeps the souls of his acolytes in pots, the lieutenant still had my identity, my passport; and that, this being the fifth day after Tabaski, we were on a wasted journey.

We had passed a side-track that Lamine said led to some gold mines; he had been there once a few years ago. In any other circumstances I would have made the digression to that corner of the fourteenth-century Eldorado. But now nothing would have diverted me from the road to Niagassola, not all the gold in Guinea.

Soon after, we had driven through an abandoned village. Its mud houses were dissolving back into the dust, guttering away like candles. That had been the fate of IB's lost City of Mali. Elsewhere on my travels with him, places and buildings had often been my first destinations. Here, though, it was people, and things – one thing in particular, the Sosso Bala, enshrined in an architecture of memory that was more solid than that of mud, guarded by beliefs that weathered time. My whole travelling life with IB had been an attempt to pick up the vibrations of his age; to echo-sound the centuries. And here, a few miles ahead of us, was an object that could make the resonances audible. Except that I knew it would be silent, guarded by mute old men.

And now we were in the dark in Niagassola and Djigui Kouyaté, in whose house we were to sleep, was telling us it was time. For what?

★

Lamine and I sat in the dark in an empty row of chairs. Somewhere behind us there was a gunshot – an assault rifle by the sound of it. It was followed by the boom of a shotgun shell. Then came the metallic cough of a small generator clearing its throat, and two dim

bulbs began to glow in the air in front of us. They were slung on a
line across an open space of dust. To the right, the feeble light fell
on a row of dark shapes, reflected softly from burnished wood and
bulbous calabashes: not one, but six balafons!

There was another gunshot, close this time, then voices. We
stood and turned. A group of men were approaching, led by a large
and resplendent figure in banana-yellow trousers and a black, lime-
green and raspberry-pink batik shirt. He was followed by a thinner
man who wore a fawn safari suit, a matching fedora worn back-to-
front, and the air, strange out here in the sticks, of a *boulevardier*,
then came another – the owner of the assault rifle – in battledress, then an assortment of other faces dimly recognized from our
arrival in Niagassola. There was Djigui, now in a parka with a fur-
lined hood, exotic here in the tropics. And among them all an old
man stood out, slender and upright despite his years, wearing a
white Arab-style robe and a red checkered headscarf. The others
waited till he had taken his seat, then the large man in the fruit-
cocktail outfit came forward and announced him to Lamine and
me: '*Messieurs . . . Monsieur le Balatigui*'. The Lord of the Balafon.

'*Excellence*,' I said, inclining my head.

The bulky popinjay, Judge Siriman Kouyaté, was a younger half-
brother of the Balatigui, as were the professor in the reversed fedora
and the officer in battledress. They had all come from the capital,
Conakry, to spend the Tabaski holiday in their ancestral village.
This was the last night of the Kouyaté family get-together. I
couldn't believe my luck.

More chairs were coming out, more voices approaching. The
women came on, magnificently proportioned and attired. One was
draped in golden cloth so heavy it might have been chain mail;
another was in puce satin checkered with squares of enormous
silver sequins and wore her hair dyed gold, a helmet of glittering
curlicues; the oldest woman was in black with giant scarlet poppy
heads. Others followed, gleaming and glittering with sequins and
smiles. Each was crowned by a turban that matched her draperies,
tied with the airy insouciance of a vol-au-vent. The effect was both
solemn and psychedelic. And one of the woman looked familiar . . .
As I tried to think why, Lamine leaned over and whispered, 'You
see the woman on the left in the front row? She's Kaniba! Kaniba

Kouyaté, the famous singer!' Then I remembered where I'd seen the quizzical eyebrows and the almond eyes: on television on my arrival in Mali, declaiming to the rippling backing of a balafon. And now the ripple began again.

Six players had taken their places behind the rank of balafons. They played in unison, a simple, repeating four-bar refrain, touched now and then by the lightest of rhythmic decorations. The refrain, the riff, the ripple proceeded in a gentle and regular cascade of notes, of beats, marking time, mesmerizing. One of the central players wore bands on his wrists that were hung with small silver bells. They added a thin and gleaming thread to the skein of sound that unspooled into the darkness that embraced our brilliant gathering. We were on an island of sound in a sea of silence.

Five small boys came and sat in the gaps between the players. Their shining eyes followed the blur of sticks. And in my mind I saw a longer line of balafons, of players and pupils stretching into the dark down the generations of Kouyatés, marking time, marking centuries of festivals, back to Dugha the Dragoman and another watcher from a distant land; back beyond them, to the dark tower of Sosso where the Orphic ancestor of these people had charmed the serpent and the severed heads and the sorcerer king.

The dancing began with the extremes of age. First a few tiny children, tentative but unselfconscious, taking careful steps, one small girl biting the end of her tongue in concentration. They were soon swept off the floor by the irruption of the oldest of the women, splendid in her coruscating poppy heads. She paced the dust in a circle, head and shoulders thrown back, arms jerking as if twitched by invisible strings, shuffling in time to the beat of the balafons.

Suddenly the rhythm elided into a new and quicker one and four middle-aged matrons took the floor, statuesque as caryatids and topped by their intricate capitals of turban. Each carried a short length of metal tube and, tied to it with cord, a small metal bar. They began to clang these instruments, at first in time with the balafon riff, but then digressing from it. Keeping in line with each other, they circled the floor, sometimes going into reverse, a radius that advanced and retreated. One of the women, the one with the helmet of gold curls beneath her turban, was a virtuoso clanger who wandered off the beat and back again in ever more complex cross-rhythms. She was enjoying herself hugely; they all were. But I felt a vein of seriousness pulsing in all this: there was something sacerdotal in the women's bearing, an echo of the sistrum in their clangs, as if they were concelebrating mysteries. Two places along from me the Balatigui, the Lord of the Balafon, looked on, grave and motionless, while the women wheeled and clanged and that hypnotic backing-track rippled on.

Kaniba rose. As she did so, Lamine's neighbour said something to him. He passed the message on to me. 'I didn't know before, but Kaniba is the daughter of the Balatigui.' She looked about her, head erect, smiling. I noticed that in profile she had faint sideburns, darkened by sweat, and the beginnings of a Queen Anne chin. Then she threw her head back and – the power of the live voice hit me unawares – poured out a flood of sound, half sung, half declaimed, a waterfall of words dark with a sediment of earth. She looked about her again, laughing, as the four older ladies clanged, the six balafons rippled, and the wave of sound washed back in a choral echo from the seated women. Once more came the liquid surge of words with its timbre of earth, then the choral undertow of the women and the melodic patter of the balafons, water cascading through pebbles. Kaniba laughed again; her father permitted himself a slight nod of the head. She poured out another recitative, her voice warming, *Sprechgesang* gaining new notes of smoke and rosewood. 'This is the way the *jeli*s sing,' Lamine whispered. I remembered that day in 1352 when the *jeli* Dugha had sung and his gorgeously dressed womenfolk had replied in chorus.

Eventually Kaniba retired, smiling. The four caryatids intensified their clanging; their syncopations became more intervolved, adding a hint of madness to the incessant rhythm of the balafons. Four Kouyaté men took the floor, Djigui – also, I learned, a younger brother of the Balatigui – among them in his furry parka, and danced in a slow round, their feet advancing in a shuffle, their upper bodies following in controlled spasms. Against the background of rhythmic ticking and mad chiming they might have been automata on an ancient clock. Now Djigui began to dip and rise, picking up each time he did so a handful of dust which he let fall from his fingers in a thin stream. I remembered that dust-abasement before the old emperors. (Djigui himself later gave another reason: 'No, it is not that. It is to bring to mind our ancestors who are now dust.')

Now the dancers and the clangers left the floor, and the resplendent judge and another man took their place. The judge began to declaim, in measured, forceful phrases. In the background the balafons ticked over. And between the phrases the judge's companion stared, almost glared, around the audience, and uttered loud Arabic ejaculations: '*Na'am!* . . . *Wa'llah!* . . . *Wa'llahi* . . . *Na'amu!*' Indeed, by God, the words were true! As the words in question were in Bambara I wasn't the wiser at first. But then I began to recognize names in the judge's litany: Sundiata . . . Bala Faséké . . . Dogha –

. . . *Dogha*? It had to be IB's Dugha! The judge was reciting the family history. And there he was again, Dogha/Dugha. *Wa'llahi!* I listened, enthralled. The traveller's tale had gone its own way while memory marked timed at home; but they had kept in step for 650 years. The balafons ticked on.

The moon rose, just past the full. The night cooled. And suddenly the rhythm hotted up. Kaniba returned to the dust-stage with two other women and resumed those cascading recitatives, the clangers clanged again as if to raise Osiris. Then the soldier-Kouyaté came on and added a new cross-rhythm of rifleshots – and the clangers went mad. They strutted and twitched and jerked, shoulders flying back and swooping forward with growing violence, haunches shuddering and shimmying. Now all the women flooded on, screaming with laughter, and the night became a blur of buttocks and breasts bucking and plunging like waves in a storm on a sequinned sea. I felt myself being dragged in – by Kaniba. She pulled off a sash and tied it round my loins and I kicked off my Dubai boots and danced: I, most awkward dancer in the world, giving myself to the rhythm, to the child of time.

I flopped back into my seat, exhausted. Then the Lord of the Balafon himself rose. Everything fell silent; except for the balafons, which entered into a new and stately measure, a slow and steady drip as if from a gallery of water-clocks. And now the judge was pulling me to my feet again, guiding me to the Balatigui's side, joining our hands, raising them in the air. All the other men rose too, and we sashayed forward in time to the harmonious clepsydral rhythm, past the smiling women and along the line of balafons, Dugha's chief descendant looking slowly left and right, our hands still joined in the air as he solemnly, silently acknowledged the smiles.

Round we went and round again in our memorious loop, our dance to the music of time, in which even the dust beneath our feet held memories, and the past was only a few paces ahead, or behind.

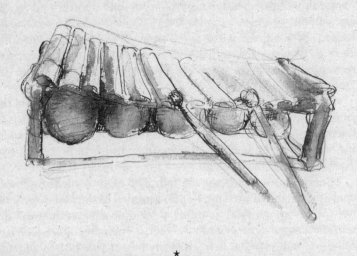

*

'This is the description of your *grandpère*,' I said the following morning, holding up the copy of IB's *Travels* and looking round the circle of Kouyaté men, 'as written by my *grandpère* . . .' I threw a glance at Lamine. In his role as my temporary unofficial *jeli*, he had somewhat embroidered the relationship between me and IB. Quite how Dr (another embroidery) Mackintosh could be the *petit-fils d'Ibn Battoutah* would be hard to explain; fortunately, no one asked for an explanation. As for the Kouyatés' *grandpère*, we were on firm ground. The judge, as chief spokesman of his brother the Lord of the Balafon, had enumerated several Dughas – or Dökkas, as the Kouyatés spell the name born by their ancestor* – among the early generations of their ascendants. Which of them was IB's man would

---

* The second consonant, the Kouyatés' *kk*, is not quite the *ghayn* of IB's 'Dugha', a voiced velar fricative similar to the Parisian *r*, but to my ears is not far from it.

be hard to tell; perhaps it was Dökka Mamu, the grandson of the Orphic Bala Faséké. In any case, the name stuck, and the Kouyatés bear it still as an alternative surname – literally, in the Balafon Lord's case. Today he had put on a robe of locally woven cotton in yellow and chocolate, embroidered with balafons and, on the back, with the word 'Dökkala', the plural form of the name. I had never expected human survivals from IB's book to be so legible.

I read out IB's written memories of Dugha, repatriating them in my excruciating French: memories of the man who was 'one of the most excellent and distinguished of all the Blacks', of his speeches as mouthpiece of the emperor, of his festival performances on the balafon with his chorus of magnificently attired women, of his own splendid dress, 'standing at the door of the audience chamber in his superb robes of figured *zardkhanah*' – I looked at the superbly robed current Lord of the Balafon – 'and wearing on his head a turban with borders, which they tie in a most elegant manner . . .' Today the Balatigui too had put on a turban, of sulphur yellow, elegantly tied with a projecting 'tail' and bound by a band of silver phylacteries . . . I had the distinct impression that those silver amulet-cases were a detail IB forgot; that the fourteenth-century original was unfaithful to the twenty-first-century copy.

'Copy' is the wrong word. When I had finished reading, the judge told me that the Kouyatés, the Dökkas, had never heard this sole eye-witness description of their forebear. I felt I had achieved something by bringing our *grandpères* back together after so long.

Whether it was in recognition of this service to the collective memory of the family, or in deference to the signature on my hard-won permission *pour voir le Sosso Bala* – the signature, I'd only realized this morning, of Commissaire *Keita* (the old loyalty of Kouyaté to Keita, *jeli* to royal, being stronger by far than that of citizen to state) – I finally made it over the threshold of the sacred house of the ancestor of all balafons.

'The Sosso Bala is 803 years old,' the judge announced to me before the assembled family outside the round thatched hut in which the instrument is kept. 'Only the Lord of the Balafon may play it, and only on certain occasions. It may never travel in a vehicle or on the backs of beasts, but only on the heads of men. We must enter the house of the Sosso Bala unshod. Remember the sanctity of the Sosso Bala. Remember', his voice took on an even more portentous tone, 'that even if a fly landed on it, its first master the king of Sosso would pursue that fly, wherever it might go – ' he looked from face to face; I thought, I wouldn't want those eyes on me in a court room ' – *pour l'écraser.*' I winced at the idea of being similarly crushed by the enormous judge in his lime and raspberry shirt.

The House of the Sosso Bala looked small from the outside. Within, it seemed miraculously to accommodate all the grown-up men and women, and a good number of the children. The latter, however, were shooed out; they squatted in the entrance, eyes glowing. Slowly, my own eyes adjusted to the dark. Against the wall leaned a row of spears, one with a metal haft blackened by age. The Balatigui took hold of this and stood as if on guard ('Dugha holds two short spears,' IB remembered, 'one of silver and the other of gold'). 'This is the silver spear of the king of Sosso,' the judge said, his voice now soft in the sacral gloom. I wondered where the gold spear had got to.

Also leaning against the wall was a large trapeziform object, as tall as a man, in a fitted cover of white linen. Kaniba and one of the other women tenderly removed this – and there it was, calabash-side out, the whole instrument patinated to a rich and burnished brown; made richer still by all those ancient libations of blood? Only one small tie at the upper right corner was of a lighter colour. (Later, thinking about the authenticity of the Sosso Bala and remembering Article 17 of the Manding Charter – the one saying that lies that have been believed for forty years are thereafter thought of as truths – I tackled Kaniba on the subject. She was shocked by my doubt: '*No!* It is absolutely original, from the time of the king of Sosso! Except for a few of the ties, nothing has been renewed – *ni une calebasse, ni une pièce de bois!*')

The Balatigui, still holding his silver spear, covered his free hand with a cloth and placed it protectively on the top of the instrument. Kaniba and the other women dusted the calabashes with respectful flicks. I edged closer. 'Don't touch it!' Lamine hissed. I didn't need to be reminded; not with the prospect of *écrasure* by the judge.

'The Sosso Bala is only lowered to the ground, to the playing position, if a ram is sacrificed,' the judge went on. I asked him if its sound had ever been recorded. 'The attempt was made once,' he replied. 'But nothing came out.'*

Not only the Sosso Bala itself, then, but even its voice was too sacred to be transmitted by any other vehicle than the human one – and only that of the Balafon Lord. Dugha's instrument holds the voice of history, but it needs Dugha's chief descendant to release it . . . Of all the material relics I had seen on all my travels, this was the one in which what I was searching for was most deeply immanent. And without these people it would mean nothing. They were right to keep it here in its reliquary of mud and memory; move it to a museum and it would become an assembly of bits of old wood.

I left without hearing the voice of the Sosso Bala, that epitome of my quest for the material and human traces of IB's journey. And as I said farewell to the gravely smiling Hajji Sékou Kouyaté, Lord of the Balafon, I realized that he hadn't spoken either. But I had danced with him.

★

'There's one question I forgot to ask,' I said as the Land–Rover set out along the red dust lanes of Niagassola. 'Where did the king of Sosso get the Sosso Bala from?'

Kaniba laughed from the back seat. Beside her was her aunt, the virtuoso clanger of the night before. Above our heads a large balafon was strapped to the roof-rack. We were giving them all a lift into Siguiri. 'We must keep *some* things secret!' she said. 'We can't tell you everything on your first visit.' I knew, however, that there would be no more visits. The secret, and many others, would remain.

Something caught my eye as we turned left on to the main track out of Niagassola – something to the right. It was a limp string hanging across the red dust between two twigs . . .

'Yes,' Kaniba said in answer to my next question, 'that's the frontier with Mali.'

I stared back at the diminishing thread, and thought of the policeman with the extra finger, of Lieutenant Diawara, the Hôtel

---

* An alleged recording does exist. It may be of a replica of the instrument.

Tamtam, the million-franc ransom. 'Lamine, why don't we go the other way, straight back into Mali?'

'Because', Lamine said, as I remembered the infuriating fact myself, 'Diawara has your passport. And there is another . . . small problem. You couldn't get a visa when we crossed into Guinea. And I couldn't get a laissez-passer for the car.'

Like a draught of hemlock, the mind-numbing implications of this news spread from the pit of my stomach to my brain . . . we had no evidence of when and how we had entered Guinea, neither we nor the car; we could have stolen the car; we could, in this country notorious as a channel for narcotics, have spent a year running drugs, or people-trafficking, or engaged in any number of nefarious pursuits. Guinea was the very homeland of the trumped-up charge. In short, we were in the shit, and we really could end up *en prison*, and for a good long stretch. I voiced these fears to Lamine, trying not to sound too panicky. He didn't answer.

Kaniba did. 'Don't worry. Everything will be fine.'

Mad murderers, Ebola viruses and Lieutenant Diawara loomed, and she was telling us not to worry . . . I looked in the rear-view mirror. She was smiling. At least the image would be something to cherish in my prison cell, along with the *Golden Treasury*, if they let me keep it.

And yet there was something in the tone of her voice that spoke of more than platitude.

*

Lieutenant Diawara kept us waiting in the dark outside the gate of his villa for half an hour. At last, it creaked open and he emerged. Without his shades he looked vulnerable, not a spider but a snail without a shell.

He caught sight of the balafon on the roof of the car; looked at me, then back to the instrument. '*What?* You are removing the patrimony of the Republic of Guinea!' He looked vulnerable; he sounded venomous. '*Vraiment, on doit te mettre en pri –*'

I heard Kaniba's barely suppressed snigger as her husband stepped from the shadows. At the sight of his superior's features, which had been rendered more than usually hangdog by the wait, the lieutenant froze; then unfroze just enough to perform a slow and shaky salute.

'Monsieur Mackintosh's passport,' Commissaire Keita said.

Some hours later, just before midnight, as I sat in the car still savouring the sweet taste of *schadenfreude*, Lamine presented the Commissaire's letter to the commander of the border post on the main Guinea–Mali road. It demanded, on prefectoral authority, that we be allowed to pass without hindrance. '*Je sais compter*', the Commissaire concluded, '*sur votre diligence habituelle.*'

We sailed out of Guinea without a check, without a stamp. For once, I'd got the better of a border.

Andalusia

The Dark Matter of History

It does not seem to me, Austerlitz added, that we understand
the laws governing the return of the past.

W. G. Sebald, *Austerlitz*

Gibraltar – Granada

No, the taxi driver said. It wasn't a trick of the light. It really was
that close: the Spanish colony of Ceuta on the coast of Morocco,
a promontory seen across the strait dividing Europe and Africa,
over a royal-blue sea that danced with ships and white horses, so
near, so clear I might have been looking through a zoom lens. But
I was lucky, the driver said; today the *poniente* was blowing, the
west wind. In an easterly *levante* Africa was often invisible. I
looked up at the western sky half expecting to see a team of
puffing putti, Atlantic zephyrs cracking their cheeks as they blew
all the fug into the Med.

It really was that close – less than twenty miles, less than Calais to
Dover. I remembered looking across from the other side ten years
before, from IB's birthplace of Tangier, and failing to see Europe;
it must have been blowing a levanter then. And I remembered that
Ceuta, the Arabs' Sabtah, now so clear, so close, was the birthplace
of those two brothers IB met, one on the eastern rim of China, the
other on the shore of the Sahara. 'How far apart the two of them
were!' IB said. And yet how much further still it is today, in all but
distance, across this narrow gulf between the continents.

But why end up here in Spain with what for IB was the penulti-
mate journey, and not with his own triumphant ending, summoned

from the Sahara by the sultan of Morocco and commissioned to record his travels? Partly because the conclusion of my own African journey was less than triumphant: I ran out of money in Timbuktu. Partly too because I want to end in Europe, in Christendom, where my own journey began: after so long abroad I want to ask myself – in this liminal place, like a wanderer pausing on his doorstep to look back on the world he's travelled – where I'm at home. But mainly to look for a garden.

In the garden of Abu 'l-Qasim Ibn Asim, somewhere outside the walls of Granada, IB had one of the most fateful meetings of his life. His early encounters with the two sufi seers in Egypt had shaped his travels. This one shaped his *Travels*. As Sir Henry Yule noted, 'the four most remarkable Asiatic itineraries of the middle ages' – those of Marco Polo, Odoric of Pordenone, Nicolo Conti and IB – were all put into the form we have them in by literary assistants. In IB's case it is not the whole story, as Yule suggests, to say that he dictated his book. The process was more complicated: IB's assistant, Muhammad Ibn Juzayy, says that he both 'gathered together the loose ends of what was dictated' by IB and made what he calls 'an abridgement of the record set down' by the traveller (an abridgement: O for a look on the cutting-room floor . . .). And Ibn Juzayy is more than a scribe or a copy-editor. Often he steps into the text – 'Ibn Juzayy adds . . . Ibn Juzayy comments . . .' He is IB's fellow-*Traveller*, and the Granada garden was where they first met, in the spring of 1350. 'I was with them in that garden,' Ibn Juzayy wrote, straying into IB's frame. 'Shaykh Abu Abdallah [Ibn Battutah] delighted us with his tales of travel, and I noted down from him the names of the eminent people he had met on his journeys. He edified us all most marvellously.' There is something, in the young man's first encounter with the colossus of travel, of the young Boswell's first awed experience of Johnson, in Davies's Covent Garden bookshop.

IB also met someone else in that garden who was to shape his future – not that of his travels, actual or literary, but of his reputation. The octogenarian Ibn al-Balafiqi* was one of the most

---

* Elsewhere I have followed Gibb in transliterating the surname, derived from the Andalusian town of Velefique, as 'Balfiqi'. 'Balafiqi' is probably more correct.

respected scholars in the western Islamic world; when he passed judgement, other mortals listened. From the surviving evidence, it is clear they listened with interest to what he had to say about IB. 'He had a trifling share of learning,' his verdict on the traveller began. After summarizing IB's eastward itinerary, he continued,

> The king of India paid him a massive retainer even though, both in outward appearance and inner disposition, he travelled in the guise of a sufi. In time he returned to Morocco and went to the peninsula of al-Andalus, where he told tales of the East and of what he had gained from people there. He was, however, disbelieved. I met him in Granada, where we stayed a night in the garden of Abu 'l-Qasim Ibn Asim at the village of Niblah. That night and the day preceding it he recounted his travels in the East and elsewhere. He informed us that he had entered the great church in Constantinople, and that the church was the size of a city and roofed all over, and that in it there were 12,000 bishops.

In not much more than a hundred words, Ibn al-Balafiqi managed to damn IB with faint praise, to trash, implicitly, his credibility as a scholar, as an unworldly sufi and as a reporter of facts, and to insinuate that he was a money-grubbing charlatan.

One hesitates to say it, but there are some grains of truth in the accusations. And for me, at least, Ibn al-Balafiqi grew in my estimation when I found verses by him in praise of his wife's pearlescent thighs, and of a cheesecake; he was not merely a sneering and crotchety old academic. But the fact is that – even if IB perhaps got carried away by spring on the plain of Granada and embroidered his oral account to the audience in the garden – the particular tall story cited is at odds with what he wrote in his book. There are indeed 'thousands of priests and monks' in the Aya Sofiya at Constantinople, he says. But of the 12,000 bishops there is no trace. As for his own visit there, he specifically states that he *didn't* enter the building: to do so would have meant prostrating himself to the cross, he says – something which as a Muslim he could never agree to. Still, the unfortunate truth remains that, other than IB's own sprawling but fragmentary self-portrait in the *Travels*, Ibn al-Balafiqi's gently damning depiction is the only character sketch of the traveller actually done from the life (or, as we shall see, the only sketch that bears a caption). It sparked off a discussion on the veracity of travellers in general in which some of the greatest minds of the day participated. This, then, is why I wanted to find the garden at Niblah: it was the point of departure both for the other journey, from travels to *Travels*, and for the debate about the truth of those travelling tales. It is a debate that still goes on.

I'd always had such a clear picture of that Granadine *fête cham-pêtre*; it is the picture from the Preamble to this journey. To one side there is Ibn Asim, the wealthy civil servant who owned the garden, to the other, a group of *wujuh* – 'faces', or notables – from the city. In the middle are Ibn Juzayy the future amanuensis and Ibn al-Balafiqi the future nemesis. And at centre-stage sits IB, the garrulous little man holding his audience, both fascinated and dubious, beside a pavilion on a plain whose confines are the many-towered green hill of the Alhambra and the snows of the Sierra Nevada, all on an Islamic island in a Christian peninsula. The picture is sharp, jewel-like, a miniature seen through a hole in time. The only thing I can't make out, that refuses to resolve itself, is the face of IB.

Gardens are fitting places for farewells: the Garden of Gethsemane, gardens of remembrance. Paul Theroux once said that travellers don't know where they're going (and that tourists don't know where they've been). I'd known all along that the garden at Niblah was where my journey with IB would end; wherever Niblah was, for that was what I didn't know.

★

At the border crossing from Spain into Gibraltar I dug in my pocket for 'that indescribable nuisance and curse of continental travel', as Richard Ford called it a century and a half ago, 'to which a free-born Briton can never get reconciled, and is apt to neglect, whereby he puts himself in the power of the worst and most troublesome people on earth'. But unlike Lieutenant Diawara, the ghastly Guinean policeman, neither the Spanish nor the British frontier officials were interested in my passport.

In outward appearance, Gibraltar ('Jabal Tariq' – the Mount of

Tariq, Muslim conqueror of Spain) was almost parodically British. Having walked across the border and the adjacent airport runway, the first objects I saw were a red telephone box and a road sign that said 'Winston Churchill Avenue'. It was as British as Trafalgar Square ('al-Taraf al-Agharr', the Resplendent Cape of the Arabs). The doughty Rock has survived the end of the British empire; long before, however, it was the steadfast citadel of the rulers of IB's Morocco. When IB arrived here in the spring of 1350, it had just sat out a ten-month siege by 'the Christian tyrant Adfunus' – Alfonso XI of Castile. 'He had deluded himself', IB says, 'into thinking he could take the portion of al-Andalus that still remained in Muslim hands. But instead, God took him unawares, and he died of the plague.' For Ibn Juzayy, in one of his many Jack-in-the-book appearances to add an anecdote or a verse to IB's Spanish chapter (he was, after all, himself a Spaniard),

> Earth's other mountains quake with fear. This Rock
> Stands firm through time, immune to every shock.

And so, I saw as I looked up at its north-west flank, does the hard core of Moorish resistance to the Christians, the Calahorra Tower: 'Our master Abu 'l-Hasan, God have mercy on him, built the great Qalahurrah Tower at the top of the fortress,' Ibn Juzayy says in his long Gibraltar interpolation.[*] Externally, the enormous keep looked unchanged, except for a Union Jack flapping on its summit in the brisk *poniente*. The flag marked a meeting point between IB's world and mine.

There were more such meetings to come. The first thing I saw in the courtyard of the small and creaky hotel I'd booked into was another enormous military installation with a Union Jack – rippling, in this case, on his biceps: a huge squaddy, scowling over his lager. It was only when I was in the bar and studying the Gibraltar street-map that I realized my billet was next door to the great mosque of IB's time, now effaced by the Roman Catholic cathedral. The Englishwoman who ran the hotel was unaware of the historical significance of its location. In fact she didn't even particularly feel

---

[*] The Calahorra is also known today by a later name, 'the Tower of Homage'.

that she was abroad. 'Gib? It's just like England, really, but with this great lump of rock and a load of monkeys on it. 'Nother pint, luv?'

I could sort of see what she meant. Outside, Main Street might have been the high street of some lovably seedy Olde Devon fishing port, complete with the cries of gulls and drunks, limp pasties in the pubs and a pavement crusty with three centuries of honest English vomit. Inside, I was followed upstairs to my room by the weary-cheery strain of the *Coronation Street* theme from the TV in the bar. But when I opened my window, it was the strains of IB's own dialect of Arabic and the scent of mint tea that wafted up from a table of grizzled Moroccans down on Cannon Lane.

The meetings continued that evening. Having become blasé about culinary exotica, I had an urge to dine on something really different . . . like fish and chips. I didn't have to go far, of course: back along Main Street, past Cornwallis Lane and Bell Lane with its 'ALHAMBRA MINI-MARKET: Wines, Spirits, Tobacco, Indian Spices' (the poor Alhambra – few names have been taken quite so much in vain) and into Casemates Square. Here, sitting with my fish supper at Rock Fish & Chips, I was overlooking what had been an inter-tidal beach fronted by the arched openings of IB's *dar al-sina'ah* or 'house of manufacture' – another Arabic name that has gone, garbled, into English, as 'arsenal'; in this case it meant a naval dock-yard. Given that the remains of the dockyard were now buried under concrete and asphalt, imagining the fourteenth-century scene was hard work. But the present was more interesting. The chip-shop proprietor was a Tangerine, from IB's home town across the Straits, and as I ate I argued amicably with him in Arabic about the authenticity of the alleged tomb of the traveller in their native city. At the same time, the man's teenage son, who was sporting yet another Union Jack – this time in the form of a T-shirt – moved between the tables delivering plates and singing along to Pink Floyd: 'Hey! Teachers! Leave those kids alone!' Who said the twain never meet?

There were more meetings the following morning. 'Would you like to read the lessons?' the Precentor of the Anglican cathe-dral asked, surprised to have a congregation, even of one, at 7.15 a.m. Mattins. If he didn't mind them unrehearsed, I said. The first lesson, thick with Semitic names, was from the Book of Judges and resembled a pre-Islamic war ode ('. . . and their camels were without number, as the sand by the sea side . . .'). The wider horizons of the Gospel ('. . . and they shall come from the east, and from the west . . .') brought all into their Judaeo-Hellenistic embrace. It wasn't a brilliant performance; but it all sounded appropriate in the cathedral of the Church of England's so-called Diocese in Europe – shorthand for a see that in fact stretches from Casablanca on the Atlantic to Vladivostok on the Sea of Japan – where a stained-glass Christ floats in the Moorish horseshoe arch of the east window (the Spanish captured mosques in order to turn them into churches; the British built one).

If there is a message in all these meetings, it is probably that *métissage* isn't only for Swahili witch doctors and sufi-yogic cave hermits in Sarandib. To employ an over-used and much abused word, we're all multicultural whether we like it or not. There was, however, one marker of monoculture here in the Cathedral of the Holy Trinity: that unmistakeable musty odour of Anglican sanctity. It was the same here as in Christ Church, Colombo, the same as in the parish church of my childhood. I bet there's someone employed by Lambeth Palace to can the stuff and send it round the globe.

I liked Gibraltar. It was a place that managed to be here, there and everywhere in less than half a square mile, and I felt at home in it. Whether there'd be any more solid remains from IB's and Ibn Juzayy's joint description of the Rock, though, I doubted. But at least I had a solid starting point in that soaring Calahorra Tower.

From close to, the masonry of the tower was cyclopean in scale. As I'd thought from below, the structure was virtually unchanged from the time it was built, seventeen years before IB's visit. There were, however, a few proportionately cyclopean pock-marks on the east façade of the tower, the one that faced the flank of the Rock. These, a board said, dated to that siege by Alfonso XI of Castile – the one that was raised just before IB arrived, when the king (alone among the crowned heads of Europe) succumbed to the Black Death. Alfonso had installed three mangonels, the board explained, on the mountainside above the tower. His battery had made little impression, although the scars would have been more visible when IB saw them fresh. The interior of the keep was a series of large and forbidding rooms that needed the eye of a historian of military architecture to make proper sense of them. But the view from the roof was glorious, with that royal-blue bay and the waters of the Straits still dancing, all laid out below like an eighteenth-century naval panorama, and the rhythmic slap of the Union Jack overhead.

I climbed on up the Rock, following Signal Station Road and hoping to find fragments of the 'Wall of the Arabs' mentioned by Ibn Juzayy in his insertion in IB's account; this was a long rampart that began somewhere near the summit. The road twisted upwards between Ministry of Defence barbed wire and a spiky *maquis* of pines, lentisc and wild olives. Gulls dive-bombed me, screaming 'Oh! No! Go!' – one so close that I felt the rush of wing-air in my hair. Further up I came to one of the hang-outs of those imperial *lares et penates*, the Barbary apes, where they lolled in a squalor of superannuated veg. One of them came over to greet me, raising first a Churchillian chin, and then a leathery backside.

From here steps rose to a sudden and stupendous drop. The sheer east face of the Rock glittered with a blizzard of gulls. I followed the knife-edge to a Second World War look-out post, redolent with piss but blessed with the view of all views: the *poniente* had dropped, vapour was rolling into the Straits, Africa disappearing, and you could indeed imagine Hercules heaving the continents asunder at this *ne plus ultra* where the world came to an end at the Circumambient Sea. Just north of the main look-out was a small cuboid room, not old but built on a few courses of what could have been some ancient turret belonging to the Moorish rampart. By the old masonry was a declaration in spray paint: DARREN LOVES ZULAIKA. The twain were meeting up here too.

*

The Ronda train pulled out of the station at Algeciras (al-Jazirah al-Khadra, 'the Green Peninsula') as the first sunlight tumbled over the rim of hills, gilding the city's undistinguished buildings and promising warmth and oranges. Soon the line climbed, we rounded a bend and I looked back for a last sight of Africa, dissolving in the haze. Nearer to hand, to the west, the promontory of Tarifa crouched like a heraldic beast at the foot of Iberia; and there was the Rock, a monstrous dorsal fin rearing up from the deep.

Other than the Calahorra Tower, I'd only found fragments from

IB's age in Gibraltar: that possible bit of rampart, and perhaps some more sections that were unreachable behind MoD barbed wire; the remains of a little mosque at Europa Point, long since built into a shrine to Our Lady; part of a *hammam*, a public bath, in the cellars of the museum; and, upstairs in the museum, a fourteenth-century child's whistle that had turned up on the ex-beach near the defunct dockyard (there was no one about . . . I had a sudden urge to blow it – *O whistle and I'll come to you, my lad* – but the case in which it lay was locked). Unlike, say, a village in the sticks of inland Guinea where the flow of time is dammed by isolation and inertia, here on the Straits it swept by, a tide-race of history. Too much flotsam had snagged on Gibraltar, too many trampling feet made landfall. Anything that might have linked me at all intimately to IB's visit was utterly destroyed or irretrievably buried. From all the years of Arab rule not a single inscription remained.

Looking out of the train window, I could see what drew the Arabs to Spain: it was like home. The line rose higher, taking us into a delightful land where castles crowned tors and villages tumbled down the slopes below them in a white scree of houses. Jimena de la Frontera might have been a shaykhly stronghold in the High Tihamah in my adoptive home of Yemen. But as we climbed further, burrowing through tunnels and gorges, we emerged into uplands where mist swirled round sparse forests of cork oak and parted now and then to reveal a backdrop of cloud-smoky peaks. We seemed to have left those glimpses of Arabia behind, and I wondered what I'd find of the seven centuries of Arab presence in Ronda. In the railway carriage the heater was on full, in summer, in the southernmost corner of mainland Europe, and it was still cold. The promise of oranges was broken.

Arrived in by train, Ronda looked dull, a grey town oppressed by lowering cloud. It could have been somewhere much further north and less distinguished. I thought of the Brit I'd chatted to in a pub in Gib, who thought I was going to Rhondda, in Wales. To look at the view, he might have been right.

But on trains you tend to see the best of the country and the worst of the town. Away from the station, Ronda is a city of small but splendid palaces, cleft by the chasm of the Guadalevín (Wadi al-Laban, 'the River of Milk', although it was more the colour of the veins in a Stilton). Down between the walls of the gorge, chatterings of choughs wheel and cry *cheow!*, while chatterings of French tourists up on the *mirador* above it admire and exclaim *Ah, oui!* As chasms go, Ronda's is particularly deep and romantic. Looking at the architecture of the extraordinary bridge-with-rooms that spans the gorge, the Puente Nuevo, I was reminded of its down-to-earth contemporary, Pulteney Bridge in Bath; but more forcibly of another daredevil span, the Bridge of Shaharah in Yemen. (Pre-Arab Ronda was situated sensibly down below. The present cliff-top city, crouching as if in ambush along the scarp, was an Arab foundation – and I suspect the founders were Yemenis, whose urban planning has always been inspired by the nests of eagles.) It all had the light-and-dark-smitten drama of El Greco's Toledo, but with the increased thrill of the perpendicular.

And yes, there were fragments of IB's age. The strangest was constructed, or rather excavated, by Abu Malik, who a couple of decades before IB's visit ruled Ronda on behalf of his father the sultan of Morocco, builder of that great citadel in Gibraltar. Now called La Mina, the Mine, it is a sort of negative of the Gibraltar tower, a dank and dripping stronghold hewn from the bowels of the gorge, all slippery stairs and Beckfordian vaults and galleries haunted by echoes and lit by sudden views down to the verdigris stream of the Guadalevín. Emerging hundreds of feet down on to a ledge at the level of the river, I found a post-Romantic foil to Abu Malik's Gotho-Mooresque: lying on its side in the shallow stream was an abandoned supermarket trolley.

Upstream the gorge was less abysmal and here, next to an IB-period bridge, an almost complete IB-period *hammam* had survived. Inside among the horseshoe arches, light entered in slanting columns through star-shaped holes in the vaults ('It is as if the celestial sphere were overhead,' said the Andalusian poet Ibn Shuhayd of a similar bath). This being the age of EU funding, there was also a *centro de interpretación* in the now cold *caldarium*, with a video that sprang to life, making me jump, as I entered the empty room. The film explained the various stages of heat and cold through which the bathers went ('First a sweet and burning fire,' said another poet, Ibn al-Zaqqaq, 'such as lovers feel . . .'). It was all very well done, even if the bathers were the sort of animated androids who star in aeroplane safety videos. And the commentary was warmed by the inclusiveness of newly liberal Spain: 'This was the Moors' land, and in it they left an imprint of their art, culture and customs . . .' – a far cry from Philip II's ban on bath-houses, those hotbeds of Morisco sedition and cleanliness. (For centuries after, the toilette even of the grandest of grandees consisted of rubbing the face occasionally with the white of an egg.)

A dry bath is as much use as a dry bar; but the lack was partly made up for by the piped recorded sounds of running water. I could almost picture IB as one of those video androids – he spent five days in the city, and after the long and sweaty slog up from Gibraltar it is highly likely that he would have bathed here, in Ronda's main *hammam*. Highly likely too that, on the steep path up into the centre of town he would have rested, as I did, on El Sillón del Moro, a four-seater stone bench – 'the Moor's Sofa' – now comfortably eroded by centuries of backsides . . . 'Highly likely': I have to resort to the struggling biographer's let-out since, other than saying that Ronda was a great stronghold and listing the people he met there, IB tells us nothing about the place.

Over the next days I found a few more highly-likelys, pieces that added something to the picture of Ronda IB fails to give us. There was a fourteenth-century mini minaret, a brick tower ten feet square and thirty feet tall called the Alminar de San Sebastian. Some tiny bits of glaucous tile had clung on above the doorway, but it cut a pathetic figure – doubly orphaned, having lost both its mosque and the church that replaced it. As in Gibraltar, a cathedral had wiped out the Friday mosque (in which, since he mentions meeting its preacher, it is highly likely that IB prayed); but not completely. A couple of inscribed stucco arches had survived – somewhat ironi-cally, for the most prominent inscription was the anti-trinitarian Qur'anic verse on divine unity, 'He begot no one, nor was He begotten'. I sighed for the lost mosque. The stucco work was the best thing in a building described shortly after I saw it, by a critic of impeccable taste, as looking 'like an old pub that's been ripped out and done again in the 1970s'. And then there was a building that illustrated a bigger picture than IB's Ronda.

The Church of the Holy Spirit glowers on the southern brink of the city, looking with its all but windowless elevations more like a

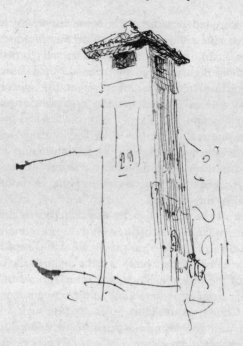

military redoubt than a place of prayer. Almost the first act of the reconquistadors when they took Ronda in 1485 was to raze the mosque that had stood here, prominent in the city's skyline, and build this blind-walled bastion of their most Christian faith. But, again, the demolition party left something from the earlier structure: not in this case dainty stucco arches, but the great rectangular masonry plinth on which the mosque had perched, built out over the rocky slope. The west end of this platform, approached by a ramp and bordered by the stumps of felled mosque columns, forms a small forecourt to the church. The church is orientated to the east; the surviving ramp, forecourt and plinth of the mosque are aligned to Mecca. To enter the church, therefore, you climb the ramp and then take an oblique left turn.

The sight of it reminded me of a story told by the twelfth-century Syrian prince Usamah (Osama) Ibn Munqidh – on the scale of religious tolerance the polar opposite, it has to be said, of his latter-day namesake Ibn, or Bin, Ladin. Usamah was in

Christian-controlled Jerusalem and some friends of his, Knights Templar, lent him a church, converted from a mosque, for him to perform his Islamic prayers in. While he was bowing towards Mecca another knight came in and tried to shift Usamah bodily to the east, the Christian direction of prayer; at this Usamah's Templar friends appeared and kicked out the unknown crusader. 'Sorry about him,' they said. 'He's new.' Usamah finished his devotions, Mecca-ward and undisturbed.

Looking at the skewed Iglesia del Espíritu Santo in Ronda, I remembered the story, and thought: we all pray to the same God; we just have slightly different angles on Him. Here the difference was less than twenty degrees.

And what of the features of Ronda that IB *did* mention – the people? They include one of the very few other members of his family whose names have been preserved: Muhammad ibn Yahya Ibn Battutah, our IB's first cousin and the judge of the city. He and all the rest of the Moorish Rondeños are lost, it seems, to history. But there is a clue as to where some of them might have ended up. Below the Church of the Holy Spirit, and through a little square littered with *los excrementos de los perros* that unheeded signs tell the lapdog-loving Spaniards to remove, is the Puerta de Almocábar – the Arabic Bab al-Maqabir. It is a fine edifice with a pair of portly bastions and the usual holes for dropping *excrementos* and other nasty things on to the heads of attackers, and it was rebuilt in stone in its present form not long before IB came here (it is highly likely, of course, that he passed through it). Outside the gate is a large paved open space; open, because the Christians of Ronda have avoided building on *al-maqabir*, the burial places of the Moors. Presumably they find the idea of living on top of a graveyard macabre (and yes, *maqabir* is a possible origin for that word).

I turned my back on the Muslim dead and retraced my steps. In Ronda I had a rendezvous with the living: from the Puente Nuevo I could see him almost vertically below, just the dot of a straw hat down in the olive groves, standing at an easel.

★

'It's the view Bomberg kept painting,' Martin said. I remembered seeing one of Bomberg's oils of the Puente Nuevo done from far below, arcing over the gorge in a parabola of fauve colour. Martin's palette was less riotous, but he had captured the *sol y sombre* of the chasm in all its drama.

The scene we were driving through now was less theatrical, a gorsey plateau pocked with hollows and scattered with long low farmsteads. Then the road dropped down the forested side of the massif, and we descended into golfland. Golf-villa complexes sprouted all the way down to the *autovía* CN340. We passed the turn-off for IB's 'Marbalah, a pretty little town'; Marbella today is neither so pretty nor so little and, besides, he had nothing else to say about it. There were more important things to look for.

'So this is the Costa del Sol,' said Martin.

'The Costa del Solid Concrete,' I said, looking at our surroundings. 'Where's the sea?'

'I think they built over it.'

But the sea did make an appearance at last, distant and bleary. 'Have you heard of Tossa del Mar?' Martin asked.

'Any relation of the conductor – what was his name? – Norman Del Mar?'

'No, it's a place, up the coast I think. But you're on the right lines.' Martin told me the story of his uncle, who had a wicked sense of humour. 'He and my aunt used to go on holiday to Tossa del Mar. And when they got this dog, he said to her, "Why don't we call it 'Tossa del Mar'?" She thought it was a great idea. Anyway, you can guess what they called it for short. I can still hear my poor aunt, calling out to the dog in the park, at the top of her voice: "Tossa! *Tossa!*" She was very innocent, my auntie . . .'

The road swung closer to the coast. A small round tower flashed past, bang on the *autovía* and overlooking the sea. Suddenly IB's world flooded back.

IB's reason for visiting Spain, he said, was for *jihad*. The word, of course, touches off fuses today; but we can safely dismiss images of IB wearing explosive underpants, or their fourteenth-century equivalent. For several hundred years before his time, ever since the Christians had begun to retake al-Andalus, Muslim tourists had gone there for *jihad*, 'the fight for the faith', and *ribat*, 'defending the frontiers'. It was a cliché of travel, like 'See Naples and die' – not many people actually did it. As it turned out, IB only just missed seeing action. He was lucky: his travels might have ended up in some fourteenth-century Guantánamo, or in a roadside grave.

As we drove along the *autovía* I read Martin IB's account of what he saw on this same road, the CN340.

At Marbalah I found a group of horsemen who were heading for Malaqah [Malaga], and decided to set off in their company. But it so happened that God Almighty by His grace protected me, for they set out before me and were taken captive on the road, as I shall presently relate. I left in their tracks. When I had reached the end of the territory of Marbalah and entered that of Suhayl [Fuengirola], I came upon a dead horse in a ditch.

Then I came upon a basket of fish, abandoned on the ground. I was filled with foreboding at the sight of these things.

In front of me was a look-out tower, and I said to myself, 'If the enemy had appeared here, surely the officer of the tower would have raised the alarm.' I went on to a house that was nearby and found by it another horse that had been killed. While I was there I heard shouts from behind me. I had gone on ahead of my own companions, and I now returned to them and found them with the commander of the castle of Suhayl. He told me that four enemy galleys had appeared here and that some of their company had come ashore. The look-out had not been in the tower at the time. Just as the enemy landed, the horsemen coming from Marbalah, twelve in number, were passing by.

The Christians had killed one, one had got away, and the other ten had been taken captive. A fishmonger who was travelling with them was also killed. It was he whose basket I had found abandoned on the ground.

It is a vivid and disturbing passage. The step-by-step discovery of an aftermath – of what? – make it all the more ominous. Even now I've been there, it still seems more real than the four-lane highway and the hoardings and the villas and our hired Lancia hatchback.

The ominousness doesn't let up in IB's account. The commander of the castle of Suhayl put him up for the night – and there, moored beneath its battlements, were the four enemy galleys. When IB got to Malaga the following day, he found the worshippers in the mosque collecting money to ransom the captives. We never learn their fate. There but for the grace of God . . .

The story was important for me not just because it brings to life, through one small incident, the fears of an age and a place. It also provided me with that great rarity – so rare, in fact, that I couldn't think where I'd last found one (it must have been back in India): the precise location of an IB overnight. The exact setting of his disturbing discoveries would of course be impossible to pinpoint, I thought. There are old look-out towers dotted all along this coast, like the one we saw outside Marbella. But the castle at Fuengirola is still there, and still known by its Arabic name, the Castillo de Sohail. That was where we were heading now, and it was more than a mere highly-likely.

For a while we drove along in silence. The images and sounds of that day in 1350 went round inside my head like a video clip on auto replay ... 'God! Did you see *that*?' Martin's exclamation came as I caught it too, in the periphery of my vision, to the left. We turned off at the first exit, came on to the *autovía* again and drove back on ourselves. Another slip road. Back again along an access road, heading the way we'd first been going. It detoured through villa-land, then ran parallel to the *autovía* once more.

'It was somewhere here,' I said. 'In a parade of shops.' We reached the place. An American-looking scene: business units of equal size, the whole set-up designed round car access. And there it was: 'BATTUTA Bistro Bar Lounge: Fine Food, Great Mood.'

Some enterprising Moroccan must have opened it; probably a Tangerine like IB. I doubted whether the traveller would approve of a bar ... But no: the owner was a German called Thor, snake-hipped, Jaggeresque, with long hair and bright blue eyes.

'It used to be an *immobiliaria*,' Thor said, jiving slightly to a background electronic thump as he mixed my cocktail. 'And then when all the flats and villas round here had been sold it closed down. So I took it on and turned it into a bar. The name? Well, you know, they're all called "Thor's Bar" or something like that. I was looking for something a bit more interesting.' His eyes twinkled. We sat down at an outside table, overlooking the *autovía*. 'And then I just came across "battuta" by chance, in a dictionary.'

'In a *dictionary*?'

'Yeah. It means, "keeping time". Like with a ...' He wagged his finger rhythmically from side to side in time to the recorded beat from the bar.

'A metronome.'

'That's it. A metronome. *Battuta*: not a lot of people know that.' I certainly hadn't. (But it's there, in the dictionary: 'The beating of time; a strong beat; the regular beat.' An Italian term, from the verb *battere*.) 'You see, I'm into house music. Anyway, I've made it copyright. No one else in Europe can use it for a bar.'

'But you know ... the *other* meaning?'

'You mean that Battuta was a big international traveller? I found that out afterwards, on the Internet. And I thought, Hey, that's good! This place is full of Brits, but I want to give my bar an international taste.' He got up to go and finish making a pot of tea for Martin, who was as utterly bemused by all this as I was.

I studied the décor. It was exotic-eclectic, with purple silk cloths on the tables and African masks on the walls. On the door of the gents' was a sign: 'Battuta Does Not Tolerate Drugs'. A young blonde girl came in and greeted Thor in the vowels of south-east England. She was followed by a couple more Brits. Despite Thor's efforts, the clientele so far wasn't very cosmopolitan.

On the little forecourt outside, a middle-aged woman was pouring out her heart to Martin, in the way people do; all strangers are to one another kin. Her husband was mortally ill. They had to give up the villa and go back to suburban Kent. She looked out over her misted wine glass, past a pair of dwarf palms, over the *autovía*, over the speeding cars and lorries, towards the sliver of sea; towards her own widowhood. 'Ohh . . .' She shook her head and smiled through her tears. 'I love Battuta's.' I looked down at the table, and knew why.

Thor came out and sat with us, gently touching the woman's arm. There was something else I wanted to ask him. 'Thor, you know Ibn Battutah came here, came along this road, don't you?'

His blue eyes stared at me. He didn't even know IB had come to Spain.

I read out the passage I'd read to Martin. When I'd finished, Thor spoke. 'Where did he say he found these things – the horse, the basket?'

'He says it was when he'd left the territory of Marbella and entered the territory of Suhayl – that's Fuengirola,' I said.

Thor was shaking his head, smiling. 'That's where we are now. Near the Marbella-Fuengirola municipal border. And I just picked the name by chance . . . I just felt it was right.'

★

By the time we got there my guaranteed IB overnight, the Castillo de Sohail, had closed for the day. Besides, we couldn't even find the turn-off to it from the CN340. It sailed past on its hillock, looking like a toy fort, almost completely rebuilt since IB's time. We let it slip away, a castle in Spain.

We had found something more significant, but also harder to interpret. That night I wrote in my diary about liminal places and temporal fault-lines, about joints and sutures, slippages and leakages; about the ghost on the stair – for it is at points of transition (land-sea, Marbella-Fuengirola, the staircase, the slip-road) that such things seem most often to occur. 'All this could be seen as quite mad,' I wrote at the end of these musings, or ravings.

All I'll say here in these more public pages is that as well as the castles and mosques and churches and bath-houses there appear to exist other, invisible structures, built of what I can only call, by analogy to current cosmological thinking, the dark matter of history.

★

We climbed the bright bowl of mountains that rises to the Zaffaraya Pass and the province of Granada. For all he says about this road, IB might as well have done it in a Lancia Ypsilon too. 'I travelled to the town of Ballash [Vélez],' he says, with little more than a high-speed glimpse of 'a splendid mosque' in his rear-view mirror. 'I then went on to al-Hammah [Alhama].' That was where we were heading for too, for the *hammah*, the hot spring, and a bath-house that IB visited at slightly greater leisure.

We'd left the coast behind, left Spainsburys British Supermercado and Curry Fever and the Amsterdam Sex Shop, and the pedalos and deck chairs and windbreaks and apartment blocks with garden gnomes on the balconies; left the old look-out towers that could be glimpsed in the gaps between the concrete and in the place-names – Torreblanca, Torremuelle, Torrequebrada, Torremolinos . . . I wondered which was the one where the guard had been away from his post that day when the Christian attackers landed. (The two sides in the great game have changed ends; the expression now, proverbial for approaching danger, is *Hay moros en la costa* – There are Moors on the coast.) We'd left behind Malaga, where IB enthused about the gilded pottery and the grapes and pomegranates and almonds and figs, the latter, he says, 'exported to the East and the West' (al-Idrisi quotes an informant who had seen

Malaga figs in India); where Martin continued his own journey in the footsteps, or the brushstrokes, of earlier artists, and painted Sir William Nicholson's view of the bullring and the harbour seen from Gibralfaro, the Hispanic garbling of the Arabo-Greek Jabal al-Pharos, Lighthouse Hill (place-names are the haikus of history; 'Spainsburys' probably included); and where I found no more than a couple of rather-unlikelys.

Now we were over the pass and in the rocky uplands again, following the narrow gorge of the Rio Alhama. We crossed it by a small bridge. In front of us was the Hotel Balneario.

'So where's this ancient Arab bath you were going on about?' Martin asked.

I was wondering that myself. The hotel was a three-storey concrete structure in 1960s costa-turismo style, fronted by a full car park and flanked by a patch of woodland with an undergrowth of bungalows. It was all very quiet, until we heard a snorting sound from beneath the bridge. Two fat men with very hairy backs were wallowing below it in a pool in the Rio Alhama, which steamed slightly. Then two old ladies emerged from the entrance of the hotel, both in bathrobes – it was broad daylight – and both with big hair and bad hips. 'I think we've forgotten our zimmers,' Martin said.

The *Kurhaus* atmosphere continued inside. 'I know what I'm ordering,' Martin said in the bar, where we were the youngest customers by decades. 'A Sanatogen Tonic Wine . . . or what about a Wincarnis? I bet they've got tankers of the stuff reversing in. And do you fancy a game of cribbage before we turn in?' I'd recently seen a guide to 'hip hotels'. The Balneario was not so much hip as hip-replacement.

We were both in a state of barely suppressed giggles, made worse by the number of signs enjoining *silencio*. 'How's your back these days?' I asked Martin, looking at the tariff of *masajes y fangoterapia* and remembering his abortive massage in China. 'You could have a *Masaje con piedras volcánicas*. Or even an *Envoltura de chocolate*.' The possibilities of a chocolate body-wrap seemed wildly at odds with the ambience of the place. What would IB have made of it all? He spoke only of 'a bath-house for men and another for women, near the bank of the river'. Although, come to think of it, his Granadine contemporary Ibn al-Khatib wrote that the baths of Alhama were visited by crowds of valetudinarians 'and revellers'.

We found IB's baths in the bowels of the hotel, along a stark white corridor. The sight of the men's chamber was utterly unexpected in this clinical setting: an undercroft illuminated by those same star-shaped skylights I'd seen in Ronda, but whose beams here played over the mercurial surface of a pool filled by a bubbling hot spring and vaulted by honey-coloured horseshoe arches. It was just as IB had seen it, this elegant man-made grotto built around the time of his birth in the early fourteenth century.

'And I think there's some Roman masonry further down,' I said, filling Martin in on the history of the place as we undressed.

'So it's 2,000 years of verrucas.'

Scandalously, we bathed not in the gents' but in the ladies', a circular domed chamber restored in the nineteenth century (the untouched men's chamber is now only an elegant show-place). Piping hot water channelled here from the spring in the gents' bath gurgled out of a central fountain. As instructed by the *bañador*, we alternated between spells in the pool and cold showers in the next-door changing room ('Our *hammam*,' said the poet Ibn Baqi,

> burns like the dog days,
> but also contains the living cold that does no ill.
> Two opposites between which the human body
> feels great voluptuousness, like the bough
> that enjoys both sun and rain)

until the showers became too much of an effort, and we ended up drunk and oblivious on steam and heat. There was no one else there. The domed chamber might have been a flotation tank in which time itself was suspended.

Later I followed current local custom and promenaded the public parts of the hotel in my bathrobe. Despite the dated modernist exterior, time seemed in suspense here too, in the panelled passages, in the rooms furnished with writing desks and radiograms, with plush club chairs and heraldic candle sconces and Goya prints, with disinfectant smells and with the soft rustlings of newspapers and old ladies. I bowed to a pair of elderly couples silently playing whist. One of the men was actually wearing moustache-wax.

There was even an in-house chapel, with a reredos painting of Christ Crucified – rising from a depiction of the gents' bath-house down below . . . Perhaps, I thought, not as strange as it first appeared: the Muslim Arabs, for whom cleanliness and godliness were far closer neighbours than they were in largely unwashed Christendom, often incorporated a *musalla* or oratory into their *hammams*.

The Hotel Balneario was all so very far from the new Spain of EU directives and gay marriages. At 10.30 p.m. it was silent and deserted. Then again, who could guess what was going on behind all those closed doors, inspired by the lingering aroma of an *Envoltura de chocolate*?

★

A last distant look at Alhama with its church of Santa María de la Encarnación – built, as I'd expected, on the site of IB's 'superbly placed and marvellously built mosque' – like a galleon cresting a wave of hill above a sea of furrowed fields; and then we entered still higher highlands where more white-towered churches stood out sharp on the shoulders of hills (again I could see why the Arabs loved this land: I'd half-close my eyes and picture the white minaret of Dhi Ashraq seen from the pass of al-Najd al-Ahmar against the folded mountainsides of Lower Yemen); where the dark high massif of cloud was spiked with light and the olive trees tossed, spiky in a gusting breeze. As we drove we listened to a CD of de Falla's *El Amor Brujo*, also gusty and spiky.

According to a leaflet from the information office in Alhama, we were following the Ruta de Washington Irving, named in memory of the American propagator of Andalusian romance. 'Isn't there a Ruta de Ibn Battutah?' I'd asked, thinking there ought to be one, if only for the sake of the silly name.

The woman in charge of the office smiled. 'It was proposed,' she said, 'but there was no political interest. So no money.'

We were also following the route of the Christian reconquest. When the Catholic Kings Ferdinand and Isabella launched their drive to take the sultanate of Granada, the last Arab corner of Spain, it was Alhama that in 1482 was the first of its strongholds to fall. Ten years later Granada itself, IB's 'Gharnatah, capital of the land of al-Andalus and bride of its cities', was theirs.

It happened that Ferdinand and Isabella were among the first notable characters we met in Granada. That night, workmen were building what looked like a giant wedding cake opposite our hotel in the Calle Mesones. The following morning, well-dressed women were applying the final touches: the cake had turned into an altar, heaving with candles and flowers and crowned by a yard-high monstrance. The street itself had been strewn with greenery, and a crowd was beginning to gather. Today was the feast of Corpus Christi – the city's great festival, as important here as Holy Week in Seville, in which Granada celebrated its Saviour and its Christian self.

By mid-morning we were pressed against the door of the hotel by the waiting crowd. It was a genteel crush. Pearls and hairdos were in; so were panamas and moustaches. At length a waft of incense and a clatter of castanets reached us, and the buzz of anticipation subsided into suspenseful silence. At the head of the

procession came two mounted constables leading a group of women with mantillas and long sharp noses. To the accompaniment of a small band of guitars and mandolins, the women pirouetted and castanetted charmingly before the altar, then moved on.

They were followed by four outsize figures of papier-mâché, each borne by a person hidden inside. Two of the figures were dressed rather in the style of a playing-card king and queen; of the other pair, one wore a sky-blue turban and held a scimitar while his female companion had copious jewellery and a veiled face. A woman next to us, pointing the figures out to a small child, confirmed what I'd guessed: 'Los Reyes Católicos, y Boabdil . . .' The Catholic Kings, Ferdinand and Isabella, and Abu Abdallah, last Arab ruler of Granada. I didn't catch the identity of the veiled woman, but wondered if she was Boabdil's mother, mistress of the famous cutting comment ('Why do you cry like a woman', she hissed at her son as he looked tearfully back on his beloved Granada from the pass called 'The Moor's Sigh', 'for what you failed to defend like a man?'). The quartet of figures swayed past as if hobnobbing with each other at a *thé dansant* for giants.

Hot on their heels came mummers wearing over-sized heads representing a blackamoor, a Red Indian, a Japanese girl and other exotic types, who bopped us onlookers with inflated pigs' bladders; then a group of soldiers in early sixteenth-century-style helmets and doublets carrying a large treasure-chest. I picked up the name 'Cristóbal Colón' from the running commentary next to me.

This was all only the beginning of a parade that took an hour and a half to pass us: the children going for their first communion; the besuited, bemedallioned masters of the city's religious fraternities; the military band swaying to the thump of a dead-march; the massed ranks of monks and nuns and clergy and choristers; all possible personages, civil, military and ecclesiastical; and the climax of it all, the enormous flower-decked brazen dais borne by concealed bearers – sixty of them, I guessed – on whose stepped summit rode the most monstrous monstrance of them all, enshrining Corpus Christi, the consecrated Body of Christ. We touched this great siege-engine of an altar as it passed, and picked up its fallen petals, seeking blessings, *barakah*.

Throughout the spectacle, which was infused with that peculiarly Spanish mix of gravity and frivolity, sun and shadow, I had those first four outsize figures on my mind. History here, like the procession, begins with 1492, with the Moor's last sigh and that Columbian opening up of a new world and its treasures; with the beginning of the end of IB's old world, and the birth of the world so many of us have lived in up till now. Granada was unlike everywhere else I'd been on my journey round the edge. After that brief meeting of the Catholic Kings and the Muslim sultan, there would be no accommodation, no cohabitation. The Islam that had been part of Spain for 700 years (and, for that matter, the Judaism) was ritually expunged by the Inquisition, washed away with the blood of Christ, the living sacrifice that draws a red line other faiths can never cross.

A genial-looking priest had stopped to chat with us. 'Magnificent procession, Father,' I said to him.

'May its spirit fill the world!' he replied, beaming. Then he clasped his hands together and raised them. 'And may God bless you both!'

After he'd moved on, I asked the woman next to us if she happened to know him. She laughed and told us he was El Arzobispo. The Archbishop. More *barakah*.

The immense cortège ended with the *alcalde*, the mayor (the Arabic *al-qadi*, 'the judge'). Then the castanetting dancers were back again, and Ferdinand, Isabella, Boabdil and his mum, or perhaps Mrs Boabdil, and the mummers, their pig's bladders (another one in the eye for the Muslims and Jews?) much deflated, and Columbus's treasure . . . History, as they say, repeats itself.

★

How could we not go to the *corrida*? Corpus Christi, *corpus tauri*. Besides, for Martin, as for Goya and Picasso, the bulls were the great subject, that brutal delicate drama of death played out to the banality of a brass band in a circle not much bigger than Shakespeare's wooden O. What was more, El Cordobés was on the bill. At one point, just after he had knelt before his second bull, their foreheads touching, a grinning gorgon-faced woman in the row in front turned round to praise, loudly, his *cojones* . . . Did she mean those of El Cordobés, or the *bravo toro*? Both were showing off their balls, actual and metaphorical. And after the long deep silent moment of the kill, broken only by the screaming of swifts, Martin and I screamed as loudly as the rest of them for El Cordobés to be granted that rare trophy, both ears of his victim. The *presidente*, high up in his box like Domitian at the games, eventually relented. He would have been lynched by a crowd of 15,000 if he hadn't.

Really, how very far it all is from the delicacy of the Alhambra.

Or is it? IB's slightly younger Granadine contemporary (and later, as we shall see, friend) Ibn al-Khatib wrote of the passion for the bulls among the Moorish upper classes of the city and described the *corrida* of the age, in which the bullfighter was a mounted knight armed with a lance – the *rejoneador* of the subsequent Spanish rite of bullfighting. And not only this. Between bulls a granny next to us fed us cheese sandwiches, and the gorgon-faced woman in front sausage rolls. 'Strangers giving you food – it's just like being in the Arab world,' Martin said.

And so too, I realized with a shock, is *Olé!* So similar is the awed intonation with which it is uttered, and at such similar moments – histrionic swerves, balletic passes – that I feel it *must* derive from the equivalent Arabic exclamation, heard at football matches from Morocco to Oman: *Allah!*

★

'You know why Ibn Battutah didn't say anything about the Alhambra?' Martin asked. We were standing in line – a line that folded back on itself half a dozen times along a barrier, airport check-in style – clutching the tickets we'd been given in exchange for our pre-booked, pre-timed vouchers and which would admit us, eventually, to the inner sanctum of the palace of the Nasrid dynasty, to the Court of the Myrtles and the Hall of the Ambassadors, largely built by IB's Sultan Yusuf.

'Well, there are a few theories,' I said. 'For instance, there's one that claims that when IB says Sultan Yusuf was ill and couldn't give him an audience, the sultan was actually avoiding him. It was a diplomatic indisposition, if you like. He probably thought IB was an envoy from the new sultan of Morocco, and he wasn't very pleased because this new sultan had just overthrown his own father . . .'

'So he was being Yusuf the Elusive.'

'. . . And there's another idea that says IB was "palaced out" – I mean, he'd already seen so many Alhambras that this was just another one.'

We inched forward a little. Martin didn't look convinced. 'No,' he said. 'The real reason IB never got in was because the queue was too long.'

Whatever the reason, IB's silence does seem strange to us today, for whom the Alhambra − al-Madinah al-Hamra, 'the Red City', the great metropolitan fortress-palace − is the most prodigious built survival of his age. It is all the more extraordinary to think that it was created by the rulers of an embattled statelet. Muslim, Nasrid Granada was singing an architectural and cultural swan-song, the moribund principality enjoying an efflorescence of the arts that mirrors strangely the fit of building and writing that accompanied the political decline, at the other end of the Mediterranean, of Christian, Palaeologue Constantinople. And IB doesn't say a word about its showpiece. But then, he did have a recurrent blind-spot for large royal residences. He says nothing about al-Ma'qili, the Alhambra's contemporary and peer, now utterly gone, in Yemen; and nothing about Husuni Kubwa, that other great palace of the age and the most splendid building in Black Africa, with which this journey began.

Ibn Juzayy, being a Granadine himself, might have been expected to fill the gap; but he went all shy. 'Were it not that I fear accusations of favouritism towards my place of birth,' he says in one of his pop-up appearances, 'I would have described Gharnatah at length, for this is the place to do so. But of a city as celebrated as she is, there is no sense in long descriptions.' I know exactly what he means, and it is particularly true of the Alhambra. No monument of Islamic civilization has been the cause of so much wordshed. The Alhambra is trapped in a bubble of oohs and aahs like a glass dome over some fragile sculpture; the bubble at once protects, enshrines and prevents close examination. How could I, a passer-by on a day-ticket, presume to inflate it further, to add my pennyworth of words, of wind? Almost all that needed to be said was said by the building itself, even as the stucco was drying: the Alhambra is encrusted with self-referential poetry of an unblushingly narcissistic nature, boasting of

> The palace portico, so beautiful
> It bids to rival heaven's very vault,

where

> Black the shadow-darkened cornice cuts
> Across the fair light thrown by snowy marble . . .

On and on it goes, winding round the walls. In a society in which poetry and calligraphy were the highest forms of art and figurative painting a comparative rarity, such architectural verse – much of it by the belletrist viziers Ibn al-Khatib, IB's future friend, and his successor Ibn Zamrak – was the equivalent of having your palazzo frescoed by Giotto.

In the face of competition like that, and warned by Robert Irwin in his elegant book on the Alhambra* of the perils of 'fine writing', it would probably be best to follow the lead of IB and his editor and say nothing at all. But I find myself slipping, if not into fine writing, then into the rhymed prose that Ibn Juzayy was bursting to spout, even though the scene is slightly different from the one he knew at

> . . . this cynosure of travellers from Nebraska and Alaska,/ from Singapore and Seoul,/from Czech to Pole,/from pole to pole,/from all earth's climes,/clutching pre-booked tickets with fixed entry times;/this nurse of prose and verse, long serving/writers as diverse as Ibn al-Khatib and Washington Irving,/he who penned tales of al-Hamra, 'the Red',/whose prose was purple but whose book was read –/a weft of words they wove,/a tissue for *les fauves,*/of every hue between maroon and mauve/(never shall romantic tosh, myth/or other suchlike nonsense flow from the pen of Mackintosh-Smith)./ Fabled Alhambra, yours is the beauty that Time cannot alter –/so Time, enraged, has lent your name to bingo halls in Balham and to mini-markets in Gibraltar . . .

Perhaps it works better in Arabic.

It was with a sense of achievement – at surviving the queue, at

---

* *The Alhambra*, London, 2004. The verse translations above are taken from another indispensable book by Irwin, *Night, Horses and the Desert: The Penguin Anthology of Classical Arabic Literature*, London, 1999.

going one better than IB – that we stood at last in Yusuf the Elusive's audience chamber, the so-called Hall of the Ambassadors, an opulent casket of a room lined with a rich and legible brocade of stucco ('I hope you're not expecting me to draw all *this*,' Martin said, goggling at the writhing calligraphy). I spent some time reading the walls, deciphering the gorgeous self-reflexive graffiti; but I went away with one message, the one that repeats itself every-where your eye alights, the mantra of the Alhambra – *la ghalib illa 'llah*, 'There is no victor but God'. It was the motto of the Nasrid dynasty, and it begs another phrase, unspoken: Even if, in the meantime, the Castilians beat you.

In the Museum of the Alhambra I found an object that embodied the year of the Castilian victory, 1492. Among the eminent men IB met in Granada was the preacher of the mosque of al-Mansurah, down in the valley of the Darro below the palace hill. The mosque's minaret survives, now sporting a belfry and attached to the church of Santa Ana. Here in the museum was the original copper finial of that minaret, three spheres of diminishing size, one above the other, topped by a spear-like spike. It dated back to before the time of Nasrid rule in Granada; after the Christian conquest of the city, it was taken down and placed in the newly built church as a support for a banner. I saw that it was riddled with shot-holes – made by large-calibre balls, by the look of them not from rifles or muskets but from older, heavier weapons . . . I can imagine the scene: the victorious arquebusiers of the Catholic Kings, showing off by loosing a *feu de joie* at this symbol of the defeated faith; their whoops (*Olé!*) as the balls clang home echoing with the bangs up the valley to Albaicín and Sacromonte and the Generalife; Boabdil, sighing up on the pass as the wind brings the sound of the distant volleys. As the Dutch traveller Cees Nooteboom has said, 'The finest monuments are . . . those that happened at the time.'

★

'You are lucky,' Abu Faris said in English. We'd begun in Arabic – he might have been an Arab to look at – but his was rather basic. 'Because today is Thursday, we perform *dhikr* after the evening prayer. We'd be pleased for you to join us.' I'd joined in a number of sufi *dhikrs*, literally 'remembrances' of God – with the Whirling Dervishes in Anatolia, for example, and at the shrine of Nizam al-Din in Delhi; more recently, if abortively, with the Rifa'is in Sri

Lanka. Now I'd be attending one in the heart of Andalusia, the Islamic Paradise Lost. Abu Faris, a handsome Spaniard of my age with a neat beard and an open face, smiled in welcome.

I was particularly excited by the prospect of this spiritual perform-ance. Granada has plenty of material monuments to IB's age, not all as obvious as the Alhambra. There was an early fourteenth-century cara-vanserai, for instance, up an alley off the Street of the Catholic Kings. There was a *madrasah* founded by Sultan Yusuf in the year of IB's visit, across the road from the Chapel Royal but interned inside the pilas-tered and pedimented façade of its baroque namesake, the Palacio del Madraza. There was the Palacio de Daralhorra (Dar al-Hurrah, 'the House of the Free-Born Noblewoman'), at one time home to Boabdil's sharp-tongued mother, buried in the back-lanes of Albaicín (Rabad al-Bayyazin, 'the Suburb of the Falconers') and covered with graffiti; 'GRANADA ES FONKI . . .' said one, in yellow, pink and tur-quoise spray paint – not up to Arabic verses carved in floriated Kufic, but poets have to start somewhere. There were these and many other minor monuments. But so far I'd found no human links with IB's Gharnatah; or nothing more than impressions – a bedouin nose here, a Yemeni complexion there, that *Allah!* at the *corrida*.

IB, however, had given me a thread to follow. There was in Granada, he says, a group of foreign sufis of diverse origins – from Samarqand, Armenia, Anatolia, Khurasan and India. In recent years, I'd read, the cosmopolitan sufi presence in Granada had been revived by one Shaykh Abd al-Qadir al-Murabit, who in his earlier incarnation as a Scot called Ian Dallas had been a successful actor and playwright in the Swinging Sixties. Shaykh Abd al-Qadir, it seemed to me, was a spiritual descendant of those far-flung sufis of IB's day. I couldn't wait to meet him.

He was all over the Islamic Centre in Albaicín, on the covers of books, pamphlets and devotional guides, on sale along with tasteful pots, prints and postcards. Above the Centre's basement quarters rose the even more tasteful Mezquita Mayor or Great Mosque of Granada, built in 2003, mainly with money from the Gulf. It is a small building, but chaste and lovely, with a doorway – the Gate of Shaykh Abd al-Qadir the Sufi, an Arabic inscription said above it – leading in from a small parterre planted with myrtles; or it would lead in if it wasn't roped off. There is also a plain square minaret with an open horseshoe-arched chamber at the top and, on its apex, a finial like that shot-pierced one in the museum. This was the first new mosque in Granada for more than 500 years, and it had not been built without opposition. The Christian Granadines, however, would no doubt get used to it in time.

I asked Abu Faris if the Scottish shaykh would be leading the *dhikr* that night. He smiled. 'The shaykh lives in South Africa now, and has been there for a number of years.'

A disappointment. But the *dhikr* went on without him. Through an open door I could see the room where it would be held, carpeted and lined with cushions. The neo-sufis of Granada clearly weren't into messy self-wounding like the Sri Lankan Rifa'is. I wondered what their ceremony would involve. 'You said the session begins after the evening prayer?' I asked. Abu Faris nodded. 'What time is that? I'm not a Muslim, so I don't know the prayer times in Granada.'

I felt a sudden chill. The open face had shut. '*You are not a Muslim* . . . The shaykh has issued a strict ruling that no non-Muslims may be present at our *dhikr*.' This was the last thing I'd expected to hear. Were Scottish shaykhs and Spanish sufis less inclusive than Turkish or Indian ones? Slowly, Abu Faris's smile returned; a different sort of smile. 'Now, you could always pronounce the Islamic creed. Then we would let you in.'

'Look,' I said, trying not to sound prickly, 'you've heard of Ibn Battutah?' He had. I explained my quest, how I'd travelled years and continents in search of the remains of IB's world, of its resonances in the Islamic world today.

He took this in. Then he spoke again, quietly and gravely. 'If you are only here to gather knowledge, if you just want something interesting to write about, another . . . *colourful encounter*, then it is certainly best that you do not come. You are in the worst position of all. You know Arabic. You know the truth about Islam. But you do not accept it. Why do you remain in this state of ignorance? We say that *true* Christianity is part of Islam. But the Christianity of today is nothing but . . .' – his voice was still quiet, but growing more vehement in tone – '. . . but Roman paganism . . . the Trinity . . . idol-worship of saints . . . all the, the *antropofagia*.' The last word was spat out, discreetly, like a gob of phlegm.

'"Anthropophagy,"' I said, thinking how much less nasty cannibalism sounded in English. 'I suppose you're thinking of Corpus Christi.'

'*Yes!* And don't think I don't know what I'm talking about. I come from a Catholic background. My grandmother was a saint! *I studied at a Catholic seminary!*' I smiled, thinking, perhaps unfairly, of Abdul Wahhab Higgins, Michael Carson's fictional self-flagellating Jesuit who turned into a lash-wielding Wahhabi puritan.

Abu Faris wasn't smiling; but he did relent a little. 'Listen. Tomorrow, wash yourself, put on clean clothes, come at 2.15 p.m. If they ask, say you have come for *me*. Then you can come to Friday prayers.'

'Well . . . if you don't mind me watching from the sidelines . . .'

'*No!* You will join us in the front line and touch your forehead to the ground in praise of Allah!'

I told him I'd think about it. I was curious – even if curiosity was, apparently, the worst of motives – to see the Muslims of Granada at prayer. And in theory I had absolutely nothing against prostrating myself to God; for that matter, Islam had in all probability borrowed its trademark prostration from the seventh-century rituals of eastern Christianity. But it all smacked so much of borders, boundaries, barriers, roped-off doors . . . and it suddenly brought to mind IB, back in that mirror of Granada, Constantinople: '"I should like to go into the church with you,"' he said to the monk he had met at the door of Aya Sofiya, the great church of Divine Sagacity,

> but the monk said to the interpreter, 'Tell him that everyone who enters it must needs prostrate himself before the great cross, for this is a rule laid down by the ancients and it cannot be contravened.' So I left him and he entered alone and I did not see him again.

Abu Faris had heard a vocation and answered from his heart. But the extremity of his self-dislocation shocked me. He was at home in the land of his birth, physically; in every other way he had made himself an alien. The sufis IB met in Granada came from distant lands, from beyond the Bosphorus and the Oxus and the Hindu Kush. Abu Faris had come no distance at all. But in another sense he had come from much further away, from the strange intense world of Christian Spain, and he had not come, I felt, without baggage.

Down the hill, I went to recover from the encounter in the *ambiente familiar* of a café run by another neatly bearded handsome middle-aged alien – a Muslim-born countryman of IB from Chefchaouen. He pulled me a beer, we talked in Arabic, and I felt at home again.

*

Few scholars of the history of Moorish horticulture would deny that the garden of Abu 'l-Qasim Ibn Asim at Niblah, now so lovingly restored, is the finest of all the suburban *jannahs* created by the Muslim aristocracy of Granada on its surrounding *vega*, or plain. Its perimeter wall of beaten earth encloses some four acres of cultivation. The outer margins of this area are at present a little tangled, with trellised vines interspersed by the dense unruly foliage of figs and mulberries. Further in, however, we come upon an ordered orchard of carefully pruned trees – apricot, almond, peach, pomegranate, quince and medlar – planted on the quincunctial plan inherited from antiquity. Hidden away in the centre of the orchard, and just audible before it is seen, is a miniature *saqiyah* or canal (the Arabic word is preserved in the name of the Patio de la Acequia, centrepiece of the famous Generalife gardens which adjoin the Alhambra and are contemporary with this more modest but perhaps equally lovely survival). The canal, lined in marble, is aligned east-west and supplied with water diverted from a stream that in turn flows into the Rio Genil.*

On either side of this canal is a long flanking bed, sunk beneath the level of the marble kerb so that the plants, which tend to run riot at this time of year, do not impede our view of the water. Nearest the kerb is a line of myrtles, clipped square like a diminutive box hedge; so recently clipped, in fact, that their faintly medicinal scent is still strong in the last of the afternoon sun. Set further back you will see, according to season, the various flowers

---

* Shanil, the river's Arabic name, was glossed by Ibn al-Khatib – with a degree of hyperbole, it has to be said – as 'Nil' prefixed with the letter *shin*, whose numerical equivalent is 1,000. The *sh*-Nil is therefore the equal of 'a thousand Niles'.

listed by al-Himyari in his *Wonders of Spring*, and more: narcissi, violets, stocks, wallflowers, roses, irises, lilies, poppies, carnations, lupins, lavender. There are also a number of herbs – basil, thyme, camomile, marjoram and mint – and a few specimens of *shawk al-yahud*, 'Jews'-spike' or acanthus, and even a *tuffahat al-jinn*, a 'jinn-apple' or mandrake, planted as a curiosity (although the head gardener fancies that it keeps the caterpillars off, ancient gardening beliefs being remarkably hardy).

Immediately to the north of the mid-point of the canal there stands a pavilion of rectangular plan surmounted by a small dome and surrounded on all sides by wooden arcades. The joinery is picked out in gold leaf and paint of powdered lapis lazuli, and a couplet carved in relief in stately *thuluth* script runs along the front overlooking the water:

THIS HOUSE WAS BUILT BY IBN ASIM FOR HIS NOBLE FRIENDS.
HERE LET YOUR SENSES LIVE A WHILE, FOR ALL TOO SOON LIFE ENDS.

Night-scented jasmine rambles up the columns of the arcades and has encroached on the inscription, as if to underline with its tendrils the transitoriness of earthly pleasure. As the verse suggests, this place is meant to delight all the senses: with the scent of jasmine and crushed myrtle, with the saturated blue of the iris, with the bloomy knap of an early apricot and the sweet burst of its sun-hot juice between the teeth, with the silver sound of the marble rill and the louder splash of a fountain that occupies the space between pavilion and canal. It seems from surviving evidence that Ibn Asim was particularly fond of this fountain. Not only did it prevent eaves-droppers listening in on his more private conversations, but he also managed to secure the services of the sultan's favourite sculptor to carve the pair of crouching lions from whose pursed mouths shoot twin jets of water. Grandiose as they are in conception, I can only think of them, with their short crinkled manes and stubby bronze spouts, as a pair of late Victorian swells in astrakhan capes with cigar holders in their mouths.

Ah. The fountain-keeper has just stopped the outlet from the raised cistern, hidden on the north side of the pavilion, that supplies the lions' spouts. The twin arcs have faltered and died, and I can

hear the softer ripple of water on marble. (*Ladhdhatuha fi sukuniha*, as they say. The joy of a fountain is in its cessation.) All else is silent but for the intermittent crooning of a ring dove somewhere in the tangled selvage of this little paradise.

That such a place has been preserved for more than 650 years is nothing less than a miracle . . .

But I confess that the remarkably preserved garden is extant only in my imagination, landscaped from texts by Ibn Luyun and Ibn Khaqan, planted with cuttings stolen from al-Himyari's flower treatise and from the genuine Patio de la Acequia, and fertilized with memories of a real place I once lived in that had a pool and a poetical pavilion and pepper trees, and is now gone. Over time the imagined garden has grown lush with detail, an ever more elaborate frame for my miniature of IB telling his tales of travel.

In reality I looked for the garden for years in books, and found no more than a couple of references to the hamlet of Niblah in Ibn al-Khatib's history of Granada, *Al-ihatah* (*The Encompassing*). There was that reminiscence by the author's teacher, Ibn al-Balafiqi, of the meeting with Ibn Battutah; and there was one other passing mention of Niblah, in a list of places on the plain outside the city wall but within the area covered by its defensive fire-power. This limited the radius of possibilities, but there were still a bewildering number of them: 'Hamlets and gardens proliferated,' Ibn al-Khatib writes elsewhere of the plain of Granada under the Nasrid sultans, 'and the daughters of these places crowded round the skirts of their mothers. Plants rustled in the breeze, and the earth in every direction was clothed with a verdant brocade.'

It was in Granada itself that I finally came across another reference to Niblah. It appeared in a compilation of Arabic documents from the city, in a fifteenth-century will. The editor, the eminent Granadine arabist Luis Seco de Lucena, glossed it as a place now known as El Nublo . . . I hadn't expected that change of vowels. Supplied now with the Spanish spelling, I found a single reference to the place in the website of a group of environmental activists.

★

The Genil, the river 'equal to a thousand Niles', was a trail of slime in its canalized bed. Across it, tour-group Granada gave way to suburban villa-land. This in turn soon petered out into a landscape of concrete canyons cutting between blocks of flats. Beneath them were shuttered shops; children's swings rusted and creaked in the wind that whistled down the streets, scattering trash. Even the graffiti lost their colour, became mere crude declarations of love or hate. Granada had ceased to be *fonki*. There was no one about, except for a single North African immigrant family dressed in grey and sitting on a bench. They looked lost, back home in their lost paradise.

My destination was off the city map, but I could see it already – glimpses of tall leaning pylons topped by floodlights, seen down the long high-rise perspectives beyond the Circumvalación Zaidín.

(Even these cement sierras are haunted by a ghostly population of Arabic place-names.)

It was out of season, and the Granada Football Club's new Estadio los Cármenes, or 'Gardens Stadium', was shuttered and deserted. It was this structure, looking like a giant jerry-built starship, that had been plonked, as its name suggested – and to the horror of the environmentalists – on top of three *cortijos* or small country estates: En medio, Alarcón, and El Nublo. I walked along one side of the stadium, looking for someone to ask. It seemed important to know where El Nublo, Niblah, had been. There was no one about.

I was the only customer in the Café Futbol Sur, with its team photos and framed football shirts. The proprietor had heard of one of the names of those lost gardens: there was a Calle Alarcón nearby, he said. But he was new here. At length an older man came in. Yes; he knew the name of Cortijo El Nublo. He wasn't sure, but he thought it had been just to the south of the stadium. I finished my beer and thanked them.

The south side of the stadium was still open ground, but it had been asphalted over and turned into a car park. It looked as if a temporary market had been set up there that morning. Now, in the dead siesta-time, all that was left was a parked van or two and some boxes of discarded and rotten fruit. Two men, West African immigrants in ragged anoraks, were picking through the boxes. Beyond, rubbish tumbled in the breeze across the tarmac towards an outer orbital road that marked the current edge of the city. El Nublo had remained a garden for 650 years after that meeting. I'd only missed it by seven.

I stood by the vans and tried to conjure up once more my imagined garden with its pavilion and fountain and seated figures, but it wouldn't come. Not here.

At first there was no one else about apart from the two Africans, refugees from the long collapse of the golden empire of the Sahel. But at the far end of the car park I found a policeman patrolling, alone, on foot. In answer to my question – I wanted to be sure this was the place – he drew an electronic device from a holster on his belt and typed in 'El Nublo'. There were no matches. He didn't know the name himself. 'But I used to come here when I was little,' he said. 'There was alfalfa growing all around, and orchards of peaches, here where the car park is. And there was a stream too.'

I thanked him and he went on his way.

I stood in the car park. At certain points in my travels with IB I'd sensed he was only a few steps ahead, or behind: tramping across the empty gravel plain of Qalhat on the Gulf of Oman, for instance, or exploring the remote Indian hollow where he'd seen a widow throw herself on her husband's funeral pyre, or dancing in the African night with the Lord of the Balafon. There was the matter of the time-difference, of course; but time, after all, is only one of the dimensions. Here, though, in the car park, in the garden of Abu 'l-Qasim Ibn Asim, IB had never seemed more distant, and in every dimension imaginable.

Speaking of time, had it all been worth a quarter of my own life? And was it *that* long? By travelling in pursuit of IB all these years I'd somehow suspended them, slowed them in some unfathomable Einsteinian way; as if the fractions of the intervening period were up in the air like a juggler's balls; as if, were the journey to end now, they would all fall down. The poet al-Humaydi put the fear in plainer words:

> How many travellers have I known? I cannot count.
> How many corners of the earth? I cannot tell.
> Now that my wanderings east and west are done,
> There is but one last corner left: my grave.

Perhaps it wasn't as bad as that, yet. Still, all I wanted to do was to sit down and give up. I'd always known my journey would end here. I'd never realized just how final the end would be.

And then I thought, No, the journey doesn't end, not when there's a book to write.

Postscript

Further Travels of a Tangerine

IB HAD A book to write too. But how did *he* feel, at the end of the first, 75,000-mile road?

Early in 1354, he 'laid down his much travelled staff in the Sublime Residence of Fez, in the realization that it was the place that possessed the distinction of absolute and unqualified superiority over all other places and, having encompassed in his travels the regions of the East and the rising-place of the full moon in the West, in acknowledgement that, as gold dust is to dross, so is this land to all other lands on earth'. That, and much more in the same vein, is how IB felt about the land of his birth on his final return there; or at any rate it is how his logorrhoeic editor, Ibn Juzayy, expressed the traveller's feelings in the Epistle Dedicatory at the start of the *Travels*, addressed to their patron the sultan of Morocco. (Alas for the passing of patronage! How happy I would be to preface my books with this sort of stuff, in return for suitable remuneration. These days one is expected to write for love, not money.)

But how did IB really feel, coming in that bitter January – the snow on the Umm Junaybah pass, he said, was the thickest he'd seen in all his travels – to the capital of Morocco, a city whose people according to Ibn al-Khatib were 'wolves . . . who greet the stranger with a doleful countenance'? Did he, like Samuel Johnson going back to Lichfield, find the streets much narrower and shorter than he thought he had left them? Visiting his parents' tombs in his native Tangier, did he find, again like Dr Johnson, that his playfellows were grown old, which forced him to suspect that he was no longer young? Did he find, like Descartes, that 'When one spends too much time travelling, one finally becomes a stranger in one's own country'? Or, like Eliot, that

> the end of all our exploring
> Will be to arrive where we started
> And know the place for the first time?

Or did he perhaps, like Whitman, 'round the world having wandered', now

> face home again, very pleased and joyous,
> (But where is what I started for so long ago?
> And why is it yet unfound?)?

Did he feel the two hungers that the Prophet Muhammad said are never satisfied – hunger for knowledge, and hunger for the material world? Or did he find like the wanderer Muhammad Kibrit that 'travel is the mirror of marvels, in which I saw the whole age so full of the marvellous that I had no appetite left for it'? Did he miss that universal kinship of strangers that the traveller felt in the ancient Arabic verse? Or the sense, experienced by Kipling's returning soldier, of being

> like all the rest, alone –
> But reaching out to all the rest?

Did he discover, like Roxanne Euben in her *Journeys to the Other Shore*, that the idea of going home is in itself impossible, because 'the meaning of "home" . . . emerges only after it is gone, built from memories, echoes and the sum of experience that fills the distance between past and present'? Or, like Djuna Barnes's Dr O'Connor, that 'remembrance of things past is all that we have for a future'? Coming home can be the most complicated and dislocating part of travel.

We'll never know. IB was, after all, 'overwhelmed by his master the sultan's most copious benefaction and by the solicitude of his most generous favour, such as caused him to forget the past in the present . . .' On it goes, and all to the effect that Morocco is the best country on earth and its sultan, Abu Inan, the best ruler in the universe. But how do ten-page eulogies weigh, in the scales of sincerity, against a sigh for a wife in the Maldives? And where in

Morocco were the junks and dhows and elephants and rubies and the landfalls on white beaches and in the dark embraces of Tamil concubines? Home, almost by definition, is the absence of these things.

Even if the true feelings elude us, we have a few facts, a few frames flickering at the tail of the final reel. The *Travels* winds up with a note of its own completion on 13 December 1355 and an effusive parting thank-you note to the sultan from Ibn Juzayy, who was determined to have the last word. (Poor Ibn Juzayy expired within a year at the age of thirty-five, spouting verse and rhymed prose on his deathbed. Among his very last recorded words was a request for a draught of *sakanjibin* or oxymel, a concoction of honey and vinegar, which he expressed in the form of an anagram. Luckily the addressee was a nifty solver; to die of an unsolved crossword clue would have been too absurd for words.) After the book was finished, IB's known appearances can be counted on the fingers of one hand. He is mentioned in a list of scholars in Fez, a sort of Sultanic Academy of the Arts and Sciences. At some point in the mid-1350s the debate about his veracity, fuelled by Ibn al-Balafiqi's scathing reminiscences of their meeting in the Granada garden, comes to a head.* Then in the early 1360s IB is working as a judge in Tamasna, the region in which present-day Casablanca is situated; we know this from a letter to him from Ibn al-Khatib, in exile at the time in Morocco and hoping to buy a plot of land with IB's help. (The Granadine writer and politician preserved some of his correspondence, including this, as examples of epistolary style. His writings on the dour citizens of Fez, on bullfights and, in stucco, on the walls of the Alhambra, have been alluded to already. We will soon turn to him again on another matter.)

We can speculate on what else might have happened. In December 1358 the greatest ruler in the universe, God's Shadow on Earth and IB's patron, Sultan Abu Inan, came to the end of his time in this battered earthly caravanserai: he was strangled by his prime minister. It is likely that in the anarchy that ensued IB, even as a minor satellite in the dead sultan's orbit, had to make himself scarce. At the very least, he would have found himself forgotten in the chaos and without patronage. A judicial posting in the provinces

---

* See *The Hall of a Thousand Columns*, p. 15.

was probably as good an option as any. The only other certain fact about him is that in AH 770 (AD 1368–9), according to a trustworthy contemporary, 'he died while holding the office of judge in some town or other'.

It is all so inconclusive. To be unplaceable in death may be appropriate for someone who had led so errant a life as IB. But I couldn't leave him like that, dead 'in some town or other', any more than I could leave him in a Spanish car park. I needed a memorial; somewhere to say farewell. I suppose I needed what bereavement counsellors call 'closure'. The alleged tomb of IB in his birthplace, Tangier, wasn't the place. On the contrary, it was in part the dubiousness of that monument that had led me to spend all these years tracking down the genuine relics of IB's life and travels.

But there was one last relic. It was the greatest of them all, more memorious than any tomb, and it was in Paris.

*

The paper was thick and polished, the ink still intensely black. You could see where the scribe had paused to dip his reed pen: *dip* . . . four, five, perhaps six words, then *dip* again . . . I had the sensation, as I did looking at the dhow scratched in the plaster of the palace wall way back in Kilwa Kisiwani, of peering over the shoulder of the person making the marks. But here there was another sensation – of collaboration, of complicity. It brought me suddenly close again to IB, this long slow slog of words that we've both done.

I began at the end, at the colophon: 'This copy was completed in . . .' *dip* 'Safar of the year seven and fifty . . .' *dip* 'and seven hundred. May God requite . . .' *dip* 'him who copied it.' Safar AH 757 was February AD 1356. The midsummer air was close in the small book-lined room above the rue de Richelieu. But I could picture February in Fez, 'city of scholars and indexes', as Ibn al-Khatib called it, and the inkpots icing over in the night. At the latest, this manuscript of the *Travels* was finished ten weeks after IB and Ibn Juzayy had put the final words of the text together. In all probability this was the first fair copy. The *umm*, the 'mother'.

The irony of it made me smile. My journey with IB went back to another close book-filled room a dozen years before and more

– to the Greater Yemen Bookshop, when I'd taken the *Travels* off the shelf and on the road. All along the way I'd thumbed my nose at those stationary scholars who travel only in libraries. And now I'd ended up in a library too. I suppose it's where we all end up, on the shelf, until someone else turns up and takes us travelling.

At least these were fitting shelves for the mother-copy of the *Travels*. The Bibliothèque Nationale is a universe of volumes, ever expanding from the nucleus of a royal library created in IB's lifetime by Charles V. Not without reason was a celebrated documentary film about it called *Toute la mémoire du monde*. And here in my hands was the memory of the fourteenth-century world. I'd started out, so long before, with a poorly printed copy. This was the pristine ancestress, and every page of it radiated the peculiar mana of manuscript that printed books cannot possess.

But whose hand, I wondered as I turned the leaves, had written it?

The expatriate Irish orientalist William McGuckin, Baron de Slane, was convinced that the copyist was Ibn Juzayy himself. I could see why. Ibn Juzayy's hand was said to have excelled that of Ibn Muqlah, the most famous of Arab calligraphers, and this script was indeed superb – precise, crisp, confident, with elegant forward-thrusting descenders, beautifully legible. IB's present-day Moroccan editor Dr Abdelhadi Tazi has, however, wondered if a noted grammarian like Ibn Juzayy would have made even the few linguistic errors to be found in this copy . . .

A small exclamation broke into my absorption. It came from Marie-Geneviève Guesdon, the librarian in charge of Islamic manuscripts. 'Did you see the *filigrane*?' she asked, excited. I didn't know the word. '*Al-alamah al-ma'iyyah*,' she explained in Arabic. The watermark. I'd never suspected that there were such things so early on; but there it was, clear in the centre of the leaf, backlit by the light from the window – a stag's head, in profile. And there were more of them, and another mark as well, the head of a bearded billy-goat. Mme Guesdon left me for some minutes, then reappeared with a manual of early watermarks. We soon turned up the stag and the goat. They had both been found, the manual said, in books produced in the mid-1350s – in Venice. The paper was probably made there too . . . Perfect dating for the *Travels*. And such costly imported paper suggested a client of the highest rank. It seemed to me even more likely that this was the copy made for the sultan by his man of letters, Ibn Juzayy.

The words of IB. The hand, perhaps, of Ibn Juzayy. And this book, I felt as I explored it further, enjoying the tactile thrill of its polished leaves – no white gloves, directly in touch – was the immediate offspring of their collaboration. And now I had it to myself, this sole survivor of the three, speaking in phrases that drew breath with each dip of the pen.

> Just as man's tongue interprets for his brain,
> So through the sharpened reed I speak for man.
> But men and all their fine words die in time,
> While yet, alone, my fine black words remain.

The 'speaker' is an inkpot belonging to IB's countryman and contemporary, Ibrahim al-Abbasi. The fancy is typical of the time; then again, Milton's books were 'not absolutely dead things' and Macaulay's spoke with 'the audible voice of history' – so why not a versifying inkpot?

From the colophon I leafed slowly backwards, putting my journey with IB into reverse. The place-names, enlarged and emboldened by the scribe, stood out like signposts on the page: landfalls on the banks of the Niger and the shores of the Sahara and of Iberia; a great leap back to China and its maritime emporia; Sarandib and Adam's fall to earth, landfalls in remote Maldivian atolls; the ports of Malabar – Calicut and Cannanore and Mangalore – and the cities of the Indian interior – Dawlatabad and Gwalior, Aligarh and Delhi with its Thousand-Column Hall. I reached the Indus and the beginning of this second volume of the *Travels*. The first volume of the mother-copy is lost; but the momentum of memory carried me on, back to Constantinople and to the coast of that other, Cimmerian, Bosphorus; to the island of Kilwa Kisiwani, misplaced in my itinerary; to the shores of Anatolia and Arabia and the Levant, to the banks of the Orontes and the Nile, to cities on the littoral of Egyptian deserts and on the coasts of the Mediterranean . . . 'all that archaeology of fragments lying around, from the broken African kingdoms, from the crevasses of Canton, from Syria and

Lebanon, vibrating not under the earth but in our raucous, demotic streets'. It was his native Antilles that Derek Walcott was speaking of, but he might as well have been writing about our wider, older world. And so to Tangier, where it all began and that Old World came to an end on the Circumambient Ocean, beyond which there were as yet no Antilles, no more landfalls.

On the way I saw how many gaps I'd left.

★

My book-travels didn't stop. On a visit to IB's native land I called on his living editor, Dr Abdelhadi, eighty-five and enthusiastic as ever. He was agog with a discovery. It was part of a three-volume manuscript – again, the first was lost – on Islamic jurisprudence, and it had recently turned up in the library of al-Azhar, the ancient university mosque of Cairo.

'Look at this,' he said. He handed me two photocopied sheets. They showed the colophons of the two extant volumes. I began to read the first one: 'The copying was completed on Friday 2nd Jumada I of the year seven hundred and twenty-seven, by the hand of one who sorely needs the mercy of his Lord, who hopes for His pardon and forgiveness, Muhammad ibn Abdallah ibn Muhammad of Tangier . . .' – I stared at Dr Abdelhadi; he motioned me to read on – '. . . may God grant him success, and of His kindness and generosity bestow on him His favours, and may He repair his broken state and bring him back to his family, to reunite them all, safe and sound, and that full soon.'

'Read on,' Dr Abdelhadi said.

The second colophon was dated 18th Jumada II, AH 727 – six weeks after the first – and stated that the copy was made in Damascus for Abu 'l-Hasan Ali al-Sakhawi the Maliki. The name was familiar.

'That is the same Sakhawi whom our shaykh stayed with in Damascus when he was ill,' Dr Abdelhadi reminded me. And to dispel any lingering doubts that this might be the work of some fortuitous namesake, Muhammad ibn Abdallah of Tangier added a patronymic this time: 'Ibn Battutah . . . *a stranger far from his homeland.*' A patronymic; and a plea for sympathy.

'You see how many problems this solves!' Dr Abdelhadi said,

twinkling with implications. 'Ibn Battutah was in Damascus much longer than the *Travels* claims.' I remembered the superhuman feat of IB attending a lecture course in the Syrian capital that involved a verbatim recitation of al-Bukhari's *Sahih* – a work that in its closest-printed versions runs to 1,500 pages – together with its detailed exegesis, of his picking up fourteen teaching diplomas, being ill with fever for a fortnight, *and* getting married and fathering a child, all in under three weeks. I remembered the lightning tour of the Levant that followed, and the multiple pile-up of places and dates further on, in Iraq and Iran. IB, it was clear from these new-found pages, had in fact spent more like three *months* in Damascus. 'Many of the places the *Travels* says our shaykh went to in AH 727 he must have actually visited a whole twenty years later,' Dr Abdelhadi continued, 'on his way back from the Far East. Ibn Juzayy simply took all of Ibn Battutah's material on each country and lumped it together, regardless of whether the dates worked or not.'

It was a discovery that would unravel many of the knottiest problems of the *Travels*. For 150 years, scholars had puzzled over IB's kinky time-line. Now there was a prospect of it finally straightening out. (As I've admitted before, most of us tie knots in our itineraries, to take up slack, to make things neat. In my case, everything I write has happened – but, occasionally, not in the exact order in which it happens on the page. It's fun now and then to lead time a merry dance.)

But for me the photocopied pages also disclosed something else. There was a spikiness to the uprights of the script, an impulsiveness in the curves, a tendency to wander in the pointing of the vowels. And when the twenty-two-year-old IB came to write his name, there was a sudden dash forward – a long impetuous line that ended in a mass of ingrown loops. It didn't need a graphologist to infer that the scribe was no shrinking violet. Energetic, erratic, proud, prickly, self-centred were the adjectives that suggested themselves to me; in a word, cocky. Looking at the script, I recalled that in Arabic the words for a volume of a book and for a journey share the same root: *sifr* is the unscrolling of the written page in the hand, *safar* the unrolling of the earth underfoot. IB wrote like he travelled.

Then again, was I reading my own preconceptions about IB into his handwriting? Perhaps. But there was no doubt about his words.

Some of them were as revealing as his script or those dates. There was the prayer to be reunited with his family; there was the pathos of that byline – 'Ibn Battutah . . . a stranger far from his homeland'. These are not the sort of expressions one normally finds in the colophons of works on Islamic law. The form may be cocky, but the content betrays a surprising vulnerability. The written picture of IB was more complicated than it seemed at first.

It was to become more complicated still.

★

My own literary discovery was of a portrait of a much older IB, by another hand, but done from the life. It wasn't a slick caricature like Ibn al-Balafiqi's, dashed off after a single meeting in a garden. It was carefully observed, not without cruelty, but also with affection. There have been several glancing references to it in this book; it is, for example, the mysterious source of the comments by IB's 'more effusive self' on the palms and scorpions of Sijilmasah. But I wanted to leave it to its proper place, here, to the end, if it can be called an end.

Of the three Andalusian men of letters who figure in IB's later life, it was Ibn al-Khatib who interested me most. Old Ibn al-Balafiqi's role was too brief and damning; Ibn Juzayy disappeared from the scene by dying. Ibn al-Khatib, however, got to know IB in Morocco during his three-year exile from Granada in the early 1360s, and became fond of him. In the letter about his intended purchase of land that he wrote to the traveller, now provincial judge, he speaks in the warmest tones of his hope of enjoying IB's company – and his *barakah*, blessings – as a neighbour. The hope was probably never fulfilled. Ibn al-Khatib returned to Spain in 1362 as prime minister of Muhammad V, the reinstated sultan of Granada whose exile he had shared.

For a time, though, he and IB were clearly more than just acquaintances. However, I only realized just how well Ibn al-Khatib knew IB when I came across a small published volume of chapter-length topographical pieces by the Granadine.* These are written in the highly wrought rhyming prose in which he excelled.

---

* Lisan al-Din Muhammad b. Abdallah Ibn al-Khatib, *Khatrat al-tayf*, ed. Ahmad Mukhtar al-Abbadi, Abu Dhabi, 2003.

One of the pieces, dating from his Moroccan exile, caught my particular attention as it both described many towns in IB's homeland and, in its first half, followed IB's route through Andalusia. In it Ibn al-Khatib used the literary device, one that goes back to the earliest days of Arabic rhyming tales, of the author meeting a picaresque narrator.* The encounter with the story-teller took place in that locus of travel, that metaphor of the ephemeral world – a caravanserai. The translated extracts that follow preserve most of the meaning of the original, but not its strange rococo music.

'Night embraced me,' Ibn al-Khatib says. 'The hermit of the dark had let his tresses fall; the thief of night had snatched the sun's disc from the hand of yesterday.' Thus benighted, he finds shelter in the caravanserai, and there meets

> an old man who had wandered round the world . . . the whiteness of whose hair had judged in favour of his gravity; who wound around his arm a serpent rosary of banded beads both black and white, colours in whose meeting met the Negro and the Frank. To his right, a brimming jug; on his left a lad, a young disciple; and, before the two of them, a braying ass.

The old man with his rosary and youthful acolyte is clearly of a sufi bent. His gravity somewhat undermined by the donkey's sobbing interjections, he begins to bewail in verse his lost youth, then reverts to rhyming prose:

> He sighed . . . and said, 'To the world I bid farewell. I've gained all I desire, I've mounted danger's steeds, I've flown both far and wide, I've kissed my hand to many lands; I've milked the teats of Time.'

But exactly what, his disciple asks, has his master done that is so amazing?

'"Insolent boy," he exclaimed. "Does one speak in these terms to such a *qutb* as *I*?"' The *qutb*, or 'axis', is the highest rank of sufi

---

* The rhyming tales, *maqamat*, are still a living literary genre: my old friend Hasan, direct descendant of IB's host in Yemen, composes them. I sometimes appear as his picaresque narrator.

sainthood. The old man goes on to brag in detail about his many accomplishments, which range from hunting 'both the lizard and the whale' and subduing the jinn 'in the manner of Solomon' to 'paying off debtors' and 'spurring on many a brisk mule'. The last phrase, I realized, is a sexual double entendre whose English equivalent might be 'riding many a fine filly' . . . I was beginning to have my suspicions about the identity of the well-travelled old man with spiritual pretensions, cash-flow problems, a big libido and an equally big ego.

They were confirmed when he began listing all the lands he had seen: China, India, Constantinople ('where I gained mastery over the *Lateen* tongue'), Yemen, Iraq, Persia . . . The roll goes on until it extends from the Far East to furthest West Africa. No other known traveller, as IB himself rightly boasts in his own book, had been to all these places. I was certain now that Ibn al-Khatib's picaresque greybeard was a thinly disguised version of IB. And I could picture the literati of Granada and Fez sniggering at him, rather as readers in Regency London would later laugh at Raspe's fictional Baron Münchausen dining, like the real James Bruce, off live Abyssinian oxen.

The satire went on, mercilessly. This was the burlesque reverse of IB's own self-portrait in the *Travels*. And it depicted a much older, grumpier and more cynical IB than the cocksure but homesick young man who had copied that manuscript in Damascus, nearly forty years earlier. Here is the great traveller, down on his uppers in a grotty flop-house, still recounting his tales, still missing home; except that home is now the world. How telling it all was. And how disturbing: old travellers never die, I thought, they only blather away.

I was beginning to feel that Ibn al-Balafiqi's caricature of IB was kind in comparison. And then the tone changed.

The old man slips into poetry and self-pity once more, and concludes,

> 'Not one of my good brethren have I left.
> Of all support and friendship I'm bereft.'

'On hearing this,' the author says, 'I was overcome by sympathy for him.' This being Ibn al-Khatib in full rhyming flow, he is overcome at some length. And then he quotes the Arabic verse that had echoed through my own travels with IB:

> *We two are strangers here,*
> *And strangers are to one another kin.*

So too now are author and narrator, joined by the cousinhood of the road. And after these seven pages of dense scene-setting, Ibn al-Khatib finally comes to the point and asks the old traveller for a full and true account of his journey to al-Andalus. I was by now hardly surprised to find that the old man follows the same road travelled by his non-fictional self, from Gibraltar, via Marbella and Fuengirola – beware here, he warns, of attacks from the sea – up to the baths of Alhama and on to the bride of Andalusian cities, Granada.

Following in the footsteps has a venerable literary history. In IB's case it began within a decade of him laying down his staff in Fez.

As I read on, a thought came: could there be any clues in all this to the conundrum that had always intrigued me – what IB looked like? I turned back to the lines describing the old traveller. There was nothing beyond the white hair. The face remained a blur.

The character, though, was there in loving detail, and if any speck of doubt remained in my mind that the old man was IB,* it was dispelled by the way in which the account of his Spanish journey ends. Just as his real self had told tales of travel to potentates across the hemisphere and then, in his ingratiating but apparently irresistible way, touched them for a purse of gold, so too does his fictionalized *alter ego* solicit a donation: '"Henceforth I'll be your guest if I'm pleased with your largesse, and I'll be your kinsman if your kerchief smiles at me"' – in other words, if he sees the gleam of money from an open purse. The mix of smarm, charm and impecuniousness is IB to a T.

Just like all those sultans, Ibn al-Khatib pays his dues for the tales of travel. He then nods off for a minute or two. When he wakes again, he sees in the lamplight that the old man has gone. 'I looked at his sleeping-place and saw nothing but a few threads from his ragged

---

* Something which does not seem to have occurred to Ibn al-Khatib's editor, even though he quotes IB in a footnote about the dangers of attack on the Andalusian coast.

clothes, and the dung of his donkey. So I went out to search for him, following in his footsteps – and it was as if the circling heavens had enfolded him in their revolutions. On I went; but he had gone, and gone too was all trace of him. I contemplated the gulf that lay between us now, and my heart was seared with pain. And I said in consolation to myself, *Two dear friends meet; and yet such meetings must needs end in parting.*'

The feeling of loss, I sensed, was real. I'd felt it myself.

But in the strange world of Ibn al-Khatib's rhyming tales, endings are not that final. Not long after the old man's disappearance, the author finds himself in a crowded market, 'one of the suqs of dust'. Here he comes across an itinerant hawker of amulets. Like IB's fictional double, the man goes on to recount his travels, this time in Morocco. Only when he finishes – 'whereupon he drew me near to him and took my hand in his and passed his fingers between mine' – does it dawn on Ibn al-Khatib . . . that the amulet seller is in fact his companion from the caravanserai: 'I saw through his trick – and it was the old man! . . . He had dyed his hair and put on a disguise . . .' And, even as he marvels at the transformation, his elderly friend 'smote the flank of his donkey and was gone, lost in the surging crowd, leaving me to ponder his traces. *All that is joined together shall be cast asunder*'.

Like the holy mages and mesmerists he met on his actual travels – like Burhan al-Din the Lame of Alexandria and the disappearing hermit of Guangzhou – IB had turned into a master of illusion. It was appropriate; but I knew now that I'd never get to see his true face. His features were as mobile as his home; he wore the face of Everyman. But this end was more fitting than that rapture into the folding circles of the sky, or the double solitude of a forgotten tomb which is the fate of the real IB. Here was the greatest traveller in human history, disappearing into the crowd on a donkey.

★

It isn't the end, of course. As long as people read, and travel, and write, as long as readers take to the road then go home – whatever it is that home has become – to tell their stories, the journey never ends. It is both circular and linear, a double helix inscribing itself back into the past and forward into the future.

And then where? At Abbadan, at the head of the Arabian Gulf, as near as anywhere to the geographical mid-point of all his travels and another of those liminal places – between Arab and non-Arab, land and sea, west and east – IB met a hermit in a ruined mosque. 'He took my hand', he remembered, 'and said to me, "May God help you to attain all you desire in this world and in the world to come."' And then, as IB sets down the memory twenty-five years on, in Fez, he steps outside the narrative – pauses to look back into his past, and onward into his future:

> I have indeed, thanks be to God, attained my desire in this world, which was to travel the earth; and in these travels of mine I have achieved what no one else has achieved, to my knowledge. There remains the world to come. And my hope is strong in the mercy of God, that He will pardon my offences, and that I will gain my desire, which is to enter the Garden.

Antum al-sabiqun, as one says in Arabic on passing the resting-places of the dead, *wa nahnu al-lahiqun*. You have gone before, and we will follow.

Acknowledgements

This book is (to paraphrase the 'Warning to the Reader' that prefaces Peter Fleming's *One's Company*) set in eleven countries scattered over three continents. Their combined land area is more than 2.5 million square miles; their combined population is nearly 1.5 billion. They cover the whole of human history going back 2 million years to the primitive hominids of the Olduvai Gorge.

The author of this book is 48 years old. He has spent less than a year altogether in the countries concerned. He does not speak Kiswahili, Dhivehi, Sinhala, Tamil, Chinese, Bambara or Spanish. He has therefore needed all the help he could get.

It has of course simplified things to be following the itinerary of one man through these lands in a particular period of time. On the language front, Arabic can be useful in the most surprising places and French, however execrable, in West Africa. However, I would still have got nowhere without the help of a large number of people. Some of them have appeared earlier in this book but should do so again here to be thanked formally. They include, in Tanzania, Athumana Limonga of Kilwa Masoko, Mohammed Hassan Mwanga of Kilwa Kisiwani, and Pascal Bacuez; in the Maldives, Ahmed Tholal and Naseema Mohamed of the National Centre for Linguistic and Historical Research, Zuraa Rasheed of Vaadhoo, and Hassan Sobir, former High Commissioner of the Maldives in London; in Sri Lanka, Sharm Aboosally, Roshana Aboosally Mohamed and A. Denis N. Fernando; in China, Chris and Francesca Pratt of Hong Kong, Professor Li Guangbin of Beijing, Dr Ding Yuling, Wang Liangmao and the rest of the staff at the fascinating Maritime Museum in Quanzhou, and members of the Ding clan in Quanzhou and Chendai; in Mauritania, Sayyid

Bati ould Baba al-Mahjubi and Talib al-Saduq ould Abba of Walata; in Mali, Namankoumba Keita of Kangaba, Ali Maïga of Gao and Djibril Doucouré of the Institut Ahmed Baba in Timbuktu; in Guinea, the Kouyaté family of Niagassola and in particular the Lord of the Balafon Hadji Sékou Kouyaté, Judge Siriman Kouyaté and Kaniba Oulen Kouyaté; in Andalusia, Thor of the Battuta Bar and Father Charles Azzopardi of Gibraltar; and in Paris, Marie-Geneviève Guesdon, librarian in charge of Islamic manuscripts at the Bibliothèque Nationale.

Dan Edge, Maggie Gu, Martha Haxworth, Alexandra Henderson, Sara Ramsden and Jamie Wightman together ensured that the making of our BBC television series on IB was memorable and enjoyable. With them I had the peculiar experience of following in my own footsteps as well as in IB's, and in a few places I got ahead of myself. I beg their forgiveness for editing them out of the occasional points in this book where they should by rights have appeared.

Various other forms of help and encouragement have been given from places as far apart as Boston and Borneo, by Jay Butler, Professor Steven Caton, Lala Corpuz, Sofia Fonseca de Oliveira Braga, Monica Esslin-Peard, Nigel Kotani, Dr Abdulla Abdul Wali Nasher, Abdulwahhab al-Sayrafi, Hasan al-Shamahi, Chris Scott, Christopher Tanfield, David Tatham, Frances Wood, Denyse Woods and George Yeoman. Dr Abdelhadi Tazi of Rabat, IB's countryman and editor, continues to inform and enthuse. Roland Philipps and Caroline Westmore at John Murray have supported me from afar. My peerless editor, Gail Pirkis, and my sagacious agent, Carolyn Whitaker, have as ever been indispensable companions on the writing road. I only wish my old friend and fellow-traveller Martin Yeoman could have been with me along the whole of the physical road, to show me more of the beauty that hides in the ordinary.

I thank them all.

The translation of the verse on Pate on p.14 I found in the House of Wonders in Zanzibar. The extract from the Dhivehi copper grant on p. 64 was translated by H. C. P. Bell, and that from Marignolli's description of Adam's Peak on p. 99 by Sir Henry Yule. The verses from the *Mathnawi* on p. 117 were translated by

Reynold Nicholson; those from Xue Neng on p. 165 and Bao He on p. 199 are done from the French versions by Chen Dasheng and Ludvik Kalus; those on *hammams* on pp. 307 and 318 come from Carlos Vílchez Vílchez's *Arab Baths*. The fragments of Alhambra mural poetry on pp. 325–6 were translated by Christopher Middleton and Leticia Garza-Falcon. All other translations are mine.

Finally, without the friendship and hospitality of Ianthe Maclagan, Tim Morris and their children, my other travels – in the Bodleian and other Oxford libraries – would have been a lonely business. To them this book is dedicated, with thanks and love.

*

IB is an enormous subject, and I wish Godspeed to those who will continue the journey with him and fill in the many gaps I have left. Part of the enormity is the result of IB's curiosity, his love of side-tracks and byways. For me, it has meant that what was originally intended to be one book has grown into three – over a thousand pages, and perhaps the biggest narrative of travel since IB's own book came out at the end of 1355. By way of apology I can do no better than to quote John Dunton's excuse in his *Voyage round the World* (1691), a book that purports to follow the adventures of Don Kainophilus, a man who was born in a coach and who spent his entire life on the road:

> Nor think, Dear Friend, I ramble now from you,
> My Subject Rambles, and I but pursue.

San'a, Yemen
May 2010

Index

Note: Arabic *ibn/bin*, 'son of . . .', is abbreviated to b.